Embattled Korea

About the Book and Author

This comprehensive book examines the history of Korea's division and the political and economic development of both Koreas, their military confrontation, and their efforts at dialogue. Mr. Clough focuses on the international rivalry between the two, including relations with big power supporters and diplomatic competition inside and outside the UN and the nonaligned movement. The first book to explore in detail the competition between Seoul and Pyongyang outside the diplomatic circuit—from overseas construction projects to international athletic contests—Mr. Clough's study breaks new ground, analyzing South Korea's growing contacts with the USSR and the PRC, as well as North Korea's relationship with Japan and the United States. He views these contacts as probable precursors of diplomatic recognition of both Koreas by all four big powers. Identifying the problems and the choices for the United States in the rapidly changing environment in and around Korea, Mr. Clough makes recommendations for the future direction of U.S. policy.

Ralph N. Clough is professorial lecturer and coordinator of the SAIS China Forum, School of Advanced International Studies, The Johns Hopkins University.

As a Foreign Service officer, he spent thirteen years in China, Hong Kong, and Taiwan. He served as director of the Office of Chinese Affairs in the Department of State. After his retirement from the Foreign Service in 1969, he spent eight years at The Brookings Institution as a senior fellow and guest scholar. He was then a fellow at the Wilson Center, the Institute for Sino-Soviet Studies, George Washington University, and the Washington Center of The Asia Society. He has also taught at American University.

He is the author of *East Asia and U.S. Security* (1975), *Deterrence and Defense in Korea: The Role of U.S. Forces* (1976), and *Island China* (1978). He is coauthor of *The United States, China, and Arms Control* (1975) and *Japan, Korea, and China: American Perceptions and Policies* (1979). He is coeditor of *Modernizing China: Post-Mao Reform and Development* (Westview, 1986).

Embattled Korea

The Rivalry for International Support

Ralph N. Clough

Westview Press / Boulder and London

To Awana

Copyright © 1987 by Westview Press, Inc.

Published in 1987 in the United States of America by Westview Press, Inc.; Frederick A. Praeger, Publisher; 5500 Central Avenue, Boulder, Colorado 80301

Library of Congress Catalog Card Number: 87-50072
ISBN: 0-8133-7324-7

OCLC 16753053

Printed and bound in the United States of America

(∞) The paper used in this publication meets the requirements of the American National Standard for Permanence of Paper for Printed Library Materials Z39.48-1984.

10   9   8   7   6   5   4   3   2   1

Contents

Preface

The confrontation between the two Koreas constitutes one of the most difficult and complex problems in international politics. A relentless military buildup has gone on for more than thirty years on both sides of the demilitarized zone established at the end of the Korean War. Attempts at sustained dialogue between Seoul and Pyongyang have produced meager results. Unlike the two Germanys, the two Koreas have been unable to agree on reciprocal trade, travel, or even the exchange of letters between separated families. Intense hostility and suspicion persist between North and South.

The two Koreas have competed doggedly for international support and recognition. Each government has sought to prevent acceptance of the other by the international community. Both failed. Today, sixty-seven nations maintain diplomatic relations with both Koreas. But the four big powers whose support is most essential to Seoul and Pyongyang remain locked in the pattern established during the late 1940s and early 1950s. The United States and Japan have diplomatic relations only with South Korea, and the Soviet Union and China have diplomatic relations only with North Korea. The pattern and climate of international relations in East Asia have changed radically over the past thirty years, but the Korean confrontation continues essentially unchanged.

Trends in the 1980s, however, foreshadow significant changes in the situation of the two Koreas. Both face difficult succession problems. South Korea continues to outperform North Korea in economic development and international relationships, gradually compelling North Korea to emerge from its shell and become more active in the international community. The big powers, impatient with the inability of the two Koreas to lower tension and the risk of war, are pressing for a fruitful North-South dialogue and are expanding unofficial contacts with the part of Korea with which they lack diplomatic relations. Movement toward a new framework of international relations in which both Koreas will have diplomatic relations with all four big powers is underway, although years may pass before that framework is in place.

As Korea steadily became more important on the world scene, it seemed to me that a book was needed that would give the reader in one place a comprehensive survey of the political and economic development of the two Koreas, their military confrontation and intermittent dialogue, and their international relations over the period from 1945 to the present. In addition to covering these topics, this book contains a final chapter with recommendations on U.S. policy.

The names of Chinese and Koreans are given surname first, in accordance with practice in those countries. Japanese names, however, I have written surname last, as they generally appear in English language newspapers and other publications. Spelling of Korean names varies considerably. I have tried, insofar as possible, to use the spelling favored by the individual. The names of Chinese cities are given in the *pinyin* system, except for Peking (Beijing) and Yenan (Yan'an). Dollar values in the text refer to U.S. dollars, unless otherwise specified.

Those whom I consulted in doing the research for this book are too numerous to list. They include officials, scholars, journalists, and businessmen in the United States, the Soviet Union, China, Japan, South Korea, and North Korea. To all of them I express my deep gratitude for the time they made available and the insights they provided. I am particularly grateful to Congressman Stephan J. Solarz for the opportunity to travel to North Korea with him and to be present at his conversation with Kim Il Sung. I should like also to express my heartfelt appreciation to the Ford Foundation, the Luce Foundation, and the Rockefeller Brothers Fund for their generous support and to the Woodrow Wilson International Center for Scholars of the Smithsonian Institution and the School of Advanced International Studies of The Johns Hopkins University for providing me with congenial surroundings in which to do my research and writing. Thanks go also to William Gleysteen, Lawrence Krause, and William Shaw for helpful comments on the manuscript and to Libby Barstow, Lauri Fults, and Christy Stebbins of Westview Press for expediting its publication.

The opinions in this work are entirely my own and should not be attributed to any of the persons consulted or to the foundations and institutions that provided support for the project.

Ralph N. Clough

Acronyms

ANSP	Agency for National Security Planning
ASEAN	Association of Southeast Asian Nations
CAAC	Civil Aviation Administration of China
CICA	Confederation of International Contracting Associations
CMEA	Council for Mutual Economic Assistance
CPC	Central People's Committee
CPSU	Communist Party Soviet Union
DCRK	Democratic Confederal Republic of Koryo
DFRF	Democratic Front for the Reunification of the Fatherland
DJP	Democratic Justice Party
DKP	Democratic Korea Party
DMZ	Demilitarized Zone
DPRK	Democratic People's Republic of Korea
DRP	Democratic Republican Party
ECA	Economic Cooperation Administration
EEC	European Economic Community
FAO	Food and Agricultural Organization
GSP	Generalized System of Preferences
IAEA	International Atomic Energy Agency
IBRD	International Bank for Reconstruction and Development
ICAO	International Civil Aviation Organization
IISS	International Institute for Strategic Studies
IMF	International Monetary Fund
IOC	International Olympic Committee
IPU	Interparliamentary Union
ISA	International Security Affairs
ITU	International Telecommunication Union
JCP	Japanese Communist Party
JETRO	Japan External Trade Organization
JSP	Japanese Socialist Party
KAL	Korean Air Lines

KCIA	Korean Central Intelligence Agency
KCNA	Korean Central News Agency
KDP	Korean Democratic Party
KDPR	Korean Democratic People's Republic
KNDF	Korean National Democratic Front
KNP	Korean National Party
KOTRA	Korean Trade Promotion Corporation
KPA	Korean People's Army
KPG	Korean Provisional Government
KPR	Korean People's Republic
KWP	Korean Workers' Party
LDP	Liberal Democratic Party
MAC	Military Armistice Commission
MDL	Military Demarcation Line
MITI	Ministry of Trade and Industry
NATO	North Atlantic Treaty Organization
NCNA	New China News Agency
NDP	New Democratic Party
NKDP	New Korea Democratic Party
NNSC	Neutral Nations Supervisory Commission
OAU	Organization of African Unity
PLO	Palestine Liberation Organization
PRC	People's Republic of China
ROC	Republic of China
ROK	Republic of Korea
RPR	Revolutionary Party for Reunification
SNCC	South-North Coordinating Committee
SPA	Supreme People's Assembly
UNC	UN Command
UNCURK	UN Commission for the Unification and Rehabilitation of Korea
UNDP	UN Development Program
UNESCO	UN Education, Scientific, & Cultural Organization
UNGA	UN General Assembly
UNKRA	UN Korean Reconstruction Agency
UPU	Universal Postal Union
USIS	U.S. Information Service
WHO	World Health Organization
WMO	World Meteorological Organization

1

Korea:
Victim of the Cold War

On October 14, 1945, the Soviet military command in North Korea introduced the "patriot hero," Kim Il Sung, to a mass rally in Pyongyang. Kim, who had entered Korea a few weeks earlier with Soviet forces, spoke to the crowd, praising "the heroic champions of the Soviet army" for liberating Korea from Japanese imperialism.[1] On October 17 General John P. Hodge, commander of U.S. forces occupying Korea south of the 38th parallel, held a press conference to introduce another Korean patriot, Dr. Syngman Rhee. Rhee had arrived the day before on a U.S. military plane from Tokyo. On October 20 he delivered an address at the welcoming ceremony for U.S. forces.[2] These almost simultaneous ceremonies of foreign sponsors presenting Korean leaders to the Korean people were an omen of Korea's star-crossed destiny after World War II. Liberated from thirty-five years of Japanese colonialism and anticipating a joyous rebirth as an independent unified nation, the Korean people were trapped in a divided condition by the sharpening cold war confrontation between the United States and the Soviet Union.

The contrast between the two Korean leaders was great. Kim Il Sung, born Kim Song Ju in 1912 to a lower middle-class family near Pyongyang, was only thirty-three years old when he addressed the Pyongyang rally. He had emigrated with his family to Manchuria, where he attended a Chinese middle school. Briefly imprisoned by the Chinese authorities for attempting to organize a Communist youth group, Kim later fled to the hills of eastern Manchuria to join Chinese Communist guerrillas fighting the Japanese who had occupied Manchuria in 1931. For eight to ten years Kim, with a small group of Korean comrades, was a guerrilla. He advanced through the ranks of the Chinese Communist military

1

organization to the position of division commander. He never commanded more than a few hundred men, however, operating much of the time in parts of Manchuria near the Korean border among a sizable Korean population. Finally, probably about 1941, Japanese counterinsurgency operations forced him to withdraw his unit into Soviet territory in the vicinity of Khabarovsk, where he apparently spent most of his time until 1945. Thus, when Kim returned to Korea with the Soviet army, he was a seasoned guerrilla commander, despite his youth, and brought with him a small group of other Korean guerrilla fighters with whom he had forged strong personal ties. He had been closely associated with the Chinese Communists in Manchuria and had developed relationships with the Soviets during his sojourn in the Soviet Union.[3]

Syngman Rhee was seventy years old when he returned to Korea. Born to an upper-class family in the southern part of Korea in 1875 during the Yi dynasty, he had studied the Confucian classics as a youth and then attended an American-run Christian missionary school. He became active in the movement to keep Korea free from domination by the Japanese or Russians, who were struggling fiercely to control the Korean royal court. Arrested and tortured in 1897, Rhee spent seven years in jail and emigrated to the United States on his release. He continued his education at George Washington University, Harvard, and Princeton, receiving a Ph.D. in international law from Princeton at the age of thirty-five. For the next thirty-five years he remained in the United States, devoting himself to the Korean independence movement, supported by contributions from the Korean community and sympathetic U.S. citizens. By 1919 he was sufficiently well known to be elected president in absentia of the "Korean provisional government" established by a small group of Korean exiles in Shanghai, only to lose the designation a few years later in one of the squabbles endemic among Korean exile politicians.

Thus, the two men who were to become the most important political figures in the two parts of Korea during the fifteen years following their return in 1945 differed greatly in age, family background, education, experience, outlook and foreign associations. In certain respects, however, they were similar. Neither had close associations with the political leaders inside Korea who emerged, many from jail, after the Japanese surrender. Both were deeply committed to Korean independence and had spent a large part of their lives abroad working to this end. They were tough-minded and possessed enormous self-confidence and political skills. Each had special relationships with the big power in occupation of his part of Korea. They were adept at exploiting those relationships for political advancement, but in the end both proved to be truculent, obdurate Korean patriots, not easily kept in line.

Drawing the Line

When U.S. and Soviet forces entered Korea, their governments had agreed in only the most general terms on the future of that country. President Franklin D. Roosevelt, Prime Minister Winston Churchill, and Generalissimo Chiang Kai-shek announced at Cairo in 1943 that Japan would be stripped of all territories "taken by violence and greed" and that "in due course Korea shall become free and independent." Roosevelt, having in mind the U.S. experience in the Philippines, was attracted to the idea of placing the Koreans under trusteeship for a time in order to prepare them for independence. In February 1945 at Yalta he discussed with Joseph Stalin a trusteeship over Korea by the United States, the Soviet Union, China, and Great Britain that might last as long as twenty to thirty years. Concerning the length of the period, Stalin responded, "the shorter the period the better," but he concurred in the trusteeship idea. No attempt was made at Yalta to discuss details or to reduce the agreement to writing.[4]

The sudden Japanese surrender on August 14, 1945, caught the United States unprepared to deal with the Korean problem. The Soviet Union had declared war on Japan just six days before, and its forces were already advancing into Korea. No agreement had been reached with the Soviets, however, concerning military occupation of the country or arrangements for setting up an international trusteeship over it. In an all-night meeting in the Pentagon on August 10–11, two colonels proposed that the Soviets accept the surrender of Japanese forces north of the 38th parallel and that U.S. forces accept the surrender in the south.[5] This proposal, which was incorporated into General Order No. 1 directing the surrender of all Japanese forces, was accepted without comment by Stalin. Soviet forces in Korea consequently halted their advance at the 38th parallel.

The Impact of Decolonization

The first mission of Soviet and U.S. forces entering Korea was to accept the surrender of the Japanese forces and repatriate both military and civilian Japanese. Thus, their intrusion not only divided Korea, it also severed the important economic links between Korea and Japan and removed at one stroke the bulk of the managerial and technical elite. Under such handicaps the military commanders' tasks of remolding the economy and superintending the emergence of a new Korean political structure were extraordinarily difficult.

During their thirty-five years in power, the Japanese had radically altered the Yi dynasty's lethargic Confucian bureaucratic state characterized by its self-contained agrarian economy. Their modernizing drive turned Korea into a far more productive area, shaped to meet the needs of the Japanese empire. They governed it through a highly centralized bureaucracy, headquartered in Seoul and staffed at the upper levels by Japanese. The governing apparatus was huge compared to those of other colonial regimes of the period. For example, in 1937 the French governed 17 million people in Indochina through a thin layer of 2,929 administrative personnel, 10,776 regular French troops, and 38,000 indigenous employees. In contrast, Japanese rule over Korea's 21 million people in the same year required 246,000 Japanese in public and professional positions, supported by 63,000 Koreans in subordinate positions.[6]

The swollen bureaucracy reached deeply into Korean society, placing Japanese policemen in every village and giving the central government powers of control, mobilization, and extraction of resources far exceeding any in previous Korean experience. New roads and railroads in remote rural regions opened these areas to outside influence and gave them access to urban markets. Cadastral surveys regularized land ownership, enabling the state to extract larger amounts of taxes and furthering the concentration of land in fewer hands. The population grew rapidly, increasing 25–30 percent during each decade,[7] sharply reversing the population decline that had prevailed during the nineteenth century. Peasants poured into the towns and cities, and the Japanese recruited large numbers of them to perform unskilled labor in Japan and Manchuria, particularly during World War II.[8]

The Japanese left behind a relatively modern infrastructure: roads, railroads, communications facilities, schools, hospitals, improved agricultural techniques, a body of experienced lower-level bureaucrats and police officers, and a very few Korean entrepreneurs in commerce and small industry. But, for most Koreans, the benefits of Japanese rule were far outweighed by the repressive and discriminatory way in which that rule was exercised. The Japanese owned most of the industry and much of the land in Korea. Illiteracy was high among Koreans, and only 5 percent of them went beyond primary school. In 1936 less than 1 percent of college-age Koreans were in college.[9] The privileged Japanese residents of Japan's Korean colony looked down on the locals as second-class citizens. Strict police controls squelched manifestations of Korean nationalism; thousands of Koreans were imprisoned. As Japan itself became more militarized during the war against China, the Japanese sought to assimilate the Koreans completely, closing down the Korean press and forbidding the use of the Korean language in schools and business. Koreans were compelled to adopt Japanese names. In the period after the Japanese left, hatred engendered by Japanese colonial rule often produced violent actions against those accused of having collaborated with the Japanese, particularly the Korean police.[10]

The economic consequences of the division of Korea were serious and immediate, for the two areas had been heavily interdependent. Most of the best mines were in the North. Eighty-six percent of heavy industry was in the North, whereas 75 percent of light industry, including 88 percent of textile production, was in the South. The South produced two-thirds of Korea's grain, but obtained the needed fertilizer from the North. Eighty-five percent of Korea's electricity and gas was produced in the North, where only one-third of the population lived.[11]

The U.S. and Soviet military commanders in Korea faced similar problems. They had to create a mechanism for maintaining law and order, devise a framework that would keep the economy running, and begin the political process of producing a Korean government to replace that of the departed Japanese. Lacking instructions as to how the vaguely agreed trusteeship was to work, each was confined to working within his own zone of occupation. Hodge did attempt to carry out a directive received in mid-October, five weeks after he had landed in Korea with his forces, to agree with the Soviets on ways of maintaining normal trade, transportation, and communication between the two zones of Korea, but the Soviet commander rebuffed his approaches on the ground that the two governments had not reached an agreement on these matters. Representations to the Soviet government by the U.S. Embassy in Moscow produced no results.[12] By the time the foreign ministers of the United States, the Soviet Union, and Great Britain met at the Moscow Conference in late December 1945, it was more than four months after Soviet forces had entered Korea and three months after the U.S. entry. The two commanders had already gone far toward setting up systems within their zones that reflected the contrasting political and economic concepts of their own countries.

Although the commanders faced similar problems, conditions in the two parts of Korea differed in important respects. The U.S. zone contained not only two-thirds of the population, but also the city of Seoul, the nerve-center of what had been a highly centralized system under the Japanese. Thus, the majority of Korean bureaucrats were in the South, especially those at higher levels; their numbers were further increased by the flight from North Korea of a large number of senior bureaucrats.[13] No comparable political center existed in North Korea; administrative lines had radiated directly from Seoul to each of Korea's provinces, both north and south of the 38th parallel. The Soviet commander lacked a ready-made center from which to administer his zone. Problems in the South were compounded by Koreans flooding in from Japan, Manchuria, and North Korea, a process already begun in 1945. This influx, which was to rise to nearly two million persons by the end of 1947, could not be absorbed quickly by the South's damaged economy. The North Korean population, on the other hand, declined during these years.[14] Another difference between North and South that would significantly affect the politics of the two zones was the smaller number of tenant farmers in the North and the flight to the South of considerable numbers of landowners, along with senior officials and police.

Soviet Occupation: The Early Months

Throughout Korea in the weeks after the Japanese surrender, Koreans spontaneously organized themselves into local and provincial "people's committees," which in many places took over governmental functions from the Japanese. Thousands of Koreans, imprisoned for anti-Japanese activities, were freed from jail, and many of them became members of these newly formed, self-appointed governing bodies. The exprisoners included many Communists, who had been the chief targets of Japanese suppression. People's Committees did not appear in every locality. They varied greatly in composition, and they did not answer to a central administration, although many declared allegiance to the Korean People's Republic (KPR) that was announced by a group of political leaders in Seoul two days before U.S. forces arrived. Politically, most inclined to the left, advocating a new order in Korea in which peasants and workers would benefit from the disposition of Japanese agricultural and industrial properties. They generally were hostile toward those who had staffed the bureaucracy and the police under the Japanese and toward Korean landlords and businessmen who had collaborated with the Japanese.[15]

The Soviets made an early decision to work through these local committees in governing their zone, rather than set up a military government.[16] Where committees did not exist, they created them. Where Korean Communists were inadequately represented, they reorganized the committees to include more. The Soviets were experienced in working through united front organizations, where a minority of disciplined Communists could exercise control behind the scenes. They also had brought with them a group of Korean residents of the Soviet Union trained for political and technical tasks; the members of this group, many of them from the Soviet Communist Party, were variously reported as numbering from several hundred to several thousand. In addition, they had brought Kim Il Sung and his small group of partisans, later to be known as the "Kapsan" faction—after the Kapsan mountains, one of their former guerrilla bases.

The Korean Communists were far from unified when Korea was liberated. Those in the Soviet Union had few ties with the Korean

Communists associated with the Chinese Communists in Yenan. Neither of these groups had strong connections with Communists inside Korea, most of whom had been jailed by the Japanese. The Korean Communists were notorious for factional infighting, which accounted in part for the effectiveness of their suppression by the Japanese. Consequently, an early task for the Soviets was to encourage the formation of a unified, disciplined Korean Communist Party, which would become a reliable instrument for controlling affairs in Korea.

Kim Il Sung was a suitable candidate for Soviet support for several reasons. He had never been involved in the factional disputes that had afflicted the domestic Communists in the past. As one of the few leading anti-Japanese guerrilla fighters who had not been captured or killed by the Japanese, he could be presented to the Korean people as an authentic national hero. He had presumably convinced the Soviet officials with whom he had worked between 1941 and 1945 of his leadership qualities. His lack of supporters within Korea and his youth would make him dependent on Soviet backing and therefore, they must have thought, amenable to Soviet direction.

Time would be needed for Kim to become the leading figure among the Korean Communists and for the Korean Communists to gain the dominant position in the Soviet zone, even with the benefit of Soviet support. When Soviet forces reached Pyongyang on August 24, they found the city in the hands of a committee headed by Cho Man-sik, a respected noncommunist nationalist who had been asked by the Japanese provincial governor to assist in maintaining order after the Japanese surrender. The Soviets left Cho in charge, but reorganized the committee to include more Communists. In October 1945 Cho became the chairman of the Five Provinces Administrative Bureau, a body set up to provide loose coordination among the provinces of the Soviet zone.

Thus, Kim Il Sung did not become the top governmental figure in the Soviet zone at the October 14 rally presentation. Neither did he assume leadership of the North Korean Branch Bureau of the Korean Communist Party, which was organized later that month and continued to regard itself as a part of the national Korean Communist Party based in Seoul and headed by the leading domestic Communist, Pak Hon-yong. At a party meeting on December 17, however, Kim became head of the North Korean Branch Bureau and immediately launched a party purge to weaken the power of the domestic faction in the north and consolidate his own position. Party historians later described this meeting as a critical turning point in Kim's fortunes.

By the eve of the December 1945 Moscow Conference the Soviets had put an end to an orgy of rape and pillage by their occupation forces that had badly stained the Soviet image among the Koreans. They had ordered the dissolution of armed units established by the people's committees, permitting their reestablishment after screening by the Soviet military command to make them reliable adjuncts to Soviet forces in maintaining order. They had supervised the formation of an administrative structure, an economic system, and a small but growing Communist party organization for the northern zone, headed by a leader whom they had helped to gain power. The skeleton of a separate political system existed in the north, but the Soviets continued to subscribe to the concept of a unified Korean government centered in Seoul.[17]

U.S. Occupation: The Early Months

During the three-week interval between the Japanese surrender on August 15 and the landing of U.S. occupation forces at Inchon on September 8, Korean political leaders began positioning themselves for the struggle for power. On one side was the KPR, which claimed jurisdiction over the people's committees throughout Korea. It was the outgrowth of a committee originally established by a leftist political leader, Yo Un-hyong, at the request of the Japanese governor-general to keep the peace in the weeks immediately after the Japanese surrender. Dominated by moderate leftists and Communist politicians, including many who had been incarcerated by the Japanese, the KPR stood for the punishment of collaborators with the Japanese and for sweeping social and political change, including the nationalization of banks, mines, and factories. In an effort to dilute somewhat its strongly leftist composition, the KPR named to its shadow cabinet several well-known rightists, including Syngman Rhee as chairman, Kim Ku as minister of interior, and Kim Kyu-sik as foreign minister. All three were outside the country, Rhee still in the United States and the two Kims in Chongqing where they were members of the Korean Provisional Government (KPG), long in exile there.

Conservative landowners and businessmen, worried by the influence of Communists within the KPR and alarmed by the radical policies it advocated, banded together in an opposition movement under the name of the Korean Democratic Party (KDP). They backed the KPG as the legitimate government of Korea and named as leaders two of the same politicians in exile chosen by the KPR—Syngman Rhee and Kim Ku. Initially, the activities of the KDP were limited to members of the conservative elite in Seoul, in contrast to the KPR, which launched an early effort to mobilize support from the congeries of people's committees and other local organizations that had sprung up throughout the country.

General Hodge had two tasks to perform when he brought his occupation forces into Korea: first, to administer the zone south of the

38th parallel in an orderly manner and, second, to encourage the emergence of political leaders who would be able to form the nucleus of a Korean government when agreement had been reached with the Soviets on a trusteeship formula. The first task was difficult but doable. Hodge was supplied with military government teams, most of them trained for the occupation of Japan but diverted to Korea when the U.S. government decided to govern Japan through the existing governmental machinery. The teams utilized the Korean bureaucracy and the national police, promoting Koreans to the top-level positions vacated by the Japanese. Reliance on Koreans seen by many of their compatriots as having collaborated with the hated Japanese was to create political problems for the military government later, but the bureaucracy provided an efficient, centralized mechanism through which to administer the occupation zone.

For the second task, Hodge lacked experience, qualified personnel, and adequate guidance. He soon discovered that the very idea of trusteeship was anathema to Koreans of all political persuasions, thus placing the military government at odds on a fundamental issue with those it was administering. To carry out his instructions to encourage the emergence of political leaders, Hodge, unlike the Soviets, had no cadre of trained political operatives of Korean origin. Neither was he free to throw the decisive weight of the military government behind a political leader or organization. On the contrary, while he was instructed to encourage the formation of democratic political parties, he was forbidden to recognize or utilize for political purposes "any self-styled Korean provisional government or similar political organization."[18] Recognition of either the KPR or the KPG, the two leading contenders in the Korean political struggle, was therefore ruled out.

Syngman Rhee, too, was far from being a chosen instrument of the U.S. government when he returned to Korea in October 1945, even though his return was sponsored by the U.S. military. The State department, which had opposed his return, took exception to his extreme anti-Soviet views and his opposition to trusteeship. Hodge himself was taken aback at the stridency of Rhee's anti-Soviet rhetoric in his first public address. Later, Hodge was to write, after clashes with Rhee over policy: "I've had a couple of stormy sessions with the old rascal, trying to keep him on the beam."[19]

Rhee's stature as a longtime fighter for Korea's independence from Japan enabled him on his return to take a position above the fray and briefly draw leaders of right and left together in a Council for the Rapid Realization of Korean Independence, a cause on which all could agree. But the deep differences between right and left, together with Rhee's own unconcealed hostility toward the Communists, soon caused this group to fall apart. Rhee began to draw closer to the KDP and to KPG leaders, who arrived in Korea in November from Chongqing. Financial backing from a number of wealthy Koreans helped Rhee to strengthen his political position.

In mid-December 1945 the U.S. military government banned the KPR for its refusal to abandon its claim to be a government. KPR leaders continued active political maneuvering as party heads but had to contend with U.S. opposition to the radical policies they espoused. Local organizations affiliated with the KPR came under growing pressure. U.S. authorities increasingly favored the conservative KDP, although without giving it any formal endorsement.

The growing opposition of the U.S. military government to left-wing groups resulted in part from the influence of the Korean bureaucracy, particularly the Korean national police. Knowing that if the KPR should come to power they would be punished for collaboration with the Japanese, it was in their interest to weaken the left and strengthen the right, and they worked hard to push the military government in that direction.

The sharpening confrontation between right and left in the political arena, complicated by stormy factional disputes within each camp, increasingly hobbled Hodge's efforts to produce a unified political leadership that would cooperate with the United States. Serious economic and social problems, including inflation, declining industrial production, spreading unemployment, and a rising crime rate added to his troubles. Demands by politicians for immediate independence for Korea drew enthusiastic responses from Korean crowds.

On December 16 Hodge warned that the U.S. occupation was drifting toward "a political-economic abyss." Every day of delay in positive action to unite Korea, Hodge said, made its division more permanent; Koreans were becoming increasingly resentful toward the United States, which they blamed for the partition. Their desire for immediate independence was so strong, in Hodge's opinion, that they might "physically revolt" against any attempt to impose trusteeship on them. Hodge urgently recommended the unification of Korea and the abandonment of the trusteeship concept.[20] On the very day that Hodge made these recommendations the Moscow Conference convened to work out the details of a trusteeship.

The Failure of Trusteeship

At the Moscow Conference the United States and the Soviet Union agreed that their respective Korean commands were to meet promptly to resolve urgent administrative and economic problems. A Joint Commission of representatives of the two commands was to formulate recommendations in consultation with "Korean democratic parties and social organizations," for the establishment of a provisional Korean democratic government.

The announcement of the Moscow agreement brought a storm of protest from all political groups in the U.S. zone. Massive demonstrations erupted in the cities. The Korean Communist Party in the South, after initially opposing trusteeship along with the other political parties, soon reversed itself and lined up with the Soviet-dominated Communist Party in the North. As a result of having taken this unpopular position, the Communists lost ground in the South and the polarization of politics there hardened. In the North the refusal of Cho Man-sik, the leading noncommunist nationalist, to support trusteeship led to his arrest and disappearance.

Meetings of representatives of the two commands to coordinate the economies of the two zones made little progress. The United States wanted broad arrangements: a unified operation of railroads and electric power, a single currency, and the free interflow of goods between zones. The Soviet Union wanted only to negotiate specific exchanges of products, in particular the exchange of electricity, raw materials, and chemical products for rice. But their proposals came to nothing because of a shortage of rice in the South.

The meetings of the Joint Commission during 1946 and 1947 to set up a provisional Korean government were no more successful than the effort to break down the administrative barrier at the 38th parallel. By January 1946 each occupying power had established a firm grip on the part of Korea it occupied. The Koreans on whom each had come to rely—Kim Il Sung and the Communist Party in the North, the rightists, bureaucrats, and police in the South—were deadly enemies and bitter rivals for dominance in a unified Korea. U.S. and Soviet representatives on the Joint Commission could not agree on which Korean political groups to consult in developing recommendations for a provisional government. Neither the United States nor the Soviet Union would accept arrangements that the other could exploit to gain a predominant position in the Korean peninsula. Confrontations elsewhere in the world cooled relations between Washington and Moscow, causing each to become more determined to cling to its foothold in Korea.

Crystallization of Two Regimes

The emergence of different and separate regimes in North and South was already well under way by the end of 1945. During the next two years the process gained momentum, while U.S. and Soviet representatives in the Joint Commission squabbled over how to carry out the Moscow agreement. As Hodge had accurately noted, every day of delay in unifying Korea made the division more permanent.

In the North Kim Il Sung systematically isolated his adversaries and strengthened the position of the Communist Party. Cho Man-sik's opposition to trusteeship gave Kim an opportunity with Soviet assistance to destroy the political influence of Cho and his noncommunist nationalist supporters. Kim became chairman of a new governmental body established in February 1946, the North Korean Provincial People's Committee, with Kim Tu-bong, a Yenan faction leader, as vice chairman. During the next few months the committee promulgated a series of basic laws for the northern zone, which set in motion a sweeping social revolution and put in place the basic structure of a socialist state. Land reform, the most important of these measures, won much popular support as it benefited hundreds of thousands of peasants. It became a potent propaganda instrument for the Communist Party and other leftists in the southern zone, who advocated similar measures there. In August 1946 the Yenan faction, which had for a few months operated as a separate party, rejoined the mainstream Communist Party, now renamed the North Korean Workers' Party. The Central Committee elected Kim Tu-bong chairman and Kim Il Sung one of two vice chairmen. Kim Il Sung still had to share leadership, but he was steadily gathering support for ascent to the top.

In late 1946 the North Korean Provisional People's Committee, following a decision by the U.S. military government to elect an interim legislature in the South, held elections for local and provincial peoples committees, representatives of which, in early 1947, elected a People's Assembly for North Korea. The Assembly, after endorsing legislation previously enacted by the Provisional People's Committee, replaced it with a new People's Committee, headed by Kim Il Sung, as the top Korean governing body in the Soviet occupation zone.

The creation and consolidation of the political system in the Soviet zone did not go as smoothly as suggested in the brief description above. At least one prominent political leader was assassinated, others disappeared. Here and there opposition to Soviet policies had to be put down by force. Whether Major General Romanenko, the officer responsible for guidance to the Soviet Koreans and the Kapsan group, had any "stormy sessions" with Kim Il Sung we do not know. Perhaps Kim was more tactful and effective in managing his foreign sponsors than Syngman Rhee, whose outspokenness and stubbornness were legendary.

In the South, where the U.S. authorities operated from the center of the stage instead of behind the scenes, problems proliferated. Assassinations removed several political leaders on both right and left. Following instructions from Washington, the military government spent several months trying without success to organize a coalition of moderate politicians in the center, shunning both Syngman Rhee and Kim Ku on the extreme right and the Communists led by Pak Hon-yong on the extreme left. Pak Hon-yong's resistance to the coalition and other disruptive activities by the Communists caused the military government to issue a warrant for his arrest. He subsequently fled to North Korea. General Hodge deplored Syngman Rhee's clamorous opposition but took no reprisals. The election in October 1946 of a South Korean Interim Legislature was boycotted by the leftists; as a result it produced a body almost exclusively from the right.

Not only did U.S. efforts to form a broadly based political body fail, but severe disorders broke out in the U.S. zone in the fall of 1946. The military government had come to rely increasingly on the centralized Korean national police organization to assert its control over the zone, bypassing and working to weaken leftist-dominated local people's committees. Dissatisfaction with the forcible collection of rice from the peasants by the police, rising rice prices, the refusal to confer power on the people's committees, and the lack of jobs for the tens of thousands of workers who had returned to the U.S. zone from Japan, Manchuria, and the Soviet zone had created a combustible mixture, which burst into flames in September 1946. Strikes and demonstrations soon led to pitched battles in many places between mobs and the police in which hundreds of policemen and rioters were killed and thousands arrested. In Gregory Henderson's words, South Korean society stood "at the gates of chaos," and U.S. troops had to intervene directly to restore order.[21]

When the smoke of battle lifted, the Korean national police had strengthened their position; they had smashed the power of the leading people's committees and had cowed the peasant agitators. The military government at the time suspected that the Communists in the Soviet zone had orchestrated the uprisings, but subsequent analysis of the contemporary records shows little evidence of direct northern involvement. Communists in the South took part, but they could not control and coordinate the opposition, which erupted sporadically in reaction to local grievances. By the end of 1946, the U.S. military government and the well-organized Korean bureaucracy had restored order, greatly weakened the leftists, and driven underground the radical advocates of revolution against the old order.[22]

Syngman Rhee's obdurate opposition to a trusteeship and his public excoriation of the Communists and the Soviet Union, at a time when General Hodge was trying to negotiate with the Soviets and organize a group of moderate Korean leaders who would accept trusteeship, created a deep rift between the two men. Rhee, a stirring speaker, stumped the South, adding to his popularity and reinforcing his patriotic credentials with emotional demands for Korean independence. Factional disputes crippled attempts by his opponents of right, center, and left to organize against him. He quietly built bases of support within the bureaucracy and police, while some of his backers organized youth groups and unions to counter those organized earlier by the left. His financial support from conservative Koreans was threatened temporarily by his exclusion from the Korean interim government set up in the South by the United States as a basis on which to resume negotiations with the Soviets on trusteeship. But by the time trusteeship negotiations had collapsed for good in August 1947, Rhee had positioned himself to become the unchallengeable political leader in the U.S. zone. Despite their distrust of Rhee, many U.S. officials increasingly shared his suspicion of the Soviet Union as the cold war intensified.

The status Rhee had achieved in Korea would give the U.S. government little choice but to support him.[23]

By September 1947 the U.S. government had concluded that the impasse between the United States and the Soviet Union on the establishment of a provisional government for a unified Korea could not be broken and proposed that the question of Korea's independence be referred to the UN General Assembly. The Soviets countered with a proposal for the withdrawal of all foreign troops from Korea, which the United States rejected. In November 1947 the General Assembly, overriding Soviet opposition, voted to establish a United Nations Temporary Commission on Korea to observe free elections by secret ballot to choose a national assembly. The Temporary Commission, refused admission to the northern part of the country, decided that it would observe elections in that part of Korea accessible to it, which contained two-thirds of the population.

The Soviets and Kim Il Sung condemned the proposed UN action as a scheme instigated by the United States to dismember Korea. Prominent Korean politicians Kim Ku and Kim Kyu-sik broke with Syngman Rhee over the issue of separate elections in South Korea. They attended a "unity conference" in Pyongyang in April 1948, providing a public demonstration that significant political opposition to separate elections existed in South Korea, but the conference did not dissuade the United States and the United Nations from going ahead.

The elections, held in May 1948, were certified by the Temporary Commission as "a valid expression of the free will of the electorate in those parts of Korea which were accessible to the Commission."[24] The elections produced a 198-member National Assembly dominated by conservative forces. One hundred additional seats were left open, to be filled by members from North Korea when elections could be held there.

The Assembly promptly drafted a constitution establishing the Republic of Korea and elected Syngman Rhee as its first president. On August 15, 1948, authority was transferred from the U.S. military government to the Republic of Korea (ROK), which was soon accorded diplomatic recognition by the United States.

Parallel actions occurred in North Korea during the autumn of 1948 free from the scrutiny of the United Nations: the election of a Supreme People's Assembly (SPA), the adoption of a constitution, the establishment of the Democratic People's Republic of Korea (DPRK) with Kim Il Sung as premier, and the recognition of the new government by the Soviet Union and other Communist states.

Thus, within three years after Korea had been liberated from Japanese control it had been formally divided into two separate states, each supported by one of the superpowers. The 38th parallel had become, without anyone's having planned it, one of the main lines of confrontation in the developing cold war.

Consolidation and Confrontation, 1948–1950

As premier of the newly established DPRK, Kim Il Sung pressed ahead with the transformation of North Korean society into a socialist state. By 1949 90 percent of industrial production and more than half of trade was in the hands of the government.[25] A two-year economic plan, adopted in 1949 and backed by Soviet economic assistance, favored development of heavy industry. The government launched a large-scale program for the elimination of illiteracy and the expansion of education.

In June 1949 Kim became the chairman of a unified Korean Workers' Party, thus consolidating his power over both party and state. Pak Hon-yong, separated from his political base in the South, which itself had been severely weakened as a result of the Communists' policy of militant confrontation with the U.S. military government, became a vice chairman of the unified party. He was necessary to Kim for the influence he still had over the depleted Communist Party to the South but was no longer a real threat to Kim's leadership. The other vice chairman, Ho Ka-i, was a Soviet Korean, as was the director of the party's organization bureau. The former chairman of the North Korean Workers' Party, Kim Tu-bong, of the Yenan faction, was shunted aside to become chairman of the Supreme People's Assembly, a ceremonial position with little power. The Soviets maintained strong influence over the new government in the North through Soviet advisers in the ministries and Soviet Koreans throughout key party organizations and agencies of government. Many of these Soviet Koreans held dual citizenship. Satisfied that North Korea was bound firmly to the Soviet camp, the Soviets had withdrawn their forces in December 1948 and demanded that the United States do the same.

From the time of its founding, a primary objective of the DPRK was to extend its power over the South. In its view, which the Soviet Union vigorously backed, the UN had acted illegally in sponsoring the elections in the South and the founding of the ROK. The DPRK claimed that the election of the Supreme People's Assembly in August 1948 had taken place throughout Korea, with more than 8 million people in South Korea participating secretly. Of the 572 SPA members, 360 were said to represent South Korea, where the majority of the Korean people lived. DPRK leaders saw the demonstrations and riots in the fall of 1946 in opposition to the U.S. military government as evidence of widespread southern support for the North's new socialist system. They set about strengthening left-wing resistance to the rightist-dominated government of Syngman Rhee and sent in armed agents to organize guerrilla warfare against that government. In his speeches in 1949 Pak Hon-yong accused the United States of having imposed slavery on the people of South Korea. He urged the unification of Korea in accordance with proposals made by the Democratic Front for the Unification of the Fatherland, established in North Korea in June 1949, and he described unification as the most important and immediate task of the party and people.[26]

During 1949 and 1950 the Korean People's Army (KPA), formally established in February 1948 but based on the organization and training of military units by the Soviets begun as early as 1945, gained rapidly in strength. At least 30,000 Korean soldiers who had fought with the People's Liberation Army in China joined the KPA's ranks after the decisive defeat of the Kuomintang in mainland China in 1949. U.S. intelligence estimated that 80 percent of all officers in the KPA had served with Chinese forces.[27] In 1950 Choe Yong-gon, who, like Kim Il Sung, had fought the Japanese in Manchuria and spent the years 1941 through 1945 in the Soviet Union, was defense minister. Kang Kon, another Kapsan comrade, was chief of staff. Altogether some 10,000 military men had received training in the Soviet Union. Equipped by the Soviets with heavy artillery and medium tanks and supported by fighter aircraft and attack bombers, the 150,000 strong KPA was becoming a formidable fighting force.[28]

In South Korea, although the National Assembly had elected Rhee president by a vote of 180 to 16, it immediately set about to weaken his power and increase its own. The Assembly attacked Rhee's cabinet appointments; proposed a constitutional amendment changing the presidential system to a parliamentary system; and attempted a purge of Japanese collaborators in the bureaucracy, Rhee's main base of support.

Rhee succeeded, barely, in beating back these challenges, but at the cost of weakened support. He did shrewdly enhance his popularity among farmers and weaken the political influence of landlords (his erstwhile backers) by pushing through the Assembly a land reform bill in February 1950 that gave landlords a share in former Japanese industrial plants in exchange for land turned over to tenants.[29]

A far more serious threat to the Rhee government than the maneuvers of opposing politicians was armed insurrection by the Communists in South Korea during 1948 and 1949, backed by North Korea.[30] A bloody rebellion led by Communist guerrillas had broken out in Cheju-do in April 1948 in opposition to the forthcoming UN-sponsored elections. In October 1948, just two months after the establishment of the ROK, a constabulary unit in Yosu, being sent to reinforce troops struggling to suppress the Cheju-do rebellion, revolted and fled to nearby mountains to establish a guerrilla base. The Rhee government responded with a purge of suspected Communists in the military and widespread arrests of others accused of procommunist leanings. North Korea infiltrated guerrillas into various places in South Korea in an effort to instigate a general armed rebellion against the Rhee government. But the government forces launched a counteroffensive and by the winter of 1949 and 1950 had broken the back of the insurgent movement. North Korea's attempt to unify the country by supporting uprisings in the south had failed.

Demands for unification were not limited to the North Koreans. During 1949 and 1950 Rhee and others in his government called publicly for a march north. Clashes occurred along the 38th parallel with both sides mounting incursions and counterincursions. These border clashes dropped off sharply in the months before the Korean War broke out in June 1950.

Rhee's calls for a march north and raids by his forces across the border troubled U.S. officials. Other problems cropped up between him and the United States: differences over the administration of U.S. economic aid, Rhee's unwillingness to raise taxes to combat inflation, his threat to delay scheduled National Assembly elections, and U.S. unresponsiveness to Rhee's requests for additional military aid. But the most serious difference arose from a decision to withdraw U.S. forces from South Korea.

For the United States Korea was a distant and troublesome burden. Maintaining forces there was costly and ran counter to the prevailing desire in the United States to demobilize forces and reduce the military budget. China was rapidly falling under the control of victorious Chinese Communist armies. From the military viewpoint Korea was an exposed salient, difficult to hold in a general conflict, and the forces deployed there were needed elsewhere. Consequently, the Joint Chiefs of Staff recommended their withdrawal and General Douglas MacArthur concurred. Shortly after the establishment of the new South Korean government the United States quietly began a phased withdrawal of U.S. forces from Korea.[31] The withdrawals were halted briefly after the Yosu rebellion of October 1948, but were resumed early the next year and completed in June 1949.

Although the U.S. government wanted to disengage militarily from Korea, it did not wish to abandon South Korea to military conquest by North Korea. It adopted a three-pronged strategy to reduce that risk. It persuaded the United Nations to assume a long-term responsibility for the future of Korea; it sought to strengthen the South Korean economy through economic aid; and it continued equipping and training a South Korean military force.

The United Nations had already had a role in the establishment of the government of the Republic of Korea. Now, by a resolution of December 12, 1948, over the strenuous opposition of the Soviet bloc, the General Assembly declared that government to be a lawful government based on elections observed by the United Nations Temporary Commission. The elections were said to be a valid expression of the free will of the electorate in that part of Korea accessible to the commission. The resolution added: "this is the only such government in Korea." It also called for the withdrawal of foreign occupation forces as early as practicable and established a permanent UN Commission on Korea with a mandate to use its good offices to bring about a unification of the country and to observe the withdrawal of the occupation forces.[32]

The involvement of the United Nations in Korean affairs had far-reaching consequences. It facilitated UN intervention in defense of South Korea in 1950 and for many years thereafter provided a basis for the claims of the government of the ROK to be the only legitimate government on the Korean peninsula.

The second facet of U.S. policy, intended along with UN involvement and army-building to ensure the survival of a noncommunist South Korea after the withdrawal of U.S. forces, was economic development. During the occupation, the United States had contributed over $400 million in economic aid, but this contribution consisted almost entirely of emergency relief supplies, mainly in the form of food, clothing, fuel, and other commodities. Although these met the most urgent needs of a people that increased by 27 percent from 1944 to 1949, owing largely to the influx of 1.7 million Koreans from outside South Korea, it did not resolve the problems of low agricultural and industrial production and severe inflation. With the establishment of an independent South Korean government in 1948, the United States instituted a program of aid under the Economic Cooperation Administration (ECA) designed to further economic development.

The ECA-administered grants were intended not only to provide fertilizer, food, and industrial raw materials, but also to initiate a capital development program aimed at increasing coal production, electric power capacity, and fertilizer output. Some progress resulted. Agricultural production increased in 1948 and 1949, spurred by the distribution of land to tenant farmers instituted by the military government, and even industrial production increased substantially in the latter year. This increase provided some reason for optimism that the new economic aid program would significantly stimulate economic growth.[33] Unfortunately, it was interrupted by war when it was just beginning.

As early as November 1945 General Hodge had advised Washington that Korean police would not suffice to preserve order in South Korea and had suggested the establishment of Korean military forces. Washington deferred action on this suggestion pending international agreement on the future of Korea.[34] Hodge was permitted, however, to organize a national constabulary of some 20,000 men trained along infantry lines and equipped from a stockpile of Japanese rifles. In September 1947 Lieutenant General Albert C. Wedemeyer, after conducting a survey of conditions in China and Korea, warned that the North Korean army of 125,000 men was much stronger than the South Korean constabulary and recommended that the United States train and equip a South Korean army. Although MacArthur opposed this course of action on the ground that the U.S. occupation forces lacked the capability to organize and train an army, the U.S. government instructed Hodge to begin converting the constabulary into an army so that the withdrawal of U.S. forces could proceed.

After U.S. combat forces withdrew, a military advisory group of 500 men remained to continue training South Korean armed forces. By June 1950 the ROK army consisted of about 98,000 men, only 65,000 of whom had received unit training. They were furnished with equipment and supplies left behind by the withdrawing U.S. forces. In addition, a military aid program of $10.9 million had been authorized in January, but almost none of the equipment being purchased under this program had arrived in Korea by June. The force lacked heavy artillery, tanks, and aircraft.[35] It was no match in numbers, training, experience, or equipment for the far more powerful North Korean force.

Outbreak of the Korean War

The rationale for the withdrawal of U.S. forces was spelled out in a top secret decision of the National Security Council.[36] The document judged the Soviet aim in Korea to be the domination of all Korea through the DPRK and acknowledged the risk that the withdrawal of U.S. forces might be followed by a North Korean invasion. Nevertheless, it rejected a U.S. policy of defending South Korea "by force of arms if necessary" on the grounds that U.S. forces stationed in Korea might be destroyed or forced to withdraw in the event of a major hostile attack "in an area in which virtually all the natural advantages would accrue to the USSR." The Joint Chiefs of Staff approved a Department of the Army study of June 1949 rejecting U.S. military intervention in Korea in the event of a North Korean attack. They commented bluntly: "that Korea is of little strategic value to the United States and that any commitment to United States' use of military force in Korea would be ill-advised and impracticable in view of the over-all world situation and of our heavy international obligations as compared to our current military strength."[37]

North Korean superiority in weapons over South Korea was well-known within the U.S. government.[38] Even so, the small strategic importance attached to Korea hindered the efforts of those within the bureaucracy who pressed for more weapons for the South Koreans. At a meeting on May 10, 1950, Ambassador John J. Muccio urged that South Korea be furnished combat aircraft to match those possessed by the North Koreans. Major General Lyman L. Lemnitzer reminded him that military assistance to South Korea was essentially a political matter of concern principally to the State department because "South Korea was not regarded as of any particular value to the overall American strategic position in the Far East."[39]

The withdrawal of the last remaining U.S. combat forces from South Korea in June 1949 was a significant indicator to interested observers of the relative unimportance of the peninsula in U.S. strategic thinking. Conclusions to that effect must have been strengthened by MacArthur's statements during 1949 placing Korea outside the U.S. defense perimeter in the western Pacific. He told one correspondent: "Anyone who commits the American army on the mainland of Asia ought to have his head examined."[40] On January 12, 1950, Secretary of State Dean Acheson in a formal speech followed MacArthur's precedent by drawing the U.S. defensive line from Japan through the Ryukyus to the Philippines. He added that the defense of other areas would have to depend initially on the people attacked and then on "the commitments of the entire civilized world under the Charter of the United Nations."[41] Senator Tom Connally, chairman of the Senate Foreign Relations Committee, further confirmed the improbability of U.S. military intervention in Korea. When asked whether Korea was an essential part of U.S. defense strategy, he said: "No. Of course, any position like that is of some strategic importance. But I don't think it is very greatly important. It has been testified before us that Japan, Okinawa and the Philippines make the chain of defense which is absolutely necessary. And, of course, any additional territory along in that area would be that much more, but it's not absolutely essential."[42]

Based on U.S. actions and statements, Kim Il Sung's apparent conclusion that the United States would not intervene if his army moved south is understandable.[43] His attempt to reunify Korea by promoting insurrection in the South had failed, making invasion the only remaining option. According to Nikita Khrushchev's memoirs, Kim visited Stalin late in 1949 to propose an armed attack to unify Korea under his regime.[44] At first Stalin was doubtful, but he finally agreed to Kim's proposal after obtaining Mao Zedong's concurrence. Kim had good reason for confidence that his surprise attack would succeed quickly, for his military forces were much stronger than those in the South, and substantial quantities of new equipment arrived from the Soviet Union in the spring of 1950. Moreover, political support for Syngman Rhee was declining as severe inflation created much public dissatisfaction, and serious disagreements had developed between Rhee and the United States over Rhee's political and economic policies.[45] Kim was no doubt disappointed that his invasion did not trigger popular uprisings against the Rhee government, as he had predicted to Stalin. But even without that form of assistance, his judgment that his forces could quickly overrun the South proved correct. Only the unexpected U.S. military intervention thwarted his plan.[46]

President Harry Truman's decision to intervene militarily in Korea was one of the most dramatic policy reversals in U.S. history. His order to General MacArthur to land U.S. GIs in Korea to rally the routed South Korean army and conduct a last-ditch defense of the "Pusan perimeter" converted the security of South Korea overnight into a vital interest of the United States. Leaders of both political parties, the majority of U.S. citizens, and the Western European allies applauded the decision. Moscow's tactical error in absenting itself from the Security Council in protest over the exclusion of the People's Republic of China made possible Security Council resolutions calling on UN members to assist in repelling the armed attack on South Korea and setting up a UN Command with a commander to be designated by the United States. Although only 44,000 troops from 15 other UN-member countries took part in the Korean War, compared to the 350,000 U.S. soldiers eventually involved,[47] their presence provided evidence to the U.S. public and others that U.S. intervention had international support and sanction.

The original UN objective had been to push the invading forces out of South Korean territory, but the spectacular success of the Inchon landing in September 1950, leading to the disintegration of the North Korean army, opened the possibility of unifying Korea. The UN General Assembly (the Soviets had returned to the Security Council, thus ruling out the passage in that body of resolutions authorizing further UN intervention in Korea) called for UN-supervised elections to establish a "united, independent and democratic government in the sovereign state of Korea." It also authorized the creation of the UN Commission for the Unification and Rehabilitation of Korea to carry out this recommendation after the UN Command had "ensured conditions of stability throughout Korea."[48] As UN forces advanced toward the Yalu, meeting little resistance, the victorious allies discounted warnings from the Chinese that they could not stand idly by in the face of an advance menacing their security.

When the Chinese poured across the Yalu, the United States faced, in MacArthur's words, "an entirely new war."[49] The hope that the United Nations could unite Korea wilted. Chinese armies had punched their way well inside South Korea before U.S. and South Korean forces could halt their advance. Pushing them back to the vicinity of the 38th parallel was painful and costly. MacArthur's proposal to carry the war to China itself, rejected by Truman and his military advisers, and the general's subsequent recall for publicly disagreeing with the president's policy, reflected deepening divisions in the United States concerning the conduct and purpose of the war. Truce negotiations, begun in July 1951, dragged on while fighting continued.

The Armistice Agreement was finally signed on July 27, 1953, by General Mark W. Clark for the UN Command, by Marshal Kim Il Sung for the Democratic People's Republic of Korea, and by Peng Dehuai as commander of the Chinese People's Volunteers. It provided for a cease-fire and a military demarcation line cutting across Korea in the vicinity of the 38th parallel with a demilitarized zone two kilometers wide on either side to provide a buffer. The agreement also established a Military Armistice Commission composed of representatives of the two sides to supervise the implementation of the armistice and a Neutral Nations Supervisory Commission composed of representatives from Sweden, Switzerland, Poland, and Czechoslovakia to ensure that the armistice was observed. Additional articles of the agreement covered the repatriation of prisoners of war and forbade the introduction of reinforcement in the form of either men or weapons into Korea. Finally, the agreement stipulated that a political conference to settle the question of withdrawal of foreign forces and the peaceful settlement of the Korean question should be held within three months.

Outlook at War's End

When the war ended both Koreas lay devastated and exhausted. The hope of the Korean people for a unified independent nation had been destroyed for decades, perhaps for generations. The governing elites had acquired a profound hostility and suspicion of each other, which they passed on to their children. The Korean War marked a new stage in the global rivalry between the United States and the Soviet Union. When it ended, each part of Korea had become inextricably attached to one of the two contending camps. In the climate of the time, the political conference held in Geneva in 1954 to seek agreement on the unification of Korea was foredoomed to failure.

Kim and Rhee, the paramount leaders on either side of the 38th parallel, not only weathered the ordeal of war, but emerged strengthened by it. Each had come close to achieving his dream of unifying Korea under his leadership, only to see the dream shattered by the intervention of a foreign power. Each had survived only through the support of a foreign power. Neither abandoned the resolve to preside eventually over a unified nation.

Kim Il Sung took advantage of the war to eliminate some of his principal rivals. Mu Chong, the leading military figure of the Yenan faction, had greater military experience than Kim himself. Kim might have feared that he would exploit his connections with the Chinese, on whom the Korean Communists had become dependent for survival after the near-destruction of their own forces. Accused of having failed to defend Pyongyang after UN forces landed at Inchon and advanced north, Mu Chong was cashiered and eliminated as a political rival. Kim also built a case against Pak Hon-yong, leader of the domestic faction, who had served as foreign minister during much of the war, and a number of his associates. Kim accused them of having been agents of the United States and, after show trials, had them executed, thus decapitating the domestic faction.[50]

Rhee also found opportunities in wartime conditions to shore up his precarious position. He beat back renewed attempts by the National Assembly to replace the presidential system by a parliamentary system. By resorting to police power, he forced through the Assembly a constitutional amendment providing for election of the president by popular vote, rather than by the Assembly. In 1952 he was reelected by an overwhelming majority. Through control of appointments to top positions in the rapidly growing South Korean army, by diverting a portion of U.S. aid to political purposes, and by establishing his own political party, Rhee consolidated his position.

Rhee almost caused an irreparable break with the United States by insisting on continuing the war until the Chinese had been driven from Korea and the nation unified under his government. By mid-1953 fighting had continued for two years after peace negotiations had begun, and the early support for the war in the United States had crumbled. In an attempt to torpedo the negotiations, Rhee unilaterally released a large number of Korean prisoners of war who had declared themselves anticommunist. So intractable had he become that the U.S. government at one time prepared a secret plan for the U.S. military to take him into custody. In the end he agreed to respect the terms of the armistice, although he refused to sign it. In exchange, the United States agreed to conclude a mutual defense treaty with the ROK, to equip air and naval forces and an army of 20 divisions, and to provide generous postwar economic aid.

Whether Kim Il Sung created similar problems for the Soviets and Chinese by insisting on the continuation of the war we do not know. He was certainly no less determined than Rhee was to see Korea unified under his government. He did, however, sign the armistice, whereas Rhee did not, giving Kim a tactical advantage in later years in his maneuvering for international advantage.

Caught from their very inception in the web of big power politics, the two Koreas have had to be more sensitive than most countries to the changing international scene. Outside influences profoundly affected the nature of their political and economic systems. Their security and their pace of economic development have depended heavily on the connections they succeeded in establishing with other countries. During the early years after the Korean War, both were preoccupied with physical reconstruction and army-building, tasks for which they required above all close relations with their big power sponsors. The respective relationships of South Korea to the United States and of North Korea to the Soviet Union remain basic to the security of both Koreas. Yet with the Sino-Soviet split and the increasing multipolarity of the international system, rivalry between the two Koreas for connections, prestige, and influence in the world at large has become steadily more important.

Notes

1. Joungwon A. Kim, *Divided Korea: The Politics of Development, 1945–1972* (Cambridge: Harvard University Press, 1975), p. 92.

2. For a picture of Kim at the rally with Soviet officers in the background, see Robert A. Scalapino and Chong-Sik Lee, *Communism in Korea* (Berkeley: University of California Press, 1972), vol. 1, p. 332; for a picture of Syngman Rhee speaking, with General Hodge in the background, see Bruce Cumings,

The Origins of the Korean War: Liberation and the Emergence of Separate Regimes, 1945–1949 (Princeton, N.J.: Princeton University Press, 1981), p. 157.

3. Almost nothing is known about Kim's activities while in the Soviet Union. Reports that he held the rank of major in the Soviet army and that he had made one or more trips to Moscow cannot be confirmed. The most detailed and reliable account of Kim's early life can be found in Scalapino and Lee, *Communism in Korea*, vol. 1. Baik Bong's three-volume *Kim Il Sung: Biography* (Tokyo: Miraisha, 1969) is the official hagiography, presenting Kim as a godlike figure from his earliest years. See also Dae-Sook Suh, *The Korean Communist Movement, 1918–1948* (Princeton, N.J.: Princeton University Press, 1967) and Sung Chul Yang, *Korea and Two Regimes: Kim Il Sung and Park Chung Hee* (Cambridge, Mass.: Schenkman, 1981).

4. Carl Berger, *The Korea Knot* (Philadelphia: University of Pennsylvania Press, 1957), pp. 36–41; U.S. Department of State, *Foreign Relations of the United States* [hereafter cited as *FRUS*]: *Diplomatic Papers, Conferences at Malta and Yalta, 1945* (Washington, D.C.: U.S. Government Printing Office, 1945), p. 770.

5. The colonels were Dean Rusk, later to become secretary of state, and C. H. Bonesteel, who was to be named commander of U.S. forces in Korea in the 1970s. Rusk's recollection of that hectic night five years afterward was that the 38th parallel was chosen because it was thought important to include the Korean capital, Seoul, within the area of U.S. responsibility, even though Soviet forces would probably reach the demarcation line before U.S. forces could. Rusk recalled being somewhat surprised that the Soviets accepted a line that far north. *FRUS, 1945*, vol. 6, p. 1039.

6. Cumings, *Origins of the Korean War*, p. 12.

7. Ibid., p. 54; Kim, *Divided Korea*, p. 11.

8. Cumings, *Origins of the Korean War*, p. 56. Cumings estimates that over four million Koreans worked in Japan at some time during the colonial period and at least two million in Manchuria.

9. Gregory Henderson, *Korea: The Politics of the Vortex* (Cambridge: Harvard University Press, 1968), p. 89.

10. For more detailed analyses of the Japanese colonial period, see Cumings, *Origins of the Korean War*, Chapters 1 and 2; and Henderson, *Korea: The Politics of the Vortex*, Chapter 4.

11. Kim, *Divided Korea*, p. 33.

12. *FRUS, 1945*, vol. 6, pp. 1073–91.

13. Cumings, *Origins of the Korean War*, p. 154.

14. Ibid., pp. 60–61.

15. Ibid., Chapters 8 and 9 contain the most thorough study of the emergence and treatment of people's committees in the U.S. zone of Korea, based largely on U.S. official records from the period. In the absence of comparable Soviet documentation, no similar study can be made of the emergence and treatment of people's committees in the Soviet zone. Cumings, in Chapter 11 of *Origins of the Korean War*, and Scalapino and Lee in *Communism in Korea*, vol. 1, Chapter 5, do the best they can with the skimpy documentation available.

16. Nothing is known of Soviet planning for the occupation of Korea; Soviet aims must be inferred from behavior. We do not know whether there were

differences within the top leadership in Moscow concerning policy toward Korea or between Moscow and the commander in the field. Even the relationships between the Soviets and the Koreans in Korea have to be reconstructed largely from statements by Korean participants, often made much later and with axes of their own to grind. Soviet contemporary documentation, except for public orders and statements, is unavailable, in striking contrast to the wealth of U.S. documentation made available to scholars in recent years, ranging from originally top secret National Security Council papers to formerly classified reports from U.S. diplomats and military officers in Korea.

17. According to Cumings, "there is simply no evidence to support the assertion that the Soviets or their allies planned for a separate regime in the north before February 1946" (Cumings, *Origins of the Korean War*, p. 393). The absence of evidence is not necessarily conclusive, as Soviet internal records of the period are unavailable. See note 16 above.

18. *FRUS, 1945*, vol. 6, p. 1081.

19. Cumings, *Origins of the Korean War*, p. 250.

20. *FRUS, 1945*, vol. 6, pp. 1145–47.

21. Henderson, *Korea: The Politics of the Vortex*, pp. 137–147.

22. See Cumings, *Origins of the Korean War*, Chapter 10, for an account of what he calls "The Autumn Harvest Uprisings."

23. For a sympathetic account of Rhee's activities during this period, see Robert T. Oliver, *Syngman Rhee and American Involvement in Korea, 1942–1960* (Seoul: Panmun Book Co., Ltd., 1973), pp. 24–91. Cumings is critical of Rhee and his right-wing supporters, but describes his successful manipulation of politics in the south as "a virtuoso performance" (*Origins of the Korean War*, p. 431). See also Kim, *Divided Korea*, pp. 60–79.

24. Leland M. Goodrich, *Korea: A Study of U.S. Policy in the United Nations* (New York: Council on Foreign Relations, 1956), p. 60.

25. Kim, *Divided Korea*, p. 171.

26. Scalapino and Lee, *Communism in Korea*, vol. 1, p. 390.

27. Bruce Cumings, "Introduction," in Bruce Cumings, ed., *Child of Conflict: The Korean-American Relationship, 1943–1953* (Seattle: University of Washington Press, 1983), p. 39.

28. Scalapino and Lee, *Communism in Korea*, vol. 1, pp. 390–393. Soon Sung Cho, *Korea in World Politics 1940–1950: An Evaluation of American Responsibility* (Berkeley: University of California Press, 1967), pp. 255–258. David Rees, *Korea: The Limited War* (Baltimore: Penguin Books, Inc., 1964), pp. 16–17.

29. In 1947 and 1948 the U.S. military government had sold to half a million tenant farmers land formerly owned by Japanese, thus reducing tenancy from 75 percent to 33 percent. This action did much to weaken Communist influence in rural areas (see Henderson, *Korea: The Politics of the Vortex*, p. 156). Rhee had opposed military government sale of Japanese lands, wanting the credit for that enlightened and politically costless move to accrue to the soon-to-be established South Korean government.

30. For an account of this insurrection and the concurrent clashes between the forces of the two Koreas along the 38th parallel, see John Merrill, "Internal Warfare in Korea," in Cumings, *Child of Conflict*, pp. 133–162.

31. Cho, *Korea in World Politics*, p. 230.

32. For the texts of the United Nations resolutions on Korea, see Goodrich, *Korea: A Study of U.S. Policy in the United Nations*, pp. 215–234.

33. Data on U.S. economic contributions to Korea are from Paul W. Kuznets, *Economic Growth and Structure in the Republic of Korea* (New Haven, Conn.: Yale University Press, 1977), pp. 30–36.

34. *FRUS, 1945*, vol. 6, pp. 1137 and 1157.

35. For additional details on the withdrawal of U.S. forces and the buildup of the South Korean armed forces, see Cho, *Korea in World Politics*, pp. 226–236 and 246–255; also David Rees, *Korea: The Limited War*, pp. 13–16.

36. National Security Council, NSC 8/2, approved by President Truman on March 23, 1949. It was a revised version of the statement of policy on Korea contained in NSC 8 of April 2, 1948. See *FRUS, 1949*, vol. 7, Far East and Australasia, Part 2, pp. 969–978.

37. *FRUS, 1949*, vol. 7, Far East and Australasia, Part 2, pp. 1046–57.

38. See, for example, a CIA estimate of June 19, 1950, concurred in by State, Army, Navy, and Air Force. *FRUS, 1950*, vol. 7, Korea, pp. 105–124.

39. *FRUS, 1950*, vol. 7, Korea, p. 79.

40. Statement to William R. Mathews of the *Arizona Daily Star* quoted in Richard H. Rovere and Arthur M. Schlesinger, Jr., *The General and the President* (New York: Farrar, Straus, 1951), p. 100. See Cho, *Korea in World Politics*, p. 260.

41. Dean Acheson, *Present at the Creation* (New York: W. W. Norton & Co., 1969), p. 357.

42. "World Policy and Bipartisanship: An Interview with Senator Tom Connally," *U.S. News and World Report*, May 5, 1950. See *FRUS, 1950*, vol. 7, Korea, pp. 65–66.

43. Stalin, if not Kim Il Sung, may even have known of statements in highly classified U.S. internal documents that U.S. forces would not intervene in the event of a North Korean attack as the Soviet spies in Britain, Kim Philby and Guy Burgess, had access to large quantities of U.S. classified materials.

44. Strobe Talbott, ed., *Khrushchev Remembers* (New York: Bantam Books, 1971), p. 401.

45. See Kim, *Divided Korea*, pp. 115–132. Kim concludes, "When the Korean war broke out, the South Korean political system, under the leadership of Syngman Rhee, was in an advanced state of political disintegration, its initially weak political bases nearing internal collapse" (p. 132).

46. The U.S. intervention in Korea is discussed in many books; some of the most useful are Dean Acheson, *Present at the Creation;* Matthew B. Ridgway, *Soldier* (New York: Harper, 1956); Harry S. Truman, *Memoirs, Vol. II, Years of Trial and Hope* (London: Hodder and Stoughton, 1956); Trumbull Higgins, *Korea and the Fall of MacArthur* (New York: Oxford University Press, 1960); Robert Leckie, *Conflict: The History of the Korean War 1950–53* (New York: Putnam, 1962); Glen D. Paige, *The Korean Decision, June 24–30, 1950* (New York: Free Press, 1968); David Rees, *Korea: The Limited War;* Richard Rovere and Arthur Schlesinger, Jr., *The General and the President;* John W. Spanier, *The Truman-*

MacArthur Controversy and the Korean War (Cambridge: Harvard University Press, 1959); Allen S. Whiting, *China Crosses the Yalu* (New York: Macmillan, 1960). Revisionist interpretations of the war appear in I. F. Stone, *The Hidden History of the Korean War* (London: Turnstile Press, 1952); Joyce and Gabriel Kolko, *The Limits of Power: The World and United States Foreign Policy 1945–1954* (New York: Harper & Row, 1972); and Robert R. Simmons, *The Strained Alliance: Peking, Pyongyang, Moscow and the Korean Civil War* (New York: Free Press, 1974).

47. Rees, *Korea: The Limited War*, pp. 32–33.

48. Ibid., p. 108.

49. Ibid., p. 157.

50. For details, see Scalapino and Lee, *Communism in Korea*, vol. 1, Chapter 6, "The War Years," pp. 383–462.

2

Political Change and External Influence, 1953–1979

From a distance the political systems of the two Koreas had a foreign look in 1953—a constitutional democracy in the South and a socialist state in the North—but on closer inspection both showed the strong influence of traditional Korean political culture. The long-lived Yi dynasty had bequeathed to the Korean people concepts of politics and government that persisted with important modifications through the period of Japanese colonialism. These concepts were more congenial in some respects to the new government in the North than to that of the South, but they affected both.

During the Yi dynasty (1392–1910), Korea was a Confucian bureaucratic state, governed by a king and a group of scholar-officials drawn from a class of landowning aristocrats. The government was highly centralized, but relatively weak, because the king and the bureaucracy checked each other's power. Moreover, officials devoted much of their energy to factional quarrels and intrigue, further reducing the government's effectiveness.

No one was permitted to question Confucianism, the officially established ideology, but Confucianism itself placed an obligation on scholars to remonstrate against acts by officials that violated Confucian precepts. Society was hierarchically structured with a wide gap between the official class and the mass of people. The ruler was seen as a father to his people, governing by ethical example. Royal benevolence toward the people was to be reciprocated by loyalty to the ruler. In fact, however, the primary object of an individual's loyalty was his extended family. In this society dominated by scholar-officials supported by rents and taxes from land, the merchant and the soldier both were relegated to low social positions.[1]

Although scholars debate the extent to which Korean political culture was modified by the colonial experience under the Japanese, there is little doubt that important changes occurred. The Japanese colonialists increased centralization and expanded the size and function of the bureaucracy, while improving its efficiency. They maintained the distance between officials and the people. The concept of development supplanted the Yi dynasty's ideal of preserving the status quo. The social status of merchants and industrialists rose. The Japanese established elaborate controls on dissent through laws regulating education, the press, and assembly and through a large police apparatus. Resistance to Japan spawned modern Korean nationalism, in the forefront of which were anti-Confucian leaders from the indigenous Chondogyo church and Christian churches. The colonial experience reinforced some Confucian concepts, but weakened others.

Koreans made some advances in education and technical skills under the Japanese, but were denied experience in political activity. Western concepts of freedom of speech, assembly, and press and the equality of the individual under the law were as lacking for Koreans under the Japanese as they had been under the Yi dynasty. Representative government was an aspiration for a few highly educated Koreans but had never existed in Korea.

Since the end of the Korean War, the two Koreas have continued to follow the divergent political paths they started down in the late 1940s with the encouragement of their foreign sponsors. But the pressures of traditional Korean concepts have changed those imported models into distinctively Korean variants of the original. Kim Il Sung's paternalistic posture toward the people and his demand for their loyalty echoes Confucian maxims, but the power he wields exceeds by far that of Yi dynasty kings who were restrained by the aristocratic Confucian bureaucracy. The official ideology, as in Yi times, cannot be questioned, but it has been transformed from Confucianism into a mutation of Marxism-Leninism known as "Kimilsungism." Party and government bureaucrats, under the firm guidance of Kim Il Sung, have assumed an even more enveloping role than the Japanese colonial bureaucracy, and the gap between officials and people, although narrowed, remains significant. Society retains a hierarchical structure. Education is highly esteemed as a means to position and power.

In South Korea the influx of western ideas and the social change resulting from a modernizing free enterprise system have overlaid and blurred traditional political values. Yet scholars have noted their persistence in the importance of the bureaucracy's role, the relations between officials and people, the high value placed on education and deference to superiors, and official restrictions on dissent.

Both Korean societies have been profoundly affected by the trauma of war and the division of their country. Born in an atmosphere of confrontation and conflict, the Korean governments place a high value on military preparedness and domestic security controls. Military concerns and the existence of large military establishments have shaped the political systems North and South in important respects.

The two Korean governments chose radically different ways of dealing with the outside world, reflecting in part the nature of the foreign model they had adopted and in part the experience and predilections of their leaders. Communist systems everywhere tend to seal off their societies from outside influence much more than noncommunist systems. Extensive controls by the state over the individual make this possible. Kim Il Sung was acutely aware that in the past ambitious Koreans had frequently used support by a powerful neighboring state to gain political power. He himself had come to power with foreign help, but had seen his position challenged by rivals backed by the Chinese or the Soviets. In order to minimize the risk of foreign interference in domestic politics he chose to turn North Korea into one of the most reclusive societies in the world, rivaled, perhaps, only by Albania. He did not, however, want his country to become a decaying, anachronistic relic like the Hermit Kingdom of the late Yi dynasty; North Korea would have to industrialize and modernize its armed forces in order simply to survive in the face of the more populous South Korea. To do so required relations with the Soviet Union, China, and Eastern Europe, particularly in the years of reconstruction and army-building in the 1950s. Kim Il Sung held such interaction to a minimum, however, isolating even foreigners from friendly states from contact with the Korean people. He preached extreme self-reliance as the only way for Korea and other developing nations to avoid falling under foreign domination. In practice, as will be shown later, North Korea has been less self-reliant than it has professed to be.

The South Korean government adopted a radically different policy. Even if Syngman Rhee had wanted to exclude outside influence, the political and economic system adopted by South Korea lacked the controls that Kim was able to apply in the North. In order to maximize economic and military aid from the United States and keep U.S. forces in South Korea, Rhee risked U.S. interference in South Korea's domestic affairs. Differences with Washington over his policies repeatedly strained relations. Furthermore, during the 1960s, with Park Chung-hee in power, the Korean government adopted a policy of promoting exports in order to accelerate economic growth, a policy that required the increasing involvement of South Korea in the world economy and a proliferation of relations between South Koreans and foreigners. South Korea maximized relations with the outside world, while North Korea minimized them. Kim Il Sung has maintained dictatorial control over North Korea for more than thirty years in part by insulating its political system from outside influence, while South Korean leaders, governing a rapidly changing society open to diverse currents from outside, have had to cope with a growing opposition movement that drew many of its ideas from abroad.

SOUTH KOREA[2]

The Changing Political Scene

In the 1954 National Assembly election, Rhee's Liberal Party, amply funded through its government connections, captured almost two-thirds of the seats, enabling Rhee to squeeze through a constitutional amendment the following year removing the limitation of two terms for presidents. But public resentment against corruption and Rhee's strong-arm tactics in dealing with the Assembly had diminished his popularity. Running for the third time in 1956 at the age of eighty-one, he was reelected by a margin of only 55 percent compared to 72 percent four years before, despite the death of his chief opponent on the eve of the election. His handpicked candidate for vice president, Yi Ki-pung, lost to Chang Myon, the candidate of the opposition Democratic Party.

The Liberal Party, fearing that the aging Rhee might die in office leaving the presidency in the hands of the opposition, resolved at all costs to secure the election of Yi Ki-pung as vice president in the 1960 election. By a police lockout of opposition assemblymen, the Liberals passed a new national security law, couched in such vague terms that it could readily be used against the political opposition. When the election occurred, the ruling party rigged the balloting so blatantly that a public outcry occurred at the announcement that Rhee had won 92 percent of the vote and Yi had defeated Chang by 8.2 million to 1.8 million. Students poured into the streets, where more than a hundred were shot down by the police. Continuing demonstrations against the government in all the principal cities and the unwillingness of the military to forcibly suppress them finally convinced Rhee that he must resign.

The Second Republic, which succeeded the First Republic under Syngman Rhee, lasted less than a year. It was the freest period in the short history of the ROK but also the most chaotic. In reaction against Rhee's autocratic ways, the constitution was amended to replace the presidential system with a parliamentary one, greatly weakening the power of the president. Chang Myon, elected premier by a narrow margin, found his ability to govern hamstrung by intense factional fighting among the politicians. Rhee's Liberal Party had totally disintegrated, to be succeeded as ruling party by the Democratic Party, which promptly split into feuding factions. To satisfy assemblymen's demands for political office, Chang turned his cabinet into a game of musical chairs, in which the tenure of ministers averaged only two months.

Lacking a strong hand at the helm, the economy drifted; prices shot up, production declined, and unemployment rose. Street demonstrations to exert pressure on the government on one issue or another occurred daily. Students even invaded the floor of the National Assembly to force the passage of an *ex post facto* law imposing criminal punishment on officials and politicians whom they considered to have misbehaved during the Rhee regime. Sections of the press, no longer subjected to government restrictions, turned to extorting money by blackmail. Crime increased, as the police—discredited, purged, and demoralized after the failure of their bloody attempt to suppress student opposition to the Rhee regime—became less effective in maintaining public order. Students openly advocated talks with North Korea on unification, warmly encouraged by broadcasts from North Korea.

In May 1961 a group of military officers, headed by Major General Park Chung-hee, carried out a swift, nearly bloodless coup that caused the abrupt demise of the Second Republic. Park and his coconspirators, a few generals and a small group of young colonels and lieutenant-colonels, had become increasingly disturbed at the corruption among senior generals, the lack of promotion opportunities, and the feckless performance of the Chang Myon government. They installed a military government, declared martial law, dissolved the National Assembly, banned political parties, closed down all news publications except the principal newspapers and news services, replaced scores of civilian officials with military officers, launched a sweeping campaign against corrupt military and civilian officials, and began a roundup of common criminals.

General Park announced that the government would be restored to civilian hands by 1963, after the country had been cleaned of corruption and other social evils. The military junta drafted a new constitution, which was approved in a national referendum in December 1962 by 78.8 percent of the voters. The constitution provided for election of the president by direct popular vote limiting him to two four-year terms and gave him wide powers, including the authority to appoint a premier and cabinet without the consent of the National Assembly. In order to prevent subversive activities against the junta mounted from either inside or outside the country, Park established the Korean Central Intelligence Agency (KCIA), directed by a relative, former Colonel Kim Chong-pil.

By early 1963 preparations to turn power over to a civilian government were well underway. The junta had lifted the ban from all but 74 of the more than 4,000 politicians who had been banned from political activity, and Kim Chong-pil had created a new political party, the Democratic Republican Party (DRP), to support Park. In March Park, apparently assailed by doubts that the country was ready for return to civilian rule, announced plans for a referendum on extending military government for four years. He dropped the idea, however, under strong pressure from the United States.

In the presidential election held in October 1963, Park, who had resigned his military commission only six weeks before, eked out a victory over his principal rival, Yun Po-son (who had been president during the Chang Myon regime), by a plurality of only 47 percent to 45 percent. The National Assembly elections held a month later gave nearly two-thirds of the seats to Park's Democratic Republican Party; the rest were divided among four opposition parties. The Third Republic, founded in December 1963 with the inauguration of Park Chung-hee, then in his forty-sixth year, lasted until Park installed the Fourth Republic in 1972. The new constitution, adopted in that year, ensured the retention of power in his own hands. His authoritarian rule ended in 1979 when he was assassinated by the director of the KCIA.

During his eighteen years in power, Park presided over an astonishing surge in economic growth. South Korea's per capita GNP shot up from $87 in 1962 to $1500 in 1980.[3] Next to defense of the country from the North Korean threat, economic growth was the main preoccupation of the government. Because its benefits were widely spread among the population, Park's success in promoting growth was the primary source of support for his continuance in office, despite resentment among politicians, intellectuals, and students at his authoritarian practices.

Park faced a grave challenge early in his first term when he resolved to normalize relations with Japan. Opponents of a treaty found it easy to fan the embers of anti-Japanese feelings, and the opposition among students and intellectuals became so violent that Park declared martial law to bring it under control. Diplomatic relations with Japan brought economic benefits that contributed to popular support of Park, however, and he was reelected in 1967 by a margin of 51 percent to 41 percent over his old rival, Yun Po-son. In the National Assembly elections held the same year, the ruling DRP won a decisive victory over the opposition New Democratic Party (NDP) with 129 seats to the latter's 45, although many reports of election fraud caused the NDP to boycott Assembly sessions for six months.

By 1969 a division appeared within the ruling party between supporters of Kim Chong-pil, who saw himself as Park's successor, and those who favored amendment of the constitution to allow Park to run for a third term in 1971. Rather than weaken the party by a factional split in the face of growing NDP strength, DRP members in the end rallied in support of Park and passed the constitutional amendment, which was subsequently supported by 65 percent of the voters in a national referendum. In the 1971 presidential election, Park, who had publicly promised not to run for a fourth term if elected for a third, faced a vigorous young opponent in Kim Dae Jung, the NDP candidate. Park won with 53 percent of the vote to Kim's 45 percent. But in the subsequent National Assembly elections, the DRP fell well below a two-thirds majority, with 113 seats to the NDP's 89.

Park saw threatening clouds building up both within South Korea and abroad. His grip on his own party was weakening, while his opposition grew stronger. In 1971 the United States ended its economic aid to South Korea, withdrew one of its two divisions there, pressed ahead with the withdrawal of U.S. forces from Vietnam, and announced a radical change in relations with the People's Republic of China. Park responded with bold moves: the opening of negotiations with North Korea and a sweeping revision of the political structure of South Korea to bolster his position.

In October 1972 Park declared martial law, dissolved the National Assembly, closed the universities, imposed press censorship, and suspended political activities. He submitted a new constitution to a national referendum; the *yusin* or revitalization constitution would allow him to serve an unlimited number of six-year terms. The constitution provided for the president to be elected by a National Conference for Unification composed of 2,000 locally elected members who did not belong to political parties. It authorized the president to appoint one-third of the members of the National Assembly and gave him a broad range of emergency powers to use at his discretion, including the power to dissolve the Assembly. The new constitution was reportedly approved by 92 percent of the voters in the national referendum. The National Assembly elections of February 1973 gave the DRP only half of the elected seats, but these, together with the one-third appointed by the president, still gave Park a large majority.

The remaining years of Park's rule were marked by recurrent resort to emergency measures to suppress opposition, particularly attacks on the *yusin* constitution. Abduction of opposition leader Kim Dae Jung from a Tokyo hotel by the KCIA in 1973 severely strained relations with Japan. Further strains resulted in 1974 when a Korean youth from Japan, attempting to assassinate Park, shot and killed his wife. In 1976

Park jailed Yun Po-son, Kim Dae Jung, and other prominent political leaders for issuing a declaration calling for the restoration of democracy. Internal and external problems did not, however, prevent a continuing high rate of economic growth, which had a stabilizing effect politically because of the unwillingness of many to upset the economic applecart, however dissatisfied they might be with political repression.

Despite a widespread feeling that Park had been in office too long, he insisted on reelection in 1978. National Assembly elections that year showed further erosion of support for the DRP. The opposition won a majority of the popular vote, although the majority of seats continued to be held by the combination of DRP elected members and assemblymen appointed by the president.

In 1979 a sharp confrontation between the government and Kim Young Sam, the new leader of the NDP, caused the government to oust Kim from the National Assembly, at which all the opposition members of the Assembly resigned in protest. Student demonstrators in Pusan and Masan clashed with police, causing the government to place those cities under military control. KCIA Director Kim Jae-kyu objected strongly to the rough suppression of student protestors favored by Park's tough personal security chief, Cha Chi Chol, and suspected Cha of conspiring to remove him from his position. Kim Jae-kyu invited Park and Cha to a dinner in the KCIA compound in October 1979 and murdered them, thus bringing the Fourth Republic to an end.

Political Structure and Dynamics

Politics in the ROK have thus been characterized by continual tension between democratic form and authoritarian content. Leaders extolled democracy in their rhetoric but often gave it short shrift in practice. As an offspring of the United Nations, which in those days was dominated by the United States and other Western democracies, the ROK's international legitimacy depended upon the willingness of the ruling elite to have the constitution approved and the president and legislature elected by a democratic process. The vital U.S. commitment to defend South Korea and to supply badly needed economic and military aid also depended on the ROK's satisfying the U.S. public that it was a democracy or at least that it was making satisfactory progress in that direction. Western-educated Koreans valued democratic concepts and wanted to see them take root in Korea, although many acknowledged the difficulty of nurturing so delicate a plant in the inhospitable conditions that prevailed there. Activists attempting to create a more democratic system in South Korea have had to contend with severe restrictions on freedom of speech, press, and assembly enforced by authoritarian leaders.

The constitution provided a framework for conducting politics; so long as it served the leader's purposes, it survived intact. But whenever support for his continuance in office could no longer be assured under the existing constitution, that leader would have it amended or replaced, if necessary, by draconian methods such as those used by Syngman Rhee in 1952 or by Park Chung-hee in 1961 to 1963 and in 1972. Replacement of presidents has occurred only by extraconstitutional means.

The executive branch has dominated the legislative branch, except during the brief interlude of the weak Chang Myon government. The Assembly elected Rhee in 1948 under the first constitution, but when it turned against him, Rhee used the police to remove that power from the Assembly and to appeal to his personal popularity with the public to be returned to office. He subsequently relied heavily on the police to ensure the election of assemblymen from his party and in the disastrous attempt to have Yi Ki-pung elected vice president in 1960. The student revolt against that maneuver and the wide support the revolt received from key groups showed that the society's tolerance for violation of democratic norms had its limits. Parks' *yusin* constitution of 1972 ensured the dominance of the executive branch by giving him power to appoint one-third of the assemblymen, thus eliminating the need to resort to extralegal pressures in National Assembly elections. The president's power to dissolve the Assembly also gave him a club for emergency use.

A marked characteristic of the South Korean political system has been its high degree of centralization. Local officials were elected during much of the Rhee period, but in 1958 a constitutional amendment placed in the president's hands the power to appoint provincial governors and the mayors of principal cities. Briefly revived under Chang Myon, local elections disappeared with the advent of Park, who was given the power to appoint not only governors and mayors, but even county heads and ward chiefs. A 1980 study described the Park government as "one of the most centralized in the non-communist world."[4] Seoul, with its high concentration of government offices, corporation headquarters, leading universities, national newspapers, and one-fifth of South Korea's population epitomized this centralization. Gregory Henderson, in his path-breaking study, *Korea: The Politics of the Vortex*, traced the tendency toward the concentration of power in the capital to cultural traits and political practices of the Yi dynasty.[5] Koreans were accustomed to a hierarchical structure, with a leader to give orders and followers to carry them out. The military background and training of many of those placed in high position by Park strengthened this tendency in the political system of the ROK.

The tendency of power to flow from the top down is evident in the development of ruling political parties. The party did not select the leader, the leader created the party. Thus, Syngman Rhee established the Liberal Party as his personal political base, and Kim Chong-pil (with the help of the KCIA, of which he was director) created the Democratic Republican Party as an instrument for the election and support of Park Chung-hee. When the leader fell, the party disintegrated. Most of the time from 1948 through 1979 South Korea has had two main parties: a ruling party and an opposition party. The opposition party was formed in reaction to the monopolization of power by the ruling party. The opposition party suffered from serious limitations in access to funds and in freedom to attack government policies. Whenever dissatisfaction with the government increased to a point where the opposition party, in spite of these limitations, threatened the position of the leader, he changed the rules. The game has always been zero-sum with little scope for compromise with an adversary. Even the opposition parties tended to split into factions, as aspiring leaders battled fiercely for the top position. Parties were coalitions of faction leaders with followers attached by personal loyalty, rather than coalitions of interest groups in society.

Although the form was Western, the way that politics in the ROK actually worked during its first three decades owed more to traditional political culture than to imported ideas. People generally approved strong leadership, giving the executive dominance over the other branches of government, so long as the leader was respected and his policies were seen to bring practical benefits to the lives of the people. The public held politicians in low esteem. The National Assembly had little influence, and the people viewed most of its members as squabbling, self-seeking individuals who contributed little to the governing process and sometimes amassed sizable fortunes by questionable means.

The Rhee, Chang, and Park governments imposed no official ideology comparable to Confucianism under the Yi dynasty or Kimilsungism in North Korea. Yet an ideological stance underlay and shaped the policies of those governments. In part it was negative: anticommunism. The expression of sympathy with Communist or even socialist ideas was vigorously suppressed, and for the first two decades, contact with Communist countries was prohibited. During the 1970s, in response to the shift toward a multipolar world, Park eased restrictions on contacts with Communist states for practical reasons without softening ideological opposition to the political philosophies of those states. The positive ideological position, which emerged during the Park period, was a commitment to a free enterprise market economy and a heavily emphasized goal of rapid economic growth. Under the guidance of the leader, with the advice and assistance of technocrats, the government intervened more deeply in economic affairs than in most market economies and, through a shrewd combination of firmness and flexibility, produced remarkable results. Anticommunism aimed at ensuring the security of the state. At the same time, rapid economic growth, which brought increased national prestige and a rise in the living standard of the people, served as a means of retaining popular support for the leadership, or, if not support, at least tolerance of the leader's retention of power.

Active opposition to the authoritarian practices of the leaders developed principally among intellectuals—university students and faculty, the independent press, opposition politicians, and certain leaders of the Christian church. The dissenters focused on the gap between the form and content of politics in South Korea, demanding that the government live up to its professions of democracy. The leaders viewed dissent as disloyalty or even treason—serving the purposes of the enemy in the North. The concept of a "loyal opposition" seemed to most Koreans a contradiction in terms. As the leader prolonged his time in office, opposition tended to increase and the leader resorted to harsher and more arbitrary methods to suppress it, until the eruption of violence ended his rule. Park succeeded, however, in avoiding the cruder displays of force seen during the Rhee period, such as using police to herd opposition assemblymen into the Assembly hall to vote for government measures. Under Park, both the opposition and the government became more sophisticated in handling their confrontations.

Leadership

Among the three leaders who headed governments from 1948 to 1979, two were strong men whose personalities and governing styles distinctively marked their long periods of rule. The third, Chang Myon, was a moderate, cautious man, seen by the public as lacking in self-assurance and leadership, who governed the turbulent Second Republic for less than a year. A U.S.-educated superintendent of a Catholic commercial school in Seoul for seventeen years before 1945, Chang had presented Korea's case effectively as envoy to the United Nations in 1950 and had briefly served as premier under Rhee the following year. During Chang's short tenure as paramount leader in 1960 and 1961, he presided over a Democratic Party riven by factional disputes that had come to power less through its own effort than by default, when the student revolt toppled Rhee and his ruling party disintegrated. Chang's inability to provide effective leadership resulted not only from the popular reaction against authoritarian rule that had weakened the power of the executive, but also from his own indecisiveness and his susceptibility to pressures from his colleagues.

Syngman Rhee's outstanding characteristic was his self-confidence, his conviction of his own infallibility. Stubborn, intolerant of criticism, resistant to pressure, he went his own way. He was an effective orator and a consummate politician. Building on his reputation as a lifelong fighter for Korean independence from Japan and the leader of the defense of the ROK against Communist aggression, he "came close to being an indispensable man in the crisis-ridden young republic."[6]

Rhee became skillful at extracting money for political purposes from the flow of U.S. aid and in return for advantages granted to Korean businessmen. But he paid the price of growing corruption that fed popular dissatisfaction with his rule. He used his control over appointments with great effectiveness to place supporters in key positions in the police, the military, and the bureaucracy. But the criterion for such appointments was more often personal loyalty than qualifications for the job. Rhee's political skills were not matched by administrative ability. He had little administrative experience and had not learned to delegate power. He strongly resisted any sharing of power and whenever a political figure gained a stature that threatened to rival his, Rhee did not hesitate to crush him ruthlessly.[7]

Rhee showed particular astuteness in dealing with the United States. In his many disputes with U.S. officials, he had a keen sense of how far he could push in order to extract the best deal. He came close to pushing too far in his attempt to frustrate the armistice negotiations, but ended up with a strong U.S. commitment to the defense of the ROK and generous promises of economic aid. He understood how important the ROK was to the United States in its confrontation with the Soviet Union and used his connections with influential U.S. citizens to exploit this asset.

In the final years of Rhee's rule, he was handicapped by advancing age, which prevented him from stumping the country and limited his contacts. He became increasingly dependent on a few close associates and was cut off from wider sources of information. He was insensitive to the political implications of rapid social change, particularly urbanization, the expansion of the politically attentive press, and the explosion of higher education, all of which led to increasing public restiveness at the corruption and repression of the Rhee government. The hard-liners in the Liberal Party, most of whom had been police officers, prosecutors, or judges under the Japanese, together with other close Rhee associates, were more inclined to try to prevent change than to adapt to it. They resorted to the stepped-up police repression and electoral fraud that produced the student revolt.

Rhee's charismatic personality and his authoritarian methods served South Korea well during the infancy of the new republic, when it had to contend successively with armed rebellion, external attack, and recovery from a long and devastating war. He contributed much to bringing into being the political and administrative framework on which future development would be based. During the early period through the end of the Korean War, when Rhee was concerned primarily with consolidating his power position, he relied on political lieutenants such as Yi Pom-sok, who came as Rhee did from the Korean independence movement. During the recovery period from 1953 to 1957, Rhee appointed as ministers technocrats of considerable administrative ability, who brought about some economic recovery and improvement in administration. Thereafter, however, as his energies waned and his judgment faltered, the top political elite came from the ranks of exbureaucrats turned politicians, who were less interested in economic development than in exploiting their positions for personal gain, suppressing the political ferment produced by social change, and maneuvering to control the succession to Rhee.[8]

Park Chung-hee, like Rhee, would brook no rival and was equally determined to retain his hold on power. In other respects, however, he was a very different leader. He was more administrator than politician. A small, dour, aloof individual, who rarely smiled and who was an indifferent public speaker, Park lacked charisma. He was Confucian in his sense of hierarchy, his commitment to public service, and his paternalistic concern for the welfare of the people. His style of rule and his choice of associates owed much to his experience in the military, where he had spent his adult life.

Park's father had been educated in the Confucian classics, but failing to obtain an official post had turned to farming. Park grew up on the farm, entered middle school by competitive examination, graduated from a Japanese military academy in Manchuria, and served two years as a Japanese army lieutenant before the end of World War II. He became an officer in the ROK army in 1946, but in 1948 was arrested and sentenced to death for complicity in the Communist-instigated Yosu rebellion. The sentence was later commuted, and he was reinstated in the army at the outbreak of the Korean War. He advanced more slowly in the military hierarchy than some of his colleagues, attaining the rank of major general in 1958, three years before he came to power by military coup.

Even before the coup, Park had a reputation in the military as the most political of the generals, in the sense of being concerned about what was going on in the country outside of the military. His familiarity with rural poverty as a youth and his war experience imbedded in him a deep conviction that the country must be modernized in order to improve the lot of the poor and to provide an adequate defense. Thus, he took a much keener interest than Rhee had in economic development, making it the chief goal of his administration. His philosophy held that "in human life, economics precedes politics or culture,"[9]

In his use of people, Park displayed the talents of a good administrator. Placing exmilitary colleagues in many key positions, he rewarded those who performed well and did not hesitate to remove those who did not. He listened to the advice of experts and assembled around him a competent group of senior officials from both military and civilian backgrounds. He became personally involved in setting goals, drawing up plans, and following closely the implementation of the plans.

Park tolerated the National Assembly and the debates and maneuvers of politicians, but saw such activities more as interfering with than contributing to the orderly process of government. His Confucian up-bringing and military experience caused him to prize unity and discipline above the confrontations of politicians and the tortuous working out of political compromises. He had little patience with attacks by students and the media on policies that he considered in the best interests of the nation, and when it seemed necessary, as during the negotiations for the normalization of relations with Japan, he rode roughshod over their opposition. Acutely conscious of the military threat from North Korea, he brandished it frequently to rally his supporters and intimidate his opponents.

In Park's later years in office he became, like Rhee, more isolated and less willing to listen to advice that might conflict with his own preconceptions. Attempts on his life by North Korean agents made him more suspicious and more reliant on the KCIA, which expanded in numbers and in the scope of its operations. He maintained good contacts within the military, removing senior officers suspected of conspiring against him. South Korea's transition to the status of a "newly indus-trialized country" owed much to Park's firm hand on the helm, but his failure to create a mechanism for orderly political succession set the stage for another military coup following his sudden death.

The Bureaucracy

During South Korea's tumultuous history, the bureaucracy has been an important stabilizer of the system. Leaders changed, ministers suc-ceeded one another (often in rapid succession), and major upheavals drastically altered membership in the political elite. Throughout it all, the bureaucracy carried on with its routine tasks. In the hands of a strong, development-oriented leader, the bureaucracy became in addition an effective instrument for promoting economic and social change. From the latter part of the Yi dynasty, Koreans had been accustomed to "centralized, uncontested bureaucratic rule."[10] The chief aim of ambitious *yangban*—Korean aristocrats—was to pass the civil service examinations and thereby secure an official post, with its desirable prestige and perquisites. The Japanese greatly expanded the functions of the bureaucrats as well as their numbers: from a few thousand in late Yi times to over 90,000 by 1945, including 45,000 Koreans.[11] Recruitment continued to be through strict examination and promotion was by merit, but the great majority of senior and mid-level positions were reserved for Japanese.

The advent of the U.S. military government in Korea opened doors for Korean bureaucrats. Many were promoted to positions vacated by the Japanese. The United States also brought some foreign-educated, English-speaking Koreans into senior positions and recruited other Koreans to fill the ranks depleted by the departure of the Japanese. The Korean War brought a rapid expansion of the bureaucracy, and further increases occurred during the period of rapid economic growth under Park Chung-hee. Purges of bureaucrats accused of corruption or other wrongdoings, particularly the large-scale dismissals following the changes in political leadership in 1960 and 1961, restrained the pace of growth somewhat and made room to bring in fresh blood.[12]

Bureaucrats of the pre-Park period saw their function primarily as performing the routine tasks required of them to maintain the status quo. Rhee himself took little interest in promoting economic change through the bureaucracy, and the senior political figures of his later period, themselves exbureaucrats, took a similar view. A Korean scholar wrote: "Korean bureaucrats may actually want modernization, but they are imbued with a value system which is incompatible with modernization."[13] In his view, Confucian concepts of loyalty primarily to family and secondarily to school ties resulted in factionalism, nepotism, and corruption, which interfered with rational decisionmaking, efficient administration, and the selection of the most competent officials. Overemphasis on hierarchy and excessive deference to superiors inhibited the free expression of views by subordinates and produced a tendency to refer all problems to the top for solution. Exaggerated concern with "face" and overreliance on personal relationships hindered effective rational action to resolve problems, as did the preoccupation with legalistic niceties carried over by older officials from their early training as clerks under the Japanese.

The Park government revitalized the bureaucracy and infused it with a new sense of purpose. The military had become the most modernized sector of society after a decade of intensive training in organizational techniques and decisionmaking not matched elsewhere. Generals with managerial experience became cabinet ministers, and field grade officers moved into positions in the upper bureaucracy, along with relatively young reformist civilian officials promoted to replace older bureaucrats who were unable to free themselves from attachment to the status quo and to the concept of promotion by seniority rather than merit.[14]

A survey of senior bureaucrats in 1971 and 1972 showed them to be young and highly educated.[15] Their average age was forty-six, and a high percentage were college-educated. Seventy-five percent could read or speak English. One-fourth were former professional soldiers. (Half of these had advanced degrees, a larger proportion than among their civilian counterparts.) Senior bureaucrats came from middle-class and upper-class families. They evinced a commitment to long-range planning and to achieving tasks assigned to them by whatever means might be necessary. Placing a lower value on democratic political norms than on national security and economic growth, they accepted a need to limit freedom of the press and civil liberties during the struggle against communism. The emphasis on hierarchy and on the importance of personal relationships that had marked the earlier generation of bureaucrats continued to be evident in this one. The public stereotype of a bureaucrat as arrogant, selfish, and corrupt showed little change in this survey.

The rejuvenated, goal-oriented bureaucracy made a vital contribution to the rapid economic growth of the Park period. Although private enterprise was the main source of growth, it operated under firm government direction. Government leaders gave competent bureaucrats an unusual degree of discretion in applying incentives, disincentives, and command procedures to private business in order to stimulate growth.[16]

The bureaucracy was the key link between the leadership and the public, far more important than political parties or the National Assembly. Bureaucrats paid little attention to legislators; interest group representatives sought out senior bureaucrats rather than legislators to urge government actions favoring their interests. Under Park the bureaucracy improved greatly in the quality of its personnel and in its effectiveness in carrying out the central policy of the government—the promotion of economic growth. Its stress on hierarchy and prompt decisionmaking by a small circle of senior officials, together with the commitment of subordinates to vigorous implementation of policy, generally produced the desired results. If the policies failed to produce the desired results, the decisionmakers did not hesitate to change them.

The Military[17]

The ROK armed forces have combined to an unusual degree military professionalism and intervention in the country's politics. Their chief task has been to defend South Korea against the threat of a military attack from the North. Planning, training, and conducting maneuvers to prepare for such a contingency have absorbed most of their time and energy. The majority of senior officers have had battle experience, either in the Korean War or in Vietnam.[18] They are a professional fighting force that takes pride in capability and readiness.

Although the armed forces are committed to military professionalism, military leaders have also become the most potent force in South Korean politics since 1961. The defense establishment has not meddled as an organization in the day-to-day business of government, but many of the leading figures in government have come from the military. Indeed, so dominant were exmilitary men in the government and ruling party as of 1969 that one of the most perceptive of Korean analysts described it as a "quasi-military" government.[19] Military training and outlook have had a significant effect on government policies and performance. Military leaders also have implicitly arrogated to themselves the right, if not to select the country's paramount leader, at least to reject anyone in whom they lack confidence.

The ease with which Park Chung-hee had seized power at the head of a tiny band of conspirators tempted other military men to emulate him in the early years of his tenure. Between 1961 and 1970, Park foiled 16 attempted countercoups.[20]

Gradually, through improving salaries and other conditions in the military, winning over disaffected generals by offering them positions in the government, and establishing new security organs responsible directly to him to maintain surveillance over senior officers, Park consolidated his power. The final challenge came, not from within the military, but from a former military colleague whom he had appointed to head the KCIA.

Military men held strong anticommunist views, based not only on theoretical grounds, but also on personal and institutional experience. The ROK was barely two months old when its fledgling army was racked by the Yosu rebellion, instigated by Communists infiltrated into the armed forces. In the suppression of that rebellion 5,000 died, and subsequent purges removed 4,750 commissioned and noncommissioned officers, affecting 10 percent of army personnel.[21] During 1948 and 1949 the main task of the army was to suppress widespread Communist uprisings. In 1950, the nation was plunged into war by the overt North Korean attack. The rapid expansion of the South Korean army took place during battles against North Korean and Chinese Communists. Later, South Korean troops fought Vietnamese Communists. In light of this history, it is not surprising that military officers, whose professional duty is to defend the nation against the North Korean military threat, are strongly opposed to communism. They give a high priority to internal security, tend toward worst-case analyses of North Korea's military capabilities and intentions, and react with suspicion toward views of North Korea less hard-line than theirs. The North Koreans have done much to reinforce anticommunism in South Korea, not only among the military but among the population in general, by their own hostile behavior.

In addition to stiffening the anticommunist orientation of South Korean society, the presence of such a large and powerful institution has had other far-reaching effects on social change. Military men achieved a level of public respect they did not have during the Yi dynasty or the Japanese colonial period. A military career provided an upward path in society for many Koreans. The training of hundreds of thousands of military conscripts in modern skills such as auto and aircraft mechanics, electronics, and heavy construction poured a stream of skilled workers into the Korean economy as the conscripts completed their military service. Thousands of retired officers put to use in private business managerial skills learned in the officer corps. No other sector of society had so extensive and continuous an exposure to U.S. training and example. The military became a thoroughly professional force, patterned after the U.S. armed forces, as well as a channel through which skills and concepts acquired from the United States passed into society. In the intervention by the military into politics, however, the Koreans broke away from the U.S. model over the outspoken opposition of U.S. military and civilian authorities.

Political Impact of Social Change

The emergence of Korea from Japanese colonial rule, the trauma of the Korean War, and the rapid economic growth since the mid-1960s transformed Korean society in the short space of thirty years—a single generation. A predominantly rural society became predominantly urban. A largely illiterate society became literate.[22] The number of students in elementary schools quadrupled, the number in middle schools increased by 700 percent, and in high schools by 1,200 percent. In higher educational institutions the number of students in 1975 was 37 times what it had been in 1945.[23]

The greatly increased mobility of the population made possible by urbanization and modern transportation facilities attenuated traditional ties to family and place of origin. Old class barriers tumbled. Military officers and businessmen, held in low regard in traditional society, moved up to become part of the new elite. Newspapers, radio, and television proliferated, penetrating the most remote hamlets and stimulating interest in national and international affairs.[24] The popularity of Christianity grew remarkably so that by 1979, South Korea had 1.2 million Catholics and 6 million Protestants.[25]

In some respects modernization improved the capability of a centralized authoritarian government to retain power. The educational system had a socializing effect on the great bulk of students, preparing them to fit into South Korean society and to view with antipathy the contrasting society to the north. Modern transportation and communication greatly facilitated the maintenance of security by the police and the KCIA. Rapid economic growth bolstered the Park government's claim to legitimacy. A rising standard of living held out for most people a realistic hope that tomorrow would be better for them than today and thus kept down dissatisfaction with the existing state of affairs.

At the same time, modernization accentuated the discrepancy between the democratic professions of the government and its authoritarian practices. The growing intellectual class became more critical of the government and resorted to attacks through the media until the government was compelled to suppress the criticism by censoring newspapers, having journalists dismissed, and otherwise exerting pressure against opponents. Some Christian leaders joined in the criticism and suffered government reprisals as a result.

Throughout the short history of the ROK, university students have been the most unruly and the quickest to demonstrate against real or presumed abuses of power by government. Student activism has its roots in part in the Confucian tradition of the scholar's obligation to oppose bad government, in part in what students learn in school of democratic principles and practices elsewhere, and in part in their nationalistic feelings. Students tend to be idealistic, impractical, and both susceptible to and suspicious of foreign influence as well as readily aroused. They are proud of the tradition of student activism going back to their participation in the March 1, 1919, independence movement against the Japanese and the successful deposing of Syngman Rhee in 1960. Student political activists have been few in number within the student body as a whole, but they organized antigovernment demonstrations on a greater or lesser scale almost every year during Park's rule, causing the government to adopt a variety of measures including arrests, expulsions, and the stationing of plainclothes police on campus in order to keep their activities within bounds.[26]

NORTH KOREA[27]

Evolution of the Political System

The 1950s were the critical formative years for the political system of North Korea. In 1953 when the war ended, the political system was essentially that established under Soviet guidance between 1945 and 1950. Soviet influence remained strong during the early years after the armistice. North Korea's need for Soviet and Chinese aid to rebuild its shattered economy gave those governments and their friends within the top leadership of the Korean Workers' Party (KWP) considerable leverage. But by 1955 serious policy differences among senior leaders surfaced. In speeches at party meetings Kim Il Sung criticized by name certain leaders of the Soviet and Yenan factions, charging them with trying to introduce foreign concepts and practices incompatible with the Korean revolution.

In December 1955, shrewdly exploiting the strong nationalist sentiments of Koreans, Kim introduced formally the concept of *chu che*, or self-reliance, which was to become the lodestar of Kimilsungism. Some of Kim's opponents took issue with the high priority that Kim gave to heavy industry in the three-year plan (1954–1956), urging greater investment in light industry and agriculture to relieve severe shortages of food and consumer goods. Kim disagreed, insisting that heavy sacrifices were needed in order to repair war damage quickly and create the heavy industrial base needed to develop a self-reliant economy.

At the Third Congress of the KWP in April 1956, which convened only a few weeks after Khrushchev's denunciation of Stalin at the Twentieth Congress of the Communist Party of the Soviet Union, the Soviets openly supported the views of Kim Il Sung's opponents. The Soviet representative, Leonid I. Brezhnev, criticized the newly drafted five-year plan as unrealistic, placing insufficient emphasis on agriculture and on improving the people's living standard. More important, Brezhnev praised the restoration in the Soviet Union of the principle of collective leadership and expressed confidence that the KWP Congress would "help to fully establish in the Party organizations from top to bottom the Leninist principle of collective leadership, the enforcement of which lends a powerful force to each Marxist Party and keeps it from making mistakes related to the cult of personality."[28] This was a direct slap at the spreading manifestations of the Kim cult.

The dispute between Kim and his domestic adversaries came to a head in the summer of 1956. Taking advantage of a two-month European tour by Kim to raise additional aid funds for North Korea, his opponents in the Soviet and Yenan factions opened a campaign in the media attacking his personality cult and formed a political coalition aimed at bringing Kim down.

The putsch against Kim failed and he succeeded in having his chief antagonists removed from their positions, only to be forced to reinstate them in response to urgent representations by senior Chinese and Soviet officials, Peng De huai and Anastas Mikoyan, during a hurried trip to Pyongyang.[29] By 1958, however, Kim had strengthened his position enough to purge them and all other senior figures belonging to the Yenan and Soviet factions. Kim thus took firm and unchallenged command of the Korean Workers' Party and the Korean People's Army, the prime instruments of power in North Korea. Furthermore, he surrounded himself chiefly by longtime, trusted comrades from his days as a guerrilla leader in Manchuria. He never forgave the Chinese and Soviet intervention, and in later years publicly denounced meddling by the Communist parties of large countries in the domestic affairs of Communist parties in small countries.

In 1960 Kim could look back with considerable satisfaction on the progress made during the previous decade in consolidating the political system under his leadership and shaping it according to his design. He had eliminated as serious rivals for power the leaders of the domestic, Yenan, and Soviet factions. Introduction of the *chu che* concept as the philosophical basis for North Korean communism appealed strongly to the aroused nationalism of the Korean people. It provided a rationale for rejecting attempts by the Soviet and Chinese parties to control North Korea and for blocking the traditional Korean tactic by political rivals to seek personal advancement through foreign support. By stressing the need for the whole nation to learn from the experience of the Manchurian guerrillas, Kim not only imparted a distinctively militant flavor to life in North Korea, but also justified placing close associates from the Kapsan group in leading posts. An emergent cult of personality had begun the process that in later years was to approach deification of Kim Il Sung.

By 1960 difficult problems had been surmounted. Massive economic aid in the immediate postwar period had rebuilt the economy and initiated a period of substantial economic growth. By 1958 all privately owned farms had been incorporated into agricultural cooperatives. The KWP, rapidly expanded during and just after the war, had become a more effective instrument for managing the country as the result of large-scale purges of unfit and politically unreliable members and the establishment of training schools and courses for the rest. The KWP was a highly centralized mass party with a membership of 1 million in a population of 10 million directed by a small elite group at the pinnacle of power. The KWP mobilized and indoctrinated the nonparty majority of the population through mass organizations of industrial workers, agricultural workers, intellectuals, women, youths, and children.

During the 1960s Kim Il Sung further consolidated his position, bolstered by the rising tide of the personality cult and by the support of his Kapsan colleagues, who constituted a majority of the Political Committee, the top governing body of the KWP.[30] A struggle occurred within the Kapsan group itself in the late 1960s, probably arising from differences over economic and military policies and the failure of a violent campaign to instigate revolution in South Korea.[31] Fifteen Kapsan members of the Central Committee, including five members of the Political Committee, lost their positions between 1966 and 1969. Kim replaced them with other Kapsan partisans, thus continuing the practice of surrounding himself with trusted associates from his Manchurian guerrilla days.

A dominant feature of the 1960s was the effort "to turn the whole country into an impregnable fortress." Kim declared in 1962 that a growing threat from "American imperialism" required an all-out drive to improve military preparedness. North Korea poured one-third of its national budget into strengthening the armed forces and building extensive underground military installations. Nearly all able-bodied men and women were organized into a "people's militia."[32] Forced draft militarization and the suspension of Soviet economic and military aid in an attempt to force North Korea to take the Soviet side in the Sino-Soviet dispute hobbled economic growth.[33] The seven-year plan, originally scheduled for completion in 1967 had to be extended to 1970.

By the early 1970s, Kim Il Sung had created a personal kingdom in North Korea. Praise of his name and his *chu che* philosophy resounded throughout the land. The KWP had become a reliable instrument for his exercise of power. He began cautiously to prepare the ground for passing the power on eventually to his son.

The constitution of 1972, replacing the obsolete constitution of 1948, reflected the realities of power as they had developed during the 1950s and 1960s. The new constitution created the office of president of the republic (previously the chairman of the presidium of the Supreme People's Assembly had performed the formal function of head of state), and Kim Il Sung became president and supreme commander of the armed forces. The SPA was no longer designated the highest state authority. Instead, the constitution declared that the DPRK was to be guided in its activity by the *chu che* idea of the KWP, implying the superiority of the party to the state apparatus. Because Kim was general secretary of the party's Central Committee, as well as president and supreme commander, he held all the commanding heights in the party, government, and army.

The new constitution stripped the SPA of most of its functions, transferring them either to the president or to a newly created organ, the Central People's Committee (CPC), "the highest leadership organ of sovereignty of the DPRK." The latter was composed of top party leaders, including most of the members of the Political Committee of the KWP's Central Committee. This extensive concurrent holding of top offices in party and government accurately reflected the concentration of power in a few hands. Chong-Sik Lee concludes that "the CPC was created and power was concentrated in it to dispense with the myth of legislative supremacy as well as the fiction of the separation of power and authority between party and state."[34]

Conforming the structure of government to the realities of power was not the only remedy Kim applied to the slow economic growth that worried him and his associates in the 1960s. Kim sought other remedies to lessen the sharp contrast with South Korea's economy, which grew at an accelerated pace after 1965. One was the Three-Revolution Team movement launched in 1973, headed by Kim's son, Kim Chong Il. Too many old cadres, Kim felt, were handicapped by outdated ideas in carrying out the ideological, technical, and cultural revolutions needed to turn North Korea into a modernized socialist state. Teams of young intellectuals fanned out all over the country to provide up-to-date guidance to local cadres in industrial enterprises. Another effort to speed the pace of economic development was the large-scale purchase of plants and machinery from Japan and Western Europe between 1970 and 1974, which ended abruptly with default by North Korea on its debt repayment.[35]

North Korea, under Kim Il Sung's firm hand, was one of the most stable political systems in the world in the 1970s. Its stability, however, was symptomatic of a fundamental problem: bureaucratic rigidity that hindered innovation and adaptation to a rapidly changing external environment. The mind-set imposed by the *chu che* principle stood in the way of expanded access to the benefits of the swiftly moving technological revolution in East Asia. Preoccupation with military preparedness placed a heavy strain on resources and manpower. The easing of tension with South Korea, which could have lightened the burden of armaments, was made difficult by stubbornly held misconceptions of conditions in South Korea and inflexibility in Pyongyang's approach to North-South relations.

Leadership

The most arresting feature of Kim Il Sung's rule in North Korea has been the extraordinary scope and intensity of his personality cult. He has outdone both Stalin and Mao Zedong and stands unrivalled in the extremes of adulation lavished on him by his countrymen. The North Korean media refer to him as "peerless patriot," "ever-victorious, iron-willed brilliant commander, the greatest military strategist the world has ever known," "the greatest philosopher politician in the annals of human history," and "the most profound revolutionary genius of all time."[36] He is credited with creating the Korean Workers' Party, liberating Korea from the thrall of Japanese militarism, and throwing back the attempt by "American imperialism" to conquer Korea. All of the successes in building socialism in North Korea since 1945 are attributed to his genius. His theoretical writings centered on the *chu che* principle are held out as a beacon for the people of the whole world. He has become the symbol of the nation, portrayed as a fatherly figure with unbounded compassion for his people and worthy of the greatest loyalty and self-sacrifice. Kim-worship has taken on a religious fervor and in some homes his picture stands on the altar where tablets of ancestors once stood.

The flamboyance of Kim cult rhetoric has been matched by the grandiosity of the structures dedicated to Kim's greatness. The Korean Revolution Museum, opened in 1972, has over ninety rooms filled with objects glorifying his revolutionary exploits. In front stands a heroic bronze statue of Kim 75-feet tall. The International Friendship Exhibition Hall, established in 1978, displays thousands of gifts to Kim from all over the world, aimed at convincing the streams of Korean visitors that their leader is universally admired. Kim's boyhood home at Mangyongdae, on the outskirts of Pyongyang, has become a shrine visited by hundreds of Koreans daily and is a required stop on tours of the capital by foreign visitors.

Numerous statues of Kim adorn public parks and plazas. The entrance to every public building has a large painting, mural, or mosaic of the leader, as do the subway stations. All citizens wear Kim buttons on the left breast. Every room visited by Kim on one of his continual on-the-spot guidance tours is marked by a red plaque with gold letters giving the date of his visit. Every briefing on a factory, hospital, school, or other institution gives Kim the credit for its establishment and achievements. Glorification of Kim is the main theme of dances, songs, operas, and films. Everyone is expected to devote several hours daily to the study of Kim's works. One diligent student, held out by the press as a model, was reported to have memorized the entire text of Kim's report to the Fifth Party Congress of 1970 and recited it more than one hundred times to audiences totalling 47,000 people.[37]

How Kim has actually exercised his power behind the screen of the Kim cult myth is difficult to discern. Little is known of his day-to-day relations with his principal associates. A few general characteristics of his rule are evident. Most important, he has allowed no one to create a position of power remotely approaching his own. The rapid turnover in the membership of the Central Committee over the years probably has resulted in part from the need to eliminate any person or group that threatened to become too powerful. Personal loyalty has been the prime criterion for high position, although competence must have been important, too. North Korea could not have accomplished what it has in organization, industrialization, military strength, and foreign relations without a substantial number of competent officials in senior positions.

Kim has sat at the apex of a highly centralized pyramidal structure, the KWP, assisted by a small number of senior officials whom he has come to know intimately. All members of this hierarchical organization from top to bottom have been subjected to endlessly repeated injunctions to be loyal to the leader, to observe rigid discipline, and to carry out the orders of the leader without the slightest deviation. Thus, Kim has tried to fashion an organization as responsive to his will as fallible human beings could be.

Kim has not committed the error of staying in the capital, dependent on self-serving official reporting and unaware of what was actually going on in the country. He has been constantly on the move, checking up on local officials, observing personally the stage of completion of large projects, and judging for himself the state of the grain crop and the mood of the people.[38] The value of the incessant detailed "on-the-spot guidance" Kim has reportedly given on every conceivable subject may be questionable, but his determination to keep in touch with developments throughout the country is impressive. He has insisted that bureaucrats follow his example by frequently leaving their offices to check on what is happening at lower levels.

Kim has also taken possession of the ideological heights. His thought alone has been disseminated as holy writ. Other writers have been restricted to lauding the thought of "the great leader," rather than advancing original ideas.

Another distinctive aspect of Kim's style of rule has been the repeated exhortation, often couched in wartime language, to stir people to greater efforts. The Manchurian partisans have been held out as models for people to follow in austerity of living, dedication to struggle, and willingness to take risks and work hard. Life has been likened to a military campaign, with people urged to throw themselves into "speed battles" to set new records in production. Under Kim North Korea has been portrayed to its people as engaged in a continuing war with imperialism that requires a wartime spirit of dedication and sacrifice.

During the 1970s Kim took steps to ensure that his personalized form of rule would continue after his death. For a short while his younger brother, Kim Yong-ju, seemed to be in line to succeed him. He became director of the powerful organization department of the KWP in 1966 and by 1970 had risen to sixth position in the power structure. But he suffered demotion in 1973 and soon faded entirely from the scene.[39]

Coincident with the disappearance of Kim Yong-ju, Kim Il Sung's eldest son, Kim Chong Il, began to play an increasingly important role. Thirty years younger than his father, Chong Il graduated from the Mangyongdae Revolutionary Academy, an exclusive school for the children of high level cadres, and from Kim Il Sung University. In 1972, after ten years of experience in party work, he became party secretary in charge of organization, propaganda, and agitation, and in 1973 he took charge of the Three-Revolution Teams.[40]

Although Kim Chong Il's growing importance was widely known within North Korea, where pictures of him began to appear in homes next to his father's picture, the North Korean media avoided using his name, referring to him instead by a code word: "the party center." The reason for this curious reticence seems to have been Kim Il Sung's concern that other Communist countries might be critical of his attempt to install a system of dynastic succession in Communist North Korea. As recently as 1970, the DPRK itself had criticized hereditary succession in the *Dictionary of Political Terminologies* as "a reactionary custom of exploitative societies whereby certain positions or riches may be legally inherited. Originally a product of slave societies, it was later adopted by feudal lords as a means to perpetuate dictatorial rule." Not surprisingly, the item was deleted in the 1972 edition of the dictionary.[41] References to Kim Chong Il as "the party center" occurred frequently from 1974 to 1977 when they ceased abruptly, just after the Japanese press published a leaked confidential document of the pro–North Korean association, Chochongnyon, hailing Kim Chong Il as Kim Il Sung's "sole successor," and did not reappear until 1979.[42]

Glorification of Kim Il Sung had been expanded gradually to encompass his ancestors going back to his great-grandfather, who was said to have led the attack on "the U.S. imperialist pirate ship *General Sherman*" on the Taedong River in 1886.[43] When Kim Chong Il began to be groomed as successor, his mother, Kim Jung-sook, who died in 1959, received special attention. She was lauded as an outstanding revolutionary fighter and has been honored with statues, portraits, and a revolutionary museum dedicated to her memory. Thus, Kim Chong Il has been portrayed as the latest in an unbroken line of zealous revolutionaries.

Ideology

Ideology in North Korea derives from Marxism-Leninism and incorporates its basic tenets: the ownership of all means of production by the state, a vanguard party that holds power on behalf of the masses, the exercise of power by the party by means of "democratic centralism," the suppression of individualism and the exaltation of the collective life, the existence of a continuing world struggle between communism and imperialism, and the ultimate victory of world communism.

Although based on Marxism-Leninism, North Korean ideology has taken on a unique national character from the extraordinary emphasis placed on the principle of *chu che* (or *juche*), hailed as a profound original contribution of Kim Il Sung to Marxism-Leninism and defined as follows:

> Establishing *juche* means, in a nutshell, having the attitude of master towards the revolution and construction in one's own country. This means holding fast to the independent stand of rejecting dependence on others and using one's own brains, believing in one's own strength and displaying the revolutionary spirit of self-reliance, and thus solving one's problem for oneself on one's own responsibility under all circumstances, and it means adhering to the creative stand of opposing dogmatism and applying the universal principle of Marxism-Leninism and the experiences of other countries to suit the historical conditions and national peculiarities of one's own country.[44]

As suggested by the foregoing definition, the essence of *chu che* is Korean nationalism, which has its roots in Korean history and in Kim Il Sung's personal experience. Historically, Korea has been dominated by or threatened with domination by larger neighboring states. Korean individuals or factions have sought outside support for domestic political gains, as Kim's adversaries did in the 1950s. Koreans traditionally have prized foreign products and ideas over those produced in Korea. Kim's stress on self-reliance is a reaction against these past practices and present dangers. He has sought the greatest possible self-sufficiency in economic development and defense production to minimize dependence on others. His experience as a guerrilla, where he had little choice but self-reliance, has contributed to the development of this philosophy. He uses *chu che* not only to maximize the use of North Korea's own material and human resources, but also as a weapon against the government of South Korea, which he condemns as totally dependent on the United States, and therefore a puppet. North Korean propaganda touts *chu che* as a philosophy that should appeal to all Third World countries striving to free themselves from the bonds of imperialism.

Appeal to Korean nationalism is not, of course, limited to North Korea. Syngman Rhee and Park Chung-hee both used nationalistic themes to mobilize support for their policies. South Koreans share with North Koreans the historical experience of domination by a big power, and both Koreas face the problem of being unable to dispense with foreign support and assistance while striving to avoid domination. Park even used the term *chu che* in his speeches when stressing the need for South Korean self-reliance. But, as B. C. Koh points out, *"chu che* is an all-pervasive phenomenon in North Korea, whereas it is little more than a political slogan in South Korea."[45]

It is the pervasiveness of reference to *chu che* in North Korea and its identification with the all-wise great leader that strikes the outsider. North Korean media urge the suffusing of the entire society with *chu che* thought. A central theme of the personality cult, it has been elevated to the status of a panacea, virtually supplanting Marxism-Leninism as material for study. Kim Il Sung made not a single reference to Marxism-Leninism in the ideological section of his lengthy address to the Sixth Party Congress in October 1980, devoted to the need to model society on the idea of *chu che*. Kim declared in that address: "The whole party is rallied rock-firm around its Central Committee and knit together in ideology and purpose on the basis of the *chu che* idea, and no force can ever break its unity and cohesion based on this idea."[46]

North Korean ideology resembles Korean Confucianism, not in its content, but in its function as the official dogma and in the stress on study. The memorization and recitation of the words of Kim Il Sung is reminiscent of the memorization and recitation of the writings of Confucius by the scholars of old. Articles on *chu che* have a ritualistic, repetitive quality, at times approaching incantation.

Those who have carefully studied Kim Il Sung's ideas and compared them with Marxism-Leninism and the writings of Mao Zedong find little that is original.[47] He has elaborated a few simple themes present in the writings of earlier Communist theoreticians. He has been more original in practice than in theory. Kim Il Sung himself acknowledged to Japanese journalists in 1972 that the *chu che* idea was not original. He reportedly said: "We are by no means the first to discover this idea. Anyone who is a Marxist-Leninist thinks this way. I have merely laid a special emphasis on this idea."[48] Kim's modesty has been overwhelmed by the extravagant praise since heaped on the *chu che* idea by North Korean propagandists, who have hailed Kim as a great revolutionary theoretician who has made an immortal new contribution to human thought. Ideology in North Korea, as Scalapino and Lee point out, is a secular faith, not a creative and evolving political theory.[49] It serves as an instrument for mobilizing the people and ensuring uniformity of belief among them. Because it discourages independence of thought, even among the elite, it is more effective in perpetuating stability in the political system than in facilitating its adjustment to change.

Mobilization and Control

The fundamental elements of the political system in North Korea, as in other Communist states, are mass participation and elitist control. Kim Il Sung holds the ultimate authority, advised by a small group at the top of the KWP pyramid. The party exercises power through an elaborate network of organizations embracing the entire population. Individuals receive party instructions and indoctrination in their government offices; production teams; military, factory, or classroom units; or other small groups to which each belongs. At this grassroots level occur the study sessions, self-criticism meetings, and mutual supervision that confirm loyalty and guard against dissidence. In addition, nearly everyone belongs to mass organizations, such as those for children, youths, women, workers, and professionals that can be called out as needed to engage in speed battles to boost production, to cheer visiting foreign dignitaries, or to celebrate Kim Il Sung's birthday. Citizens also vote regularly in elections at which the turnout is invariably 100 percent and the single slate of candidates nominated by the KWP is invariably elected. Political participation is universal, but political decisionmaking is reserved to a small circle.

A primary mechanism for controlling society is compulsory participation of all citizens in a wide range of after-work collective activities that absorb nearly all their waking hours and leave no time for individual pursuits. Training in group activity begins in nursery school or kindergarten, where small children are taught to give thanks to the fatherly leader, Kim Il Sung, for their blessings. Extracurricular activities throughout the school years include political study and self-criticism sessions, sports, music, attendance at political ceremonies, and helping farmers bring in the harvest or working on national construction projects.

Control over movement is strict. Any travel away from the home village or urban place of residence requires documents and police permission. Police promptly challenge any stranger appearing in their local jurisdiction. A striking feature of Pyongyang remarked on by many visitors is the scarcity of people on the streets, except during morning and evening travel to and from work. In this respect the capital of North Korea presents a very different appearance from any other Asian city. Few bicycles can be seen in North Korea, in sharp contrast to the swarms of such vehicles on the streets of Peking and other Chinese cities. Lack of bicycles significantly limits individual mobility.[50]

Legal emigration rarely if ever occurs, although relatively small numbers travel abroad in various official delegations and athletic teams. The Chinese list 8,800 "tourists" from North Korea as having visited China in 1981 (compared to 2.2 million Japanese and 1.3 million U.S.

citizens).[51] This figure probably includes members of official delegations as well as visitors to the Korean Yan Bian Autonomous District just across the border, where many residents of North Korea have relatives. Emigrants to North Korea from the Korean community in Japan are not allowed to make visits back to family members remaining in Japan. A few such family members in Japan have been allowed to visit their relatives who emigrated to North Korea, but their contacts with these relatives were strictly monitored and controlled.[52] The people of North Korea have almost no access to information from outside the country except for that carried in the officially controlled media. Foreign visitors to North Korea, even those from the Soviet Union and China, travel with escorts and are not permitted to converse freely with ordinary people.

Every individual in North Korea is classified into 1 of 51 categories according to his *songbun*—his family's class background. The elite group at the top of the hierarchy includes anti-Japanese guerrilla fighters and their families; orphans of parents killed in anti-Japanese activites or in the Korean War; and the families of party members, government officials, and military officers. The elite receive preferential treatment in access to food and other consumer goods. Those at the bottom of the ladder include descendants of landlords, capitalists, rich peasants, collaborators with the Japanese, and members of religious groups as well as the families of persons who fled to South Korea. Their "complicated" background subjects them to suspicion of potential disloyalty to the regime. Persons with a good *songbun* find their entry into the best schools and their rise in the bureaucracy facilitated. Those with a bad *songbun* have little chance for a good education or a good job. Marriage between a person of good *songbun* and one of bad *songbun* tends to drag the couple down the social ladder and is strongly discouraged. Because family background is passed on from parents to children, stratification seems to be hardening, and opportunities for those at the bottom of the ladder seem to be declining.[53]

The leadership controls society primarily through organization, indoctrination, social pressure, and distribution of psychic and material rewards for desired behavior. The task is facilitated by the isolation of the population from outside influence. In the background, however, is a large and powerful public security apparatus to guard against activities deemed threatening to the state. How many persons have been imprisoned on suspicion of being spies or subversives is unknown, but South Korean sources assert that North Korea operates labor camps with thousands of political prisoners.[54] A few foreigners working for the North Korean regime have suffered imprisonment. A Venezuelan poet, Ali Lameda, wrote a detailed account of his seven years in prison. His account was circulated by Amnesty International, which assisted in his release.[55]

Political Impact of Social Change

In North Korea, as in South Korea, industrialization has transformed society. By 1979 the farm population, which had numbered about 70 percent of the population in 1949, had dropped to 28 percent in South Korea and 30.6 percent in North Korea. Urban population, which had been less than 10 percent of the total population in 1945, grew by 1976 to 46 percent in South Korea and 47 percent in North Korea. Both Koreas virtually eliminated illiteracy. Education expanded greatly. North Korea, which had extended compulsory education to eleven years in 1972, had 14 percent of its population in high schools in 1979, as compared to 10 percent in South Korea. But South Korea had a larger proportion of its population in college than North Korea—1 percent, compared to 0.6 percent.[56] Modernization had produced a great increase in scientists, engineers, administrators, skilled labor, and technicians of many kinds. North Korea did not suffer the downgrading of expertise in favor of political criteria that occurred in China during the Cultural Revolution. One could be both "red" and "expert."

So far, modernization in North Korea probably has helped the governing elite to maintain itself in power. It can point convincingly to dramatic improvements in health, in access to education, and to a lesser extent, in housing for the average citizen. Food and clothing, although not of the quality and variety available to South Koreans, are better than in colonial days. Thoroughly indoctrinated through modern means of communication and lacking an opportunity to compare their daily lives with those of people elsewhere, most North Koreans might well be reasonably satisfied with the material improvements in their lives under Kim Il Sung. Any expression of dissatisfaction can be quickly suppressed by well-equipped security forces. The society is so thoroughly regimented that no scope exists for the rise of an open opposition movement, as in South Korea, regardless of the effects of social change.

In other Communist countries, notably China, Hungary, and Poland, the emergence of a stratum of younger technocrats who are gradually replacing the original revolutionary generation has had a significant political impact. The younger generation has less veneration for ideology and relies more on pragmatic means of stimulating economic growth, often means with a pronounced capitalistic tinge. No similar trend could be discerned in North Korea in the late 1970s. Even though younger technocrats were appearing in the North Korean bureaucracy, including a few senior party and government positions, the ruling group was still dominated by Kim Il Sung and his associates of the revolutionary generation. Desire for modification of the rigid political system might have been building beneath the surface, especially among those stigmatized and relegated to the lower ranks of society by bad *songbun;* but, if so, such desires were masked by the Kim cult's all-embracing insistence on loyalty, discipline, and ideological conformity.

External Influence[57]

Foreign influence on domestic politics in Korea was strongest during the late 1940s, when foreign intervention determined the basic structure of the political systems established in the two Koreas: a constitutional republic in South Korea patterned on the United States and Western Europe and a "people's republic" in North Korea patterned on the Soviet Union. After the Korean War, foreign influence on Korean politics took two principal forms: direct official pressure by an ally to affect the political behavior of the ruling group and a wide variety of unofficial and often indirect influences.

The Soviet Union and China intervened directly in the mid-1950s to influence domestic politics in North Korea. After that experience, Kim Il Sung publicly and emphatically denounced big power intervention in the internal affairs of small allies. There is no evidence of later intervention by Moscow or Peking in Pyongyang's domestic politics, although Khrushchev exerted crude pressure on Kim Il Sung in an attempt to force him to take the Soviet side in the Sino-Soviet dispute. Soviet and Chinese officials and scholars in conversations with third parties have privately criticized the Kim cult and the plan for dynastic succession in North Korea, but insisted that these were internal matters in which they could not interfere. Given the rivalry between Moscow and Peking for influence in Pyongyang and their awareness of Kim Il Sung's sensitivity to meddling by outsiders, refraining from intervention would be a logical choice for them. Moreover, Kim Il Sung had demonstrated that he could prevent the Soviet Union from turning North Korea into a Mongolia, and Pyongyang's confrontation with Seoul and the United States ensured that it could not escape from the Soviet orbit like Yugoslavia. Thus, the incentive for Moscow's attempting to manipulate North Korea's internal politics was not strong.

Influence by example has occurred in North Korea, even though it has not been acknowledged by Kim Il Sung, who was intent on demonstrating the independence and self-reliance prescribed by the *chu che* principle. The most obvious illustration is the Chollima campaign, clearly inspired by Mao's Great Leap Forward.[58] In general, however,

Kim Il Sung appears to have been quite successful in excluding foreign influence that might have affected North Korea's political system.

In South Korea, foreign influence has had greater impact on politics. In the 1950s and 1960s, when U.S. military and economic aid was a large proportion of the ROK budget, the U.S. Embassy on occasion pressed vigorously for a particular course of action, as, for example, in 1963 when Park Chung-hee was deterred from seeking a prolongation of military government. After 1966 the United States probably was somewhat constrained from criticism by the ROK's participation in the Vietnam War. In the 1970s, although some U.S. newspapers, members of Congress, and individual U.S. citizens criticized the repressive actions taken by Park Chung-hee under the *yusin* constitution, the U.S. government was unwilling or unable to bring strong pressure to bear on him to modify his political behavior. U.S. economic relations with South Korea were now conducted almost entirely by the private sector, in which the U.S. government could not readily intervene to apply political leverage on an allied government. Moreover, the concern with the North Korean military threat and the desire for political stability deterred the U.S. government from withholding or threatening to withhold military aid as a means of exerting political pressure on Park.[59] The U.S. government did, however, express its disapproval, both publicly and privately, of the denial of human rights in the ROK.

Park Chung-hee no doubt resented foreign interference in domestic Korean politics, just as Kim Il Sung did in North Korea, but he could not exclude foreign influence as Kim did. Foreign organizations and individuals in the United States and Japan supported opposition to Park and urged their governments to press the ROK to ease restrictions on democratic freedoms. How much impact this diffuse and indirect political influence had on politics in South Korea is difficult to say. It could not prevent the paramount leader from taking actions he considered crucial to his hold on power, but, given the importance of the U.S. connection to South Korea's security and prosperity, rising U.S. criticism may have deterred him from taking more extreme measures than he actually took. It may have strengthened the influence on him of moderates in his administration and weakened that of the hard-liners.

The late Yi dynasty practice of seeking the backing of foreigners to strengthen one's own position in domestic politics (an extension of the common domestic practice of seeking a powerful patron) continued to flourish in South Korea. But instead of looking to different foreign governments for support, competing political groups looked to different elements in the United States. Supporters of the ROK government appealed to U.S. citizens sympathetic to the need for political stability in the face of the North Korean threat, while the opposition appealed to those more concerned with fostering democracy and respect for human rights. As the leaders in South Korea and the United States were committed in principle to constitutional democracy, those who defended authoritarian practices in South Korea excused them as temporary expedients necessary in current circumstances. Thus, although the short-term impact of U.S. influence on the politics of South Korea was difficult to discern, it helped to keep alive the spirit of democratic resistance to authoritarianism.

Notes

1. James B. Palais, "Political Leadership in the Yi Dynasty," in Dae-Sook Suh and Chae-Jin Lee, eds., *Political Leadership in Korea* (Seattle: University of Washington Press, 1976), pp. 3–35; Hahm Pyong-Choon, *The Korean Political Tradition and Law* (Seoul: Hollym Corp., 1967), pp. 1–84.

2. The principal works drawn on in writing this section are Hahm Pyong-Choon, *The Korean Political Tradition and Law*; John Kie-chiang Oh, *Korea: Democracy on Trial* (Ithaca, N.Y.: Cornell University Press, 1968); Dae-Sook Suh and Chae-Jin Lee, *Political Leadership in Korea*; Edward Reynolds Wright, ed., *Korean Politics in Transition* (Seattle: University of Washington Press, 1975); Frederica M. Bunge, ed., *South Korea: A Country Study* (American University for U.S. Department of the Army, Washington, D.C.: U.S. Government Printing Office, 1982); Se-Jin Kim and Chi-won Kang, eds., *Korea: A Nation in Transition* (Seoul: Research Center for Peace and Unification, 1978); Henderson, *Korea: Politics of the Vortex*; Kim, *Divided Korea*; Sung-joo Han, *The Failure of Democracy in South Korea* (Berkeley: University of California Press, 1974); Oliver, *Syngman Rhee and American Involvement in Korea*; Hahn-been Lee, *Korea: Time, Change, and Administration* (Honolulu: East-West Center Press, 1968); Se-Jin Kim, *The Politics of Military Revolution in Korea* (Chapel Hill: University of North Carolina Press, 1971); and Sung M. Pae, *Testing Democratic Theories in Korea* (Lanham, Md.: University Press of America, 1986).

3. Bunge, *South Korea*, p. 109.

4. Edward S. Mason and others, *The Economic and Social Modernization of the Republic of Korea* (Cambridge: Harvard University Press, 1980), p. 47.

5. See especially Chapter 1, "The Single Magnet."

6. Bae Ho Hahn, "The Authority Structure of Korean Politics," in Wright, *Korean Politics in Transition*, p. 303.

7. For example, he masterfully undermined the political power of Yi Pom-sok, head of the Youth Corps, between 1952 and 1953 (see Kim, *Divided Korea*, pp. 139–141), and he had executed in 1959 the head of the leftist Progressive Party, Cho Pong-am, for alleged illicit contacts with North Korean agents (Han, *The Failure of Democracy in South Korea*, p. 85).

8. Lee, *Time, Change, and Administration*, Chapter 5, pp. 74–108.

9. Mason and others, *Economic and Social Modernization*, p. 251.

10. Henderson, *Korea: Politics of the Vortex*, p. 2.

11. Ibid., p. 212, and Kim, *Divided Korea*, p. 22.

12. Figures on the size of the bureaucracy vary greatly and are hard to reconcile. For example, Henderson (*Korea: Politics of the Vortex*, p. 216) states that the bureaucracy had expanded to 300,000 by the end of the Korean War. Kim (*Divided Korea*, p. 269) says that the bureaucracy increased from 235,000 to 356,000 during the early Park period, 1961 to 1967. Bunge (*South Korea*, p. 174) refers to "continuous" efforts to stamp out malfeasance, resulting in disciplinary actions against 132,500 officials between 1963 and 1980.

13. Wanki Paik, "Psycho-Cultural Approach to the Study of Korean Bureaucracy," in Kim and Kang, *Korea: A Nation in Transition*, p. 222.

14. See Lee, *Time, Change, and Administration*, Chapter 8, pp. 144–175.

15. Dong-Suh Bark and Chae-Jin Lee, "Bureaucratic Elite and Development Orientations," in Suh and Lee, *Political Leadership in Korea*, pp. 91–131.

16. Mason and others, *Economic and Social Modernization*, p. 293. Chapter 8 of this book, "Government and Business," analyzes in detail the ways in which the political leadership employed the bureaucracy to stimulate economic growth primarily through the private sector.

17. The best analysis of the political role of the ROK armed forces is Se-Jin Kim's study, *The Politics of Military Revolution in Korea*.

18. Over a five-year period more than 250,000 Korean troops had combat duty in Vietnam (Kim, *The Politics of Military Revolution in Korea*, p. 158).

19. Ibid., p. 164.

20. Ibid., p. 99.

21. Ibid., p. 55.

22. In 1950 only 18 percent of South Korea's population lived in urban areas, about the same proportion as in other developing countries. By 1975 the proportion of urban population had risen to 51 percent, nearly twice that of other developing countries and about the same as the average developed country in 1950. See Mason and others, *Economic and Social Modernization*, pp. 391–392. In 1945 78 percent of the population was illiterate; by 1970 less than 12 percent (Mason and others, p. 351).

23. Ibid., p. 348.

24. Between 1945 and 1975 newspaper circulation rose from 380,000 to 3.5 million; the number of radios rose from 60,000 to 4.8 million; and television ownership increased from 25,000 in 1961 to 5.13 million in 1979 (Bunge, *South Korea*, p. 85).

25. Ibid., p. 101.

26. For a detailed account of political opposition and government repression, see Asia Watch Committee, *Human Rights in Korea* (New York, 1985).

27. The principal works drawn on in writing this section are Scalapino and Lee, *Communism in Korea*; Kim, *Divided Korea*; Baik Bong, *Kim Il Sung*; Yang, *Korea and Two Regimes*; Suh and Lee, *Political Leadership in Korea*; Frederica M. Bunge, ed., *North Korea: A Country Study* (American University for U.S. Department of the Army, Washington, D.C.: U.S. Government Printing Office, 1981); Jae Kyu Park and Jung Gun Kim, eds., *The Politics of North Korea* (Seoul: Institute for Far Eastern Studies, Kyungnam University, 1979); Robert A. Scalapino and

64   *Political Change and External Influence, 1953–1979*

Jun-yop Kim, eds., *North Korea Today: Strategic and Domestic Issues* (Berkeley: Institute of East Asian Studies, University of California, 1983); Ilpyong J. Kim, *Communist Politics in North Korea* (New York: Praeger, 1975); Gavan McCormack and Mark Selden, *Korea, North and South: The Deepening Crisis* (New York: Monthly Review Press, 1978); Tai Sung An, *North Korea in Transition: From Dictatorship to Dynasty* (Westport, Conn.: Greenwood Press, 1983); Chong-Sik Lee, *The Korean Workers' Party: A Short History* (Stanford, Calif.: Hoover Institution Press, 1978); C.I. Eugene Kim and B. C. Koh, eds., *Journey to North Korea: Personal Perceptions* (Berkeley: Institute of East Asian Studies, University of California, 1983).

28. Kim, *Divided Korea*, p. 190.

29. See Scalapino and Lee, *Communism in Korea*, vol. 1, pp. 512–515, for details of this curious episode, which was to have lasting effects on Kim's attitude toward the Soviet Union and China.

30. In the Political Committee, announced after the Third Party Congress of 1956, the Kapsan group outnumbered other factions; they became a majority in that body from the Fourth Party Congress in 1961 after the purging of senior members of the Yenan and Soviet factions. Until the Fifth Party Congress in 1970 no member of the Kapsan group was dropped from the KWP Central Committee, despite a high turnover in the membership of that body at the party congresses from 1945 to 1961. Those Kapsan members dropped from the Central Committee in 1970 were replaced by new appointments from the Kapsan group. See Suh Dae-Sook, "Communist Party Leadership," in Suh and Lee, *Political Leadership in Korea*, pp. 159–191.

31. See Chapter 4.

32. Scalapino and Lee, *Communism in Korea*, vol. 1, pp. 594–596.

33. See Chapters 3 and 7.

34. Chong-Sik Lee, "The 1972 Constitution and Top Communist Leaders," in Suh and Lee, *Political Leadership in Korea*, p. 209.

35. See Chapter 3.

36. An, *North Korea in Transition*, p. 135.

37. Thomas Hosuck Kang, "Changes in the North Korean Personality," in Park and Kim, *The Politics of North Korea*, p. 91. The ubiquitousness of Kim's presence is difficult to convey to anyone who has not experienced it in North Korea. One Korean-American scholar, a longtime student of North Korea, commented on his impression of the Kim personality cult during a 1981 visit: "Neither prolonged exposure to the North Korean press and publications nor familiarity with reports by previous visitors prepared me for what I actually saw, heard and felt in North Korea" (B. C. Koh, "The Cult of Personality and the Succession Issue," in Kim and Koh, *Journey to North Korea*, p. 25).

38. Kim told Congressman Stephen Solarz in 1980 that he tried to visit each province and centrally governed city for ten to fifteen days each year. As there are thirteen provinces and cities, he would have to be on the road for four to six months out of each year to meet this schedule. He is reported to have had comfortable residences built for his use in each province and major city.

39. Although Kim Yong-ju was appointed the North Korean cochairman of the North-South Coordinating Committee, established in accordance with the

agreement between Seoul and Pyongyang announced in July 1972, he did not appear at any of the meetings of the committee. A Soviet Korean specialist told me that Kim drank heavily and underwent a serious operation in the early 1970s to remove one of his kidneys.

40. See An, Chapter 7, "Dynastic Succession," in *North Korea in Transition*, pp. 149–172, for a more detailed discussion of the subject.

41. Ibid., pp. 150–151. For a discussion of the North Korean practice of avoiding use of Kim Chong Il's name, see Morgan E. Clippinger, "Kim Chong-il in the North Korean Mass Media: A Study in Semi-Esoteric Communication," *Asian Survey* 21, no. 3 (March 1981):289–309.

42. An speculates that the two-year suspension of references to "the party center" may have resulted from Kim Chong Il's having been responsible for the ax murders of two U.S. officers at Panmunjom in August 1976, a widely circulated rumor in South Korea. But the fact that frequent mention of "the party center" continued for eight months after that incident, until March 1977, confers greater plausibility on the leaked document explanation. See An, p. 153.

43. See An, pp. 138–139, for a genealogical table of Kim's ancestors and living relatives and the accolades bestowed on them.

44. "Let Us Thoroughly Arm Ourselves with *Juche* Idea of Our Party," *The People's Korea*, August 26, 1971, p. 1, in Park and Kim, *The Politics of North Korea*, pp. 98–99.

45. Byung Chul Koh, *The Foreign Policy Systems of North and South Korea* (Berkeley: University of California Press, 1984), p. 76.

46. *Foreign Broadcast Information Service, Daily Report, East Asia and Pacific* [hereafter *FBIS*], October 15, 1980, p. D18.

47. See Scalapino and Lee, *Communism in Korea*, vol. 2, pp. 867–868; An, *North Korea in Transition*, p. 65.

48. Koh, *The Foreign Policy Systems of North and South Korea*, p. 72.

49. Scalapino and Lee, *Communism in Korea*, vol. 2, p. 1300.

50. I observed the emptiness of Pyongyang's streets during a trip in 1980. A foreign diplomat, who had spent a year in Pyongyang, said that officials ascribed the lack of a bicycle industry in North Korea to an unwillingness to divert valuable resources to this end, but he thought the true reason was to limit individual mobility. A Chinese who grew up in Pyongyang during the period of Japanese occupation told me that during that period only Japanese were allowed to own bicycles and that the DPRK had continued to employ this method of control by not producing bicycles. That policy may be undergoing change, however, for reference to a bicycle plant appeared in the North Korean press in 1984 (see *FBIS*, August 16, 1984, p. D19).

51. PRC State Statistical Bureau, comp., *Statistical Yearbook of China, 1983* (Hong Kong: Economic Information and Agency [sic], 1983), p. 442.

52. A poignant account of such a visit was published in Japan in 1984 under the title *A Disillusioned Trip to North Korea—A Frozen Land*. See excerpts in *Korea Herald*, April 6, 7, and 8, 1984.

53. Scalapino and Lee, *Communism in Korea*, vol. 2, pp. 831–836; Changsoo Lee, "Social Policy and Development in North Korea," in Scalapino and Kim, *North Korea Today*, pp. 118–120; Bunge, *North Korea*, pp. 74–77.

54. *Korea Herald,* July 2, 1982. See also Bruce Cumings, "Human Rights in the Democratic People's Republic of Korea," in Asia Watch Committee, *Human Rights in Korea,* pp. 340–364.

55. *Washington Post,* July 2, 1979.

56. Sangwoo Rhee, "North Korea Ideology, Social Change and Policy Toward the South," in Scalapino and Kim, *North Korea Today,* pp. 247–248.

57. For a fuller discussion of big power relations with the two Koreas, see Chapters 7 and 8.

58. See Chapter 3.

59. An exception was the $20 million in military aid withheld by the Congress in 1974 as a gesture of dissatisfaction with political repression in the ROK. See Chapter 4.

3

Interdependence Versus Autarky

Economic growth has been a high priority national goal for both Korean governments. Military preparedness, declining dependence on allies, the leader's continuance in office, and, ultimately, survival as a political entity, all demanded a respectable rate of growth. Outsiders and the Koreans themselves saw economic growth and the benefits it conferred on the people as a standard by which to judge the success of the rival regimes. Economic power became a factor in their competition for international prestige and influence. Beginning with a common cultural background and historical experience, but with differing endowments of natural resources, the two Koreas chose radically different methods to promote growth.

All Koreans shared the Confucian commitment to education that helped to create a hospitable climate for rapid economic growth in the countries of Northeast Asia.[1] Japanese colonialism, although slanting economic development in Korea to benefit mainly Japanese rather than Koreans, left behind a foundation to build on in agriculture, industry, education, and administration that was considerably more advanced than had existed in 1910. The sense of rivalry between North and South lent an urgency to the drive for economic development not present in most developing countries. Commitment to eventual reunification through a winner-take-all solution made winning the race for economic growth vital to political survival.

Division of Korea gave the North most of the country's mineral resources, electric power plants, and heavy industry: the South, the bulk of the light industry and the most productive agricultural land. North Korea began its reconstruction after the Korean War with a labor shortage. South Korea, which had gained population through an influx of Koreans from North Korea, Japan, and Manchuria, including many with training and experience in industry, commerce, and administration, had a labor surplus.

Differences in resource endowments had little effect in the long run on the rates of economic growth achieved by the two Koreas. The crucial differences were in the systems and the policies chosen to foster growth. The chief features of the North Korean system were state ownership of the means of production, a command economy, policies giving priority to heavy industry over light industry, large expenditures for defense, and minimal dependence on external economic relations. South Korea developed a mixed economy, primarily private enterprise, but with government ownership of a significant share of the economy. It was a market economy, but subject to substantial government management and intervention. South Korea initially gave priority to light industry, developing heavy industry later. The South Korean economy depended extensively on external sources of raw materials, markets, capital, and technology. The North Korean economy grew more rapidly than that of South Korea during the first decade after the Korean War, but in the mid-1960s South Korea's economy took off and posted higher rates of economic growth than North Korea through the 1970s.

SOUTH KOREA

Growth Trends

The South Korean economy, renowned for its high rate of growth over the past twenty years, got off to a faltering start. From 1945 to 1948, the division of the country, the repatriation of Japanese administrators and technicians, the return of a million or more jobless Koreans, and fumbling management by temporary U.S. military administrators inhibited growth. The infant ROK government of Syngman Rhee, harassed by guerrillas supported from the North, had little opportunity to foster economic expansion before it came under all-out attack by North Korea. The war caused over a million deaths in South Korea and destroyed much of the country's industry, housing, and transportation facilities. Thus, although accurate statistics on economic trends between 1945 and 1953 are lacking, economic output in 1953 was significantly lower than it had been in 1939 to 1940.[2]

Economic growth was a secondary objective of the Syngman Rhee government from 1953 to 1960. During the first four years, the most urgent need was the repair of war damage. Thereafter, stabilization of prices became the chief objective. Defense expenditures absorbed 4 percent of GNP. The annual real growth rate during the Rhee years and immediately thereafter was only 4.1 percent. Rapid population increase held the growth in per capita GNP down to 1.7 percent.[3]

Park Chung-hee took office determined to speed up lagging economic growth and to make South Korea less dependent on U.S. aid. His first five-year plan (1962–1966) set a growth target of 7 percent per annum, a steep increase over the average of previous years.

Park's economic managers adopted new monetary, fiscal, and trade policies, which created a favorable environment for manufacturing and export. Led by an average annual increase in exports of nearly 30 percent, composed almost entirely of manufactured goods, the economy grew at an average rate in real terms of 9.6 percent per year from 1960 to 1962 through 1974 to 1976. Aided by decline in the rate of population increase, per capita GNP rose during this period at 7.2 percent annually, a dramatic increase over the 1.7 percent of the earlier period.[4]

During the latter half of the 1970s, the high growth strategy of the Park administration was severely tested. The jump in oil prices and the consequent world recession of 1974 to 1975 increased the cost of South Korea's imports and cut back sharply the growth in exports, causing large balance of payment deficits. Real economic growth dropped from a record 16.9 percent in 1973 to 8.6 percent in 1974 and 8.3 percent in 1975. It surged back into the double digits from 1976 to 1978, but dropped to 7.1 percent in 1979 as a result of the second round of oil price increases and the world recession of 1979 and 1980. Still, the average annual growth rate for the five years from 1975 through 1979 exceeded 10 percent, an impressive record, but it was achieved at the cost of inflation ranging from 10 to 30 percent annually and a rapidly rising foreign debt. When Chun Doo Hwan took over the leadership in 1980 following the death of Park Chung-hee, confronted both by political disorder and economic recession, many questioned whether Chun could restore momentum to the economy.

Rural Economy

A shortage of farmland to produce food for its growing population has severely limited South Korea's economic policy choices. Few nations have less arable land per person.[5] During the colonial period, when the population was much smaller than it is today, South Korea was an exporter of rice to Japan, but even then only because landlords squeezed a surplus out of an impoverished rural population. After land reform and the resulting increase in domestic consumption of grain, South Korea became a grain importer. Grain imports increased substantially from 1965 on, as rising income enabled people to enjoy a more varied diet.[6] Farmers produced less grain and more fruit, vegetables, and livestock, which gave them a higher return, but required increasing imports of grain, including feedgrain for livestock.

Not much land remained that the ROK could develop for agriculture except at very high cost. Moreover, expanding cities were absorbing agricultural land. Consequently, greater agricultural production had to come almost entirely from increasing production per hectare rather than adding to the acreage under cultivation. Farmers achieved substantial increases in production averaging 3.4 percent annually from 1954 to 1975, primarily through the introduction of high-yielding plant varieties and the use of increasing amounts of fertilizer. By 1975 South Korean farmers were using more chemical fertilizer per hectare than the Japanese and reaping rice yields close to the high Japanese level.[7] Initially, South Korea imported fertilizer, but by the late 1970s, the newly established chemical industry had made the country virtually self-sufficient in fertilizer. Of course, the raw materials going into fertilizer, mainly oil and its derivatives, still had to be imported.

Land reforms carried out by the U.S. military government and the Rhee government between 1947 and 1950 laid the foundation for South Korea's productive farm economy. At the beginning of World War II 60 percent of all cultivated land had been owned by landlords, who took half of the tenant's product. The land reforms reduced rented land from 60 percent to 15 percent and enabled 95 percent of the farmers to acquire their own land.[8] The reforms did not produce an early increase in productivity, for the distribution of land was not accompanied by other measures to extend irrigation and give farmers access to credit, improved seed, cheap fertilizer, and extension services. South Korea had no organization comparable to the Joint Commission on Rural Reconstruction in Taiwan, through which U.S. and Chinese specialists focused attention and resources on the rural sector.[9] The immediate result of the land reform was to increase the income of the mass of farmers and eliminate large disparities in income throughout the countryside. The pattern of small owner-operated farms, one hectare or less in size, established at that time has continued to the present.

After a period of neglect of agriculture in the 1950s and early 1960s, the government undertook a number of measures to help the farmer. It established an Office of Rural Development with 10,000 extension workers to provide advice to farmers and a National Agricultural Cooperatives Federation to purchase on behalf of the government most of the rice produced in South Korea, to sell fertilizer, and to provide credit at rates below those available elsewhere. Like other government agencies in the country, both of these were highly centralized bureaucracies. The most publicized of the government actions in support of rural people was the Saemaul Undong (New Community Movement) established in 1971 and designed to encourage self-help by villages through small government grants. These grants were used to improve roads and water supplies, build village meeting halls, and carry out other local community projects. The most effective government action to improve the farmer's welfare was the policy adopted in the early 1970s to increase the price paid by the government for grain, to be sold at a lower price to the urban population, despite the resulting increase in the budget deficit and inflationary pressures.

The twenty years from 1955 to 1975 brought a dramatic improvement in the quality of life for the rural population. Paved roads, extensive rural electrification, and a rapid increase in country schools opened new opportunities for farm youth. Mechanization of farm tasks, necessitated by labor shortage and encouraged by government subsidies, reduced the heavy physical labor required to irrigate and plow fields and to thresh grain. Infant mortality dropped and health conditions improved, although the rural resident lacked the ready access to modern medical facilities available in the cities. Television aerials began to sprout from the roofs of farm dwellings. The pronounced income gap between farmers and city dwellers of the late 1960s narrowed in the 1970s, but did not disappear. In 1975 rural household income was 84 percent of urban per capita income.[10]

The principal South Korean government actions that produced a rural standard of living closer to that of city dwellers than in most developing countries were

- the land reform, that greatly reduced disparities in rural income and caused technological improvements to spread relatively evenly throughout the countryside;
- a great expansion of the road network, giving the farmers better access to markets, and rural electrification;
- grain purchase policies in the 1970s designed to raise rural incomes; and
- the decision to permit the import of substantial amounts of cheap imported grain, rather than pushing for national self-sufficiency, thus enabling many farmers to raise their income by shifting from grain production to higher value farm products.

Although the bulk of the population lived in the countryside when South Korea began its march to modernization, rapid industrialization was not based, as in some countries, on squeezing the needed investment capital out of the rural sector. Taxes amounted to only 2 or 3 percent of farm household income, and no net cash outflow from rural areas occurred until the 1970s. The rural contribution to the urban sector, aside from food, consisted mainly of people: the farm population declined from 62 percent of the total population in 1955 to 38 percent in 1975.[11]

External Dependence

Rural development in South Korea followed upon industrial development. The rapid growth of urban industry had a spillover effect that benefited the farmer. Rapid industrial growth, in turn, depended initially on large amounts of foreign economic and military aid and later on foreign loans. South Korea was one of the world's largest beneficiaries of foreign aid. During the thirty-year period between 1946 and 1976 it received $12.6 billion in economic and military assistance from the United States, $1.9 billion from international financial institutions, and $1 billion from Japan, a per capita aid level exceeded only by South Vietnam and Israel. The larger portion of U.S. aid—$6.8 billion—was military assistance.[12] Later, South Korea became one of the largest borrowers of foreign funds, although after the early 1960s domestic savings rose rapidly and dependence on foreign funds for investment drastically declined. Economic development from the end of the Korean War fell into two distinct, radically different periods: 1953 to 1962, a period of slow growth, and 1963 to 1979, a period of rapid growth.

Slow Growth, 1953–1962

The invasion by North Korean and Chinese forces in 1950 and 1951 heavily damaged the South Korean economy, but during the last two years of the war substantial recovery took place. The South, unlike North Korea, had escaped aerial bombing, and as the front stabilized around the 38th parallel, large amounts of U.S.-financed relief supplies arrived.

By 1953 the output of agriculture and manufacturing had come back up to the 1949 level. Like many other developing countries at that time, South Korea was predominantly agricultural with many of its people living at a bare subsistence level. Forty-seven percent of GNP came from agriculture, forestry, and fisheries and just 9 percent from manufacturing. Per capita GNP was only $134 at 1970 constant prices.[13]

Heavy dependence on U.S. aid characterized the 1953 to 1962 period. Aid financed 70 percent of South Korea's imports and 70 percent of its investment. Counterpart funds generated by sales of agricultural products supplied under Public Law 480 accounted for one-half of the government's budget.[14]

The period was marked by sharp disagreements between the U.S. government and the ROK over economic policies. The Korean government wanted new factories and heavy industry financed by foreign aid, whereas the U.S. government favored the rehabilitation of light industry and better use of existing capacity. The Koreans pressed for a higher level of aid, while the United States wanted to reduce the aid level and urged the Koreans to do more to increase domestic savings and tax collections to make the country more self-reliant. The United States sought devaluation of Korean currency in order to encourage exports and reduce demand for imports; the Korean government resisted, grudgingly devaluing twice under U.S. pressure, but not by enough to compensate for the high inflation of the period. Annual increases in the wholesale price index, caused primarily by large government deficits, ranged from 25 percent to a high of 81 percent in 1955. The U.S. aid mission eventually prevailed on the government to curb deficits, bringing inflation down sharply in 1958 and 1959, but economic growth slowed in 1959 to 1960, dropping below 2 percent in the politically turbulent year 1960.[15] U.S. officials became discouraged at the lack of progress in the South Korean economy, which seemed to have become permamently dependent on U.S. aid. Economic growth in South Korea lagged behind that of North Korea during this period.

Although the overall rate of economic growth during this period was discouraging, changes were taking place in the economy and in society that would improve the prospects for success when a growth-oriented government came to power. During the first several years large amounts of aid went to the repair of the infrastructure and the rebuilding of war-damaged factories. High tariffs and quantitative restrictions encouraged the development of an import-substitution industry, producing mainly consumer goods but also some intermediate products used in manufacturing. From 1953 to 1960 the composition of imports changed from three-fourths consumer goods and one-fourth intermediates to one-third consumer goods and two-thirds intermediates.[16] Rapid expansion of education raised literacy to a level far above that of most developing countries and produced swiftly rising numbers of high school and college graduates. Thousands of men completed their military service and returned to civilian society experienced in functioning in a highly disciplined organization and trained to handle automotive, electronic, and mechanical equipment.

During this period U.S. aid made a crucial contribution to the Korean economy. The Harvard-Korean Development Institute study concludes that the high level of U.S. aid made the difference between the 1.5 percent annual real increase in per capita income achieved and no growth at all. "Without this growth, the economic condition of the population would have remained desperate, political cohesion would have deteriorated, and the foundations for subsequent high growth would not have been forged."[17]

Rapid Growth, 1963–1979

The South Korean economy recovered a little from the low point of 1960 after the seizure of power by Park Chung-hee in 1961, but did not take off until 1963, when real economic growth for the first time reached 8.8 percent. Thereafter, annual growth averaged close to 10 percent through 1976. No other Third World country except Hong Kong, Singapore, Taiwan, and the large oil exporters has grown so fast. Industrialization transformed the structure of the South Korean economy between 1962 and 1976, raising the industrial sector's share of GNP from 18 percent to 35 percent and reducing the share contributed by agriculture and mining from 45 percent to 26 percent.[18]

From the beginning the Park government committed itself to promoting economic growth. It produced the first five-year plan (1962–1966), setting a goal of 7.1 percent annual real growth and creating a precedent for the future by exceeding it. Park's economic managers relied on a policy of rapid expansion of labor-intensive manufactures as the primary engine of growth. The first and most important step was the exchange rate reform of 1964 and 1965, which devalued the won by 50 percent and instituted a unitary rate to replace the previous multiple exchange rates. Periodic subsequent devaluations as necessitated by domestic inflation kept the foreign exchange value of the won at a level that stimulated exports. More direct incentives, such as tariff exemptions on imports of raw materials for export production, preferential loans, and tax benefits also helped to attract manufacturers into producing for export. The government established the Korean Trade Promotion Corporation (KO-TRA) in 1964 to assist exporters in developing foreign markets.

Exports, which had been negligible before 1960, increased rapidly to reach 30 percent of GNP by 1976. Eighty-five percent of this greatly enlarged export volume consisted of manufactures, as compared to only 17 percent fifteen years before.[19] The ROK had the good fortune to begin its export drive during the 1960s, when world trade was expanding rapidly at about 8 percent annually.

The high priority given by the Park government to stimulating export growth and the policies adopted toward this end were the most important reasons for its economic success. Other factors also contributed. The existence of a strong, stable government provided an environment in which businessmen could plan confidently. The government had and used the power to carry out measures that furthered growth, even though some were unpopular with significant segments of the population. Another source of growth was the increase in government revenue from improved collections of taxes and more realistic pricing of the products of government-owned corporations, which enabled the government to increase investment in infrastructure and productive enterprise. Increased revenues, along with restraint in spending for social services, reduced budget deficits and brought inflation down to the one-digit level from 1966 through 1971.

The rapid growth of South Korean exports based on labor-intensive manufactures could not continue indefinitely, for the steady increase in the real wages of Korean workers made their products less competitive with goods produced by countries with lower wage levels, such as Indonesia and China. From 1968 on, capital-intensive industries, such as shipbuilding, steel, and the chemical industry contributed an increasing proportion of South Korean exports. The surge in oil prices in 1973 and 1974, although boosting the cost of essential imports, opened an offsetting opportunity in the form of construction contracts in the Middle East. Korean companies, experienced in construction work in their own country and in contract work for the U.S. military in Vietnam, were in a position to provide managers, engineers, and skilled labor for large-scale construction projects in Saudi Arabia and other oil-rich Middle Eastern countries at highly competitive prices. Construction contracts won by South Korean companies shot up from $260 million in 1974 to $2.5 billion in 1976 and $8.1 billion in 1978.[20] From 1975 through 1979 90 percent of such projects were in the Middle East.

South Korea's high growth performance resulted from an unusual combination of private enterprise and government direction. The bulk of increased industrial production came out of the private sector. Thousands of small, family-owned companies competed fiercely for a share of the market. The number of failures was high, but successful companies grew rapidly. Competition encouraged efficiency and fostered a growing class of able enterpreneurs and business managers. By 1975 the leading firms had developed into some 46 very large industrial and commercial conglomerates (*chaebol*) that produced 13 percent of the gross domestic product.[21] The *chaebol* resembled the large clusters of Japanese firms, such as Mitsui and Mitsubishi, with one important difference: the *chaebol*, unlike the groups in Japan, did not include private commercial banks, for the banks in Korea were government-owned. Business concentration increased rapidly in South Korea, but in 1975 was still substantially less than in India or Pakistan.[22]

The government sector, although smaller than the private sector, was larger than in most capitalist countries, roughly comparable to that of India. The government not only owned a controlling interest in the

banks, it also ran the railroads, the postal service, the principal broadcasting networks, and most public utilities. It controlled about one
hundred enterprises producing 9 percent of GNP, including some of the
largest industrial complexes, such as the Korea Electric Company, the
Pohang Iron and Steel Company, the Korea Oil Corporation, and the
Korea General Chemical Corporation. In the late 1960s and early 1970s
about 30 percent of investment went into the government sector. Government enterprises in South Korea operated more efficiently than those
in most developing countries, although they probably were less efficient
than the best of the private enterprises.[23]

More important than the contribution of government-controlled enterprises in speeding growth was government guidance of the private
sector. President Park and a handful of top bureaucrats, committed to
a high growth policy, monitored the economy closely. They met frequently
to assess its performance and promptly altered or replaced policies that
did not work. The pragmatism and flexibility of the economic managers,
their understanding of what was required to promote high growth, and
the fact that they were few in number made possible rapid response to
changing conditions. For example, in response to the oil crisis of October
1973, which quadrupled the price of imported oil, the government took
a series of drastic measures by January 1974, including the quadrupling
of gasoline prices. Few governments reacted so promptly and decisively.
As a result of these and other measures, the loss of growth momentum
was less than in most developing countries. The GNP growth dropped
to 8.7 percent in 1974 and 8.3 percent in 1975, but shot up to 15.5
percent in 1976. The economy paid a price for growth in high inflation
during those years: 42 percent in 1974 and 26 percent in 1975.[24]

Control of bank loans gave the government a powerful instrument
for stimulating growth through expansion of exports. Doubling of the
interest rate on time deposits from 15 percent to 30 percent in 1965
produced a rapid increase in such deposits, expanding the capacity of
banks to make loans for investment. Government-approved loans at low
interest rates, linked to export performance, gave exporters a persuasive
incentive to invest in expanding their scale of production and to increase
their sales in foreign markets. Businessmen with good government
connections, particularly those heading the *chaebol*, had an advantage
in obtaining low interest loans. But unlike the Rhee period, when
cronyism was the main criterion for loans, under the Park government
borrowers had to demonstrate a contribution to national economic goals.
Businessmen who could not meet government criteria for low-interest
bank loans had to resort to the private curb market, where interest rates
were much higher. The government also largely controlled access by

private firms to foreign loans, by granting or withholding the government guarantee usually required by foreign lenders.

In the close government-business cooperation that resulted in the remarkable rate of economic growth achieved during the Park period, government was the dominant partner. The authoritarian nature of the government enabled it to take prompt decisions and carry them out without extensive public debate, even in the face of substantial popular opposition. The rise of the giant *chaebol* gave the top businessmen increased influence, but the government still held the upper hand. Business probably had less influence on government than in Japan because the *chaebol* lacked the access to large private financial resources possessed by Japanese conglomerates.

The distribution of the rising income resulting from economic growth was relatively equitable in comparison with other developing countries. In the rural sector land reform had a powerful equalizing effect, turning former tenants into small landowners. The pattern of widely distributed land ownership changed little after that time. A gap existed between rural and urban incomes, which narrowed during the 1970s. In the cities wages and salaries rose rapidly, roughly keeping pace with economic growth, but an increasing difference between white- and blue-collar workers became apparent in the 1970s. The incomes of those at the top end of the income scale rose more rapidly than incomes in general, as the size of businesses increased and opportunities for high profits multiplied. Some of those profits went to corrupt government officials, land speculators, and financial manipulators, but most went to the productive enterpreneurs and managers responsible for the bulk of the economic expansion. Park Chung-hee and the influential Korean military frowned on the display of opulence; conspicuous consumption was less common among the wealthy in South Korea than in many developing countries.

Excessive Emphasis on Heavy Industry

In the late 1970s, particularly from 1977 to 1979, Park Chung-hee decided to speed up the development of heavy industry in order to reach a higher level of national self-sufficiency in this area. Concerned by the implications for Korea of the Nixon Doctrine and the withdrawal of a U.S. division, Park had pressed the development of certain heavy industries such as steel and shipbuilding early in the decade. But later, alarmed by Carter's decision to withdraw the remaining U.S. division, he urgently increased the number of heavy industries being promoted and the funds devoted to that purpose. Gross investment increased 26 percent annually from 1977 to 1979, as compared to an average of 16 percent over the entire 1962-1981 period. Much of this accelerated investment went into heavy industry, particularly into the machinery industry, which received 30 percent of all manufacturing investment compared to 20 percent in 1975.[25]

The concentration of investment in heavy industry had a number of adverse consequences. It reduced funds available for investment in light industry. The stress on national security as a criterion for allocation of investment resources instead of single-minded concentration on the criterion of export competitiveness diminished effectiveness in the use of limited investment funds. Moreover, the haste with which the program was implemented increased the concentration of industry in the *chaebol*, and resulted in duplication of facilities and overcapacity. Even when the government recognized that mistakes had been made, the large size of the investments and the time required to complete a heavy industrial plant made more difficult the prompt correction of errors and change in course that the government had been so successful at in the past. The drive to expand heavy industry rapidly also drove up wages, worsened the distribution of income, caused high inflation, and adversely affected South Korea's competitiveness on the world market. By 1978 the government recognized the need for a change in policy, which was underway when Park was assassinated.[26]

Interdependence

By 1979 South Korea had moved from a position of almost exclusive dependence on the United States to a complex involvement with the international economic community. In many ways its resembled other countries with few natural resources and a high level of foreign trade. But South Korea's concern with the threat from the North, the South's large military establishment, its dependence on the United States for advanced weapons, and, above all, the presence of sizable U.S. combat units on its soil perpetuated a special relationship with the United States. During the quarter of a century following the end of the Korean War a society evolved in South Korea that was "permeated by outside influences to an extent that would be hard to match in the Third World."[27]

The military relationship between South Korea and the United States will be examined in Chapters 4 and 6. Here, it suffices to point to that relationship as a principal channel for U.S. influence. A sense of dependence on the United States to deter a second Korean War underlay the tie. The geographical remoteness of the United States and the ever-present fear that it might decide, as in 1949, that South Korea was not a vital national interest, caused South Koreans to feel at a disadvantage compared to North Korea, whose allies were next door. Consequently, a prime national goal was to keep the United States militarily involved in South Korea. Koreans of all political persuasions in the South were deeply alarmed in 1977 when President Carter announced his intention to withdraw U.S. combat ground forces. The military relationship had created multiple channels of influence: the service by hundreds of thousands of U.S. military men in South Korea, the training of thousands of Korean military in the United States, frequent joint maneuvers, and the flow of new equipment and technology from the United States to the South Korean armed forces. The sense of dependency and the flow of influence was not entirely one-sided, for the United States regarded the military relationship with South Korea as a crucial link in its worldwide security system.

Between the 1950s and the 1970s the nature of South Korean dependence on external sources of investment capital and foreign exchange changed radically. By the mid-1960s the United States phased out grant aid almost entirely, replacing it with loans at concessional rates of interest. The importance of U.S. aid in financing imports dropped sharply from 67 percent of imports in the 1953 to 1962 period to only 4 percent in 1970 to 1974. Exports, Japanese concessional loans, foreign commercial loans, and direct investment provided rapidly expanding new sources of foreign exchange and investment capital. Not only did the contribution of total foreign aid in financing imports drop to a marginal level after 1970, but the U.S. share of that assistance fell below 50 percent.[28] Moreover, the interest rate reform of 1965 and other factors brought about an increase in domestic savings until by the mid-1970s it approached 25 percent of GNP. The share of foreign savings in investment financing fell from 75 percent in the early 1960s to 10 percent in 1976.[29] Thus, by the mid-1970s, although still dependent on access to the world capital market for investment and growth, South Korea had greatly reduced reliance on foreign capital and had significantly diversified the sources from which it came.

South Korean economic development depended heavily in other ways on the world economy, particularly on trade relations with Japan, its principal source of imports, and the United States, its principal market. Total exports amounted to 25 percent of GNP in 1977, a high level. The rapid industrial development that produced the rising level of exports was based almost entirely on imported technology, acquired through the purchase of turnkey plants and machinery; through direct foreign investment and licensing agreements; and through a wide variety of informal methods, including imitation, guidance by foreign buyers of Korean exports, and experience gained by Koreans working or studying abroad.[30] Construction contracts overseas, mainly in the Middle East, which reached a cumulative total of $21 billion in 1979, not only boosted

South Korea's foreign exchange earnings, but improved the managerial and technical skills of the construction companies involved, particularly when they worked closely with more experienced U.S. or European construction companies.[31]

Other elements in the proliferating network of links with the rest of the world were tourism, which brought nearly a million foreign visitors to South Korea in 1979; study abroad by thousands of graduate students; and a surge in the emigration of Koreans to the United States that raised the number of residents of Korean origin to over 370,000. The privately owned Korean Air Lines (KAL) provided worldwide service to 27 points in Asia, the Middle East, Western Europe, and North America, carrying almost 3 million passengers in 1979. Over 500 Korean flag vessels operated throughout the world, as well as a large fishing fleet.

During the 1950s and early 1960s the ROK's heavy dependence on economic aid gave the U.S. government substantial leverage on domestic policy. Heavy pressure, including express or implied threats to cut back on aid, brought about currency devaluations in 1953 and 1955 and forced the adoption of currency stabilization programs from 1957 through 1960. In 1963 and 1964 the U.S. government compelled the Park government to reinstate the stabilization program that it had abandoned and devalue the won by 50 percent.

The United States also used its economic leverage to influence domestic politics in South Korea, insisting that Syngman Rhee hold National Assembly elections on schedule in May 1950 and compelling Park Chung-hee to live up to his promise to replace the military regime with an elected civilian government in 1963. In general, however, U.S. pressures to promote democracy were less effective than insistence on economic reforms. A thorough study of elections in South Korea up to 1960 concludes that, although external influence affected the conduct and style of elections, the basic political institutions and the way that they functioned changed little.[32]

A primary objective of Park Chung-hee's drive for economic development was to make South Korea more self-reliant and thus less subject to U.S. economic pressure. The phasing out of economic aid eliminated the primary U.S. government instrument for influencing economic decisions in Seoul. By the 1970s, although the South Korean economy remained dependent on the United States for a substantial portion of its markets, technology, and capital, diversification of international economic relationships had diminished the extent of that dependence. To some degree the dependence had become reciprocal, for South Korea had become one of the largest overseas markets for U.S. agricultural products. Moveover, unlike the earlier dependency on U.S. government aid, the South Korean involvement in the U.S. free enterprise system could not be manipulated readily by the U.S. government to affect the policy decisions of a trading partner. South Korea's extensive interaction with the world economic system made its economy subject to the fluctuations of that system, such as the jump in oil prices in the 1970s and the recession that began at the end of the decade. But Seoul's policymakers now reached their domestic economic decisions independently; they no longer had to respond to official pressures from Washington.

NORTH KOREA

Judging the pace of economic development in North Korea and comparing it with that in South Korea is difficult because of the scarcity of reliable statistics on the system in the North. Since the mid-1960s the North Koreans have released little concrete data on the economy. Analysts have had to extrapolate from the scattered figures given and make educated guesses based on nonquantitative official statements claiming successes or pointing to problems in the economy. The difficulty is aggravated because the methods or bases of calculation used by North Korea differ from those generally used by Western analysts. For example, North Korea measures the overall performance of the economy by the "gross agricultural and industrial output" defined as the total monetary value of goods produced and technical services rendered by agriculture and industry. When compared to the gross national product used by Western economists, the North Korean calculation contains much double-counting and excludes many valuable services. Agricultural comparisons are made difficult by the use in North Korea of gross tonnage rather than nutrient content of fertilizer and the reporting of crop yields in terms of unhulled rather than hulled grain. Figures on North Korea's foreign trade are more reliable than on domestic trends because they can be obtained from the published statistics of Pyongyang's trading partners.

Rural Economy

North Korea is a mountainous country, with less favorable climatic and soil conditions than South Korea. It is 23 percent larger in area, but has approximately the same amount of arable land as South Korea, 2.2 million hectares. Its shorter growing season permits little double-cropping, whereas nearly one-third of South Korea's rice and barley fields are double-cropped.[33] Consequently, although North Korea has less than half the population of South Korea, it has had difficulty in achieving self-sufficiency in food production. It has had to import grain in most years, sometimes exporting rice and importing wheat in order to take advantage of the higher price of rice on the world market. Land reform in North Korea took place in two stages. In 1946 land formerly owned by Japanese and all of an owner's land exceeding 5 hectares was allocated free to landless peasants, creating for a few years a rural economy of small, owner-operated farms. After the Korean War, from 1954 to 1958, these individual farms were combined into agricultural cooperatives averaging about 300 households each. The cooperatives owned the land, farm animals, and implements, and the work was done by work teams, the members of which earned wages in cash or kind for work done. The amounts received depended upon whether the cooperative met production quotas assigned by the state.

In the early 1960s the state brought the cooperatives under more centralized control by establishing county farm-management committees to establish production targets, allocate resources, and supervise the financial operations of the cooperatives in each county. About the same time the government adopted a variety of material incentives to stimulate production, such as paid vacations and bonuses. Families were allowed private plots on which to produce foodstuffs for their own use or for sale at open markets. In 1977 the government reduced the authorized size of private plots from 260 square meters to 66 to 99 square meters.[34] In the early 1960s Kim Il Sung introduced the "Chongsan-ni method" in agriculture, requiring administrative personnel to emulate Kim's example by going to the fields to talk over problems with farmworkers.

Kim Il Sung has declared the goal for rural society to be the transformation of all cooperatives into state farms, known as "ownership by all the people." On state farms workers are employees of the state; they receive fixed wages like workers in state-owned industrial enterprises. Usually larger than cooperatives, state farms tend to be more mechanized and specialized. The transformation, which Kim Il Sung has referred to as "a very difficult and complicated socio-economic reform," has progressed very slowly, and the great majority of rural people continue to be members of cooperatives.[35]

As in South Korea, the scarcity of arable land has forced the government to concentrate resources on increasing production per hectare of cultivated land. Efforts to terrace mountain slopes and reclaim marshes and tidelands have received considerable publicity, but such projects have proved costly and have not added appreciably to the total amount of cultivable land. Substantial expansion of irrigation has contributed to increased agricultural production. Most of the production increase, however, has resulted from increased use of fertilizer and improved crop varieties. The government reports the use of large and steadily increasing amounts of fertilizer per hectare and claims average yields of rice per hectare exceeding those in South Korea and Japan. However, comparisons of either fertilizer use or yields are difficult because North Korea calculates them differently. Government investment in agriculture, relatively low during the 1950s, increased to 20 percent of total state investment between 1961 and 1969, dropping to 18 percent between 1971 and 1976.[36]

Estimates of the results achieved from the collectivization of individual farms and the increased government investment in agriculture during the 1960s indicate that grain production increased slowly during the seven-year plan period (1961–1967, later extended to 1970). An indication of disappointing results was the halt in the publication of data on grain production after 1966. The 1970s showed evidence of a substantially higher rate of increase. According to an estimate by the UN Food and Agriculture Organization (FAO), rice production increased at 7 percent annually during this period. The production of corn, barley, wheat, and other cereals rose at less than one-third this pace, suggesting a shift of acreage to rice at the expense of other grains.[37] The U.S. Central Intelligence Agency estimated that the increase in grain production averaged 5.4 percent from 1965 to 1976, a higher rate than South Korea's.[38] The estimated rise in grain production exceeds by a wide margin even the highest estimates of the rate of population growth.[39] Vegetable and fruit production increased substantially, as did meat production, mainly from pigs, sheep, goats, and poultry, secondarily from cattle.

North Korea met the basic food needs of the population during the 1970s and made some progress in providing a richer diet that included more meat and fish. Rice, the grain that most people preferred, constituted less than half of total grain production, and some of that was exported. Consequently, rice remained in short supply, was strictly rationed, and many people had to substitute corn, wheat, or barley for rice in their diet.

As in South Korea, the rural population declined as industrialization absorbed growing numbers of workers. In 1976 the rural population was about 42 percent of the total, compared to South Korea's 38 percent.[40] Judging from the fragmentary data available, living conditions in the countryside improved significantly during the 1960s and 1970s. Electricity was extended to most rural households. Considerable mechanization of farming occurred. According to official figures, 6 to 7 tractors per 100 hectares were in use in 1980.[41] The average farm family lived more frugally than its counterpart in the South, limited by shortages and high prices of consumer goods.

Rapid Industrial Growth, 1953-1960

North Korea had a better physical base than South Korea on which to build industry after the Korean War. Large reserves of coal and iron ore lay ready to be drawn on for domestic use, and quantities of nonferrous metals were available for export in exchange for needed industrial machinery. The Japanese had located over 90 percent of Korea's power-generating capacity in the North, taking advantage of the numerous suitable sites for damming rivers. The Japanese had also developed many mines and constructed a sizable heavy and chemical industry, although it was unbalanced, notably by the almost total absence of machine-building plants. The Japanese-built factories were heavily damaged by bombing during the Korean War, and many skilled workers were killed or fled south. Nevertheless, a nucleus remained on which to build.

Massive reconstruction aid poured in from the Soviet Union, China, and Eastern Europe during the years immediately after the Korean War, roughly comparable on a per capita basis to the aid received by South Korea from the United States during this period.[42] Kim Il Sung insisted on maximizing the growth rate and giving top priority to heavy industry, overriding the advice of Soviet advisers and some of his colleagues to move at a slower pace and to allocate a larger share of investment to agriculture and the production of consumer goods. Kim's goal was to create as quickly as possible a balanced and largely self-sufficient industrial base so that he would not be dependent on and subject to pressures from the Soviet Union and China. For the same reason he declined to join the Soviet bloc economic organization, Comecon, which would have given the Soviet Union a mechanism through which to influence the structure of the North Korean economy.

By 1957 reconstruction had been largely completed and North Korea launched a five-year plan (1957-1961). In 1959, no doubt influenced by the Great Leap Forward that had begun in China the year before, Kim Il Sung introduced the Chollima movement,[43] in which workers were urged to work harder and faster, vying with others to produce more in a shorter time. The campaign resulted in imbalances in the economy, poorer quality products, and exaggerated claims, but was less disruptive than the Great Leap in China. The government declared the five-year plan completed two years ahead of schedule, but designated 1960 as a year of adjustment before a new multiyear plan could be started.

Despite the disruptive effects of the Chollima campaign, industry grew at a rapid rate during the 1950s, hitting a high of 36 percent annually between 1956 and 1959.[44] The low base from which growth started, the large amounts of foreign aid, and the responsiveness to central planning of a relatively simple economy in the early stages of growth combined to produce a high growth rate. During the 1960s, affected by a variety of domestic and international factors, industrial growth slowed.

Slowed Industrial Growth, 1961–1970

During the 1960s industrial growth was erratic—high in some years and low in others. In two years, 1966 and 1969, industrial production actually dropped below the previous year.[45] The original seven-year plan (1961–1967) had to be extended three years to 1970 and even then industrial growth failed to reach the planned goal of 18 percent annually. After 1966 Pyongyang stopped publishing annual production figures on most products. In his speech to the Fifth Congress of the KWP in November 1970, Kim Il Sung acknowledged that economic development had fallen short of expectations.[46] Despite the slowdown, the rate of growth of North Korean industry during this period was relatively high compared to other developing countries. Not until the second half of the 1960s did the pace of growth in South Korea begin to outstrip that of the North.

Over 80 percent of industrial investment went into heavy industry. The most striking change in the structure of industry was the continued rapid growth of the machine-building and metal-processing industry. It shot up from a negligible level in 1944 to more than half of total heavy industrial output by 1967.[47] Heavy industry was the domain of the central government, which also managed large factories producing consumer goods, such as textile mills. Provincial, municipal, and county governments ran local enterprises, including food processing plants and other producers of consumer goods, depending largely on local materials. Thus, a degree of decentralization existed in the consumer goods industry. In an effort to stimulate efficiency of production, the government instituted a system of independent accounting for enterprises, which gave managers the right to retain a portion of profits for use by the enterprise. It also introduced an incentive system of bonuses for labor brigades and other production units within enterprises.

The slowdown in industrial growth occurred for a variety of reasons. The official explanation was the rise in defense expenditures, which reached a level of 15–20 percent of GNP by the end of the decade. The diversion of resources to military purposes, particularly to such nonproductive activities as excavating underground shelters for arms factories, did contribute to the slowdown, but is not the entire explanation. Another important factor was the sharp drop in foreign aid, especially between 1963 and 1964, when Khrushchev withheld aid in an attempt to force North Korea to take a pro-Soviet position in the Sino-Soviet dispute.[48] The decline in foreign aid limited the import of new technology needed to expand industry. Another drag on growth was the increasing complexity of the economy, making it more difficult for decisionmakers to manage efficiently the allocation of resources. Bottlenecks inevitably developed, causing affected factories to produce below capacity. Kim Il Sung in his Fifth Congress report pointed to shortages in fuel, power, and raw materials as hindrances to the full capacity operation of the industrial plant. He called for holding back on new construction until the supply of these basic requirements had been augmented.[49] The Chollima movement in its rush for records affected the subsequent plan period through the production of poor quality products, notably machine tools, and through exaggerated claims that misled planners as to what was realistically possible.

By 1970 the main features of the North Korean industrial system were firmly established. These were a high degree of centralization and planning; a pronounced bias toward investment in heavy industry; a large defense budget; repeated resort to campaigns in place of pecuniary incentives to induce higher output; and strong emphasis on education, including nine-year compulsory education introduced in 1967, with special emphasis on technical training. North Korea had been transformed from an agrarian to an industrial society, with industry's share of the national income reaching 65 percent in 1970 compared to 25 percent in 1956.[50]

Opening to the West, 1971–1979

The six-year plan (1971–1976) placed heaviest emphasis on the areas that Kim had identified as bottlenecks during the 1960s: mining and electric power. It also stressed the need to raise the quality of industrial products. The bulk of investment continued to go to heavy industry. In a striking departure from past practice, Kim Il Sung decided to import large quantities of plants and machinery from Japan and Western Europe. He was probably disturbed by the accumulating evidence in the late 1960s that industrial growth in South Korea had begun to outstrip that of the North. Eyewitness reports of Seoul from senior North Korean representatives taking part in the North-South talks of 1972 may have impressed him. Imports from noncommunist countries, which had been only 11 percent of total imports in 1971, shot up to 60 percent by 1974. Exports to noncommunist countries rose also, but only from 20 percent to 38 percent of total exports.[51]

North Korea could not increase its exports rapidly enough to meet the payments due on the sudden surge in imports, especially when the prices of some of its chief export products such as metals and minerals dropped during the recession following the unexpected jump in world oil prices in 1973. In late 1974 Pyongyang began to default on debt payments and by the end of 1976 had accumulated a hard currency debt estimated at $1.4 billion and an additional $1 billion owed to Communist countries.[52] In 1979 it negotiated a stretch-out in payments of interest and principal owed the Japanese, its chief noncommunist creditors, but had not reached comparable agreements with the Europeans.

Industrial growth continued during the six-year plan, but at a pace well below that in South Korea and short of the targets set in a number of key sectors, including iron ore, chemical fertilizers, textiles, and cement. In spite of the emphasis placed on mining and power at the outset of the plan, these continued to be problem areas and the government singled out transportation as still another sector requiring special attention. In an attack on bureaucratic inefficiency, the government instituted the Three-Revolution Team movement in 1973, sending hundreds of teams of young specialists directed by Kim Chong Il to improve production techniques and to whip up revolutionary enthusiasm. Another mass campaign was the Seventy-Day Speed Battle of 1974, aimed at speeding up production to meet or surpass targets. When economic growth fell short of planned goals, despite such draconian measures, Kim Il Sung declared 1977 to be a year of adjustment to provide a needed respite while a new plan was readied.

U.S. government analysis estimated that between 1965 and 1976, while South Korea's real economic growth averaged close to 11 percent annually, North Korea's averaged 7.4 percent. North Korea was handicapped in its efforts to expand more rapidly by high defense expenditures and by the concentration of investment on heavy industry. Its emphasis on self-reliance hindered access to modern technology. Between 1965 and 1976 North Korea imported only $2.5 billion in machinery, while South Korea imported almost $11 billion.[53] The attempt to remedy this problem by turning to the West failed, in part because of bad luck in the timing, but also because of inexperience in trading on the world market and the failure to realize that the North Korean industrial plant would have to be modified drastically in order to produce the salable exports needed to finance so large an increase in imports. Moreover, by not forcing its manufacturing industry to compete on a large scale on the world market, meeting international standards of price and quality, North Korea had failed to take advantage of one of the most effective ways of ensuring efficient production and high quality products. Pyongyang also suffered from the endemic problem of command economies, the difficulty of planning in advance every aspect of a complex economy, and having to rely on a sluggish bureaucracy to make the myriad adjustments required without the benefits of a market pricing system to steer the allocation of resources. Although the North Koreans reached the end of the 1970s faced with difficult economic problems and lagging behind South Korea in the rate of economic growth, they could take comfort from North Korea's fairly rapid growth rate compared to other developing countries and substantial additions to its industrial plant.

External Dependence

In a basic sense, North Korea depended on the Soviet Union for its security in 1979, just as South Korea depended on the United States. The security treaty of 1953 between the United States and the ROK was matched by the security treaty of 1961 between the Soviet Union and the DPRK. China had signed a security treaty with North Korea in the same year, but China lacked the capability to supply North Korea with modern arms and to pose a threat to the United States with strategic nuclear weapons.

North Korea's security dependence on the Soviet Union differed in important respects, however, from South Korea's dependence on the United States. No Soviet troops were on North Korean soil. The number of Korean military trained in the Soviet Union was far smaller than the number of South Koreans trained in the United States. No joint maneuvers of Soviet and North Korean forces took place in the DPRK. Through early emphasis on heavy industry and the production of military equipment, North Korea had acquired a much higher degree of self-reliance than South Korea, producing a wide range of weapons, including tanks and submarines. Still, it remained dependent on the Soviets for aircraft, missiles, and other types of advanced military equipment.

During the 1950s the North Korean economy was heavily dependent on aid from the Soviet Union, China, and Eastern Europe. Much of the aid was in the form of grants to be used for the reconstruction of war-battered industry. The Soviet Union provided a two-year grant of $250 million in 1953, and in the same year the Chinese made a grant of $325 million to be used over four years.[54] These, together with additional grants and loans from the Soviets, the Chinese, and the East Europeans, enabled the North Koreans by 1960 to complete the rebuilding of damaged plants and begin the expansion of heavy industry.

Loans replaced grants in the 1960s, as had happened in South Korea during the same period, and the amounts declined substantially. North Korea's foreign trade steadily expanded. By 1969 it had reached $696 million, over 10 times the very low level of $68 million in 1954. South Korea's foreign trade, starting from the much larger base of $272 million in 1954, grew a little more slowly during this period, increasing 9 times to reach $2.4 billion in 1969, more than 3 times the size of North Korea's trade.[55]

North Korea's trade changed during the 1960s, both in direction and composition. Up to 1963 over 90 percent of its trade was with the Communist bloc, but by 1969 this figure had fallen below 75 percent. Japan had become an important trading partner, accounting for half of North Korea's trade with noncommunist countries. During the three years immediately after the Korean War, minerals were North Korea's principal exports, but these were replaced by ferrous and nonferrous metals as soon as plants for processing minerals could be repaired or built. The principal import throughout the period was machinery, including whole plants, but by 1969 fuels and fuel oil became a close second.

The pace of expansion in the foreign trade of the two Koreas, which had been roughly the same during the fifteen-year period ending in 1969, diverged dramatically during the 1970s, as South Korea entered a period of phenomenal trade growth. By 1979 North Korea's trade had increased 3.8 times, from $761 million in 1970 to $2.9 billion, but South Korea's trade increased over 12 times, from $2.8 billion to $35 billion.[56]

South Korea financed the rapid expansion of its economy in part by heavy borrowings on the international capital market, boosting its foreign debt to nearly $11 billion by 1979. Its debt-service ratio was only about 12 percent, however, relatively low for a developing country, and its credit rating was good. North Korea, on the other hand, had difficulty in making payments on its much smaller debt and after 1976 was unable to make purchases on credit. Imports from the Soviet Union, North Korea's principal creditor and trading partner, exceeded exports to that country from 1968 through 1976, creating a cumulative deficit of more than $900 million. Balanced bilateral trade in 1977 and small surpluses in favor of the Soviet Union in 1978 and 1979 indicated that North Korea was beginning repayments on this indebtedness.[57]

Despite North Korea's stress on self-reliance, imports of plants and machinery were crucial to its industrial growth. Soviet writers assert that plants built with Soviet assistance accounted for 60 percent of North Korea's output of electricity, 45 percent of its oil products, 40 percent of its iron ore, 34 percent of its rolled steel, 30 percent of raw steel, and 20 percent of fabrics.[58] China assisted in the construction of power plants, a petroleum refinery, textile mills, and factories producing consumer goods. Large quantities of machinery, including whole plants, were imported from Japan and Western Europe in the early 1970s until the flow was choked off by the inability to pay. North Korea was also totally dependent on imported oil and coking coal, which came mainly from the Soviet Union and China. Clearly, self-reliance had its limits.

Autarky, as practiced by North Korea, accepted the reality that imports of technology were essential to growth, yet it failed to concentrate, as South Korea did, on maximizing the production of high quality consumer goods readily salable in a growing world market as a means of increasing rapidly its capability to import technology. North Korea's principal exports, the products of mines and heavy industry, were difficult to expand rapidly, and their prices tended to fluctuate widely. Concentration on heavy industry not only deprived North Korea of opportunities to exploit world markets for light industrial products, but resulted in shortages of consumer goods for its own people. By the end of the 1970s, while realizing that the country was falling behind South Korea in economic growth and was badly in need of an infusion of modern technology, the North Koreans had not devised a strategy for rapidly increasing exports.

North Korea's problem was not so much an unwillingness to become less autarkic by expanding foreign trade as it was a fear of contamination by outside influence if it opened its society to the extent required by extensive and growing foreign economic relations. Political requirements took precedence over economic needs. The unique view of the world propounded in North Korea, based on the Kim cult, would be threatened by the multiplication of contacts with foreigners and an influx of information and ideas from outside the country. If South Korea was "permeated by outside influences to an extent that would be hard to match in the Third World," North Korea was at the opposite end of the spectrum. Foreign trade was fine and would be encouraged, but only in ways that did not conflict with overriding political requirements.

Kim Il Sung's experience had taught him that economic dependence on a big power constrained the smaller power's independence of action. Consequently, while accepting the need to increase North Korea's foreign trade, he sought to diversify its trading partners. The Sino-Soviet split enabled him to play one Communist country against another to some extent, but China, being a developing country itself at a low level of development, could not satisfy North Korea's need for modern industrial technology or modern weapons. Only in the supply of crude oil, coking coal, power plants, and machinery for light industry did it provide an alternative to dependence on the Soviet Union. Kim Il Sung had perceived in the early 1970s that trade with the private firms of Japan and Western Europe promised more advanced technology with less risk of political interference, but those sources could not be fully exploited until the debt problem had been resolved and exports increased.

In short, at the end of the 1970s further economic development in both Koreas depended heavily on the continued influx of advanced technology to modernize old plants and to equip new ones. Both had greatly diversified trading partners after 1965, but each still carried on more than half of its trade with two big powers: North Korea with the Soviet Union and China and South Korea with the United States and Japan. Each relied almost exclusively on a single ally for advanced weapons. Thus, both Koreas remained critically dependent on links with the outside. North Korea, through its policy of limiting such links to those considered absolutely necessary, had forgone the economic advantages that South Korea obtained by maximizing external connections. In 1979 North Korea faced the difficult decision whether to cling to isolationism and continue to slip further behind South Korea in economic growth or to make a drastic change in its policies.

Notes

1. See Roderick McFarquhar, "The Post Confucian Challenge," *The Economist*, February 9, 1980, pp. 62–72; Roy Hofheinz, Jr., and Kent E. Calder, *The Eastasia Edge* (New York: Basic Books, 1982), pp. 42–45.

2. Mason and others, *Economic and Social Modernization*, p. 93.

3. Ibid., p. 97. The annual growth rate is calculated in 1970 constant prices. The period begins with a two-year base, 1953 to 1955, and extends to another two-year base, 1960 to 1962.

4. Ibid., pp. 97, 103, 105.

5. Bunge, *South Korea*, p. 58; Mason and others, *Economic and Social Modernization*, p. 226.

6. Mason and others, p. 213.

7. Ibid., pp. 11, 222–224, 226.

8. Ibid., p. 10.

9. Joseph A. Yager, "Transforming Agriculture in Taiwan: The Experience of the Joint Commission on Rural Reconstruction" (draft manuscript).

10. Mason and others, *Economic and Social Modernization*, p. 428.

11. Ibid., p. 211.

12. Ibid., pp. 165, 182.

13. Ibid., pp. 92–93. Calculation in 1970 current prices produces a higher per capita figure for 1953 than the figure for 1962 on p. 51, calculated on a different basis.

14. Ibid., pp. 93–94, 103.

15. Ibid., pp. 192–195, 331–332.

16. Ibid., p. 189.

17. Ibid., p. 204.

18. Ibid., p. 99.

19. Ibid., pp. 102–103.

20. Thomas Stern, ed., *Korea's Economy*, vol. 2, no. 8 (Washington, D.C.: Korea Economic Institute, August 1983), p. 1.

21. Mason and others, *Economic and Social Modernization*, p. 286.

22. Ibid., p. 287.

23. Ibid., pp. 272–274; Bunge, *South Korea*, p. 120.

24. Mason and others, *Economic and Social Modernization*, pp. 98, 261, 332, 486.

25. Yung Whee Rhee, Bruce Ross Larson, and Gary Purcell, *Korea's Competitive Edge: Managing the Entry into World Markets* (Baltimore, Md.: Johns Hopkins University Press [published for the World Bank], 1984), p. 68.

26. Ibid., pp. 68–70.

27. Mason and others, *Economic and Social Modernization*, p. 55.

28. Ibid., p. 190.

29. Ibid., pp. 107, 491.

30. Larry E. Westphal, Linsu Kim, and Carl J. Dahlman, *Reflections on Korea's Acquisition of Technological Capability*, Report no. DRD 76 (Washington, D.C.: World Bank, April 1984).

31. Stern, *Korea's Economy*, vol. 2, no. 8, August 1983, p. 1.

32. Donald S. Macdonald, "Korea and the Ballot: The International Dimension in Korean Political Development as Seen in Elections" (Ph.D. diss., George Washington University, 1977), p. 404.

33. Bunge, *North Korea*, pp. 50–51, 138; Bunge, *South Korea*, p. 144.

34. Bunge, *North Korea*, p. 146. For more details on the organization of agriculture in North Korea, see Bunge, pp. 139–146, and Joseph Sang-hoon Chung, *The North Korean Economy: Structure and Development* (Stanford, Calif.: Hoover Institution Press, 1974), pp. 5–43.

35. Bunge, *North Korea*, p. 146. According to Ky-Hyuk Pak ("Agricultural Policy and Development in North Korea," in Robert A. Scalapino and Jun-yop Kim, *North Korea Today*, p. 222), state farms occupied only 4 percent of arable land in 1970.

36. Chung, *North Korean Economy*, pp. 41–43.

37. Ibid., pp. 50–54; Bunge, *North Korea*, pp. 138, 253.

38. Central Intelligence Agency, *Korea: The Economic Race Between the North and the South* Report ER78-10008 (Washington, D.C.: CIA, National Foreign Assessment Center, January 1978), pp. 2, 4.

39. Bunge, *North Korea*, p. 61 cites estimates ranging from 1.6 to 3.5 percent annually.

40. Ibid., p. 61; Pak in Scalapino and Kim, *North Korea Today*, p. 225.

41. Bunge, *North Korea*, p. 137.

42. Ibid., p. 255; Mason and others, *Economic and Social Modernization*, p. 182.

43. Chollima is a mythical winged horse capable of traversing enormous distances in a day. Kim Il Sung had visited the PRC in November–December 1958 and had praised the great successes being achieved by the Chinese in the Great Leap Forward. Chin O. Chung, *Pyongyang Between Peking and Moscow: North Korea's Involvement in the Sino-Soviet Dispute 1958–1975* (University: University of Alabama Press, 1978), pp. 33, 35.

44. Chung, *North Korea Economy*, p. 76.

45. CIA, *Korea: The Economic Race*, p. 3; Chung, *North Korean Economy*, p. 76.

46. Chung, *North Korean Economy*, pp. 76, 85, and 93.
47. Ibid., p. 77.
48. Youn-soo Kim, ed., *The Economy of the Korean Democratic People's Republic* (Kiel: German Korea-Studies Group, 1979), pp. 62–63.
49. Ibid., p. 91.
50. Bunge, *North Korea*, p. 113; Pak (in Scalapino and Kim, *North Korea Today*, p. 225) gives industry's share of "social product" as 34 percent in 1956 and 74 percent in 1970.
51. Bunge, *North Korea*, pp. 255–256.
52. CIA, *Korea: The Economic Race*, p. 8. The most detailed account of North Korea's purchases from Western Europe in the early 1970s and the resulting debt problems appears in Horst Brezinski's "International Economic Relations between the KDPR and Western Europe," in Kim, *The Economy of the Korean Democratic People's Republic*, pp. 202–231.
53. CIA, *Korea: The Economic Race*, pp. 1–2, 7.
54. Chung, *North Korean Economy*, pp. 118, 122.
55. Figures on North Korean trade from Chung, *North Korean Economy*, p. 105; those on South Korean trade from the United Nations, International Monetary Fund, and World Bank, *Direction of International Trade*, vol. 9, no. 10 (New York, 1958), p. 280, and the International Monetary Fund and World Bank, *Direction of Trade Annual, 1968–1972* (Washington, D.C., undated), p. 260.
56. Figures on North Korean trade from Bunge, *North Korea*, pp. 255–256; on South Korean trade from International Monetary Fund and World Bank, *Direction of Trade Annual, 1968–1972*, p. 260, and International Monetary Fund, *Direction of Trade Yearbook, 1980* (Washington, D.C., undated), p. 229.
57. Ralph N. Clough, "The Soviet Union and the Two Koreas," in Donald Zagoria, ed., *Soviet Policy in East Asia* (New Haven, Conn.: Yale University Press, 1982), pp. 182–183.
58. *Far Eastern Economic Review*, December 3, 1982, pp. 96–97.

4

Military Confrontation
and Abortive Dialogue

The Korean War experience and the failure of the Geneva political conference of 1954 to establish a framework for peaceful coexistence between the two Koreas left the leaders on both sides of the DMZ reliant primarily on the military capability of their own forces and the backing of their allies to assure the survival of their political systems. The armistice had halted the fighting, established a narrow demilitarized zone across the peninsula to separate the combatants, and set in place two international bodies, the Military Armistice Commission (MAC) and the Neutral Nations Supervisory Commission (NNSC) to supervise the carrying out of the armistice terms.

One of the armistice provisions, aimed at preventing the strengthening of forces on either side by limiting the importation of weapons to replacements only, soon broke down, when the UN Command noted the arrival of military aircraft on airfields in the North and the North Korean government denied the NNSC the freedom of movement necessary to check on weapons imports. Since then, the two sides have competed in increasing the quantity and improving the quality of their weapons and other military equipment.

When the war ended, both sides had taken heavy losses in experienced officers and men. Existing forces had serious deficiencies in training and equipment. Korean leaders relied heavily on the armistice and the presence of foreign forces to provide a breathing spell in which to rebuild their war-damaged country and to expand and improve their armed forces. Neither Syngman Rhee nor Kim Il Sung had abandoned the hope of unifying Korea, although their foreign supporters had made clear their unwillingness to pay the price of reunification by force. The rival Korean leaders saw strengthening of the military establishment as essential to defense and as an instrument for the eventual reunification of the nation.

South Korean Force Buildup

South Korean forces increased rapidly. By 1954 the army numbered nearly 600,000 in 16 divisions deployed along three-fourths of the front. Later, the army was trimmed back to 520,000, but improved greatly with rigorous training and a steady influx of U.S. equipment. An air force, navy and marine corps, patterned after the U.S. armed forces and numbering altogether some 80,000 men, undertook a secondary role in South Korea's defense. Compulsory military service of two-and-a-half to three years for young men provided a regular flow of conscripts into the ranks. Most officers came from a two-year military academy or from reserve officer's training programs on college campuses, but the elite of the officer corps—about 10 percent—graduated from the four-year course of the Korean Military Academy, modeled on West Point.

Aggressive behavior by North Korea and concern over possible weakening of the U.S. defense commitment led to the establishment of three backup forces: the Homeland Reserve Force, the Civil Defense Corps, and the Student National Defense Corps. The Homeland Reserve Force of about 2.5 million was organized in reaction to the commando raid against the Blue House and the infiltration elsewhere of armed units from North Korea in 1968 and 1969. Manned by veterans of active duty service, some 150,000 to 200,000 of whom were discharged annually from the armed forces during the 1970s, and commanded at the field grade level and above by regular army officers, the Homeland Reserve's primary function was to defend against infiltration into rear areas.

In 1975, soon after the defeat of the U.S.-supported government in Vietnam, the South Korean government established a Civil Defense Corps in communities and at places of employment to protect lives and property in event of attack or natural disaster. In 1980 it consisted of 95,000 units. The Student National Defense Corps, also organized in 1975, gave paramilitary training to two million college and high school students.

In organization, equipment, and training, South Korea's armed forces followed the U.S. pattern closely. During the early years, weapons and equipment were of World War II vintage, but gradual modernization occurred as some of the new weapons appearing in the U.S. inventory were transferred later to the South Korean armed forces. Between 1965 and 1973, 300,000 Korean troops gained combat experience through participating in the Vietnam War. Large amounts of U.S. aid, in the form of weapons, equipment, defense budget support, and compensation for participation in the Vietnam War, enabled the government to hold its defense expenditures within a range of 4 to 5 percent of GNP, thus preventing them from becoming a serious drag on economic growth.

The U.S. Role[1]

U.S. forces in Korea, which had reached 360,000 during the Korean War, dropped to 60,000 by 1957 and consisted primarily of two infantry divisions. Although Chinese forces withdrew from North Korea in 1958, the U.S. and South Korean governments felt that they continued to pose a threat from beyond the Yalu; hostilities had been halted only by an armistice, not by a peace treaty, and intense antagonism persisted between Washington and Peking. Consequently, the U.S. government regarded deterrence of China as an important reason for the continued presence of U.S. forces in South Korea.

By 1969 U.S. attitudes toward China had changed substantially, and President Richard Nixon was signaling to Peking a desire for a change in relations. Under strong public pressure to reduce the U.S. combat involvement in Vietnam, Nixon announced the Guam Doctrine (later elaborated as the Nixon Doctrine), which proposed shifting to allies of the United States more of the burden of their defense. South Korea's vibrant economy and its strengthened military forces made it a prime target for application of the doctrine. Reluctantly, Park Chung-hee agreed to the withdrawal of one of the two U.S. divisions—about 20,000 men— in exchange for a U.S. pledge to provide $1.5 billion in military aid to South Korea's force modernization plan (1971–1975).

In 1977 President Jimmy Carter announced a plan to withdraw the remaining U.S. ground forces from South Korea. The withdrawal would be in three stages, to be completed by 1982; augmented air, intelligence, and communications units would be kept in Korea indefinitely. He based his decision on South Korea's further impressive economic growth and on an assessment that its ground forces were roughly equivalent to those of North Korea. Strong opposition to the plan arose immediately, not only in South Korea, but also in Japan, the U.S. Congress, and from within the administration itself. When new intelligence estimates showed North Korean forces to be much stronger than earlier estimates, with a substantial advantage over South Korean forces in tanks, artillery, and aircraft, Carter, in the summer of 1979, halted the withdrawals, which up to that time had numbered only 3,600 men.

The presence of U.S. forces in Korea carried with it extensive command responsibilities. At the outset of the Korean War, the UN Security Council designated a U.S. officer to head the United Nations Command, and Syngman Rhee placed South Korean forces under its operational control.

During the mid-1970s supporters of Pyongyang in the United Nations tried but failed to bring about dissolution of the UN Command. The United States and South Korea refused to agree to its dissolution unless the concerned parties reached agreement on other means of preserving the armistice. In 1978 the United States and South Korea transferred nearly all combat forces to a newly established Combined Forces Command, headed by a U.S. army general with a South Korean general as his deputy.[2] The UN Command, headed concurrently by the U.S. commander of the Combined Forces Command, thereafter concerned itself only with activities directly related to the armistice and commanded only the small number of military personnel engaged in these functions. Thus, U.S. combat forces remained in Korea not as UN forces, but pursuant to the Mutual Defense Treaty between the United States and the ROK.

North Korea has pointed to U.S. operational control over South Korean military forces as conclusive evidence that the government of the ROK is a puppet of the United States. The South Korean military doubtless would prefer to have supreme military command in its own hands. Yet South Korean leaders grant operational control to the United States in order to maximize the effectiveness of the U.S. military commitment to the defense of their country. Separate U.S. and South Korean commands would weaken the ability to effect closely coordinated defense operations. The other alternative, placing the less numerous U.S. forces under South Korean command, probably would impede rapid reinforcement by other U.S. Pacific forces in an emergency, and the U.S. public might oppose placing U.S. forces abroad under a foreign commander, particularly an infantry division that would be involved almost immediately should war break out.

U.S. command and control applies only in regard to the defense of South Korea against external attack. During peacetime each government has full control over its own forces, except that the Korean government has to notify the U.S. commander of the withdrawal for domestic reasons of a Korean unit from its assigned position under the Combined Command. The U.S. commander can object only if he believes that the proposed withdrawal would unduly weaken defenses against outside attack. This requirement created a political problem for the United States when the Korean government in 1980 withdrew an army division to quell the Kwangju uprising, for it implied to many Koreans a measure of U.S. responsibility for the tragic events at Kwangju.

Large infusions of U.S. military aid helped to transform the South Korean military into a modern and effective fighting force. From 1950 through 1968 such aid, mostly in the form of grants, amounted to $2.5 billion. The ROK acquired F-86 fighter-bombers; F-5 fighters; artillery;

tanks; frigates; destroyers; and Honest John, Nike-Hercules, Hawk, and Sidewinder missiles.[3] In this period U.S. military aid, including defense budget support, defrayed 75 to 80 percent of South Korea's total military expenditures.[4]

During the 1970s, the form of U.S. military aid changed. Rapid growth in the South Korean economy enabled the government to finance military expenditures almost entirely from its own resources. By the mid-1970s, the United States had phased out defense budget support and other forms of grant aid. At the end of the decade South Korea was buying its arms from the United States either through the foreign military sales (FMS) program or on a commercial basis. Total military aid from 1950 through 1980 amounted to approximately $5.8 billion, plus FMS credits on favorable terms of $1.2 billion.[5] South Korea continued to modernize its weapons, adding to its inventory TOW and Sparrow missiles, F-4 fighters, C-130 transports, armored personnel carriers, and sophisticated radar communication equipment. The continued substantial flow of new weapons to the South Korean forces took place in part as compensation for the withdrawal of U.S. forces—the 7th Division in 1971 and the plan to remove the remaining ground forces between 1977 and 1982. It was also an effort to overtake the North Koreans, who had armed at a faster pace and had a substantial quantitative advantage over the South throughout the 1970s.

In 1976, in order to improve the capability of U.S. and ROK forces to react promptly to a North Korean attack and to provide visible assurance of U.S. determination to fulfill its commitment to the defense of South Korea, the U.S. and ROK military inaugurated an annual large-scale combined maneuver, the "Team Spirit" exercise. The U.S. Seventh Fleet participated, along with U.S. air, sea, and ground units from Japan, Hawaii, and the continental United States. The size of this exercise increased year by year, until by 1979 it involved 100,000 Koreans and 40,000 U.S. military personnel. North Korea denounced it vitriolically as preparation for an attack on the North.

Increasing South Korean Self-reliance

Nixon's decision to withdraw the 7th Division in 1971 had come as a shock to the South Koreans. The presence of U.S. forces and the massive influx of military aid had provided a sense of security that allowed them to concentrate much of their energy and resources on stimulating economic growth. It was not the withdrawal of the division alone that disturbed them, but the implications for Korea of the sudden change in the direction of U.S. policy. The shift to détente with China, the enunciation of the Nixon Doctrine, and the intimations that more

U.S. units might be removed from Korea left Park Chung-hee troubled. The U.S. withdrawal from Vietnam and Carter's decision to remove U.S. ground forces from Korea intensified his concern.

Deterioration of relations between the United States and the ROK over other issues added to the uneasiness felt by Koreans over the effect of the Vietnam debacle on U.S. determination to stand by security commitments in the western Pacific. Park's ramming through the *yusin* constitution, the Tokyo kidnapping of Kim Dae Jung by the KCIA, and bribery aimed at U.S. Congressmen—the "Koreagate" affair—loosed a wave of criticism against the South Korean government.[6] Congress even withheld $20 million in military aid funds as a token of disapproval, and a Congressional committee recommended either relocating the U.S. division in South Korea well back of the front line or taking it out entirely.[7]

This series of disturbing developments in the 1970s convinced Park that South Korea must move quickly to become less dependent on the United States for its defense. The growth of the South Korean economy had eliminated the need for defense budget support, but nearly all the weapons and equipment needed to raise the military capability of South Korean forces to the North Korean level had to be procured from the United States. Park sought to remedy these deficiencies through two successive force improvement plans, between 1971 and 1975 and between 1976 and 1980. As the United States had phased out grant aid almost entirely in the first plan period, the South Korean government adopted a special defense tax to help fund the required purchases and raised the defense budget from 4 percent to over 6 percent of GNP. Defense spending, in real terms, rose at an average rate of 12.5 percent annually from 1971 to 1981.[8]

For South Korea, military self-dependence meant not only buying weapons from its own resources, but also developing a capacity to manufacture modern weapons. In this respect, Seoul was more than ten years behind Pyongyang, which had begun in the late 1950s to channel the bulk of its investment into heavy industry, thus creating a base for defense production. In South Korea large investments in the heavy and chemical industries began in the late 1960s and reached full-scale production only in the late 1970s. Spurred by the desire to build as quickly as possible a base for defense industry, as well as to begin the export of heavy industrial products such as steel and ships, in which state-of-the-art Korean plants would have a competitive advantage, the government provided a variety of incentives to encourage the construction of chemical and heavy industrial plants. A huge industrial machinery complex, especially designed to house and support a defense industry, was begun in 1974 in the south at Changwon. Following President

Carter's decision in 1977 to withdraw U.S. ground forces, Park Chung-hee acted to speed up expansion of the capacity and variety of South Korea's heavy industry.

At the end of the 1970s, South Korea was producing about half of the weapons and equipment required by its armed forces. This included M-16 rifles, machine guns, 105mm and 155mm howitzers, mortars, recoilless rifles, Vulcan antiaircraft guns, various types of ammunition, personnel carriers, and patrol boats. Agreement had been reached with the United States to begin coproducing F-5 fighter aircraft and helicopters, although the more sophisticated components in these aircraft would come from the United States. The ROK was refitting M-48 tanks with 105mm guns that were larger, more accurate, and faster than the 100mm guns on North Korea's T-54, T-55, and T-59 tanks.[9] It was also designing a new tank especially adapted to conditions in Korea. South Korea was still well behind North Korea in its weapons production capability, but the gap was closing.

Concern over the strength of the U.S. commitment to the defense of South Korea after the fall of South Vietnam provoked a debate among Koreans on the desirability of acquiring a nuclear weapons capability. Park Chung-hee declared publicly that if the United States should withdraw its nuclear umbrella—which he said was unlikely—South Korea would develop its own nuclear weapons.[10] Subsequently, the ROK signed and ratified the nonproliferation treaty, declaring that it had no intention of developing nuclear weapons. It agreed to permit the International Atomic Energy Agency to inspect any nuclear facilities it might acquire. Under U.S. pressure, it dropped negotiations with a French firm for the purchase of a small, laboratory-size reprocessing plant for separating plutonium from spent fuel from nuclear reactors. Even though South Korea did not develop nuclear weapons, by 1980 it had an ambitious nuclear power program, with one plant in operation, four under construction, and four more planned. The ROK was one of a number of medium-sized states rapidly acquiring the scientific knowledge and engineering skills needed to produce nuclear weapons, but there was no evidence that it was attempting, openly or secretly, to acquire this type of military capability.[11]

North Korean Force Buildup[12]

Estimates of the size of North Korea's armed forces in 1953 vary widely from a low of 257,000 to a high of 410,000.[13] Analysts generally agree, however, that in total numbers the North Korean military buildup lagged behind that of South Korea, at least through 1961 and probably until the early 1970s. North Korea's population was less than half that of South Korea, and it had suffered a proportionately larger number of casualties during the Korean War. The presence of Chinese forces in North Korea until 1958 and the involvement of both China and the Soviet Union in economic reconstruction provided a measure of assurance against attack from the South. North Korea's two big power backers formalized their commitments to its defense by signing security treaties in 1961.

Reasonable assurance against attack enabled Kim Il Sung to move at a deliberate pace during the 1950s in reorganizing, training, and re-equipping the battered armed forces of North Korea. Moreover, he had other more urgent tasks. First, he was preoccupied with consolidating his own political power and, second, with economic reconstruction and laying the foundation for heavy industry. A steady influx of Soviet weapons and equipment sufficiently augmented the fighting ability of the 300,000- to 400,000-strong military to make forced-draft militarization unnecessary.

By 1960 Kim was firmly in the saddle. During the next two years the trend of events outside North Korea convinced him that heavier emphasis on military development was necessary. The widening rift between Peking and Moscow, the Cuban missile crisis, increasing U.S. involvement in Vietnam, U.S. support of India in the Sino-Indian border clash, and Park Chung-hee's military coup in South Korea seemed to create an atmosphere of growing threat. In December 1962 the fifth plenum of the Fourth Central Committee announced a program of "equal emphasis" on military preparations and economic development, which "might affect to a certain degree the development of the national economy."[14]

Thus, in the early 1960s, North Korea began to divert large and increasing amounts of resources to building a powerful military machine. The slogans of the time indicate its scope: arming the whole people, fortifying the entire country, training the army as a cadre force, arming it with modern weapons, and building a defense industry.[15] Members of the regular forces, serving a minimum of five years in the army and navy or three to four years in the air force, were trained in the responsibilities of the next higher rank, to permit rapid expansion of the military in an emergency. The regular forces were backed up by reserves and by the Worker-Peasant Red Guard, a militia consisting of nearly all able-bodied men between the ages of eighteen and forty-five not on active military duty and many women. Officers received training in an elaborate system of military universities, academies, and specialized schools. Training and discipline were rigorous, and ordinary soldiers were granted no leave during their five years or longer period of service.[16]

Turning the whole nation into a fortress involved placing vital air bases, arms and munitions factories, and other important installations underground. Extensive networks of tunnels were dug and hardened artillery emplacements built along front lines of defense. The flow of Soviet arms declined in the early 1960s and halted abruptly when Khrushchev attempted to pressure Kim Il Sung into taking the Soviet side in the Sino-Soviet dispute. But the Soviet arms flow resumed in the mid-1960s after Khrushchev had fallen from power and Moscow and Pyongyang had restored friendly relations. This experience caused Kim Il Sung to place even greater emphasis on trying to build a self-reliant defense industry.

The increased channeling of resources into defense had an adverse impact on economic growth, acknowledged by Kim in public statements in 1965 and 1970.[17] Defense spending, which had been only about 4 percent of the total state budget in 1959, rose to nearly 20 percent in the early 1960s and to 30 percent from 1967 to 1971.[18] The sharp increase in defense expenditures in 1967 coincided with the adoption of the policy of extreme militancy toward South Korea and the United States described below.

The extraordinarily high defense expenditures of 1967 to 1971 could not be sustained indefinitely. As Kim Il Sung admitted in his address to the Fifth Party Congress in November 1970: "frankly speaking, our spending on national defense has been too heavy a burden for us in light of the small size of the country and its population."[19] In 1972, according to official figures, the defense share of the budget dropped from 31 to 17 percent.[20] Kim himself told U.S. visitors in 1972 that his government was substantially reducing its defense expenditures.[21] Pyongyang halted its paramilitary incursions into South Korea and entered into a dialogue with Park Chung-hee's government.

North Korea's moderate public posture did not, however, reflect accurately the continued heavy emphasis it was placing on strengthening its military machine. Analysts now conclude that even though military expenditures did decline somewhat as a proportion of the total budget after 1971, the drop was by no means as large as portrayed in official statistics. U.S. intelligence agencies, concentrating their effort on Vietnam during the first half of the 1970s, were not aware until 1979 of the large buildup that was occurring north of the DMZ in Korea. The army grew from 360,000 in 1971 to 600,000 in 1980. The number of tanks more than tripled, artillery pieces nearly doubled, and large increases occurred in armored personnel carriers, torpedo boats, submarines, and aircraft.[22] Thus, by 1980, North Korea possessed a large, heavily armed army, organized on the Soviet pattern, providing divisions with more tanks, rocket launchers, and artillery than U.S. divisions, backed up by highly trained reserves and an armed militia of two million for local defense. Its air force and navy, equipped with obsolescent planes and ships, although quantitatively superior to South Korean forces, offered less of a challenge to the combined forces of the United States and South Korea.

Soviet and Chinese Roles

Despite Kim Il Sung's emphasis on *chu che* and strenuous efforts to create a defense industry, North Korea has been heavily dependent militarily on its big power allies, particularly the Soviet Union, during its thirty-five-year history. Chinese military intervention in 1950 saved the North Korean regime from losing control over its territory and population. The presence of Chinese forces in North Korea until 1958 gave Kim Il Sung a breathing spell in which to consolidate his power and build a solid base for economic growth. Weapons supplied by the Soviet Union enabled him to develop a potently armed military force.

When Moscow and Peking began to quarrel in the late 1950s, Kim Il Sung faced a difficult choice. At first he tried to remain neutral in the dispute, but as it intensified and came increasingly into the open, he decided, for reasons that will be explored in Chapter 6, to take the Chinese side. From the military viewpoint, that was a serious error. Only the Soviet Union could supply North Korea with advanced weapons and the technology needed to build a defense industry. Consequently, after Khrushchev's fall, Pyongyang and Moscow seized the opportunity to patch up the rift between them, and the transfer of Soviet arms resumed.

From 1964 to 1973 about three-fourths of North Korea's imported weapons came from the Soviet Union and one-fourth from China, but after 1973 the flow of Soviet military aid diminished and that from China increased.[23] Why this occurred is unclear; probably there were a number of reasons: North Korea's tendency to tilt toward China in the 1970s, the size of its debt to the Soviet Union incurred in the late 1960s and early 1970s, its growing capability to produce many of its own weapons, and a Soviet judgment that North Korea had sufficient military power for its defense. The weapons supplied by China were copies of Soviet weapons transferred to the Chinese in the 1950s, such as the T-59 medium tank, a copy of the Soviet T-54, which was considered by U.S. military experts to be inferior to it in important respects. Chinese-supplied weapons increased the numbers of North Korean tanks and aircraft but did not upgrade their quality. China lacked the capability to design and produce more advanced weapons.

Thus, North Korea continued to depend on the Soviet Union for new weapons. In the early 1970s SU-7 fighter-bombers appeared in North Korea, apparently provided in response to the acquisition of F-4s by the South Korean airforce in 1969. During the mid-1970s, the Soviets provided the technology that enabled the North Koreans to begin the production of the T-62 tank, which had been the Soviet's main battle tank in the 1960s. The Soviets showed restraint, however, in providing advanced weapons. They did not make available to Pyongyang the T-72 tank, which they were selling to India, nor did they supply it with the advanced aircraft and surface-to-air missiles, such as the MIG-23 and the SA-6 and SA-7, which they had sent to friendly states in the Middle East, such as Libya and Syria.[24]

In 1980 North Korea's defense production capability substantially exceeded that of South Korea in both types and quantities of military materiel. Pyongyang was manufacturing AK-47 rifles, machine guns, mortars, rocket launchers, artillery, antiaircraft weapons, ammunition, personnel carriers, tanks, patrol craft, and submarines. It could not produce aircraft or missiles. The extent to which North Korea could manufacture the more sophisticated components of the weapons systems it produced is unknown. Given the relative backwardness of its electronics industry, it seems probable that fire control mechanisms and various other essential electronic items still had to be imported from the Soviet Union. The progress made in creating an armaments industry was impressive, but North Korea had not freed itself from dependence on the Soviet Union for new weapons. It had no independent research and development capability. North Korea had no nuclear power industry, and there was no evidence that it sought to acquire or produce nuclear weapons.

Unconventional Warfare

The 1953 armistice put a stop to conventional military action by either Korean government against the other. Nevertheless, tension remained high and small-scale clashes of various kinds occurred: incidents along the DMZ, infiltrations into South Korea by individuals or paramilitary units, and encounters at sea. Occasional defections and the exposure of spies in South Korea added to the atmosphere of tension.

In the early 1960s North Korea adopted a three-pronged strategy that it has pursued consistently ever since, although its tactics have changed frequently. Simply stated, the stratgy has consisted of strengthening North Korea, fomenting revolution in South Korea, and mobilizing international support for North Korea. The second prong of this strategy has utilized tactics ranging from propaganda appeals to the people of the South to overthrow their rulers, to the infiltration of agents in attempts to assassinate those leaders.

At the Fourth KWP Congress in 1961 Kim Il Sung had called for the establishment of a Marxist-Leninist party in South Korea.[25] Agents trained in North Korea infiltrated into the South and in 1964 set up an underground revolutionary organization called the Revolutionary Party for Reunification (RPR). It began organizing front groups, but before long attracted the attention of the KCIA, which broke it up in 1968, arresting 158 persons. Seventy-three were tried and nine executed.[26] Given the hostility toward communism in South Korea, its severe anticommunist laws, and the large size and effectiveness of its security apparatus, no extensive revolutionary network could survive long.

Pyongyang claimed that the RPR continued to function in South Korea. It published statements in the *Nodong Sinmun* purporting to come from the Central Committee of the RPR and established a radio station in North Korea that claimed to be operating clandestinely from South Korea. "Delegates" from the RPR appeared at meetings in North Korea. Although the RPR was supposed to be a revolutionary organization established by and representative of the people of South Korea, little attempt was made to give it an independent identity. Its statements and broadcasts were indistinguishable from those made by North Korean organs or individuals in their adulation of Kim Il Sung and their endorsement of North Korean positions and policies. Even the language used in RPR statements betrayed its North Korean origin.[27]

In 1967 and 1968 Pyongyang raised the level of violence in its southern strategy. Incidents south of the military demarcation line within the DMZ and farther south jumped from 59 in 1965 and 50 in 1966 to 566 in 1967 and 629 in 1968. In January 1968 a 31-man commando team penetrated to within the city limits of Seoul in a bold attempt to assassinate Park Chung-hee. All but one were killed. Later that year 120 highly trained men from a special forces unit landed on the northeast coast of South Korea to enlist the local population in guerrilla activities against the government. Only two survived. U.S. forces also became targets of North Korea's heightened militancy during this period. North Korean gunboats seized the U.S. Navy intelligence-collection vessel *Pueblo* in January 1968, and in October 1969 the North Koreans shot down a U.S. Navy EC-121 reconnaissance plane with 31 men aboard over the Japan Sea. Pyongyang's violence proved counterproductive. It caused Park Chung-hee to organize and arm the 2-million strong Homeland Reserve Force to guard against infiltration. It provided for the United States a forceful demonstration of North Korean belligerence, underlining the importance of the U.S. commitment to assist in the defense of South Korea.

In 1969 North Korea turned away from its ineffective campaign of violence. Incidents dropped from 629 in 1968 to 111 in 1969, 113 in 1970, and 47 in 1971, stopping entirely in 1972, when North-South negotiations took center stage.[28] Pyongyang did not, however, desist from clandestine preparations for military action against the South. In November 1974 ROK troops discovered a 3.5-kilometer tunnel from North Korea to a point 1.2 kilometers south of the DMZ, large enough to permit a regiment to pass through in an hour. In March 1975 they found a much larger tunnel in the Chorwon area of the DMZ and in October 1978 a third tunnel near Panmunjom, about the size of the second. Evidence collected by the UN Command indicated that the North Koreans had dug or were digging as many as ten undiscovered additional tunnels under the DMZ.[29] U.S. and South Korean officers surmised that the tunnels were intended to permit large numbers of North Korean soldiers in South Korean uniforms to infiltrate rapidly to points behind the front line and create confusion during the first few hours of a North Korean attack.

During the 1970s incidents continued to occur, not at the level of 1967 to 1968, but often enough to keep tension high. The most serious was the attempted assassination of Park Chung-hee in August 1974 by a Korean resident of Japan, who missed Park but killed his wife. The assassin was said to have been trained and despatched by Chosoren, the pro-Pyongyang organization of Koreans in Japan. The killing loosed a wave of outrage among South Koreans against North Korea and secondarily against Japan.

Within the DMZ, where both sides continued to construct defense works in their half contrary to the Armistice Agreement, incidents often took place. Patrols exchanged fire across the military demarcation line. Occasionally ROK troops caught infiltrators trying to sneak through the DMZ. A few officers and men defected across the DMZ, some from the North and some from the South. Often they would be produced at press conferences broadcast to the other side, condemning the miserable life in the place they had come from and praising conditions in their new home. The number of defectors either way was small, not more than two or three dozen in a decade. No high-level officials defected to the other side, although several senior figures left South Korea and denounced Park Chung-hee from the relative safety of Japan or the United States. The KCIA from time to time announced the arrest of spies trained in North Korea and sent to South Korea through Japan. Some had been in place a number of years before being detected. In 1978 the North Koreans succeeded in landing several heavily armed intruders on the coast who killed four civilians before being killed themselves.

Clashes at sea occurred two or three times a year from 1974 to the end of the decade. Fishing boats that crossed the seaward extension of the military demarcation line risked being fired upon or captured. Sometimes the boat was sunk and members of the crew killed or wounded. When captured boats were identified as genuine fishing vessels, the boats and men usually were returned after being subjected to political indoctrination, but those individuals suspected of having engaged in espionage were jailed. Some clashes involved small, high-speed boats from North Korea intercepted far south of the military demarcation line carrying agents equipped for espionage. Few of these agents escaped alive.

Control of the seas off Korea was complicated by South Korean possession of Paengnyong Island and four smaller islands west of the peninsula. These islands were south of the 38th parallel but north of the seaward extension of the military demarcation line, and they were closer to North Korea than to South Korea. South Korean access to the islands was threatened in August 1977 when North Korea declared a 200-mile economic zone and a 50-mile "military boundary." South Korean authorities feared that the North Koreans would draw the military boundary outside the five islands and attempt to cut off South Korean access to them. Tension rose temporarily, but Pyongyang did not interfere with regular ferry service from Inchon to Paengnyong Island.

U.S. forces did not escape North Korean violence, although they were much less frequently involved than South Koreans. In 1977 a U.S. helicopter that landed inadvertently north of the DMZ was shot down when it tried to take off. A more widely publicized incident was the August 1976 killing with axes of two U.S. officers who were supervising the trimming of a tree that blocked the view in the Joint Security Area at Panmunjom. After this incident the Joint Security Area was divided in half in order to separate the troops of the two sides and reduce the risk of clashes.

Outlook in 1980

The suspicion and hostility with which the two Koreas viewed each other in 1980 had abated little since the armistice of 1950. South Koreans, recalling the 1950 invasion from the north, watched uneasily the heavy investment of North Korean resources in a large and unremitting military buildup, together with calls for the overthrow of the South Korean government. Pyongyang's harsh rhetoric was accompanied often enough by border clashes and incidents of espionage, infiltration, and attempted assassination to convince most South Koreans that Kim Il Sung was determined to impose his political system on South Korea by military attack, by infiltration and subversion, or by a combination of the two. The opening of dialogue in 1972 brought a surge of hope among the people that a formula for peaceful coexistence might be found, but the hope soon faded, as dialogue degenerated into bickering and the discovery of the first tunnel raised grave doubts as to Kim Il Sung's sincerity in negotiating with South Korea.

South Korean leaders were keenly aware of two basic asymmetries in the security problems of the two Koreas. First, North Korea's allies were neighbors with permanent interests in the Korean peninsula, whereas the United States was thousands of miles away. Even though President Carter had suspended ground troop withdrawals in July 1979, who could tell when the U.S. government might decide that the security of South Korea was not a vital interest worth fighting for. Second, Seoul, which contained one-fifth of South Korea's population and produced 45 percent of its GNP, was only 30 miles from the DMZ, whereas Pyongyang was 90 miles away. Seoul was within range of North Korea's FROG surface-to-surface missiles and only a few minutes by jet aircraft from North Korean airfields.

South Korea's mountainous terrain favored defense and tended to offset North Korean advantages in numbers of tanks and artillery pieces. The attacker would be compelled to concentrate forces in confined areas where it would be vulnerable to air attack. Thus, deep penetration of South Korea by North Korean armored forces would be extremely difficult in the face of the superior air power the United States could bring into action within a few days. The main concern of South Korean military commanders was a blitzkrieg against Seoul, which they feared could be mounted by North Korean forces based near the DMZ with 24 hours warning or less. Although the traditional invasion corridors to Seoul through Munsan-ni to the northwest or Uijongbu to the north, had been heavily fortified, a sudden mass assault by North Korea's main forces, accompanied by air and commando attacks on airfields, air defense sites, and communication centers, might be difficult to halt short of Seoul if the North Koreans were prepared to suffer heavy casualties.[30]

How Kim Il Sung and other North Korean leaders viewed the military confrontation is difficult to judge. The resources allocated to the military buildup, the size and firepower of the North Korean military machine, the strength of elements stationed near the DMZ, and North Korea's strategy of encouraging revolution in South Korea strongly suggested that North Korea would use military force if conditions favored the achievement of its objectives. Encouraged by the imminent collapse of the South Vietnamese resistance in 1975 after the withdrawal of U.S. forces, Kim Il Sung declared during an April visit to Peking that North

Korea would not stand with folded arms if revolutionary forces sought
to overturn the government in South Korea.[31] The confusion following
Park Chung-hee's assassination in 1979 might have offered an opportunity
to move militarily had U.S. forces not been poised to intervene.

A minority among analysts of Korean affairs have viewed North
Korean military preparations as primarily defensive rather than offensive.
According to this view, the North Koreans, feeling themselves surrounded
by enemies and unreliable allies, had developed a siege mentality.[32]
After all, South Korea had twice the population of North Korea and
an economy over three times as large, growing rapidly. From Pyongyang's
perspective, Seoul's increasing military strength, backed by U.S. forces
with the most modern armament, including tactical nuclear weapons,
presented a serious threat. Even North Korea's extraordinary military
buildup might have seemed inadequate in the face of such an array of
military power, especially when the Soviets declined to provide them
with modern weapons.

However one might judge the motivation for the North Korean military
buildup—and the weight of evidence suggested preparations for offensive
action when the time was ripe—the dominant factor in the military
confrontation in Korea in 1980 was still the behavior of the big powers.
Although the military production capability of both Koreas was growing,
they remained dependent on their allies for critical items. Even more
important, the U.S. commitment to the defense of South Korea and that
of the Soviet Union and China to the defense of North Korea placed
military reunification of Korea by either Korean government out of reach,
regardless of progress made in developing an independent military
industry.

The Dream of Unification

Korea's long history as a unified state with a homogeneous people
and a unique culture made the division imposed upon it by foreign
powers hard to bear. Leaders in both the North and the South stressed
the necessity and inevitability of the nation's reunification, but expressed
sharply contrasting views on how to go about it. In the climate of fear
and hostility caused by the Korean War, the overtures each made on
the unification issue widened rather than narrowed differences between
North and South. South Korea branded North Korea's sweeping proposals
as propaganda, not seriously intended to initiate negotiations, while
North Korea condemned South Korean proposals to advance slowly,
step-by-step, as designed only to perpetuate division. Charges of insincerity flew back and forth. Unlike the two Germanys, where trade,
travel, and other forms of intercourse created growing links between

the societies on either side of the Berlin Wall, the two Koreas remained totally isolated from each other, except for unproductive negotiations in the early 1970s and again in 1979 to 1980. Progress toward unification or even toward contacts between the two societies remained elusive.

South Korean Position

During the 1950s, Syngman Rhee, secure in the support for his government in the United Nations, insisted that the ROK was the only legitimate government on the Korean peninsula. He refused any form of contact with the North Korean regime and favored unification of Korea by military means. After unification, free elections would be held throughout Korea under UN supervision to form an all-Korean National Assembly representative of the population, that is, two-thirds elected by the people of South Korea and one-third by the people of North Korea.

Rhee's successors abandoned the notion of unification by force. During the 1960s Park Chung-hee maintained the view that the ROK was the only legitimate Korean government and that unification should be accomplished under UN auspices. He concentrated on the economic development of South Korea, making no specific overtures himself on unification and rejecting Kim Il Sung's proposals as propaganda intended to promote a revolutionary overthrow of the South Korean government. In a 1966 speech Park defined South Korea's basic objective as "unification through victory over communism." He proposed deferring "positive approaches for unification" to 1975 through 1980, by which time South Korea would have established a "self-reliant economy as the national base for unification . . . and have seized a complete initiative in all respects."[33]

North Korean Position

During the 1960s North Korea held the initiative in proposing steps toward unification. In a speech made in August 1960, after the fall of the Syngman Rhee government, Kim Il Sung first advanced the proposal of a North-South confederation, which was to become the centerpiece of subsequent North Korean unification proposals. This concept provided for a "supreme national committee" composed of equal numbers of representatives from both sides, which would regulate the economic and cultural development of the two Koreas, while the political systems and independent activities of the two governments would continue "for the time being."[34]

Kim could hardly have expected his proposal to be taken seriously by the Chang Myon government when, in the same speech, he denied the legitimacy of the newly elected National Assembly in Seoul and called upon the workers and peasants of South Korea to form their own political party to drive the "aggressor army of the U.S. imperialists" out of Korea. Kim's overture did, however, strike a responsive chord among radical students, whose growing clamor for North-South negotiations helped to precipitate Park Chung-hee's seizure of power the following year. North Korea's continued stress on revolution in the South and its violent actions to that end between 1967 and 1969 gave Park persuasive reason for dismissing Pyongyang's repeated unification proposals as propaganda.

The Opening of Dialogue

Face-to-face talks between representatives of the two Koreas began for the first time in 1971, after more than two decades of frozen hostility. The first indication of a thaw came in a speech by Park Chung-hee in August 1970. Park proposed taking measures to remove in stages artificial barriers between North and South—provided Pyongyang ceased hostile acts and renounced its goal of overthrowing the government of South Korea. He challenged North Korea to a bona fide competition to show which society could provide a better life for its people. Although Park denounced Kim Il Sung and called the North Korean authorities puppets, his proposal to remove barriers between North and South was a significant shift from the defensive to the offensive on the unification issue.

At the KWP's Fifth Congress in November 1970, Kim Il Sung brushed aside Park's proposal as political propaganda and renewed his call for the overthrow of the "fascist military dictatorship" in the South and the establishment of a true people's government. In April 1971 North Korean Foreign Minister Ho Tam produced a comprehensive eight-point program for peaceful unification.

1. Withdrawal of U.S. forces.
2. Subsequent reduction of forces of the two Koreas to 100,000 or less.
3. Abrogation of the U.S.-ROK security treaty and the ROK-Japan normalization treaty.
4. Guarantee of complete freedom for all political parties and individuals in South Korea and release of political prisoners there.
5. Free, democratic elections throughout Korea, independent of outside control, to establish a unified central government.

6. If South Korea could not agree to elections, the establishment of a North-South confederation as a transitional step to promote cooperation and interchange between the two Koreas.
7. If South Korea could not accept a confederation, the establishment of an economic committee to promote cooperation and interchange.
8. A political consultative meeting of all political parties, organizations, and "patriotic" individuals to discuss all the foregoing matters.[35]

In August 1971 Kim Il Sung opened the door to dialogue a crack by declaring willingness to have contacts with the DRP, the ruling party in South Korea. However, in the same speech he referred to the authorities there as a "puppet clique" and continued to offer North Korean assistance to the South Korean people in their revolutionary struggle against the "U.S. imperialist aggressors."

Despite Kim's expression of openness to contacts with the DRP, the harsh rhetoric used by each side toward the other and the patent unacceptability to South Korea of Ho Tam's eight-point program gave little room for optimism in the summer of 1971 that dialogue might be possible soon. Yet a proposal broadcast on August 12 by the president of the ROK Red Cross for a joint effort to find members of separated families in North and South Korea and arrange for exchanges of letters and reunions between them brought a favorable response two days later from the head of the North Korean Red Cross. The prompt response did not, however, herald rapid progress. Disagreements emerged immediately on many aspects of the proposed talks, and 25 preliminary meetings were required between September 20, 1971, and August 11, 1972, to reach agreement on arrangements for the first full-dress meeting of the Red Cross Conference to begin in Pyongyang on August 29, 1972.

While the preliminary Red Cross talks were grinding along toward agreement on formalities, high level contacts began behind the scenes. Negotiations initiated at Panmunjom in November 1971 led to secret visits in May-June, 1972 to Pyongyang by Lee Hu-rak, director of the KCIA, and to Seoul by Vice Premier Pak Song-chol. Pak represented Kim Il Sung's younger brother, Kim Yong-ju, director of the Organization and Guidance Department of the KWP Central Committee. Lee met with Kim Il Sung and Pak with Park Chung-hee. The result was a North-South joint statement on July 4, 1972, signed by Lee and Kim Yong-ju on behalf of "their respective superiors," expressing agreement on three "principles for unification of the fatherland."

1. Unification shall be achieved through independent efforts, without external imposition or interference.
2. Unification shall be achieved through peaceful means, not the use of force.
3. A great national unity, transcending differences in ideas, ideologies, and systems shall be sought first.

In addition, "the two sides" agreed: a. not to defame each other or conduct armed provocations; b. to carry out exchanges in many areas; c. to seek the early success of the Red Cross talks; d. to install a direct telephone line between Seoul and Pyongyang; and e. to establish a South-North Coordinating Committee to settle problems between them and to solve the question of unifying the country.[36]

The announcement of such an apparently far-reaching agreement concluded in great secrecy between two implacable foes was a public sensation, but differences in interpretation arose immediately. In a July 4 press conference, Pak Song-chol stressed the agreement on achieving unification independently without external interference and declared that the "U.S. imperialists" no longer had an excuse to interfere in Korea; "they must withdraw at once, taking with them all their forces of aggression." Lee Hu-rak took a different view. In a press conference on the same day he reiterated South Korea's goal of unification through elections supervised by the United Nations and based on proportionate representation of the population in both parts of the country. He denied that U.S. forces in South Korea under the UN Command constituted "external interference" in the sense intended by the joint statement. Pak Song-chol hailed the statement as "a great historic event which . . . heralds the dawn of reunification," while Lee somberly warned his compatriots in the South against harboring illusions and referred to the new situation as "confrontation with a dialogue."[37]

An important element in the agreement, which had both practical and symbolic significance, was the installation of a direct telephone line, initially connecting the offices of Lee Hu-rak and Kim Yong-ju.[38] Often referred to as "the hotline," it was expanded to 23 circuits, mainly for the use of the Red Cross conference, and was used not only for making procedural arrangements for the two sets of talks, but also occasionally to communicate promptly concerning incidents such as the seizure of fishing boats. The line was tested daily until the North Koreans unilaterally cut it off, shortly after the ax-murder incident of August 1976.

Motivations for Beginning Dialogue

Although the dialogue between the two Koreas opened inauspiciously with conflicting interpretations of what had been agreed upon, the fact that trusted envoys of the two Korean leaders had met and hammered out an agreement was in itself remarkable. Moreover, the meetings of the leaders themselves with the principal negotiator from the other side demonstrated their serious intent. Why they decided on negotiations at this time after years of denouncing each other as puppets, and what they hoped to accomplish cannot be determined with certainty, but the trends in domestic and international affairs and the subsequent unfolding of the negotiations throw some light on these matters.

Kim Il Sung's campaign of violence against South Korea and the United States had failed. It had given its allies and the world in general an image of the North Korean regime as belligerent and unpredictable. The North Korean economy was running into serious problems, while the South Korean economy was surging ahead. South Korea continued to hold a substantial diplomatic advantage over North Korea in the United Nations and in the number of states with which it maintained diplomatic relations. A shift from a combative to a conciliatory stance could be expected to bring benefits in all these areas.

Probably more important in its impact on Kim than any of the foregoing circumstances, however, was the sudden reversal of U.S. policy toward China revealed in the dramatic announcement of July 1971 that President Richard M. Nixon would visit Peking. The implications from Kim's viewpoint were ominous. A China concerned with improving relations with the United States and with Japan, the principal ally of the United States and a firm supporter of the ROK, could no longer be relied upon as in the past to endorse a harsh, unyielding posture toward those two powers and the ROK. At the same time, Kim undoubtedly was encouraged by the U.S. decision in 1971 to withdraw one of its infantry divisions from South Korea and by indications that further withdrawals were likely. The Nixon Doctrine, together with trends in Vietnam and in U.S. opinion, might have encouraged him to believe that all U.S. military forces would soon be pulled out of the Asian mainland. A mild policy toward South Korea at this juncture could accelerate the withdrawal.

Domestic developments in South Korea also suggested that the time was propitious for North-South negotiations. In the 1971 presidential election, Kim Dae Jung, who had advocated North-South negotiations during the campaign, had won 45 percent of the popular vote. Kim Il Sung may have felt that Park Chung-hee's position had weakened and that popular support for negotiating with Pyongyang had risen, which would not only place pressure on Park to negotiate, but would improve prospects for North Korea to benefit from negotiations.

Park's decision to negotiate probably was motivated in part by the evident popularity of such a move. But he may already have had in mind a plan to use the opening of negotiations as a means of strengthening his own position, which had been threatened by growing support for the opposition in the presidential and National Assembly elections. In his press conference of July 4, 1972, Lee Hu-rak referred several times to the possible need for restructuring South Korea's political system in order to conduct a dialogue with North Korea's highly centralized and tightly controlled system.[39] When Park introduced the *yusin* constitution later that year, he justified it on that ground.

Of the various factors affecting the leaders' decisions to negotiate, the most influential probably was the shifting international environment. The Sino-U.S. rapprochement undermined their confidence in their allies. In Park's case, the effect was intensified by the U.S. withdrawal of the 7th Division in 1971. The fate of Korea had too often been decided by outsiders, and the thought of Nixon and Mao discussing Korea in Peking must have been troubling. The future of Korea should be a matter for Koreans to decide, and no decision could be reached so long as the two Korean parties declined to deal with each other.

Negotiations and Results, 1972–1979

The first full-dress session of the Red Cross conference opened in Pyongyang on August 30, 1972, in an atmosphere of hope and excitement, but it proved to be only the beginning of an exercise in frustration and disappointment. During six subsequent full-dress sessions held alternately in Seoul and Pyongyang during the next twelve months, the positions of the two sides diverged increasingly.

South Korean proposals were narrow and precise, aimed at working out detailed arrangements for locating members of separated families and bringing about exchanges of letters and visits between them, based on practices followed by the International Red Cross. North Korean delegates from the outset stressed the importance of linking family reunions to national unification. Their statements became increasingly political in tone, until by the seventh session they were demanding the abrogation of anticommunist laws and the banning of anticommunist activities in South Korea in order to ensure the safety of family members from the North who would visit there. Rejecting South Korea's proposal that separated family members be traced by the respective Red Cross societies within their own territory, North Korea proposed stationing thousands of Red Cross representatives from the other side in each part of Korea to assist individuals who would freely cross the DMZ to seek out family members themselves. They also called for positive measures to end military confrontation.

The Red Cross meetings were paralleled by a series of meetings of the South-North Coordinating Committee (SNCC), established pursuant to the joint statement of July 4 and cochaired by Lee Hu-rak and Kim Yong-ju (with Pak Song-chol acting in his place). Here also the positions of the two sides diverged widely. The North Koreans insisted that no progress could be made unless the state of military confrontation was removed. Pak Song-chol made a five-point proposal.

1. North and South to stop increasing their military strength.
2. Armed forces on both sides to be reduced to 100,000 or less.
3. No weapons or equipment to be imported.
4. All foreign troops, including U.S. forces, to be withdrawn.
5. A peace agreement to be signed between the two sides.

South Korea refused to negotiate first on military issues, proposing instead to begin with discussion of trade and cultural exchanges. North Korea demanded that all five of the agreed-upon subcommittees of the SNCC—political, military, foreign policy, economy, and culture—be activated immediately, whereas South Korea insisted on beginning with only two—the economic and cultural subcommittees. Pyongyang also introduced a proposal for a joint conference of political parties and social organizations in both parts of Korea. Seoul countered with proposals for exchanges of scientists, athletes, journalists, and others.

During the year that followed the dramatic announcement of agreement on the principles of unification, the two Koreas had agreed on the formats for conducting the parallel dialogues, but little else. Each meeting produced stiffer confrontations. Finally, on August 28, 1973, after the SNCC had met twice in Seoul and once in Pyongyang, North Korea issued a vitriolic statement under the name of Kim Yong-ju refusing to continue the meetings. The ostensible reason was the responsibility of the South Korean SNCC cochairman, Lee Hu-rak, as head of the KCIA, for the abduction of Kim Dae Jung from a Tokyo hotel several weeks earlier. The lengthy declaration also called on the South Korean authorities to withdraw their two-Koreas policy, free imprisoned "patriots," and allow representatives of various parties and organizations to participate in the activities of the SNCC. On this note, the North Koreans broke off not only the SNCC meetings, but also the full-dress Red Cross talks.

The SNCC meetings resumed at the vice chairman level in December 1973. No discernible progress had been made in the meetings when the North Koreans ended them in March 1975. Red Cross contacts also continued for a time at a lower level. From November 1973 to March 1978, 7 "delegates" meetings and 25 working level meetings took place at Panmunjom. The established pattern of talking past one another continued unchanged. The South Koreans pressed for agreement on limited exchanges, such as traditional visits to ancestors tombs on the other side of the DMZ, while the North Koreans continued to demand an end to anticommunist laws and activities in South Korea. The North Koreans broke off even the working level talks in March 1978, charging that the Team Spirit military exercise made such meetings impossible.

The North Korean decision in August 1973 to break off the formal talks may have been precipitated by Park Chung-hee's announcement on June 23, 1973, withdrawing objection to the membership of both Koreas in the United Nations and other international organizations. Park was adjusting the ROK's foreign policy to the diplomatic gains made by North Korea in 1970 to 1973, including its admission to the World Health Organization.[40] He pledged to continue to work for unification, but expressed the view that it would take a long time and would be facilitated rather than hindered by temporary membership of both Koreas in the UN.

Kim Il Sung reacted promptly to Park's announcement, rejecting the admission of the two Koreas to the UN as perpetuating the division of Korea. He proposed instead their admission as a single state, the Confederal Republic of Koryo. In addition to reiterating his earlier confederation concept, Kim renewed proposals for the withdrawal of U.S. forces; an end to arms imports; the reduction of forces of both sides to 100,000 or less; a peace agreement between North and South; the convening of a "great national conference"; and North-South cooperation in political, economic, military, diplomatic, and cultural fields.

In January 1974, Park Chung-hee proposed a nonaggression pact, which would leave the armistice in effect and contain pledges by each side not to use force against the other or to interfere in the other's internal affairs. Instead of responding to this proposal, North Korea in March 1974 proposed to the United States a replacement of the armistice with a peace treaty between Pyongyang and Washington that would lead to the withdrawal of U.S. forces. This proposal was to be repeated frequently in subsequent years. The North Koreans contended that their negotiations with South Korea had proved fruitless because they had dealt with the puppet instead of the master.

During the remainder of the decade, in contrast with the 1960s, South Korea maintained the initiative in making proposals to North Korea. On August 15, 1974, on the occasion when Park was shot at and his wife killed by an assassin, he reiterated proposals for a nonaggression pact, many-sided exchanges, and direct elections throughout the country to achieve unification. In June 1978 he proposed the formation of a consultative body for promoting North-South economic cooperation and offered to hold a ministerial conference with North Korea.

Finally, in January 1979, Park made a proposal that elicited a North Korean counterproposal. He offered meetings with North Korea at any time, any place, and any level, without preconditions, to discuss all problems between the two sides. The response came, not from the government of the DPRK, but from the Central Committee of the Democratic Front for the Reunification of the Fatherland (DFRF). It called on both sides to reaffirm the three principles of unification of July 1972 and to stop all hostile military acts and defamation against each other, including all military exercises, as of March 1 (the date on which the Team Spirit '79 exercise was scheduled to begin). It also proposed a "great national conference" for early September composed of representatives of political parties and social organizations and patriotic persons from all walks of life. Representatives of the DFRF and the Seoul side of the SNCC met three times, but the talks foundered over inability to agree on whom the delegates represented.

In July 1979, on the occasion of President Jimmy Carter's visit to Seoul, the two presidents proposed to North Korea a tripartite conference, which North Korea promptly rejected on the ground that the proposal mixed up two matters that should be handled separately. Reunification, Pyongyang insisted, should be negotiated solely between the two Koreas, without outside interference. The replacement of the armistice with a peace treaty and the withdrawal of U.S. forces should be negotiated by Pyongyang and Washington, as Seoul was not a signatory to the Armistice Agreement.

Confrontation and Dialogue: An Appraisal

To the governments of the two Koreas, military confrontation has been central, dialogue peripheral. Both Kim Il Sung and Park Chunghee came to power because of their influence within the military, and to stay in power they had to have the support of the military. The experience of the Korean War, the political power of the military, and the tendency among military personnel to view the adversary in worst-case terms has caused military preparedness to be given a high priority in both Koreas. Given their extreme suspicion of the other side, the military viewed dialogue with great skepticism. South Koreans recalled North Korean peace proposals made a few weeks before the attack in 1950 and suspected all their proposals for dialogue to be smoke screens behind which they were preparing a military attack. The North Koreans saw South Korean proposals as devices to prolong the division of Korea.

It is difficult to imagine that either Korean government could tolerate a unified Korea dominated by the other, whatever its political form might be. Kim Il Sung's proposed confederation, agreed to by some "democratic" government of South Korea after the departure of U.S. forces, clearly would be dominated by North Korea. Pyongyang's ideology, especially the virtual deification of Kim Il Sung, excludes the possibility that any southern regime or leader could dominate a unified Korea. Similarly, the South Korean government, in control of two-thirds of Korea's population and a much larger proportion of its economic power, would find it difficult to visualize a unified Korea in which the South would not be dominant. Thus, the maneuvering that has taken place under the rubric of unification has aimed at gaining a position that would ensure dominance when Korea is eventually unified and to prevent the adversary from gaining such a position.

In the maneuvering for position, time was crucial. Time was working against North Korea, for South Korea had steadily improved the advantage it held over North Korea in economic development. In the late 1970s South Korea had begun to redress the relative losses in international position that it had sustained in the early part of the decade. It was also narrowing the gap in military capability. North Korea's principal hopes were to bring about the withdrawal of U.S. forces and to encourage opposition to the Park regime. The two objectives were closely related, for the North Koreans seemed convinced that only the presence of U.S. forces propped up an increasingly beleaguered ruling group in the South. In their propaganda the North Koreans equated opposition to Park with opposition to the presence of U.S. forces; whereas, in fact, the support for the U.S. military presence was much broader than support for the Park regime.

Thus, North Korean unification proposals had two principal aims: the removal of U.S. forces and the encouragement of stronger opposition to Park. The North Koreans interpreted agreement on the three principles of unification to require the withdrawal of U.S. forces. Their sweeping unification proposals, such as the confederation concept, were designed to appeal to those in the South who hoped for early unification. They insisted on negotiating first on the military confrontation, not because they expected Park to agree, but in order to build pressure in the South and abroad for the withdrawal of U.S. forces, which they saw as the key to unification on their terms. Other proposals, such as the demands for the abolition of anticommunist laws as a condition for family reunions and the repeated calls for a grand national conference of people of all walks of life in both Koreas were designed to place Park on the defensive and attract the interest of politically conscious people in the South who felt excluded from the political process.

In their advocacy of unification, the North Koreans sought to communicate a sense of urgency; "unification brooks not a moment's delay"
was one of their favorite propaganda cliches. They brushed aside the
South's step-by-step approach as a ruse to prolong division. Time was
important to the North Koreans, but their behavior suggested that they
did not expect to achieve unification through negotiation with the Park
regime. They made no serious effort to probe South Korean positions,
to narrow differences, or to seek compromise. When they saw that the
negotiations had failed to improve the prospects for early withdrawal
of U.S. forces and that Park had utilized them as a rationale for
strengthening his political position, they dropped them.

The South Koreans took the view that time was on their side. Park
publicly declared that unification would take a long time and would be
attained only when South Korea had become much stronger than North
Korea. The South Korean gradualist approach not only minimized risks,
in the event that North Korea should agree to one of their proposed
small steps, but also coincided with their interest in gaining time. Like
the North Koreans, they did not probe the opponent's position or seek
to narrow differences and reach compromises.

Both Koreas thus undertook negotiations, not in the expectation of
being able to reach agreement on unification, but for other reasons,
including demonstrating to their own people a commitment to unification
and seeking to impress on outsiders that their attitude toward unification
was more reasonable than that of their adversary. The tactics of the
North Koreans seemed self-contradictory. Their short-lived willingness
to talk with South Korean representatives about unification did little to
overcome the sense of threat among South Koreans caused by the
continued large military buildup, the tunnel digging, the attempted
assassination of Park, the support expressed for the Revolutionary Party
for Reunification, and the repeated calls for the overthrow of the Park
regime. Even in the dialogue itself, some of the North Korean proposals,
such as the demand for the abolition of the anticommunist laws and
for a grand national conference that would include South Korean
opponents of Park, patently were designed for external effect, rather
than serious negotiation. The heavy emphasis on withdrawal of U.S.
forces and the attempts from 1974 on to negotiate with the United
States rather than the ROK on that subject strengthened the conviction
in South Korea that North Korea's overriding objective was to gain
dominance over South Korea by force and that proposals for negotiations
were a propaganda exercise, a minor aspect of Pyongyang's drive toward
that goal.

Park Chung-hee's gradualist approach to unification was clearly more
realistic than North Korea's package proposals, which prominently

featured the withdrawal of U.S. forces. It did, however, lend itself to the North Korean charge that it aimed, not at unification, but at permanent division. Park's approach, for all its realism in promoting contacts to improve understanding and diminish suspicion, presented no plan for working toward unification. His deferral of concrete proposals on unification to the vague future, when South Korea had become far stronger than North Korea, placed him on the defensive. He rejected Kim Il Sung's confederation concept, but produced no comparable counterproposal. The suspension of U.S. ground force withdrawals in 1979, the strengthening of U.S. and ROK forces, and the growing annual Team Spirit exercises, no doubt confirmed Kim's view that talks with representatives of the Park regime were of little value unless they focused on the military confrontation.

When the 1970s ended, the North-South dialogue remained in suspension. Initiatives by Park in 1978 and 1979 had produced no movement. Both sides were concentrating almost exclusively on strengthening their positions in the military confrontation. No framework for continuing contacts existed. The North Koreans insisted that the South-North Coordinating Committee created in 1972 had ceased to exist and refused to reopen the telephone hotline that they had cut off in 1976. Prospects for renewal of dialogue looked dim.

Notes

1. For analyses of U.S.-ROK security relationships, see Norman D. Levin and Richard L. Sneider, "Korea in Postwar U.S. Security Policy," in Sung-joo Han, ed., *After One Hundred Years: Continuity and Change in Korean-American Relations* (Seoul: Asiatic Research Center, Korea University, 1982), pp. 233–270; Young-Sun Ha, "American-Korean Military Relations: Continuity and Change," in Youngnok Koo and Dae-Sook Suh, eds., *Korea and the United States: A Century of Cooperation* (Honolulu: University of Hawaii Press, 1984), pp. 110–130; Tae-Hwan Kwak, "U.S.-Korea Security Relations," in Tae-Hwan Kwak, John Chay, Soon Sung Cho, and Shannon McCune, eds., *U.S.-Korean Relations, 1882–1982* (Seoul: Kyungnam University Press, 1982), pp. 223–243; and Ralph N. Clough, *Deterrence and Defense in Korea: The Role of U.S. Forces* (Washington, D.C.: Brookings Institution, 1976).

2. Certain South Korean military units were not under U.S. operational control: the Capital Garrison Command, the Special Forces Command, and the Logistics Command.

3. Levin and Sneider, "Korea in Postwar U.S. Security Policy," pp. 245–248.

4. Ha, "American-Korean Military Relations," p. 118.

5. Bunge, *South Korea*, p. 239.

6. See Chapter 6.

7. Clough, *Deterrence and Defense in Korea*, pp. 57–58.

122   *Military Confrontation and Abortive Dialogue*

8. Bunge, *South Korea,* p. 235.
9. Stuart E. Johnson with Joseph A. Yager, *The Military Equation in Northeast Asia,* p. 39; Larry A. Niksch, "U.S. Troop Withdrawal and the Question of Northeast Asian Stability," Issue Brief No. IB79053 (Washington, D.C.: Congressional Research Service, Library of Congress, June 20, 1980), p. CRS-4.
10. *Washington Post,* June 27, 1975.
11. For a fuller discussion of the risk of nuclear weapons production in South Korea, see Joseph A. Yager, "Republic of Korea," in Joseph A. Yager, ed., *Nonproliferation and U.S. Foreign Policy* (Washington, D.C.: Brookings Institution, 1980), pp. 47–65; Clough, *Deterrence and Defense in Korea,* pp. 33–34.
12. Scalapino and Lee, *Communism in Korea,* vol. 2, pp. 920–960; Bunge, *North Korea,* pp. 220–242.
13. Scalapino and Lee, *Communism in Korea,* vol. 2, p. 939; Sung-joo Han, "North Korea's Security Policy and Military Strategy," in Scalapino and Kim, *North Korea Today,* p. 147.
14. Scalapino and Lee, *Communism in Korea,* vol. 1, p. 594.
15. Han, "North Korea's Security Policy and Military Strategy," pp. 150–152.
16. For a detailed description of the North Korean armed forces, see Bunge, *North Korea,* pp. 220–245.
17. Chung, *The North Korean Economy,* p. 93.
18. Joseph S. Chung "Economic Planning in North Korea," in Scalapino and Kim, *North Korea Today,* p. 180.
19. Bunge, *North Korea,* p. 240.
20. Han, "North Korea's Security Policy and Military Strategy," p. 159.
21. *Washington Post,* July 2, 1972.
22. See table in Han, "North Korea's Security Policy and Military Strategy," p. 158, based primarily on figures compiled by the London-based International Institute for Strategic Studies (IISS) and published in the annual *Military Balance.* The table in Han is based on several issues, *The Military Balance* for 1971–1972, 1975–1976, and 1980–1981. Kim Yong-nam in 1980 told Congressman Solarz that his forces were much weaker than those of South Korea, only 350,000 to 400,000, compared to 700,000. See Stephen J. Solarz, *The Korean Conundrum: A Conversation with Kim Il Sung,* Report to the House Committee on Foreign Affairs, 97th Cong., 1st sess. (Washington, D.C.: U.S. Government Printing Office, 1981), p. 8.
23. Ralph N. Clough, "The Soviet Union and the Two Koreas," in Donald Zagoria, *Soviet Policy in East Asia,* p. 185.
24. Clough, *Deterrence and Defense in Korea,* p. 10.
25. Kim Il Sung's exposition of this strategy in a 1964 speech is well summarized in Koh, *The Foreign Policy Systems of North and South Korea,* pp. 123–127.
26. For details on the establishment and suppression of the RPR see Scalapino and Lee, *Communism in Korea,* vol. 1, pp. 647–652, and Koh, *The Foreign Policy Systems of North and South Korea,* pp. 132–133.
27. Koh, *The Foreign Policy Systems of North and South Korea,* p. 133, note 26.

28. Rinn-Sup Shinn, "Foreign and Reunification Policies," *Problems of Communism* 22 (January-February 1973):62–63.

29. *FBIS*, October 27, 1978, p. E2. See also *Washington Post*, May 27, 1975.

30. For further discussion of the military balance and possible conflict scenarios as of the late 1970s, see Clough, *Deterrence and Defense in Korea*, pp. 6–15; Johnson with Yager, *The Military Equation in Northeast Asia*, pp. 37–43; Niksch, "U.S. Troop Withdrawal," pp. CRS-8 to CRS-11.

31. *FBIS*, April 21, 1975, p. A17.

32. Manwoo Lee in "How North Korea Sees Itself" (Kim and Koh, *Journey to North Korea*) gives a thoughtful presentation of this view, based on a visit to North Korea in 1981, pp. 135–138.

33. Byung Chul Koh, "Policy Toward Reunification," in Youngnok Koo and Sung-joo Han, eds., *The Foreign Policy of the Republic of Korea* (New York: Columbia University Press, 1985) p. 82.

34. Ibid., pp. 78–79.

35. Byung Chul Koh, "Unification Policies and North-South Relations," in Scalapino and Kim, *North Korea Today*, p. 279.

36. For text of communiqué, see Republic of Korea, National Unification Board, *A White Paper on South-North Dialogue in Korea* (hereafter cited as *White Paper*) (Seoul, December 1982), pp. 85–86.

37. Koh, "Policy Toward Reunification," pp. 89–90.

38. For the full text of the agreement on the telephone line and its subsequent operation, see *White Paper*, pp. 94–95, 150–152.

39. Koh, "Policy Toward Reunification," p. 89.

40. See Chapter 9.

5

Coping with Change in the 1980s: Domestic Trends

As the decade of the 1980s began, both Koreas had to cope with unsettling changes. The assassination of President Park Chung-hee in September 1979 catapulted South Korea into a morass of uncertainty. A previously little-known general emerged as the new leader, wrestling with severe problems in consolidating his position and in dealing with the impact on South Korea of a world economic recession. In the North, Kim Il Sung also faced difficult tasks: overcoming the sluggishness of the North Korean economy and ensuring the smooth succession of his son. In the new situation each government had to review strategy and tactics for dealing with its rival.

Political Change in South Korea[1]

Upon the death of President Park Chung-hee, Premier Choi Kyu Ha became acting president in accordance with the *yusin* constitution. He declared martial law, to be administered by a Martial Law Command under General Chung Seung Hwa, which imposed press censorship and a ban on public meetings. The United States warned Kim Il Sung against attempting to exploit the situation militarily and bolstered its forces in the area.

Generals and politicians agreed that the disliked *yusin* constitution, Park's instrument for maintaining himself in power, would have to go. The leadership rejected opposition demands for its immediate abolition, however, insisting that it must remain in effect until general agreement could be reached on a new constitution. Hence, Choi Kyu Ha was elected president in early December by the National Conference for

Unification under provisions of the *yusin* constitution, but he announced that he would step down in favor of a president elected under a new constitution rather than serve out the remainder of Park's term, which ran through 1984.

The country remained stable, and the government began cautiously easing restraints on political activity. A multiparty committee of national assemblymen began work on a draft constitution, as did the government itself. On December 7, 1979, President Choi rescinded Park's catch-all Emergency Decree No. 9, bringing about the release of those arrested under its sweeping provisions, including Kim Dae Jung, who emerged from house arrest to resume political activities. Hopes rose for the replacement of Park's authoritarianism by a more democratic system.

The military seriously doubted the wisdom of granting wide scope for political activity. The Martial Law Command strictly enforced the ban on public meetings, arresting dozens of students and Christian leaders. Kim Dae Jung, in particular, was the object of deep suspicions among the military.[2] But the military itself was divided. On December 12, 1979, Major General Chun Doo Hwan, commander of the Defense Security Command, arrested his superior, General Chung Seung Hwa, head of the Martial Law Command, and a number of other senior generals. Chun, a member of the eleventh graduating class of the Korean Military Academy in 1955, was backed by other generals, most of them from the same class. Chun, who had conducted the official investigation of Park's assassination, indicated that General Chung, who had been present in the KCIA compound when the murders occurred, was suspected of complicity in the affair.

Thereafter, General Chun and his military associates exercised considerable power over President Choi's government from behind the scenes, but permitted political preparations for a new constitution and presidential elections to continue. In addition, in February 1980, 687 persons, including Kim Dae Jung and Yun Po-Son, had their civil rights restored, and in early March expelled students and dismissed professors were allowed to return to their campuses.[3] Kim Chong-pil, a former close associate of Park Chung-hee, became president of the DRP but was challenged by Yi Hu Rak, another senior DRP figure. Kim Dae Jung vied unsuccessfully with Kim Young Sam for leadership of the opposition NDP, then sought to construct a political base of his own among students and other dissidents. The "three Kims" came to be regarded as the leading candidates for president when a new constitution had been adopted.

Chun and his fellow generals from the eleventh class of the military academy continued to strengthen their positions within the military. In a purge reminiscent of Park's 1961 coup, the power-holders reportedly dismissed 33 generals and reassigned scores of others to clear the way for the promotion of younger generals and colonels.[4] General Chung Seung Hwa, found guilty of giving aid to Park's assassin, received a ten-year jail sentence. On April 14, 1980, Chun took on the concurrent position of acting KCIA director, further broadening his powers.

Resistance and Repression

Student demonstrations that had begun in the spring grew larger and more violent. Initially concerned with university reforms, they soon escalated to demands for an immediate end to martial law and the *yusin* system. An unprecedented series of strikes broke out in industrial enterprises. Workers demanded large wage increases to help them cope with rapidly rising prices. They clashed with police in some places, the most violent fighting occurring in the coal mining town of Sabuk, where workers attacked a police station, killing one policeman and injuring seventy others. Although strikes were illegal, the government did not intervene on behalf of management as it had in the past.[5]

Student demonstrations were particularly violent in the city of Kwangju, in Kim Dae Jung's native province. In Seoul they reached a climax in mid-May, when tens of thousands of students poured into the streets for three successive days, clashing with riot police and virtually paralyzing normal activities in the city center.[6] The military leadership, concerned at the size of the demonstrations and perhaps also disturbed by reports that the National Assembly, scheduled to resume sessions soon, might interfere with their plans, imposed "total martial law" throughout the entire country on May 18, 1980, augmenting the powers of the military. The government banned all political activity, closed the universities, tightened censorship of the press, and arrested a number of political leaders, including the three Kims.

The worst was yet to come. In Kwangju students reacted angrily, demanding the release of Kim Dae Jung, an end to martial law, and the resignation of Chun Doo Hwan. Paratroopers sent in to back the police in maintaining order inflamed the situation by brutal attacks on students and other civilians. Rioting grew worse, as many others joined the students in seizing weapons from the police and vehicles from the army. The government withdrew the paratroopers, armed students controlled the city, and antigovernment demonstrations erupted in other cities of Cholla Namdo, a southwestern province where the populace had long felt ill-used by a central government dominated by natives of provinces to the north and east. Efforts by a self-appointed citizen's committee in Kwangju to negotiate with the government failed, and the revolt was soon over. At 4 A.M. on May 27 the army moved into Kwangju with overwhelming force, killing or capturing the small number of students who tried to resist. Official sources placed the number of dead during the week of the Kwangju revolt at around two hundred, but dissidents claimed that it was much higher. The seriousness of the Kwangju revolt alarmed the government and strengthened the determination of the military to maintain law and order. Pyongyang portrayed it as a popular uprising that demonstrated the hostility of all the people of South Korea toward the "fascist butcher," Chun Doo Hwan.

The military tightened their grip on government with the establishment of a Special Committee for National Security Measures under President Choi, but backed by a Standing Committee with a majority of military members headed by Chun Doo Hwan, which had the real power. In a manner resembling the early days of Park Chung-hee's rule, the government now moved briskly to "purify" the bureaucracy and society. It dismissed 232 high officials and 4,760 low-level officials for corruption and incompetence. It conducted a purge of several hundred journalists and broadcasters, closed down 172 "harmful periodicals," ousted 611 public school teachers and principals, and rounded up over 57,000 hoodlums. The KCIA (Chun had resigned as acting director in early June) dropped 300 employees regarded as corrupt or inefficient. Kim Chong-pil and 9 other arrested politicians were freed after agreeing to turn their wealth over to the state and retire from politics. Kim Young Sam, who had been under house arrest, was also released on the condition that he withdraw from politics. Seventeen former cabinet ministers and national assemblymen, accused of abusing their position for profit, were arrested.[7] Public reaction to the new, military-dominated regime was mixed. Disappointment with the abrupt reversal of hoped-for progress toward democracy mingled with relief that the Kwangju uprising had not led to widespread disorders and with satisfaction that the new leaders were moving swiftly against graft, crime, and incompetence.

Military courts were active during the summer of 1980 trying and sentencing to prison students and others accused of instigating rebellion in Kwangju. The Martial Law Command tried Kim Dae Jung and 23 of his supporters on charges of sedition. Kim was accused of past connections with North Korea and of inciting students to violence in Kwangju with the aim of overthrowing the government. The government's case seemed weak to outsiders; the U.S. Department of State described the charges against him as "farfetched." Nevertheless, Kim received a death sentence in September 1980.

Chun Becomes President

Having established firm control over the state, Chun decided that the time had come to assume a position commensurate with his actual political power. During August 1980 Choi Kyu Ha resigned the presidency, Chun retired from the army, where he had recently received promotion to four-star general, and the National Council for Unification elected him president unopposed. He took office on September 1. Much remained to be done, however, to legitimize his rule. Martial law and the unpopular *yusin* constitution were still in effect.

Chun's first act as president was to name a new cabinet, which included two retired generals. The cabinet was headed by Nam Duck Woo, a respected U.S.-educated economist, who had directed the Economic Planning Board under Park Chung-hee. Chun then appointed a committee to draft a new constitution, which was submitted to the voters in a national referendum and approved by 91 percent of the votes. He named a Legislative Council for National Security as an interim legislature, replacing the National Assembly. This temporary body passed laws authorizing the formation of new political parties, strengthening the government's authority to control the media and student disorders, and prohibiting third parties from intervening in labor disputes and bargaining.

The new constitution provided for the president to be elected indirectly by a popularly elected electoral college of not less than 5,000 members. It placed certain restrictions on the president's power to declare emergency measures and to dissolve the National Assembly. More important, it limited the president to one seven-year term, providing in addition that constitutional amendments extending this term or authorizing additional terms could not apply to the president in office when the amendment was adopted.

The political parties of the Park era were dissolved with the advent of the new constitution and had to be replaced by new parties in preparation for presidential and National Assembly elections. As had happened at the beginning of each new political era in South Korea—in 1948, 1960, and 1961—the government barred from politics a large group of politicians active under the previous regime. The ban on political activity extended through June 1988 and affected 835 persons (reduced after appeals to 567), including the three Kims, former cabinet members, and most members of the previous National Assembly, all accused of responsibility for "political and social confusion or corruption."[8] Thus, most of the politicians who came forward to organize the new parties were secondary figures under the old regime. The dominant new party was the Democratic Justice Party (DJP), composed of retired military men and civilians who supported Chun Doo Hwan. The leading opposition party, the Democratic Korea Party (DKP), was organized by former members of the New Democratic Party, who had led the opposition to Park. The other sizable opposition party, the Korean National Party (KNP), was led by former members of Park's ruling party, the Democratic Republican Party.

Chun lifted martial law in January 1981. In the February elections for the presidential electoral college, the Democratic Justice Party took 70 percent of the seats. A coalition of DJP members and independents then elected Chun president with 90 percent of the votes. In the March National Assembly elections, the DJP captured 151 of the 276 seats, thus ensuring its status as the ruling party of the newly formed Fifth Republic. The DJP acquired its 151 seats by winning 90 of the 184 seats contested in the voting and then, as the party gaining a plurality of elective seats, received two-thirds (61) of the 92 additional seats allocated to parties on the basis of the proportion of seats each had won in the voting.

The Early Years of the Chun Administration

The new president, like Park Chung-hee, came from Kyongsang and had his early schooling in Taegu; otherwise, his experience was quite different. Park had to contend with the bad impression made on most Koreans by his service as an officer in the Japanese military and his alleged Communist connections in the late 1940s. Chun had no such black marks on his record. A product of the first four-year class of the Korean Military Academy, he was popular among his fellow officers, serving two four-year terms as president of the North Star Club, an alumni association of the Korean Military Academy.[9] He was an early supporter of Park Chung-hee after the 1961 coup and advanced rapidly, gaining combat experience in a year as regimental commander in Vietnam and serving as commander of the First Division on the section of the DMZ where the third infiltration tunnel from North Korea was discovered. In early 1979 he became head of the Defense Security Command, well positioned to carry out his coup after Park's assassination.

Chun ruled over a more complex and sophisticated society than Park had at the outset of his period as president. Many members of the rapidly growing urban middle class believed that the time had come for expanding public participation in political affairs. The abrupt snuffing out of their burgeoning hope for democratic competition among candidates for president was a severe disappointment. In 1980 Chun also faced a worldwide recession that had a serious impact on South Korea. The combination of economic recession and political uncertainty resulted in an unprecedented negative growth of 5.2 percent in 1980.

The dominant reactions of the public to Chun's formal accession to power were resignation and relief. Resignation among those who had hoped for a better outcome, but now saw no alternative to learning to live with the new president. Relief on the part of those alarmed by the violence at Kwangju and fearful that the North Koreans could take advantage of political disorder in the South to launch a new incursion. The need for vigorous government action to remedy the economic decline was widely recognized, and most people were willing to give Chun a chance to see what he could do.

During his first four years in office, Chun demonstrated the leadership qualities needed to maintain political stability and resume economic growth. He relied in part on close associates from the military and in part on experienced, highly qualified civilian technocrats. Exmilitary men held important positions, but Chun's government was not a quasimilitary government, as Park's had been during the early years. Chun changed his cabinet and his Blue House advisers from time to time, for the most part choosing highly qualified people. The corps of experienced and competent senior personnel in government and business had expanded greatly during the 1960s and 1970s, giving Chun a large number to choose from. The top decisionmakers, in adjusting to trends and reacting to unexpected events, displayed much of the same pragmatism and flexibility evident under Park.

Economic recovery was the most important accomplishment of Chun's first two years in office. The real growth rate reached 5.6 percent in 1982 and 9.3 percent in 1983, with inflation reduced to the unprecedentedly low range of 3 to 4 percent, thus restoring confidence in South Korea's ability to cope with sweeping external economic changes. Chun benefited from the upswing in the world economy, particularly that of the United States, and from good harvests in those years. Economic progress was not significantly set back by two serious financial scandals in 1982 and 1983, one of which involved the uncle of Chun's wife.

Chun also earned good marks in his handling of North-South relations and his efforts to enhance South Korean prestige and influence in international affairs. His 1981 invitation to Kim Il Sung to join him in talks on unification, followed by detailed South Korean proposals for North-South dialogue, took away from North Korea the initiative in this area that Kim Il Sung had held during most of the Park period. Although the North Koreans began again in 1984 to put forward proposals for North-South dialogue, they shied away from Chun's proposal for talks between the leaders and continued to denounce him in their media as a puppet of the United States.

In the foreign policy area, Chun's early proposal for a summit meeting among Pacific basin leaders evoked little enthusiasm and came to nothing.

But his trips to the United States, Canada, Southeast Asia, and Africa and the naming of South Korea as the venue for the 1983 meeting of the Interparliamentary Union, the 1985 World Bank/International Monetary Fund meeting, the 1986 Asian Games, and the 1988 Olympics produced much favorable publicity for his country. Chun's successes in foreign affairs were somewhat dimmed by his ill-fated visit to Rangoon, discussed in Chapter 6, during which seventeen members of his entourage were killed by a North Korean bomb. It was North Korea's international standing, however, that suffered greatest damage from that bloody affair.

In his public speeches Chun showed greater understanding than Park had of the obstacles to creating a more democratic system in South Korea. He criticized the extreme dominance of the executive branch over the legislature, the extensiveness of corruption, and the fondness of Korean politicians for confrontation over compromise and for personal and party advantage over national interest. His stress on the importance of political parties and of the National Assembly contrasted with Park's neglect of these institutions. He encouraged a multiparty rather than a two-party system and urged politicians to work for consensus rather than conflict.

From time to time, in moves to mollify the opposition and to counter criticism abroad, Chun released or reduced the sentence of political prisoners. In January 1981 he removed an obstacle to his trip to the United States the following month by commuting Kim Dae Jung's death sentence to life imprisonment. Later he reduced Kim's sentence to twenty years and in December 1982 allowed him to go to the United States. By February 1984, he had removed the ban on political activities for all but 99 of the 567 persons placed under the ban in November 1980. The most prominent politicians remained under the ban, including Kim Dae Jung, Kim Young Sam, Kim Chong-pil, and Yi Hu Rak. A hunger strike by Kim Young Sam in protest against the lack of democracy in South Korea gained him release from house arrest, but the government continued to keep him under close surveillance. The government took control of television and radio and kept the press under firm guidance. As of late 1984, few of the purged journalists had been permitted to return to their profession.

As during the Park regime, university students were the most unruly and troublesome element in the opposition. Student political activists were few in number, but they repeatedly drew others into campus demonstrations expressing opposition to Chun Doo Hwan and government policies. A more radical tendency appeared among students than had existed during the Park period. Dependency theory, imported from Latin America, attracted student interest and fed criticism of the United States for allegedly controlling South Korea through multinational corporations, supporting a military dictator, and drowning Korean culture in a flood of imported U.S. culture. A handful of students covertly expressed admiration for the greater national independence and equality of income distribution claimed by North Korea.

The government kept the situation under control by stationing police on the campuses and arresting the ringleaders or having them expelled from the universities. Student demonstrations evoked little sympathy from the general public. Prison sentences at first were short, and the number of students in jail at any one time did not exceed several hundred. But during 1983 the number of arrests gradually increased and judges handed down longer sentences. In December 1983 the government adopted a new strategy for coping with student activism. It removed the police from campuses, leaving the control of the students in the hands of the university administration and using the police only to confine demonstrations to the campuses. The government also approved the readmission to universities of more than three thousand expelled students and dismissed faculty members. This improved the climate. Demonstrations continued on the campuses, but on a smaller scale and with fewer arrests.

A Watershed Election

In December 1984, Chun Doo Hwan lifted the political ban from 84 of the 99 persons still excluded from political activity, leaving under the ban only 15 of the 567 banned in 1980. Among the 15 were the three Kims: Kim Dae Jung, Kim Young Sam, and Kim Chong-pil. Some of the formerly banned politicians formed a new political party in January 1985, the New Korea Democratic Party (NKDP) in preparation for the National Assembly elections scheduled for February. Kim Dae Jung, who had been in the United States since 1982, returned to Seoul just before the election with an escort of U.S. citizens (including two members of Congress) to ensure his safety.[10] Kim's twenty-year jail sentence, of which he had served less than three years, remained outstanding, but the government did not return him to prison. It kept him under house arrest, denying him freedom to meet with other politicians, although it allowed him to talk with them by telephone. He and Kim Young Sam headed a Council for the Promotion of Democracy, which maintained close connections with the NKDP.

In the National Assembly election, the month-old NKDP won a surprising 50 seats, more than anyone, including its own leaders, had expected. The ruling DJP lost only 3 seats, thus holding on to its plurality. It again received 61 allocated seats, bringing its total to 148, a clear majority of the 276-member body. The big loser was the Democratic

Korea Party, which had been the principal opposition party before the advent of the NKDP. The DJP took 35 percent of the popular vote, about the same percentage it had received in the 1981 election, and the NKDP received 29 percent.[11] The government party made its strongest showing in the smaller towns and rural areas, while the NKDP did well in Seoul and Pusan, where it outpolled the DJP by large margins in the popular vote.

The National Assembly election provided an opportunity for the urban middle class to register its dissatisfaction with the Chun government and to express support for candidates demanding liberalization of the political system. Some of the campaign speeches in Seoul and Pusan were remarkably frank, the candidates openly condemning "the military dictatorship" and claiming links to Kim Dae Jung, whose popularity had been attested to by the thousands who had turned out to greet him along the road from the airport the day he returned to Seoul. Even the usually cowed press showed an unaccustomed boldness in reporting the views of opposition candidates. The government itself gained credit at home and abroad for permitting a relatively fair election with significant gains for the opposition, even though constitutional provisions and the carefully prescribed campaign limitations favored the ruling party and ensured that it would retain its majority.

The election transformed the texture of politics in South Korea. Although it did not threaten Chun Doo Hwan's firm grip on power through control of the executive branch of government, it produced a much more vigorous opposition party than had existed in the recent past to challenge government policies in the public forum of the National Assembly. Disturbed by the success of the NKDP, Chun appointed a new head of the DJP, Roh Tae-woo, a fellow exgeneral from the class of 1955 at the Military Academy. Roh had been one of Chun's chief supporters during the military coup. The two minor parties declined in importance, as some of their members deserted to join the NKDP. Thus, contrary to the ruling party's original blueprint, the multiparty system shifted toward a predominantly two-party system.

A month after the election, Chun removed the political ban from 14 of the 15 politicians still banned from politics. Only Kim Dae Jung, because of his prison sentence, was denied the right to engage in political activity, but Kim was released from house arrest and enabled for the first time since he returned to Korea to meet face-to-face with Kim Young Sam and other opposition politicians.

The opposition made several demands of the ruling party: lift the political ban on Kim Dae Jung, mount an investigation into the Kwangju violence of 1980, and revise the constitution to provide for direct election of the president. The DJP showed no disposition to yield to any of these demands. Opposition leaders declared their determination to persist in their campaign for a constitutional revision, sometimes hinting darkly that if the ruling party refused to give ground in the National Assembly on this issue, they would have to resort to extraparliamentary action. Chun Doo Hwan reiterated his intention to remain in office until his term ended in 1988 and to carry out the first peaceful transition of power in the history of the ROK, under the provisions of the existing constitution.

Student Activism

While the NKDP, with backing from behind the scenes by Kim Dae Jung and Kim Young Sam, sought to bring pressure on the government in the National Assembly, university students stepped up antigovernment activities. Student demonstrations had broken out again in the fall of 1984 on the campuses and had culminated in a dramatic 13-hour sit-in at the headquarters of the DJP by more than 260 students, who had to be dislodged by the police. During 1985 student demonstrations gathered momentum. According to official figures, 1,352 occurred during the first six months of the year, nearly three times as many as during the same period of 1984.[12]

The student movement was changing. Students were better organized in associations that drew members from a number of universities. They were reading and circulating materials critical of capitalism, some of it with a strong anti-American slant. More serious was the increase in violence. The police reported that students had thrown some 2,700 Molotov cocktails or other homemade fire bombs.[13] Students were also exploring ways to link up with dissatisfied workers. Some took jobs in factories as ordinary workers, concealing that they were university students, and began to organize their fellow workers for confrontations with management.

The number of college students was increasing rapidly. A report by the Korea Development Institute estimated that more than one million students would graduate from college in the 1980s, as compared to 277,000 in the 1970s. In 1984, 22.5 of every 1,000 Koreans were in college. The comparable figure for the United States was 33.6, for France 18.4, for Japan 15.3, for West Grmany 14.8, and for the United Kingdom 5.3.[14] Even though only a minority of college students took part in the demonstrations of 1984 and 1985, the pool of students that could be drawn into demonstrations if dissatisfaction with the government intensified was enormous and growing.

Students became particularly active during the fifth anniversary of the Kwangju uprising in late May 1985, even though the government took into custody in advance those student leaders thought most likely to organize demonstrations. The move that attracted the greatest public attention was the occupation of the U.S. Information Service (USIS) library in Seoul for four days by 73 students from five universities. The students accused the United States of having authorized the use of Korean forces under U.S. operational command to suppress the Kwangju uprising. They demanded a public debate on the subject with the participation of U.S. Embassy officials. Although the embassy did not yield to their demand, the sit-in proved an effective means of giving wide publicity to the opposition parties' demand for an investigation of the Kwangju affair. Opposition leaders, although disassociating themselves from the method adopted by the students, expressed sympathy with their objective.

The government, which had shown greater tolerance of dissent during the year preceding the National Assembly election, adopted harsher measures in reaction to the increase in student demonstrations. The USIS sit-in intensified the government's determination to crack down. The student leader of that action received a seven-year prison sentence and 20 other students who took part were given terms of two to five years. Joint teams of police and officials from the Ministry of Culture and Information conducted raids on bookstores, publishing houses, and printshops to seize antigovernment publications and other material considered ideologically dangerous. In July 1985 police raided nine campuses and seized items prepared for student demonstrations, including dozens of homemade firebombs. During the same month the security authorities arrested 56 student leaders of the Sammin Struggle Committee, said to have masterminded the USIS sit-in. The president of Seoul National University and several other university heads were replaced for being too lenient with students. The Ministry of Education ordered the dismissal of 15 primary, middle, and high school teachers for writing articles criticizing capitalism in a *Magazine for the Masses*, and the company that published that periodical was shut down. In October, police arrested 26 persons, most of them students, graduates, or expellees from Seoul National University, who belonged to an organization called Minchuwi (Committee for the Promotion of Democracy), which was said to be affiliated with the Sammin Struggle Committee and engaged in promoting socialist revolution in South Korea. Through October 1985, 287 students were expelled, suspended, or admonished for involvement in campus disturbances. On November 14 students who occupied the U.S. Chamber of Commerce had to be forcibly removed by the police.

The government, seeking a new method of coping with the rising student unrest, put forward a Campus Stabilization Law, which would establish detention centers to which student troublemakers could be sent for up to six months of ideological "reorientation." The outcry against this idea from the opposition and others, at home and abroad, was so strong that the government put it aside for the time being.[15] At the end of 1985, the heightening confrontation between the students and the government, although considerably more tense than in 1984, had not reached the level of tension of the 1976 to 1980 period, during which 42 universities were closed for varying periods on 74 occasions. No universities were shut down from 1982 through 1985.[16]

Confrontation and Dialogue

The year 1986 began with the ruling party and the opposition at an impasse over the issue of constitutional revision. In reaction to Chun's insistence that debate on this issue should be deferred until 1989, the opposition launched a drive for 10 million signatures on a petition demanding amendment of the constitution to provide for direct election of the president. At first, the government cracked down hard. It denounced the signature collection campaign as illegal; threatened to arrest signers; placed Kim Dae Jung, Kim Young Sam, and other opposition politicians under house arrest; and roughed up reporters. The U.S. government declared publicly that it was urging the South Korean government not to oppose the collection of signatures because denying citizens the right to petition their government was inconsistent with basic democratic principles.[17] On February 24, as the struggle in the Philippines was rapidly approaching a climax (Marcos left the country on February 26), Chun abruptly moderated his position and invited the leaders of the NKDP and the KNP to meet for lunch in order to propose establishing commissions in the government and the National Assembly to study the issue of constitutional revision.

Thereafter, the government permitted the opposition to hold rallies in the principal cities during the spring. The rallies were orderly, but in some cities radical students used the occasion to clash with riot police. On May 3 at Inchon the violence prevented the rally from taking place. Hundreds of student radicals and workers hurled bricks and Molotov cocktails at police, burned a DJP office, condemned the opposition parties for compromising with the government, and shouted antigovernment and anti-American slogans. The police responded with clouds of tear gas.

The Inchon affair highlighted the growing divergence between the student extremists and the opposition politicians, who declined to endorse resort to violence and did not share the revolutionary anti-American views of the radicals. A few days earlier Kim Dae Jung, Lee Min-woo, and other opposition politicians issued a statement rejecting extremist slogans and demands. Clashes between police and students continued on campuses throughout the spring. Three students performed the ultimate act of defiance by burning themselves to death. On June 5 the Minister of Justice announced that 997 persons had been detained on political or politically related charges, 611 of them students.[18] In announcing arrests government officials pointed out that the antigovernment and anti-American slogans put forward by student protestors often were similar to or identical with those advanced by North Korea. Indeed, the Voice of National Salvation, purportedly broadcast from South Korea, praised South Korean student radicalism and offered slogans and advice. In this way, the North Koreans provided ammunition to government prosecutors and deepened the rift between student radicals and other opponents of the government, who did not wish to be viewed as serving Pyongyang's purposes.[19]

The rival parties succeeded in establishing the commission to study constitutional revision in the National Assembly. Both held hearings on the subject outside the Assembly and worked on drafts of a revised constitution. As of mid-1986 the opposing positions had not been made public, although the DJP appeared to be leaning toward a parliamentary system, whereas the NKDP continued to press for a presidential system with direct election of the president.

The Political Outlook

The political maneuvering between the government and the opposition in South Korea is essentially a struggle for power. The opposition believes that the military would retain the upper hand in a presidential election under the present constitution or under a revised constitution establishing a parliamentary system of government. They are firmly opposed to permitting Chun Doo Hwan to designate an ex-military colleague as president or premier. Consequently, they see a constitutional revision providing for the direct election of the president as the only way to elect a civilian politician president in 1988.

Both the government and the opposition recognize that pressures for a more democratic and less repressive political system are increasing within the growing urban middle class. The National Assembly election in February 1985 confirmed this trend in a striking fashion. Since 1980 the government has taken a number of steps to ease controls: lifting the midnight curfew, loosening restrictions on overseas travel, ending the political ban on the politicians excluded from political activity in 1980, reaching a consensus in the National Assembly on phasing in a system of local autonomy beginning in 1987, and removing police from the campuses and allowing the reinstatement of some professors and students expelled for political activity.[20] From the spring of 1985, however, as indicated above, government repression again increased, principally in reaction to the increase in student demonstrations.

The confrontation over revising the constitution to provide for direct election of the president, the focus of the struggle for power, will undoubtedly intensify. The opposition has been encouraged by the support it received in the National Assembly election and by student opposition to the government. Thousands of student activists worked for the election of NKDP candidates to the National Assembly. The student movement is a two-edged sword for the opposition, however. Opposition leaders have little sympathy with the anticapitalist, anti-American views of the most radical students. They also know that excessive student violence would justify in the eyes of many Koreans stern repression by the government. The middle class is overwhelmingly conservative, favoring peaceful change, and alarmed by violent confrontation. Consequently, the opposition must walk a fine line, encouraging student opposition to the government, but avoiding being tagged with responsibility for student violence, as illustrated by the cautious reaction of opposition leaders to the student occupation of the USIS library. The opposition has been encouraged by the fall of Ferdinand Marcos in the Philippines, but it glosses over the wide differences between the two situations. It also tends to exaggerate both the U.S. government's role in the Philippines and its potential role in South Korea.

Chun Doo Hwan is in a difficult position. His early successful exploitation of foreign travel to build personal prestige foundered in Rangoon where he narrowly escaped being assassinated. He cannot, as Park Chung-hee could, point to exceptional achievements in economic growth. Future prospects for the economy are murky. Criticism of Chun is widespread, not only among the overwhelmingly anti-Chun students, but also within the middle class, including businessmen and even some bureaucrats. Chun is seen as less competent than Park, less effective in delegating authority, and less willing to listen to advice than when he first took over. He lacks an understanding of the need to build political support from various groups in an increasingly pluralistic society. He is handicapped further by the almost universal unpopularity of his wife, some of whose relatives were involved in financial scandals.

The opposition suffers from more severe handicaps than does the DJP. Its two principal leaders, Kim Dae Jung and Kim Young Sam, although publicly declaring their determination to cooperate with each other, have had deep differences in the past. Each has his own faction in the NKDP, and both factions contend for influence with other smaller factions. More important, the two Kims are potential rivals in the contest for the presidency. They are very different individuals. Kim Dae Jung is charismatic, a spellbinding platform speaker, and articulate in conceptualizing his thinking. But he remains formally barred from politics and is so feared and disliked among the military that they would be unlikely to tolerate his assumption of the presidency. Kim Young Sam is no match for Kim Dae Jung in public speaking. He is, however, a skilled and experienced politician who is no longer barred from candidacy for public office and is more acceptable to the military than Kim Dae Jung. The opposition has a soapbox in the National Assembly from which it can castigate the ruling party and demand change, but it lacks the votes to effect change by parliamentary means. Its principal reliance, therefore, is on stirring up outside pressure on the government to achieve its ends.

Chun Doo Hwan has vowed to step down when his term ends, and any attempt to go back on this pledge would provoke a massive reaction, possibly even a coup by another military leader. Chun has announced that the DJP will name its candidate for the presidential election of 1988 at a party convention in 1987. The front-runner as of mid-1986 was Roh Tae-woo, the chairman of the DJP.

A major factor in the political maneuvering is the scheduled opening of the 1988 Olympic Games a few months after the presidential election, giving South Korea an unprecedented opportunity to show itself off to the world. Consequently, the government will be under great pressure to bring about an orderly presidential succession generally approved by the populace. Government leaders will not want the games disrupted by student demonstrations, but, at the same time, they will wish to avoid heavy-handed repression that would tarnish the government's international image. The opposition may see this dilemma as providing enough leverage to force the DJP to agree to direct presidential elections.

Confrontation over the election issue is likely to intensify during 1987. Political analysts differ as to whether Chun will succeed in designating his successor in an election under the present constitution or will be compelled to agree to a direct election with less predictable results. Despite the vehement criticism of the government heard in many quarters in South Korea, few of the critics would favor its violent overthrow. Thus, although the level of political disturbances may rise, the possibility that the ruling party might be forced out of office before 1988 is small. Progress toward a more democratic system probably will continue, but it will be slow—with some checks and reverses—as a strong government, determined to maintain order, gives ground grudgingly to pressure groups demanding greater influence.

Leadership Succession in North Korea

Preparations for the leadership succession dominated the North Korean political scene in the early 1980s. Kim Chong Il emerged from the shadows to become the publicly acknowledged heir to the throne. The media reported his activities and praised his writings with increasing frequency, referring to him as "the dear comrade leader." His role initially was to reinforce his father's personality cult, while assuming direction of an increasing range of government functions. Kim Il Sung remained the unquestioned leader, with final responsibility for important decisions, but Kim Chong Il was being prepared for the day when he would take over that role.

The Sixth Party Congress

Kim Chong Il's public confirmation as the number two in the hierarchy of the Korean Workers' Party occurred at the Sixth Congress of the party in October 1980. He was named to fourth position in the presidium of the Politburo, second position in the Party Secretariat, and third position in the Military Commission. No other person except his father was a member of all three of these top-level bodies.

Ten years had passed between the fifth and sixth party congresses. The high turnover in the membership of the Central Committee that had occurred in 1970 was repeated in 1980. Sixty-four percent of the committee's 145 regular members and 80 percent of its 103 candidate members were new faces.[21] Younger men moved into leadership positions. Half of the new Politburo members and all ten of the members of the Central Committee's secretariat were in their fifties or younger.[22] Midway in age between Kim Il Sung and his son, they represented the post-revolutionary generation that would soon replace the few remaining Kapsan exguerrillas at the top of the political pyramid. Political skill and technical competence doubtless were important in the rise of these younger leaders to high position, but demonstrated loyalty to Kim Il Sung and his son must have been the prime criterion. On these younger leaders rests the responsibility for carrying through the dynastic succession.

Reinforcement of the Kim Cult

The recognition of Kim Chong Il as heir apparent did not diminish adulation of "the great leader." On the contrary, one of Kim Chong Il's principal duties was to add luster to the Kim cult. Placed in charge of preparations for the celebration of Kim Il Sung's seventieth birthday in April 1982, he supervised the construction of a massive Arch of Triumph and a 170-meter Tower of the Chu che Idea, said to be the tallest stone tower in the world, on the bank of the Taedong River opposite Kim Il Sung Square in the center of Pyongyang.

Emissaries fanned out throughout the world to invite chiefs of state and other high political figures to attend the celebration. Many came, but notably absent from the festivities were the chiefs of state from the Soviet Union, China, and Eastern Europe. Nicolae Ceausescu, of Romania, arrived two days after the ceremony, having tarried in Peking. Deng Xiaoping and Hu Yaobang made a secret visit, also a few days late, to pay Chinese respects. The behavior of the other Communist parties in power unmistakably demonstrated their reluctance to endorse publicly the Kim cult and the concept of hereditary succession. Not until later in the year during Kim Il Sung's visit to Peking did the Chinese reveal Deng and Hu's secret visit.

Within North Korea, article after article in the party press extolled the virtues of Kim Il Sung, stressed the indispensable role of the leader, and called for unbounded loyalty to him and his ideas. "The first duty of a Communist revolutionary is endless loyalty to the leader. . . . whether one maintains the loyalty to the leader as a revolutionary faith and sense of obligation is the yardstick that distinguishes the true revolutionaries from those who are not. . . . those who have faith and moral sense invariably uphold the leader to the end, not fearing the trend of the times."[23] Unquestioning loyalty is demanded not only of individuals but from the party as a whole: "The leader's intentions are the will of our party and people. . . . All activities of our party are wholly aimed at implementing the ideas and intentions of the respected leader Comrade Kim Il Sung. . . . Because the respected leader Kim Il Sung brightly indicates the road to victory with the correct ideas and theory and because our party correctly embodies the leader's ideas and plans, our revolution and construction are ever-victorious."[24]

The endless repetition of praise for Kim Il Sung and of exhortations demanding unquestioning loyalty to him and his ideas gives an outsider the impression that deficiencies may exist in the quality of the loyalty extended to Kim Il Sung by the party and the people. Otherwise, why should propagandists have to dwell incessantly on the need for loyalty among a people taught from childhood to revere their great leader? Reports by the few outsiders who have observed the behavior of the people in North Korea suggest another explanation: that constant repetition of familiar and simple ideas creates an intellectual climate and habit of thinking that block out contradictory ideas. It becomes difficult for anyone enveloped every day in evidence that Kim Il Sung is a brilliant leader and loving father to believe anything else. A Korean-American who visited North Korea in 1981 described the North Korean system as "a mass manipulation so intensely and efficiently executed that the distinction between what the leadership wants and what the masses desire has for all practical purposes disappeared."[25]

The North Korean media portrayed Kim Il Sung's lengthy trip to the Soviet Union and Eastern Europe in May-June 1984 as a great achievement by a world-renowned statesman who leads the vanguard of the global struggle against U.S. imperialism.

> Our nation, which once even faded from the world map, has become a glorious *chu che* fatherland and our people have become a magnificent people of a mighty, wealthy, and civilized independent country. . . . Our people enjoy independent, creative and happy lives in the prosperous and developing socialist fatherland by upholding the great leader who is endlessly admired and respected by the world's people. . . . the several hundred million people in Europe who closely greeted the great leader Comrade Kim Il Sung highly respected and praised the respected leader as a genius of revolution. . . . when the peoples of the world assess the role which our party, country and people play in carrying out the world revolution, they think of the great leader Comrade Kim Il Sung first and highly praise his precious achievements.[26]

Buildup of Kim Chong Il

Soon after Kim Chong Il had emerged in the number two position in the KWP, the North Korean media began to refer to him by name as his father's successor. Promoters of the Kim cult stressed the need to carry on Kim Il Sung's revolutionary cause of *chu che*, generation after generation. The "dear leader" assumed the role of an inseparable junior partner of the "great leader." Descriptions of his virtues fell only a little short of those used about his father: "He is the outstanding thinker and theoretician who has fully mastered the great leader's revolutionary ideas; he is the sagacious leader of our Party and people who is possessed of brilliant wisdom, unusual insight, and refined art of leadership; and he is the real leader of the people who has unboundedly lofty virtues."[27] Books of biographical anecdotes appeared testifying to Kim Chong Il's precocity, wisdom, loyalty to his father, and love for the people.[28]

The North Korean media placed great emphasis on Kim Chong Il's theoretical writings, dating back to his student days at Kim Il Sung University (1960–1964). In 1962 he published *The Characteristics of Modern Imperialism and its Aggressive Nature*, now frequently cited as a pathbreaking revision of existing theory. In the book, Kim demonstrated that state-monopoly capitalism had replaced simple monopoly capitalism; new colonialism had replaced old colonialism; and the United States had become the leader of world imperialism, rather than coequal with other imperialist powers. Imperialism's aggressive nature would never change, Kim Chong Il wrote, but it was engaged in a last frantic effort, weakening and crumbling. In the same year he published *Let Us Strengthen the Ideological and Spiritual Unity of Party Members on the Basis of the Leader's Revolutionary Idea*. In 1964, a few days before he graduated from the university, he presented in the lecture hall his "immortal work," *The Place and Role of the County in the Building of Socialism*.[29] New works by Kim Chong Il appeared in 1982 and 1983, expatiating on the role of the leader and the party and the need to imbue society with the *chu che* idea. Scarcely any didactic article appeared in the media that did not contain a reference to Kim Chong Il's writings.

On his fortieth birthday, February 16, 1982, Kim Chong Il received the highest award granted by the DPRK, the title of "Hero" for his "shining successes throughout the political, economic, cultural and military spheres."[30] In June 1983 he made an initially unpublicized trip to China at the invitation of Hu Yaobang, where he visited Peking, Nanjing, and Chengdu and met with Deng Xiaoping, Hu, Zhao Ziyang, and other Chinese leaders. He personally arranged the itinerary of the Chinese delegation, headed by Peng Zhen, to the commemoration of the thirty-fifth anniversary of the founding of the DPRK in September 1983, and accompanied the delegation to Wonsan. Hour-long television broadcasts showed the lavish reception accorded Kim Chong Il in China and his prominent role as escort of Peng Zhen and his party. In addition, during a visit to Pyongyang in November 1984, Mikhail Kapitsa, the senior Soviet foreign ministry official in charge of Asian affairs, called on Kim Chong Il. Thus, Kim Chong Il entered the sphere of international relations, beginning with North Korea's two socialist neighbors. As he held positions only in the party, not in the government, he did not regularly meet foreign visitors.

Kim Il Sung's 50-day trip to the Soviet Union and Eastern Europe opened a new stage in the rise of Kim Chong Il and further solidified his position as his father's anointed successor. The media reported the son's activities with unprecedented frequency as he in turn visited various parts of North Korea, giving on-the-spot-guidance like his father and urging functionaries and workers to set new records in honor of Kim Il Sung's historic trip abroad. On Kim Il Sung's return, the party's Central Committee met in plenary session at Chongjin to sum up the results of his trip. A special article on the session published shortly thereafter attributed the high regard in which the KWP was held by fraternal parties to its solution of the problem of leadership succession.

Our party has become a great and proud party which has most brilliantly solved the question of inheriting the revolutionary cause, because it has held the dear Comrade Kim Chong Il in high esteem as a sole successor to the great leader Comrade Kim Il Sung. . . . Indeed, the dear Comrade Kim Chong Il is a great ideological theoretician who has brightly illuminated the future path which our people and contemporary era should follow, showing very profound and rich ideological and theoretical wisdom. . . . our party has solved the question concerning the inheritance of the *chu che* revolutionary cause in the most brilliant manner in history. . . . an immortal contribution to the strengthening and developing of the international communist movement and the carrying out of the anti-imperialist cause for independence.[31]

North Korean officials and the media increasingly praise Kim Chong Il not just for his contributions to theory, but also for his present and future leadership. For example, Premier Kang Song-san, in an article celebrating the fortieth anniversary of the KWP, declared: "Our people firmly foresee the brilliant future of the Korean revolution and of the nation from the great leadership of the dear Comrade Kim Chong Il, who is endlessly glorifying the *chu che* lineage and vigorously leading the building of the party and the revolutionary cause."[32] Prince Norodom Sihanouk, who resides three months of each year in the palace in Pyongyang built for him by Kim Il Sung, told journalists in July 1985 that Kim Chong Il "is now leading the country."[33] A U.S. scholar visiting North Korea in the summer of 1985 reported that father and son were invariably mentioned together at briefings, and plaques recording their visits to various places were mounted side by side. He even saw a news program on television in which a story on Kim Chong Il preceded one on Kim Il Sung.

Prospects for the Succession

Kim Il Sung's determination to prepare the way for his son to succeed is clear. The legitimacy and desirability of the succession has become an article of faith in the Kim cult. The North Korean propaganda organs have engaged in a massive campaign to convince people not only that Kim Chong Il is the sole qualified successor, but that Kim Il Sung's decision to transfer power to him is a brilliant stroke viewed with admiration throughout the world that precludes a struggle for power such as had occurred in other Communist countries.

Whether Kim Chong Il will in actuality be able to take over smoothly remains in question. Several factors work in his favor. The Confucian virtue of filial piety is still highly valued in North Korea. Kim Chong Il constantly displays his loyalty to his father and to his father's ideology. The idea of his succeeding is unlikely to encounter psychological resistance, especially in a country where children are brought up to revere

Kim Il Sung as the father of all the people. Even in South Korea the practice of a father's making a son his successor in a business (including the giant conglomerates) is widely accepted, provided the son subsequently proves his competence.

Another advantage is the long period of training and experience that Kim Chong Il has enjoyed. The longer Kim Il Sung lives, the smoother the transition is likely to be, as Kim Chong Il increasingly takes over decisionmaking responsibilities under his father's watchful eye. The lengthy process of grooming also has given Kim Il Sung time to build a base of political support for his son and to remove those who oppose him. This presumably was a motivation for some of the many changes in leadership that occurred at the sixth party congress, although too little is known of politics within the DPRK to judge with any assurance how much opposition to Kim Chong Il's succession may have existed at high levels within the party.

Articles in the party media during 1984, warning against factionalism and calling for steel-like unity in the party, suggest that opposition to the succession is feared. Recalling the factionalism of 1956, they urge party members "to correctly understand the essence and poisonous nature of factionalism by closely studying the experiences and lessons of our party in the struggle against factionalists, and to always be vigilant against the ideological trend of parochialism and nepotism—the hotbed of factionalism."[34] Ignoring the irony of denouncing nepotism while praising Kim Il Sung's plan for hereditary succession, the media point out that "today our revolutionary cause has developed onto a new, higher stage. With the advance of the revolution, many difficult and complicated revolutionary missions have emerged, and the class struggle has further intensified."[35] Consequently, even though the KWP has achieved great unity and cohesion "unprecedented in history" as the result of the "outstanding and tested leadership of the dear leader Comrade Kim Chong Il," that is not good enough. This article, which uses the term "unity and cohesion" forty times in the space of three pages, continues

we should never be satisfied with the results which we have already achieved in the struggle for the party's unity and cohesion. Our revolution has not ended yet. We should continue to struggle strenuously. Moreover, when imperialism exists and the class struggle continues, we should endlessly stage the struggle for the party's unity and cohesion, not stopping even a moment. We should defend, generation after generation, and further glorify the unity and cohesion of our party and revolutionary ranks, which are united as one around the great leader and the party.[36]

In the process of succeeding his father Kim Chong Il will face three critical tests: (1) accelerating economic development, (2) perpetuating the myth of the Kim cult, and (3) maintaining support among the military.

As first discussed in Chapter 3 and as will be expanded in a later section of this chapter, North Korea has encountered serious problems in its economic development, and its rate of growth has slowed significantly in the 1980s. During 1983 and 1984 Kim Chong Il's name was linked repeatedly with large projects and with campaigns to accelerate economic growth. He was credited with stirring workers to achieve the "speed of the eighties," a modernized version of the speed battles he initiated in the 1970s and the earlier Chollima campaign. He gave guidance on achieving a "revolution" in the production of consumer goods in order to provide greater material incentives for the workers. He received credit for resolving serious problems in the construction of the Nampo dike and lockgate and other major construction projects.

As of 1985, Kim Chong Il's name had not been linked with the drive to expand foreign economic relations, a major policy shift made in 1984. Kim Il Sung has been the sponsor of that move. If, as seems probable, the economic opening to the outside is a long-term strategy of critical importance to North Korea's economic growth, Kim Chong Il must eventually take over responsibility for it, as he assumes more and more of his father's duties. Success, or lack of it, in promoting North Korea's economic growth will become an important criterion by which Kim Chong Il's competence will be judged.

Another severe test for Kim Chong Il's leadership will be to maintain faith in the cloistered Kim cult, as the technocratic elite comes into increasing contact with the realities of the outside world through the expansion of foreign economic relations and through dialogue with South Korea. Already articles in the party press reveal concern over this problem.

> Anti-communist and anti-republic rackets by the treacherous puppet Chun Doo Hwan, a filthy stooge of the imperialists, a nation-selling flunkeyist, and a most vicious anti-communist lunatic, have reached their peak. The rascals are slandering and defaming our superior socialist system while embellishing their corrupt reactionary ruling system. . . . Today, the new generation, which has not experienced the trial of bloody class struggle, constitutes the main force of our revolutionary ranks. And today, the infiltration of the reactionary ideas and culture of the imperialists and their stooges is being perpetrated. . . . We should thoroughly block the infiltration of the corrupt bourgeois living style, Western customs, and all sorts of unsound ideological trends and thus see to it that our society is overflowing with the sound traits of working and revolutionary living.[37]

An article published a year later (November 1984) after the North-South dialogue had resumed, was more restrained in its denunciation of South Korea, but betrayed even greater sensitivity to the risks involved in contacts with the South. The article warned against observing only the "superficial phenomena or side aspects" of a social system, while failing to understand its essence. Party organizations should constantly remind people of the miserable life of the past in order to "make all workers more deeply realize that under such a superior socialist system they enjoy an endlessly happy life. . . . Today, our developing revolution and the prevailing situation demand that indoctrination on the superiority of the socialist system be further intensified among party members and the working people."[38]

Finally, and most important, Kim Chong Il must have the support of the military. Few countries are so heavily militarized as North Korea in the proportion of the population in the armed forces, the share of the budget allocated to military preparations, and the importance of the role assigned to the military in achieving the objectives of the leadership. Military personnel constituted 29 percent of the Politburo and 17 percent of the Central Committee elected in 1980, a larger proportion than in 1970.[39] Kim Chong Il will have more difficulty than his father in holding the support of this powerful group. He has neither wartime nor peacetime military experience and lacks a close-knit core of military backers such as the senior commanders of the Kapsan group, who were so important in Kim Il Sung's rise to power.

Kim Il Sung has taken steps to bolster his son's position among the military. When Kim Chong Il appears publicly, Defense Minister O Chin-u is his constant companion. O, two years older than Kim Il Sung and an intimate associate of his from the days of guerrilla warfare in the Kapsan mountains, ranks second in the presidium of the politburo (since the death in 1984 of Kim Il, also a Kapsan comrade of Kim Il Sung) and second in the military commission, just ahead of Kim Chong Il in both bodies. In 1979 O Kuk-yol, ten years older than Kim Chong Il, but also a graduate of the elite Mangyongdae Academy, was promoted over the heads of a number of senior generals to become chief of the general staff of the Korean People's Army. Although evidence that he is closely associated with Kim Chong Il is lacking, his age suggests that he may be closer in outlook to Kim Chong Il than older military leaders.

In July 1984 the *Nodong Sinmun* carried an article by the Vice Minister of Defense, Colonel General Paek Hak-nim, attesting to Kim Chong Il's leadership over the military forces: "Dear Comrade Kim Chong Il, who is brilliantly realizing the great Comrade Kim Il Sung's military ideology and policies, is wisely leading today the work to strengthen and develop our People's Army. . . . The firm credo of our People's Army . . . is to defend to the death the party central committee headed by the great leader Comrade Kim Il Sung and to unswervingly and unconditionally implement all lines, policies, orders and directives being put forth by the dear Comrade Kim Chong Il."[40] Again in April 1985, General Paek wrote that "Dear Comrade Kim Chong Il" was devoting great effort to strengthening and developing the armed forces. He said that all ranks were "acting only under the leadership of the party center."[41]

No matter what Kim Il Sung may do in his remaining years to give Kim Chong Il experience in governing and to build a solid base of political support for him, when the father goes the son will be on his own. Only then will Kim Chong Il's political skill and administrative competence be fully tested. In Taiwan, another political entity with a Confucian tradition and also locked in a military confrontation with a rival government, Chiang Kai-shek successfully passed the baton to his son, Chiang Ching-kuo, after a long period of training. The two situations differ, however, in important ways. Chiang Kai-shek, like Kim Il Sung, was the unchallenged paramount leader in a one-party political system, but without the extreme personality cult, the high degree of regimentation, and the closed-door policy existing in North Korea. And too, Taiwan has been outstandingly successful in export-led economic growth. Thus, when Chiang Ching-kuo assumed power he did not have the double burden faced by Kim Chong Il of maintaining the Kim cult myth, while trying to effect a drastic change in economic policy by expanding economic relations with the outside world. Chiang had only to continue long-standing and successful economic policies managed by experienced technocrats. He paid due filial respect to his father's memory, but not having to contend with an overblown personality cult, was able to adopt courses of action and a personal governing style quite different from those of his father. Moreover, his administrative experience, unlike that of Kim Chong Il, included high-level positions for extended periods in both the security services and the military, as well as posts in party and economic affairs. His was a better-rounded experience than that of Kim Chong Il, which enabled Chiang over the years to construct a network of loyal supporters in critical areas.

Economic Change in South Korea

After several boom years in the late 1970s, South Korea's overheated economy plunged into deep recession in 1980, registering a negative growth rate of 5.2 percent, the first year since the Korean War that the economy had not expanded. The slump resulted from a conjunction of several factors. Strong foreign demand for South Korean goods between 1976 and 1977, combined with Park Chung-hee's decision to expand the heavy and chemical industries rapidly, produced a surge in investment, which peaked at 36 percent of GNP in 1979. Wage increases during the boom years outpaced the rise in productivity, weakening the international competitiveness of South Korean manufactures. The too hasty expansion of the heavy and chemical industries produced excess capacity. Wholesale prices rose 11.6 percent in 1978 and 18.8 percent in 1979. Thus, the South Korean economy was in a vulnerable condition when struck by three blows in quick succession: the assassination of Park Chung-hee, the 136 percent jump in oil prices in 1979 and 1980, and the failure of the 1980 rice harvest.

Faced with a worldwide recession and burdened with overcapacity, Korean businessmen reduced investment. The Korean people saved less in order to maintain their life-style in a period of soaring prices. The wholesale price index shot up by nearly 40 percent in 1980. In order to prevent the economy from slumping further, the government maintained its public sector investment, even though it had to borrow heavily from abroad in order to do so. Total external debt rose from $20.5 billion in 1979 to $32.5 billion in 1981.[42]

Foreign borrowing and public works expenditures helped the Korean economy through the difficult years of 1980 and 1981. By 1982 domestic economic activity picked up and exports began to recover, causing the economy to grow by 5.6 percent. The level of foreign indebtedness continued to rise, reaching $40 billion in 1983, but the rate of increase slowed.

The year 1983 was good for the South Korean economy. Taking advantage of the recovery in the United States, where growth exceeded that in Japan and the European Economic Community (EEC), South Korea increased the value of its exports by 17 percent. GNP growth for the year rebounded to more than 9 percent. Moreover, Korea's economic managers succeeded in bringing inflation down sharply. The rate of increase in wholesale prices dropped from nearly 40 percent in 1980 to just over 20 percent in 1981, to 4.7 percent in 1982, and to 0.8 percent in 1983. To hold prices stable in a year of 9 percent economic growth was a remarkable and unprecedented achievement for South Korea. Unlike Taiwan, where the authorities placed a high priority on price stability, the Koreans had traditionally been willing to pay a price in inflation in order to grow faster.[43]

Growth slowed a little during 1984, but still attained a respectable 7.6 percent. Growth reflected an increase in exports of 17 percent, taking advantage of the continued expansion of the U.S. economy that took 35 percent of South Korea's exports, an increase over the 30 percent that had traditionally gone to the United States. Inflation remained low, with wholesale prices rising just 0.7 percent. Foreign debt continued to rise, but at a much slower pace than during the early 1980s, reaching $43.1 billion in 1984. South Korea maintained a good credit rating and had no difficulty in obtaining needed loans.[44] South Korea's revised five-year plan (1982–1986) put forward several objectives: to achieve an annual real growth of 7.5 percent, to maintain price stability, and to reach a balance on current account. The World Bank judged these goals to be achievable, given South Korea's past record of overfulfilling plans, but difficult, in light of the uncertainties in the world economy.[45] Slow global growth in 1985 held the increase in South Korea's GNP to 5.1 percent, but exports recovered in the first half of 1986, causing government forecasters to predict a growth rate of 8 to 9 percent for the year.

Export Growth

South Korea's economic planners considered the 7.5 percent annual growth target as the minimum needed to absorb the annual increase in the labor force of 3 percent for the next few years. Failure to provide enough jobs would aggravate the strains in the political system discussed above. Economic growth at that level will depend on the ability to increase exports by some 10 percent each year. South Korea, where exports constitute 37 percent of its gross domestic product, as compared to Japan's 14 percent, is thus critically dependent on the condition of the world economy.[46] World trade, which expanded at an 8.5 percent annual rate from 1963 to 1972 and at nearly 6 percent from 1973 to 1979, slumped to slightly over 1 percent from 1980 to 1983. It is unlikely to regain during the remainder of the 1980s the historically unprecedented rates of growth of the previous two decades.[47] South Korea faces more demanding conditions than in the past in which to strive to reach its projected rate of economic growth.

In order to expand exports at the desired rate, South Korea must continue the structural change away from labor-intensive light manufactures into capital and skill-intensive products. In the five years from 1978 to 1983, light manufactures had already dropped from 54 percent to 40 percent of total exports.[48] Countries with lower wage rates moved into South Korea's traditional markets for textiles, footware, plywood, toys, and transistors, but South Korea was able to compensate for these losses by exporting more ships, iron and steel, electronics, chemicals, and machinery. During the remainder of the 1980s the Koreans will be fighting a rearguard action to prevent further erosion of textile exports, which in 1983 still constituted 27 percent of total merchandise exports. The textile industry probably will be able to slow its relative decline by the installation of labor-saving machinery and by improving its design and marketing capability. Nevertheless, that industry, facing the twin threats of protectionism and competition from lower cost producers, can no longer be relied on as a major contributor to South Korea's export growth.

The areas where gains in exports are most likely to be achieved are steel, shipbuilding, machinery, electronics, and automobiles, although significant impediments exist in all of them. The Pohang steel complex, which has 8.4 million tons of South Korea's 13 million ton capacity, is the world's lowest cost steel producer. South Korea exported nearly half of the 12 million tons of steel produced in 1983. But prospects for large increases in exports will be constrained by rising domestic demand until the completion of a new 2.7 million ton capacity mill in 1988, as well as by resistance from steelmakers in the United States and Japan to steel imports. South Korea's shipbuilding industry is also highly competitive, but it must await the recovery of the world shipping industry. Production of general machinery is a promising field for increased exports, provided that the mostly small and medium firms in this business succeed in upgrading their technical skills and the quality of their products. A fund set up to lend exclusively to small and medium machinery firms should stimulate this process. South Korea has established itself in the lower end of the electronics industry, producing largely consumer appliances. Whether it can move up to the high-tech end of the scale, as the government hopes, remains to be seen. The pace of change and the R&D capability required in this industry dominated by the United States, Japan, and West Germany makes competition difficult for a newly industrialized country. An area certain to produce increased exports is the production of automobiles and auto parts. First introduced into Canada in 1985 and the United States in 1986, sedans produced by Hyundai have sold well. Cooperation by the principal U.S. and Japanese companies with Korean companies appears to ensure both the technological and the marketing facilities required by the South Korean automobile industry.[49]

Korean officials and businessmen have expressed grave concern that the rise of protectionism, especially in the United States (discussed in Chapter 6) would block efforts to reach export targets. The bulk of Korea's traditional exports have been in clothing, footwear, consumer appliances, and steel—industries in the United States and Europe that have been hard hit by imports and where political pressures for protection are high. Diversification of export products and markets would ease this problem but will be difficult to do quickly.

Structural and Policy Adjustments

The structural adjustments and policy changes instituted in 1979 were interrupted briefly by Park's death, then continued under Chun Doo

Hwan. These included the consolidation and rationalization of heavy industry, cuts in the proportion of loans going to the *chaebol* and increases in those going to small- and medium-sized firms, reduction in inflation and foreign borrowing, less government intervention in economic decisonmaking, and the privatization of commercial banks.

In order to eliminate the duplication in heavy industry, the government in 1980 began a process of forcing mergers and transfers of ownership, so that machinery subsectors such as large diesel engines, automobiles, and heavy electrical equipment would be produced by a single company, rather than several. Duplication and excess capacity has been reduced by these moves, but not entirely eliminated.

The oversupply of world shipping and the drop in overseas construction contracts has hurt many firms in these industries. Here, too, the government stepped in, bringing about mergers, helping in the disposition of insolvent firms, and, in general, producing a realignment, so that firms in these industries will be fewer and stronger, better able to compete under adverse conditions.

During the period of high investment in heavy industry, the *chaebol* received the lion's share of government-allocated, low interest loans, forcing small and medium firms to depend on the curb market, where interest rates were very high. The government came under attack for unjustified favoritism in lending to the *chaebol;* the conglomerates were increasingly seen by the public as symbolic of a growing inequality in the distribution of wealth. The technocrats also recognized that a sizable proportion of innovation and flexible response to market opportunities came from the smaller firms. Consequently, the government required the banks to reduce lending to the *chaebol* and increase lending to the small and medium firms. The government also took steps to limit the lines of business the *chaebol* could undertake and tried in other ways to slow their expansion. The collapse of the sixth largest *chaebol*, Kukje, in 1985 shook the business world and illustrated the danger in excessive short-term borrowing and overly rapid expansion.[50]

The economy was becoming too complex for the government to intervene to the degree that it had in the past. Hence, measures were taken to allow business decisions to be determined to a greater extent by the marketplace. The chief move in this direction was the transfer of the commercial banks to private hands, so that loan decisions would depend on commercial considerations rather than direction by the government. A problem in this connection has been the concern that control of the banks would pass to the *chaebol*, thus strengthening their oligopolistic position in the economy. The government also announced that by 1986 nearly all the discriminatory restrictions on the 42 foreign banks would be removed, allowing much freer competition between foreign and local banks.[51]

All of these policy changes have gone forward with varying degrees of success. Limiting governmental intervention is likely to be a slow and long-term process, because of ingrained practices and the reluctance of bureaucrats to relinquish power.

Foreign Debt, Investment, Savings, and Inflation

The Korean government relied on heavy borrowing to ease passage through the crisis of 1980 and 1981, but its economic decisionmakers recognized that borrowing would have to be cut back in the 1980s because of the overextended international financial system and the uncertain prospects for continued rapid expansion of exports. In 1983 South Korea had the fourth largest external debt in the world after Mexico, Brazil, and Argentina. Consequently, the revised five-year plans provided for attaining a balance in the current account by 1986.

The rate of increase in the foreign debt slowed dramatically in 1984, encouraging confidence in the feasibility of the long-term goal of reducing the size of the net foreign debt. A projection for the sixth five-year plan (1987–1991) made public by the Economic Planning Board in July 1985 showed small annual current account surpluses throughout the period and estimated the outstanding foreign debt in 1991 at $51.6 billion, with the *net* foreign debt at only $29.7 billion as a result of an increase in foreign assets. South Korean officials expressed confidence that the debt could be managed without difficulty, as the debt service ratio in 1985 stood at 15 percent, far lower than those of other heavily indebted countries.[52] By mid-1986 the surge in exports appeared likely to produce a current account surplus for the first time since the Korean War.

To maintain a satisfactory growth rate while cutting back on foreign borrowing will require an increase in domestic savings to support the level of investment needed. The official plan provides for savings equivalent to 29.3 percent of GNP, slightly higher than the 28.1 percent that prevailed during 1979, in order to permit a level of fixed investment around 31 percent of GNP. Reaching the required target will require continued low inflation, appropriate management of the financial sector so as to encourage private and corporate saving, and an increase in government saving.

Economic Change in North Korea

At the beginning of the 1980s, economic growth in North Korea continued to be governed by the second seven-year lan (1978–1984), which straddled the change of decades. The plan, presented by Premier Yi Chong-ok to the SPA in December 1977, called for increasing industrial output 2.2 times, an annual increase of 12.1 percent. The targets to be reached by 1984, as given in Yi's report, were later supplemented by Kim Il Sung in an October 1980 report to the Sixth KWP Congress[53] with a set of more ambitious targets to be reached by the end of the decade.

	1984	1989
Electric power	50–60 billion kwh	100 billion kwh
Coal	70–80 million tons	120 million tons
Steel	7.4–8 million tons	15 million tons
Nonferrous metals	1 million tons	1.5 million tons
Cement	12–13 million tons	20 million tons
Chemical fertilizers	5 million tons	7 million tons
Grain	10 million tons	15 million tons
Fabrics	800 million meters	1,500 million meters

The emphasis in Yi's report suggested that the principal bottlenecks in the North Korean economy continued to be mining and electric power. Yi particularly stressed the need for greater coal production to supply the growing number of thermal power plants. Increased steel production and the manufacture of larger numbers of heavy machines also received strong emphasis. Yi described rapid improvements in transportation as an "urgent task." Agricultural production was to be raised by the provision of more fertilizer and by the reclamation of 100,000 *chongbo* of tidal marshes to increase the amount of arable land. The 1984 target for the increase in production of consumer goods was only slightly lower than for producer goods, but received less emphasis in Yi's report. Sixty percent of consumer goods were to be produced by local industry.[54]

The most striking aspect of Yi's report was the total absence of any reference to foreign trade. Instead, he called for increasing "the *chu che* character" of North Korea's industry, accelerating the application of science to the economy, and "occupying the great heights of the second seven-year plan with our own strength, technology, and domestic resources." He urged full use of existing industrial capacity, strict conservation of electric power, fuel, and raw materials, and greater efforts to produce such products as coke and sugar from domestic resources. Even more remarkable was the speech to the SPA by Kye Ung-tae, vice premier and minister of foreign trade, in which the only reference to foreign trade was to the need to ensure domestic production of "certain industrial raw materials and machines previously imported."[55]

The heightened stress on self-reliance reflected the collapse of the policy of turning to the West for modern technology (which Kim Il Sung had personally endorsed as recently as March 1975), and Soviet demands for debt repayments. When Yi made his report, the burden of debt to the Soviet Union, China, and Western creditors must have seemed crushing. Initial arrangements for a stretch-out in payments were in place, but default had ended access to credits from Western Europe or Japan, and neither the Soviets nor the Chinese were inclined to help the North Koreans recover from the effects of their mistaken policies. Repaying debts while maintaining the flow of essential imports would strain Pyongyang's export capacity. The instinctive North Korean action, given the long-standing philosophical commitment to self-reliance, was to find ways to reduce dependence on imports.

Slower Growth

The North Koreans themselves anticipated a marked slowdown in economic growth during the second seven-year plan, as compared to the previous plan period. Kim Il Sung claimed that industrial output had increased 15.9 percent annually during the 1970s, but the target for annual increases in industrial production during the seven-year plan (1978–1984) was set at 12.1 percent.

Slower growth was inevitable as the North Korean economy became increasingly complex, particularly given the continued large commitment of investment resources to heavy industry, plus military expenditures estimated by analysts in Washington at not less than 15 percent and perhaps as large as 25 percent of GNP. The slowing growth in itself held down funds available for investments, while the trend toward more capital-intensive plants increased the amount of investment funds needed for each unit of increased output. The *Nodong Sinmun* called on all sectors and units to do more with available labor, equipment, and materials, so that production and construction could be accelerated "without tremendous investment." It inveighed against waste, asking everyone to conserve "even a watt of power, a lump of coal, or a drop of oil."[56] Foreign plants and machinery bought during the buying spree of the early 1970s were less productive than they might have been had greater attention been paid to the availability of trained technicians to operate them and to the compatibility of the new plant or equipment with the existing industrial structure.

The slower rate of growth was also attributable to the shortage of labor, the mental and physical fatigue of a workforce constantly urged to do more, and the aging of the industrial plant. Unremitting appeals to the North Korean people to work harder and faster gave the outside viewer the impression of a society strained to the limit trying to do too many things with too few resources. Everyone was urged to surpass past records by attaining "the speed of the 80s." The media conjured up an image of a nation under siege, threatened by the United States, South Korea, and Japan, and operating in a wartime atmosphere. Occasional denunciations of idleness and slackness indicated that the effectiveness of the constant exhortations probably had declined. Aging machinery, much of it dating from the 1950s and 1960s, was pushed beyond capacity to meet targets. As in the Soviet Union, the lopsided emphasis on building new plants rather than modernizing existing ones, meant that a large share of production came from obsolescent plants that were inefficient by modern standards.[57]

Frequent appeals in the North Korean media to operate plants at full capacity reflected an endemic problem in the economy: shortfalls and delays in the arrival of supplies at factories created ripple effects throughout the economy, causing many other plants to operate below capacity. Priorities shifted, as first one bottleneck and than another was singled out for special attention. For example, the Central Committee of the KWP held a plenum to criticize the inefficient operation of the railways, clearly a fundamental reason for the inability of many factories to operate at capacity. The meeting attacked practices such as "unnecessary cross-shipments of the same item between localities," "multiple transfer of cargo from one train to another," "massively" transporting cargo that could be handled by a few freight cars, and the failure of enterprises to remove trash and moisture from materials before shipment. Other weaknesses criticized were failure to observe regulations, lack of discipline, and giving priority to the interests of an agency or locality over the interests of the state.[58]

In his New Year's address of January 1985, Kim Il Sung reported that the 1984 economic plan had been successfully fulfilled, but he said nothing about completion of the 1978 to 1984 seven-year plan. He called on officials and workers to keep those familiar bottlenecks, the mining industry and railway transport, "well ahead of all other sectors" and to sharply increase the output of iron and steel.[59] In February 1985, the Central Statistics Board reported the overfulfillment of the seven-year plan in terms of gross output value. The annual growth rate of industrial output was said to have reached 12.2 percent, slightly above the 12.1 percent target.[60] U.S. government analysts calculate that much of the growth occurred between 1978 and 1980 when a number of foreign-built plants reached full capacity and that production slowed substantially during the 1980s. By the end of 1985 no new multiyear plan had been announced, so 1985 probably will be treated as a year of adjustment, as has happened in the past when a new plan was being drawn up.

Shortage of Coal and Power

From the 1960s on North Korea was unable to produce the amounts of coal and electric power required by its ambitious goals of industrial growth. These basic constraints continued to hamper growth in the 1980s. Droughts had reduced the output of hydroelectric power during the 1970s, causing the main emphasis during that decade to be placed on building thermal power stations, although hydropower stations continued to be built. In his report to the Sixth Party Congress in 1980, Kim Il Sung said that thermal power generating capacity had doubled during the decade, bringing it up to over 50 percent of total generating capacity.[61] Increased reliance on thermal power placed heavier demands on coal production, and Kim in a 1982 address, shifted the main emphasis back to the construction of new hydropower plants.[62] Until recently, North Korea had not followed the example of South Korea, where nuclear power plants produced 13 percent of its electricity in 1984. Kim called for construction of nuclear power plants in his 1980 report, but not in subsequent speeches. North Korea has been inclined to continue to rely on its relatively abundant coal and water resources rather than bring in foreign experts and incur the very high foreign exchange costs of turning to nuclear power.[63] In December 1985, however, Pyongyang enlisted Moscow's help in building its first nuclear power plant.[64]

No resource is more fundamental to North Korea's industrial growth than coal. It is consumed directly in factories as well as in the thermal power plants that produce the electricity used in industry and throughout the largely electrified railway system, which hauls 90 percent of all freight in North Korea.[65] It is the principal fuel for household use. It is combined with limestone to produce a synthetic filament—vinalon—for use in the textile industry. Production of coal has become more difficult and costly as mines go deeper. Properly scheduling the transportation of coal has also been a problem, especially in the harvest season, when the need to move crops competes with the need to stockpile coal for winter.

For twenty years the North Korean leadership has stressed the importance of increasing coal production, but rarely has the need been expressed more emphatically than in Kim Il Sung's 1984 New Year's address. "Coal is the food of our *chu che* industry," Kim declared.

Under the slogan: "Increase the coal output first, second, third" this year we should concentrate upon the coal-mining industry and bring about a new upsurge in coal production. . . . State and economic bodies should organize economic work on the principle of subordinating everything to coal production, and the whole country should give active material, technical and manpower support to coal mines. All sectors of the national economy should preferentially supply the coal mines with the equipment and materials required for their production.[66]

Increased Production of Consumer Goods?

In December 1983 a *Nodong Sinmun* editorial entitled "Let Us Bring About an Epochal Turning Point in Improving the People's Living Standard" launched a campaign to increase the production of consumer goods and improve their quality.[67] Kim Il Sung had foreshadowed this shift of emphasis a few months before in his speech on the thirty-fifth anniversary of the founding of the DPRK in which he declared that the drive toward the ten long-term goals should give priority to "a more satisfactory solution of the food and clothing problems, the most important and urgent problems in the people's life."[68] The *Nodong Sinmun* editorial, calling a rise in living standards "one of the most important tasks facing us today," said that more consumer goods "such as oil, meat, eggs, knitwear of various kinds, and textiles should be produced and supplied for production workers to further boost their zeal for production." The editorial continued, "If all people's consumer goods plants—the grain-processing plants, duckling plants, chicken plants, pig plants, and those of many other daily necessities, food and clothing plants—which we have set up through the arduous struggle of self-reliance are put into full operation, we can solve any problem, including that of oil and meat." Success in this campaign to produce more consumer goods clearly required a change in the mind-set of officials long habituated to favoring heavy industry. "The concerned agencies must intensify supervision and control over the phenomenon of ignoring the people's living and not seeking an active production of consumer goods," the editorial declared.

The *Nodong Sinmun*'s opening gun was followed by a series of articles during 1984 stressing various aspects of "the great revolution in light industry," which was "to improve especially the standard of the workers' material and cultural lives within one or two years by rapidly increasing the production of consumer goods."[69] The articles placed the responsibility for meeting the goals of the revolution in light industry primarily on local industries, which produce over half of the nation's light industrial products and which depend mainly on locally available materials. Writers asserted that by stimulating local industries to produce to their full potential, "the amount and kinds of consumer goods can be rapidly expanded without much state investment and the workers' increasing demand can be smoothly met."[70]

The authorities recognized that the "revolution" could not be placed entirely on the shoulders of local industry. The centrally controlled large-scale factories producing consumer goods would also have to increase their production, and all sectors of the economy, including transportation, would have to supply in a timely manner the equipment and materials needed by the consumer goods plants, large and small.[71] Kim Chong Il urged greater specialization in light industry. Goods to be distributed nationally should be produced in a few specialized factories, which could adopt advanced scientific production methods. Products with many components, like bicycles, should be assembled in large plants from parts made in a variety of specialized factories. The article warned, however, that specialization "cannot be realized full scope in a day or two."[72]

The flurry of articles on increasing the production of consumer goods suggests a recognition by the authorities, such as has occurred in other Communist countries in recent years, that workers must be offered greater material rewards if their productivity is to be increased. Exhortation and psychological pressures continued over many years produce diminishing returns. Kim Il Sung candidly acknowledged this problem in a speech to Labor Administration workers in September 1979: "If only the work norms are raised without increasing the reward to the working people, they will dislike the rise of work norms. But if the living allowances, bonus and incentive allowances to the workers are increased in accordance with the rise in work norms, they will actually strive to improve technique, economize labor and materials, and produce more."[73]

Kim failed to point out in his speech that increased cash rewards are of little value as incentives unless there are goods to be bought with the cash. According to defectors from North Korea, increases in wages during the 1970s were accompanied by cuts in grain and oil rations, forcing more purchases on open markets at higher prices, thus sopping up excess currency without increasing consumption. Visitors to North Korea have reported that basic needs in food, clothing, housing, medical care, and education appeared to be taken care of, but that food for the ordinary person lacked variety and most consumer goods were scarce and expensive. Grain is rationed. A Chinese specialist on North Korea estimated that half of the population had to eat a mixture of rice and corn as the principal food instead of the preferred diet of rice. Pyongyang's goal, he said, is to eliminate corn from the human diet and feed it to animals to increase the meat supply. Comparing living standards in the Korean minority Yanbian District in China with those across the border in North Korea, he found housing better in North Korea, but consumer goods more plentiful in China and food also better there, including more meat.[74] Kim Il Sung would not have stressed the urgent need to resolve the "problems" of food and clothing if supplies of such commodities were plentiful.

Efforts to increase the output of consumer goods at this time may have resulted not only from a recognition of the need to offer material rewards to boost the worker's "zeal for production," but also from the effect of the Chinese example and the intensified competition on the world stage with the highly productive South Korean economy. During the long train trip in 1982 to and from Sichuan Province, where the Chinese first tried out their successful economic reforms, Deng Xiaoping no doubt spent hours explaining to Kim Il Sung the Chinese strategy for stimulating economic growth by greater emphasis on light industry. The impact of the South Korean example must be even greater than that of China, if North Korea is to enter a period of expanded contact both with South Korea and with the outside world, prompting comparisons of living conditions in the two Koreas.

On August 3, 1984, Kim Chong Il took personal charge of the campaign to increase the production of consumer goods with the publication of a document, "On Further Upgrading the People's Standard of Living."[75] The products of this mass movement came to be known as "August 3 people's consumer goods." In his New Year's speech in January 1985, Kim Il Sung noted the need to markedly improve the people's standard of living in order to show the superiority of the socialist system, but he continued to place primary emphasis on the mining industry, railway transport, steel production, and the "great nature transformation projects," such as the Nampo lockgate.[76]

Neither Kim Il Sung's speech nor the subsequent report to the Supreme People's Assembly by the vice premier responsible for light industry, Kim Pok-sin, suggested a significant shift in investment from heavy to light industry. On the contrary, Kim Pok-sin declared that the "new upsurges" in consumer goods production were to result from "the maximum utilization of the existing foundation of light industry production." Only a single reference in her speech to the planned introduction of high-speed textile equipment indicated an intention to modernize existing factories.[77] A *Nodong Sinmun* editorial in October 1985 called on all branches of industry to give the production of consumer goods priority over other sectors and to supply light industrial plants preferentially with the materials that they needed.[78] That this editorial represented a basic shift from the priorities outlined by Kim Il Sung at the beginning of the year seems unlikely.

Much of the responsibility for increasing the production of consumer goods was placed on 700 factory work teams and 19,000 work teams in urban districts and on cooperative farms that had been organized since August 1984. These teams made use of by-products and waste materials from factories and other locally available raw materials to produce daily necessities. Production of consumer goods by such part-time efforts was referred to as a "mass struggle," and functionaries were urged to awaken the masses, heighten their will to work, and mobilize undiscovered resources.[79]

What will result from the newly evinced interest in rapidly increasing the production of consumer goods remains uncertain. Assigning workers to work teams to produce consumer goods from factory waste seems like an inefficient, labor-intensive mode of production ill-suited to a country short of labor. Shortage of labor in North Korea also rules out one of China's most effective measures: allowing the unemployed or underemployed to become private entrepreneurs, turning out a wide variety of consumer goods.

Expansion of Foreign Trade

Kim Il Sung's report to the Sixth Party Congress in October 1980 placed the traditional heavy stress on self-reliance:

> To put the national economy on the *chu che* basis we should solve before anything else the problems of raw materials, fuel and power more satisfactorily by using our domestic resources. . . . Industries which use imported raw materials and fuel must be gradually reorganized into domestically fed industries. . . . We must resolutely oppose subservience to great powers, fear of technology and all other negative ideological inclinations and make strenuous efforts to effect the modernization of the national economy in an all-people movement on the principle of self-reliance.[80]

Kim's report was not as totally negative toward foreign trade as Yi Chong-ok's report three years earlier. Foreign trade had surged in 1979 to a level nearly double the low years of 1977 and 1978.[81] Perhaps Kim was encouraged by this success to sound a more positive note; he stressed the importance to economic development of promoting foreign trade quickly, improving the quality of exports and the punctuality of delivery, and diversifying trading partners. Kim called for increasing foreign trade 4.2 times during the 1980s. An increase of this magnitude would swell two-way trade to over $9 billion by 1989, not a large figure compared to South Korea's, which was already nearly $60 billion in 1984, but a radical change for North Korea.

The North Korean economy failed to respond to Kim's call. During the years 1980 through 1983, instead of advancing toward Kim's optimistic target, foreign trade slipped back from the 1979 peak and remained there, stagnant. Kim himself turned his attention to other matters. His 1982 New Year's speech again put heavy stress on chu che, and neither that speech, his 1983 New Year's speech, nor his September 1983 speech on the thirty-fifth anniversary of the founding of the DPRK contained any reference to foreign economic relations.

Nineteen eighty-four brought a sweeping change in Pyongyang's attitude. A January resolution of the Supreme People's Assembly somewhat defensively asserted that the country had long stressed the importance of foreign trade.[82] Now that a solid, self-reliant economy had been established, the resolution continued, the time had come to expand urgently the scope of foreign trade and other forms of economic and technical cooperation. "Only by widely developing external economic relations, including trade, can we accelerate the country's economic construction and improve the people's living standard." First priority should go to cooperation with the Third World, second to economic cooperation with socialist countries—which still constituted the largest share of North Korean trade—and third priority to trade with capitalist countries "that respect our country's independence." Trade with socialist countries should be expanded "on a grand scale" increasing its value more than ten times during the next five to six years.[83]

While North Korea's new stress on foreign trade seemed a pragmatic move to attack problems created by excessive self-reliance, its insistence on Third World cooperation as "the major direction" of external economic activities continued to show a marked ideological bias. Trade with nonaligned countries had never exceeded 20 percent of North Korea's foreign trade, even in years of substantial purchases by Saudi Arabia and Iran. Political attachment to the nonaligned movement probably dictated this short-lived overemphasis on Third World trade.

Upon return from his trip to the Soviet Union and Eastern Europe, Kim Il Sung presided over a plenary session of the Central Committee that reiterated the importance of foreign economic relations and shifted emphasis from the Third World to trade with the socialist countries. A report on the meeting declared: "The realities of socialist economic construction, which has entered into a new high stage, urgently demand that external economic relations be further developed to fully meet the growing needs of the national economy for various equipment and materials." In stressing the need for "attaching primary importance to the world's socialist market in developing foreign trade," the report acknowledged that technical exchange and cooperation with socialist countries in the past had made great contributions to developing the national economy.[84] A *Nodong Sinmun* editorial in December 1984 noted that although the socialist market was smaller than the capitalist market, it was ample to satisfy the requirements of the socialist countries and "had always occupied an overwhelming position" in North Korea's foreign trade. Trade with capitalist countries was not excluded, but "in terms of the level of development of science and technology, the socialist countries are ahead of the capitalist countries in many fields. In fact, on very few occasions will socialist countries be unable to meet the demands today for what is required in economic construction by relying on the socialist market."[85]

Another *Nodong Sinmun* editorial a few days later called for an all-out effort to fulfill the export plan, pointing out that Kim Il Sung, on his return from the East European trip, had "urged drastically increasing the volume of foreign trade." Concerned government agencies "must give priority to the supply of raw materials, fuel and other resources to the plants and enterprises producing export items." Transportation units must deliver needed materials to such plants "in a preferential manner."[86]

An article by Choe Chong-kun, DPRK minister of foreign trade, published in the party's theoretical journal, *Kulloja*, in December 1984, spelled out the rationale for a rapid increase in foreign trade, pointing out not only the economic need, but also the contribution made by foreign trade to enhancing the prestige and dignity of the country.[87] A series of editorials and special articles in *Nodong Sinmun* throughout 1985 continued to stress the importance of foreign trade; they took on a tone of added urgency as the time for meeting year-end targets in exports approached. Like the appeals for stepping up production of consumer goods and meeting other high priority goals, an October 31 editorial urged that "everything should be made to serve the production of export goods, and priority should be given to the production of export goods. . . . Therefore, the entire party, the whole country, and all people must exert all-out efforts and struggle for the production of export goods and for the attainment of this year's export goals."[88]

Another indication of North Korea's intention to turn away from the excessive self-reliance of the past was a special article in *Nodong Sinmun* acknowledging the need to introduce advanced science and technology from other countries. The article urged scientists and technicians to keep abreast of world trends in their specialized fields, to learn foreign languages, and to translate foreign technical and scientific books. Among the fields marked for special emphasis was "resolving the scientific and technical problems concerning the use of atomic energy."[89]

North Korea showed heightened interest in foreign trade in actions as well as in words. Foreign Minister Kim Yong-nam and other officials inspected the special economic zones in China, including Shenzhen, near Hong Kong, which by December 1984 had hosted twenty different North Korean delegations, although a senior North Korean official told Japanese journalists that his country did not intend to set up similar zones.[90] The DPRK invited a large number of foreign visitors to Pyongyang to celebrate the twenty-fifth anniversary of the establishment of its Foreign Trade Bank.[91] The Korean Central News Agency reported that port capacity had nearly doubled over the previous ten years and that the number of ships in North Korea's merchant fleet had increased eightfold.[92]

In September 1984 the DPRK announced the text of a law authorizing joint ventures between North Korea and foreign companies.[93] According to a senior North Korean official, the law provided better tax advantages than those offered by China and Western Europe.[94] In February 1985 ground was broken for the construction of a 46-story hotel in Pyongyang in a joint venture with a French company; about the same time a department store jointly operated with a Japanese firm opened in Pyongyang. By September 1985 two additional joint ventures were reported to have been agreed upon: an instrument manufacturing plant in Nampo linked to a Japanese company and a tire factory in Hamhung with ties to a Hong Kong firm. North Korean authorities had thirty additional joint venture proposals under consideration, the Peking *People's Daily* reported.[95]

Although Kim Il Sung has clearly decided to move away from the excessive self-reliance of the past, the obstacles to a rapid increase in foreign trade are substantial. A significant increase in the level of exports is required in order to maintain imports of essential fuel and raw materials and to pay interest on the foreign debt of $2 to $2.5 billion, most of it owed to the Soviet Union and China. Chinese analysts discounted the burden on the North Korean economy of the debts to the Soviet Union and China, saying that payment of these government-to-government obligations could be postponed. They admitted, however, that acquiring the hard currency with which to repay Japanese and West European creditors was a serious problem. Interest payments on the $350 million owed to Japanese firms have been rescheduled twice, in 1979 and 1983, and as of December 1984, interest payments had again been in default since June 1983. Sizable sales of gold in Western Europe in 1984 enabled Pyongyang to resume interest payments to Sweden and Austria, but in early 1985 Premier Kang Song-san reportedly cancelled a trip to Western Europe because of differences with Sweden, Austria, Finland, and Switzerland over failure to meet debt repayment schedules.[96] In April 1985, Iraq informed all representatives from non-aligned countries at the United Nations that North Korea had flagrantly violated its obligation to begin repayment on January 1, 1985, of a $50 million loan that Iraq had made to Pyongyang in 1978.[97] In February 1986 Indonesia seized a North Korean merchant ship because North Korea failed to pay a $5 million debt owed since January 1985 to Indonesian rubber exporters.[98] Little response could be expected in Western countries to North Korea's bid for foreign capital investment until it overcame its reputation as a bad credit risk and made scheduled payments of principal and interest on its hard currency foreign debt regularly and on time.

In turning to foreign trade to resolve its economic difficulties, North Korea has been influenced by Chinese experience, as shown by the numerous official delegations to Shenzhen and the promulgation of a joint venture law, resembling that of China. But North Korea will have greater difficulty than China in following Deng's dictum: "no progress without opening to the outside (*bu kai fang, bu jinbu*). China's opening to the outside came in the context of the overthrow of the Gang of Four, which made possible comprehensive economic, political, and ideological reforms, including rejection of the closed-door policy of the discredited leadership. The expansion of foreign trade and the attraction of foreign investment was facilitated in China by the simultaneous decentralization of economic decisionmaking, the revamping of the legal system, and increasing resort to the market mechanism and material incentives.

North Korea's tentative moves to open its economy have been made under a leader whose political philosophy was built around the concept of maximum self-reliance. Kim Il Sung's *chu che* philosophy has been the basis for his claim to a preeminent position among Third World leaders and for North Korea's assertion of moral superiority over a South Korea heavily dependent on its economic connections with the capitalist world. North Korea cannot reject *chu che* as Deng rejected the policies of the Gang of Four; he must gradually redefine it so as to accommodate the idea of substantial foreign trade and investment. The process of redefinition was underway in 1984, but persisting ideological fetters and bureaucratic habits probably will impose a greater drag on change than existed in China.

A well-informed Chinese analyst denied that the *chu che* philosophy would be an obstacle to North Korea's opening to the outside. The essence of *chu che*, he said, is North Korea's ability to decide its policies independently, free of outside pressure, not the extent to which its economy is dependent on foreign trade and investment. He averred that the 70 percent self-dependence provided for in the second seven-year plan could be altered, although not so much as to make North Korea as dependent as South Korea is on external economic relations. North

Korea would prefer to develop more slowly rather than become that dependent. This Chinese analysis glosses over Pyongyang's insistence in its promotion of *chu che* to the Third World that economic self-reliance is essential to political independence.

Chinese analysts predicted that North Korea's opening to the outside would proceed more slowly than China's, but for practical, rather than ideological reasons. North Korea's basic problem, not easily remedied, is its lack of manufactured products suitable for export. Most of its factories, supplied by the Soviet Union and China in the 1950s and 1960s, are obsolescent. Their products, although usable within North Korea, are not competitive on the world market.[99] Technology in North Korea is old-fashioned, in some areas even below the Chinese level. North Koreans are unfamiliar with technological levels in the rest of the world; they are rarely invited to international technical conferences because sponsors wish to avoid political disputes between the two Koreas. Thus, backward technology is North Korea's greatest handicap in promoting exports to increase foreign trade.

North Korea's ports are inferior to those of China, and its air links with the outside are poorly developed. North Korea lacks a Hong Kong, which provided China with easy access to the outside and contained a technologically advanced Chinese society that could make an important contribution to China's modernization. North Korea has nothing comparable to the sizable corps of Chinese scientists and engineers educated in the United States before 1950 and the large number of Chinese who have risen to important positions in U.S. universities, business, and government during the past thirty years. Chinese-Americans and Chinese in key posts in China trained in the United States have been instrumental in restoring the flow of technology from the United States to China. For all of these reasons, the Chinese analysts concluded, North Korea's opening to the outside could not develop as rapidly as China's had. The one advantage held by North Korea over China is the small size of the country in which orders from the center can be quickly carried out everywhere.[100]

Like the Chinese, Japanese analysts predicted slow expansion of North Korea's foreign trade, falling well short of Kim Il Sung's goal of an increase of 4.2 times during the 1980s. They cited the lack of suitable manufactured goods to export and the difficulty of rapidly increasing production of North Korea's traditional exports to Japan, such as non-ferrous metals. The importation of modern mining machinery would accelerate mineral production, but Pyongyang lacks the foreign exchange with which to buy it. The Japanese analysts said that the big Japanese companies reacted coldly to the publication of the joint venture law. They wanted North Korea to repay its debts to Japanese companies before they would risk investments there. Small companies owned by Korean residents in Japan, however, probably would take up the joint ventures offer. These companies had been pressured in the past to contribute "patriotic factories" to North Korea as a condition for trade contracts. Compared to such contributions, from which they got no return, joint ventures promising repatriation of profits would seem attractive. The Japanese analysts believed that such investments would be small. Nevertheless, they could be useful in a small way in upgrading North Korean technology and producing products suitable for export.[101]

Economic Policy Changes

Aside from their increased stress on consumer goods and foreign trade, the North Koreans do not appear to have embarked on a wide-ranging, Chinese-style economic reform. Most economic comment in the official press combines reports of remarkable successes with adjurations to officials to carry out even better the established policies.

A comparison of the seminal article by Hu Chiao-mu, then president of the Chinese Academy of Social Sciences, with recent commentaries in the *Nodong Sinmun*, demonstrates both differences and similarities in Chinese and North Korean approaches to economic reform.[102] Hu's article, based on a speech made at a State Council meeting in July 1978, preceded the pathbreaking Third Plenum of the Chinese Communist Party of December 1978 and foreshadowed many of the reforms to be adopted by Deng Xiaoping. Several characteristics of Hu's article have no counterpart in North Korean writings. Hu quotes extensively from Marx, Lenin, and Stalin (as well as Mao Zedong and Hua Guofeng); the North Koreans quote only from Kim Il Sung and Kim Chong Il. Hu concedes the superiority of the capitalist management of enterprises and urges merging "the superiority of the socialist system with the advanced science and technology of the developed capitalist countries and their advanced managerial experience." The North Koreans make no reference to learning from capitalist countries. Hu acknowledges serious past errors in economic policies and calls for drastic reform. The North Koreans admit no errors; they do, however, imply that weaknesses exist in those areas where they press for improved performance.

A number of articles in the North Korean media during 1985 stressed, as Hu did, the importance of paying attention to economic laws, such as "the principle of value." The discussion was too general to throw much light on what is actually occurring in the North Korean economy, and it never referred to China as a model. But it suggested that the North Koreans, like the Chinese, may be giving greater autonomy to enterprises and placing greater emphasis on material incentives "to enhance the labor zeal" of the workers. Functionaries in the economic field were urged to use skillfully "economic levers" such as cost, price, and profit, "while giving priority to political work."[103]

Enterprises in North Korea had had some degree of individual responsibility and, since 1960, had utilized an "independent accounting system" aimed at improving their efficiency.[104] Now the central authorities asserted that the increasing complexity of the economy demanded that enterprises be given greater autonomy. "The individuality of the enterprises is closely tied to the treatment of the profits acquired as a result of management activities. Only when a proper share of the net income is left to be used by the enterprises, with good application of the lever of profit, can the enterprises improve and expand management on their own, take measures to improve the employees' standard of living on their own initiative, and make more strenuous efforts to increase profits." Although functionaries were to give priority to political work, they were to "pay keen attention to supporting the political work with material incentives. Neglecting or weakening material incentives in a socialist society in which the legacies of the old society remain in various fields is a harmful tendency that will have a negative effect on both development of production potential and rationalization of enterprise management."[105]

In agriculture, also, a few signs have appeared of policy changes similar to those in China, although, as in industry, the data are too scanty to permit an assessment of how far change has gone in practice. Chinese journalists visiting North Korea in December 1984 referred to the adoption of a "production responsibility system," but made no mention of a "household" responsibility system such as has been so successful in China.[106] On the contrary, a *Nodong Sinmun* editorial in January 1985 stressed the role of the party in increasing agricultural production. The editorial placed on rural party functionaries and agricultural functionaries rather than on individual farm households the responsibility for ensuring a bumper harvest. "The grand task assigned to the field of agriculture this year demands that the level of guidance of functionaries and their role increase more than ever before."[107]

The Chinese journalists noted that "according to the policy of the state worked out in the last year or so, the agricultural and sideline products produced by the farm workers themselves can be sold in rural markets." Japan's Kyodo News Service, quoted a story in Peking's *Guangming Ri Bao* to the effect that free markets had begun to emerge in North Korea in the latter half of 1984 and that one now existed in each county and in each district of the larger cities.[108] China's dramatic success in increasing agricultural production resulted not only from granting farmers greater freedom to increase their family income by producing and selling agricultural and sideline commodities, but also from making available a larger supply of consumer goods for the farmers to buy with their increased income. An urgent appeal in a *Nodong Sinmun* editorial of November 1985 to produce and supply more goods to rural areas, such as sewing machines, bicycles, television sets, and watches, which were said to be in great demand there, suggests that despite the campaign of the past two years to produce more consumer goods, the supply to the countryside still falls well short of the level needed to reach the goal of "eliminating the difference in standard of living between workers and farmers."[109]

Notes

1. For more detailed discussions of the 1980 to 1983 period, see Harold C. Hinton, *Korea Under New Leadership: The Fifth Republic* (New York: Praeger, 1983), pp. 48–77; Young Whan Kihl, *Politics and Policies in Divided Korea: Regimes in Contest* (Boulder, Colo.: Westview Press, 1984), pp. 78–90 and pp. 160–172; Bunge, *South Korea*, pp. 176–192.

2. *New York Times*, December 1, 1979.

3. *Korea Herald*, March 1, 1980; *Washington Post*, March 13, 1980.

4. *Washington Post*, March 10, 1980.

5. *Korea Herald*, April 24 and 25, 1980; *Washington Post*, May 1, 1980.

6. *Korea Herald, New York Times, Washington Post*, May 15–16, 1980.

7. *New York Times*, June 19, July 10, 1980; *Korea Herald*, June 21, July 16, 20, 21, and August 7, 1980; *Washington Post*, July 31, 1980, March 2, 1981.

8. *Korea Herald*, November 13 and 16, 1980.

9. Kihl, *Politics and Policies in Divided Korea*, p. 125.

10. Kim's return, which attracted much attention from the U.S. press, was marred by pushing and shoving at the airport when South Korean security officers separated Kim and his wife from his U.S. escort and took Kim to his house. See *Washington Post* and *New York Times*, February 10, 1985, and the accounts by two members of the U.S. escort, Pat Derian (*Washington Post*, February 11, 1985) and William J. Butler (*Washington Post*, February 17, 1985).

11. *Korea Herald*, February 15, 1985.

12. *Korea Herald*, July 13, 1985.

13. Ibid., July 13, 1985.

14. *Korea Herald*, May 1985; March 14, 1985.

15. *Far Eastern Economic Review*, August 22, 1985.

16. *Korea Herald*, July 13, 1985.

17. *New York Times*, February 15, 1986.

18. *Korea Herald*, June 15, 1986.

19. *FBIS*, May 15, 1986, p. D19; May 19, 1986, p. D7; and July 30, 1986, p. D7.

20. For a succinct statement of political progress since 1980, as seen by the DJP, see excerpts from speeches by Choi Chang-yoon, assistant to the president for political affairs, *Korea Herald*, July 4, 1985.

21. Scalapino and Kim, *North Korea Today*, p. 77.

22. Lee Dong-bok, "Hereditary Succession in North Korea and its Impact on Inter-Korean Relations" (paper presented at 2d National Symposium on Korea, LaTrobe University, Melbourne, Australia, November 1980), pp. 19–20.

23. *FBIS*, June 1, 1983, pp. D15–D17.

24. *FBIS*, June 13, 1984, p. D16.

25. Manwoo Lee, "How North Korea Sees Itself," in Kim and Koh, *Journey to North Korea*, p. 119.

26. *FBIS*, July 5, 1984, pp. D8–D11.

27. Letter of Pyongyang's Foreign Languages Publishing House, November 1982, advertising Kim Chong Il's works, quoted in Young Whan Kihl, "North Korea in 1983," *Asian Survey* 24, no. 1 (January 1984):101.

28. See, for example, Choe In Su, *Kim Jong Il, the People's Leader* (Pyongyang: Foreign Languages Publishing House, 1983), which contains numerous laudatory anecdotes from the time Kim Chong Il entered Pyongyang with his father and mother in 1945 until his graduation from Kim Il Sung University in 1964. See also Tak Jin, Kim Gang Il, and Pak Hong Je, *Great Leader Kim Jong Il (I)* (Tokyo: Sorinsha, 1985).

29. Choe In Su, *Kim Jong Il, the People's Leader*, pp. 309–310, 344.

30. *Pyongyang Times*, February 10, 1982, quoted in Rinn-Sup Shinn, "North Korea in 1982: Continuing Revolution Under Kim Jong Il," *Asian Survey* 23, no. 1 (January 1983):103.

31. "Let Us Inherit and Complete the *Chu Che* Revolutionary Cause Generation after Generation—Our Party Is the Great Party Which Has Brilliantly Solved the Question of Inheriting the Revolutionary Cause," *FBIS*, August 1, 1984, pp. D7–D11.

32. *FBIS*, July 1, 1985, p. D7.

33. *Agence France Presse*, Hong Kong, in *FBIS*, July 10, 1985, p. D1.

34. *FBIS*, September 21, 1984, p. D11.

35. *FBIS*, May 7, 1984, p. D26.

36. *FBIS*, June 21, 1984, pp. D18, D21.

37. *Nodong Sinmun* editorial, November 14, 1983, in *FBIS*, November 18, 1983, pp. D14–D18.

38. *Nodong Sinmun* editorial, November 7, 1984, in *FBIS*, November 9, 1984, pp. D11–D12.

39. See Young C. Kim, "The Political Role of the Military in North Korea," in Scalapino and Kim, *North Korea Today*, pp. 133–143. Note particularly the quotation on p. 142 from a speech by Chief of Staff O Kuk-yol in April 1980 quoting Kim Il Sung: "Officers and men of the People's Army should make full preparation to accomplish the heroic cause of the fatherland's reunification and to accomplish the revolution on a nation-wide scale."

40. *FBIS*, July 27, 1984, p. D6.

41. Article in *Nodong Sinmun*, in *FBIS*, April 30, 1985, pp. D1–D4.

42. Statistics in this and the preceding paragraph taken from the World Bank, *Korea: Development in a Global Context* (Washington: D.C., 1984), pp. 8–9.

43. Ibid., p. 12.

44. Thomas Stern, ed., *Korea's Economy*, vol. 1, no. 1 (Washington, D.C.: Korea Economic Institute, April 1985), pp. 3–6.

45. World Bank, *Korea*, p. 15.

46. "Ebb Tide for the Korean Miracle," *New York Times*, October 6, 1985.

47. World Bank, *Korea*, p. 40.

48. Ibid., p. 45.

49. For a detailed discussion of the prospects for these export industries, see World Bank, *Korea*, pp. 60–74.

50. *Far Eastern Economic Review*, August 22, 1985, pp. 98–99.

51. Ibid., May 10, 1984, pp. 68–69.

52. *Korea Herald*, July 14, 1985; Republic of Korea, International Economic Policy Council, *Korea's Economic Policy Reform* (Seoul, March 1985), p. 12.

53. *FBIS*, October 14, 1980, p. D24.

54. *FBIS*, December 21, 1977, pp. D1–D12; December 23, 1977, pp. D1–D23.

55. *FBIS*, December 23, 1977, p. D27.

56. *FBIS*, June 18, 1979, p. D9.

57. For example, the *Le Monde* correspondent, Alain Jacob, visiting the Taean machine-tool plant, one of the showpieces of North Korean heavy industry, reports that the industrial processes used are "not even remotely similar to the procedures used in modern industries" (*Le Monde*, May 18, 1984, p. 55, translated in *FBIS* May 31, 1984, p. D18).

58. *FBIS*, June 18, 1979, pp. D2–D3.

59. *FBIS*, January 2, 1985, p. D5.

60. *FBIS*, February 22, 1985, p. D1.

61. *FBIS*, October 14, 1980, p. D9.

62. Kim's policy speech to a joint meeting of the KWP Central Committee and the SPA (*FBIS*, April 14, 1982, p. D9).

63. According to the U.S. State department and the South Korean Minister of Science and Technology, North Korea in mid-1985 had a Soviet-supplied 20-year-old research reactor and was building a larger research reactor, but it had no nuclear power plants (*Korea Herald*, June 11, 1985).

64. *Korea Herald*, December 28, 1985; April 16, 1986.

65. Bunge, *North Korea*, p. 125.

66. *FBIS*, January 3, 1984, pp. D16–D17.

67. *FBIS*, December 15, 1983, pp. D13–D15.

68. *FBIS*, September 12, 1983, p. D18.

69. Article on developing local industry in *Kulloja*, the WPK's ideological journal, June 1984 (*FBIS*, July 18, 1984, p. D14).

70. Ibid., p. D14.

71. See *Nodong Sinmun* editorial, "All the Fields of the People's Economy Should Actively Help Light Industry," October, 3, 1984 (*FBIS*, October 10, 1984, pp. D18–D20).

72. *FBIS*, August 16, 1984, p. D18.

73. *FBIS*, October 2, 1979, quoted in Young C. Kim, "North Korea 1979: National Unification and Economic Development," *Asian Survey* 22, no. 1 (January 1980):61.

74. Interview, Peking, December 1984.

75. *FBIS*, March 19, 1985, p. D7.

76. *FBIS*, January 2, 1985, p. D5.

77. *FBIS*, April 11, 1985, pp. D1–D3; April 16, 1985, pp. D9–D10. See also report of Finance Minister Yun Ki-chong on the state budget for 1985 and 1986 (*FBIS*, April 11, 1986, pp. D1–D19, especially pp. D6 and D13).

78. *FBIS*, October 9, 1985, p. D9–D10.

79. *FBIS*, July 26, 1985, p. D8; August 6, 1985, p. D10.

80. *FBIS*, October 14, 1980, pp. D22–D23.

81. See Appendix 1.

82. *FBIS*, January 30, 1984, pp. D1–D10.

83. Such rhetorical flourishes seem based more on wishful thinking than on a rigorous assessment of North Korea's capabilities. A Japanese analyst calculated that reaching this goal would require trade increases of 58.5 percent annually, an extremely high rate of growth, which North Korea had little prospect of reaching. See Hiroko Kawai, "Trade of the DPRK in 1983," *China Newsletter*, no. 50 (May–June 1984) (Tokyo: Japan External Trade Research Organization):23.

84. *FBIS*, July 10, 1984, p. D10.

85. *FBIS*, October 17, 1984, pp. D6–D8. Note contrast with Kim Il Sung's statement in 1975: "We cannot satisfy our needs if we confine ourselves to the socialist market. Therefore, while relying on the socialist market, we must actively move into the capitalist market to purchase the materials, machines and equipment we need." Kim Il Sung, *Selected Works*, vol. 7 (Pyongyang, 1979), p. 178 quoted in Chong-Sik Lee, *Japan and Korea: The Political Dimension* (Stanford, Calif.: Hoover Institution Press, 1985), p. 175.

86. *FBIS*, October 22, 1984, pp. D16–D18.

87. *FBIS*, January 15, 1985, pp. D10–D15.

88. *FBIS*, November 1, 1985, p. D4.

89. *FBIS*, November 22, 1985, p. D16.

90. *FBIS*, April 1, 1985, p. D2.

91. *FBIS*, September 27, 1984, pp. D11–D12.

92. *FBIS*, September 25, 1984, p. D30.

93. *FBIS*, September 12, 1984, pp. D1–D3.

94. *FBIS*, April 1, 1985, p. D2.

95. Quoted in *Korea Herald*, September 25, 1985.

96. *Korea Herald*, February 27, 1985; February 8, 1985.

97. *Korea Herald*, May 17, 1985.

98. *Korea Herald*, February 4, 1986.

99. Interviews with Soviet, Chinese, and Japanese analysts confirmed that North Korea's technological level is low. A Soviet analyst said that commitment to *chu che* made North Korean workers resistant to advice by Soviet technicians. He added that some North Korean–built machinery was used on Soviet collective

farms, but was not suitable for "important" uses. A Japanese businessman imported a trial shipment of North Korean machine tools. They proved of such low quality that he ordered no more.

100. Interview, Peking, December 1984.

101. Interviews, Tokyo, December 1984, with Hiroko Kawai of the Japan External Trade Organization and Teruo Komaki of the Asian Institute of Developing Economies.

102. *Peking Review*, no. 45 (November 10, 1978):7–11; no. 46 (November 17, 1978):15–23; no. 47 (November 24, 1978):13–21.

103. *FBIS*, March 11, 1985, pp. D1–D3; August 7, 1985, pp. D2–D5.

104. Bunge, *North Korea*, p. 129.

105. *FBIS*, August 7, 1985, p. D3.

106. *FBIS*, January 3, 1985, pp. D2–D3.

107. *FBIS*, January 31, 1985, pp. D7–D9.

108. Quoted in *Korea Herald*, February 2, 1985.

109. *FBIS*, November 21, 1985, pp. D4–D5.

6

Coping with Change
in the 1980s:
Confrontation and Dialogue

Between 1980 and 1986, military confrontation continued to dominate relations between the two Koreas. The level of hostility remained high and both sides further strengthened their military capabilities. From late 1984, however, the authorities in Seoul and Pyongyang, under pressure from changing internal and external conditions, resumed their interrupted dialogue through several channels. By the end of 1985 they had taken several small steps ahead, despite profound suspicions of each others' motives and objectives in carrying on the dialogue. Throughout 1986, however, the dialogue was again suspended.

Military Confrontation

Military readiness continued to be the principal preoccupation of leaders on both sides of the DMZ during the first half of the 1980s. Allocations for defense remained at about the same proportion of GNP as during the late 1970s—6 percent for Seoul and around 20 percent for Pyongyang—but increased in absolute amounts as their economies grew.[1] Because South Korea's GNP was four to five times that of North Korea, its expenditures on defense had begun to exceed those of the North. However, Pyongyang spent less on personnel costs and therefore probably continued to outspend South Korea in the acquisition of additional weapons.[2] In order to alleviate its labor shortages, North Korea assigned military personnel to large construction projects and other civilian tasks.

174

The atmosphere along the DMZ remained tense. Frontline units exchanged fire from time to time and defectors occasionally crossed to the other side, but no large-scale military clashes occurred. North Korea pursued its efforts to infiltrate spies, saboteurs, and revolutionary organizers into South Korea, and its propaganda continued to call for the overthrow of the Chun government. Not content to leave that task to South Koreans, it despatched to Rangoon North Korean military officers, who narrowly missed killing Chun during his state visit to Burma in October 1983.

South Korean Military Buildup

Modernization of South Korean armed forces proceeded steadily during the 1980s, giving South Korea a qualitative edge in certain weapons systems, particularly in aircraft, but leaving North Korea well ahead in numbers of weapons. In early 1985 North Korea still had a quantitative advantage of three to one in tanks and assault guns, three to one in personnel carriers, two to one in artillery (much of it self-propelled), and nearly two to one in combat aircraft.[3]

By 1984 South Korean purchases of U.S. weapons and parts were running about $800 million per year.[4] Such purchases included components for the F-5E fighters and the Bell helicopters coproduced in Korea. They also included substantial numbers of TOW antitank missiles and Harpoon surface-to-surface missiles for South Korean destroyers and frigates. A contract for the purchase of 36 F-16s was signed in 1981 for delivery beginning in 1986.

The capacity of South Korea's armaments industry to produce certain categories of weapons began to exceed the needs of its armed forces. Excess capacity existed in factories producing M-16 rifles, M-60 machine guns, Vulcan antiaircraft guns, 4.2-inch mortars, and 155mm artillery shells. The ROK sought permission to export to third countries some of these U.S.-licensed products, but most such requests were denied on the ground that the sales would compete with similar products made in the United States.[5] South Korean efforts to produce more advanced weapons on its own proceeded slowly. As of mid-1985 the prototype of the medium tank specially designed for Korea and under development since the late 1970s was still undergoing trials.

The U.S. Role

When President Park was assassinated in October 1979, the United States immediately sent the aircraft carrier *Kittyhawk* with a flotilla of other ships to the vicinity of the Korean peninsula as a pointed warning to Kim Il Sung not to try to take military advantage of political confusion in South Korea. In early 1981 officials speaking for the Reagan administration made clear even before President Ronald Reagan took office that he would not resume the withdrawal of U.S. ground forces begun in 1977 by President Carter and suspended in 1979. Alexander M. Haig, Jr., in the hearings on his nomination to be secretary of state, declared that he saw no justification for reductions of any kind in U.S. military capabilities in South Korea.[6] The joint statement issued at the end of President Chun Doo Hwan's visit to Washington in February 1981 assured the South Koreans that "the United States has no plans to withdraw U.S. combat ground forces from the Korean peninsula."[7]

Instead of reducing U.S. military strength in South Korea, the Reagan administration added to it by modernizing the equipment of U.S. forces there. Between 1981 and 1982 a wing of 72 F-16s replaced the F-4s. A squadron of high performance, close air support A-10s, an effective antitank weapons system, arrived in South Korea during 1982. The South Koreans constructed revetments to protect U.S. aircraft on the ground, and in 1984 the United States brought in its newest surface-to-air missile, the Stinger, to improve the defense of airfields against low-flying aircraft. U.S. forces had the AH1Cobra, an antitank helicopter gunship, and 100 Blackhawk helicopters. U.S. army units began receiving M-198 howitzers, the most modern long-range artillery in the U.S. arsenal. In February 1985, U.S. forces test-fired a Copperhead 155mm precision-guided missile in Korea. This laser-guided projectile, effective against tanks and self-propelled artillery, was scheduled for deployment in Korea in 1986.

In addition to improving the capability of U.S. forces, the U.S. government took other steps to demonstrate its commitment to the defense of South Korea. Defense Secretary Caspar Weinberger visited frontline U.S. and Korean forces in March 1982 and President Reagan did the same in November 1983. Both repeated strong assurances of U.S. determination to support South Korea militarily in the event of a North Korean attack. South Korean Defense Minister Yoon Sung-min told the National Assembly Defense Committee that a high U.S. official accompanying President Reagan had said that the United States would not exclude resort to "nuclear retaliation" should North Korea launch a full-fledged attack on the South.[8] The close military cooperation between the United States and South Korea resulting from the inauguration of the annual large-scale Team Spirit exercises in 1976 and the institution of the Combined Command in 1978 continued into the 1980s, as did the annual meetings of the U.S.-ROK Security Consultative Committee. The committee brought together the defense ministers and the top military commanders of the two countries to evaluate the current military threat and preparations to counter it. The Team Spirit exercise expanded each year until it became the largest such exercise conducted by U.S. forces throughout the world, involving some 200,000 U.S. and Korean troops.

North Korean Military Buildup

The revised estimate for North Korean forces accepted by the U.S. intelligence community in 1979 showed an increase in ground forces from 440,000 to between 560,000 and 600,000, and in tanks from 2,000 to 2,600.[9] According to U.S. officials, this abrupt large increase in the estimate did not indicate a sudden surge in the pace of the North Korean buildup, but improved U.S. intelligence capabilities for detecting North Korean military units and their equipment. A steady, continuous buildup had been in progress throughout the 1970s.

The figures rose further during the 1980s. The *Military Balance 1985–1986*, published by the International Institute for Strategic Studies in London (Autumn, 1985) gave a figure of 838,000 for total armed forces, with the army at 750,000, as compared with South Korea's total armed forces of 598,000, including an army of 520,000. In July 1985 the UN Command reported that Pyongyang's total armed forces had increased to 843,000.[10] As indicated above, in 1985 North Korea also had a marked advantage over South Korea in numbers of tanks, artillery, personnel carriers, and planes. The quantitative gap in equipment widened during the early 1980s. The ROK should be able to narrow the gap during the latter half of the decade, but probably will not be able to eliminate it until the 1990s.[11]

U.S. and South Korean military commanders were disturbed, not only by North Korea's growing quantitative edge over South Korea in weapons and equipment, but also by other military preparations. North Korea continued to construct underground factories and hangars for aircraft, as well as adding to its underground fortifications along the DMZ. It converted several infantry divisions into mechanized or motorized divisions. Between 1983 and 1984 it brought forward 10 divisions from rear areas, including highly mobile, mechanized strike forces, relocating them within 40 to 60 kilometers of the DMZ.[12] North Korea continued intensive training for special forces numbering 100,000 men, some of whom could be rapidly infiltrated behind South Korean lines by numerous fast patrol craft or by 250 slow, low-flying AN-2 aircraft, capable of ducking beneath radar detection but also noisy and vulnerable to ground fire.

Between 1983 and 1985 Pyongyang pulled off a major coup by acquiring illegally through a West German firm 87 Hughes helicopters, which could easily be converted to military use, equipped with air-to-ground missiles, rockets, and machine guns. When configured for military purposes, the aircraft would be identical with some 200 Hughes helicopters used by the South Korean armed forces. The South Koreans feared that they would be deployed in battle to confuse the defense.[13]

Soviet and Chinese Roles

After Kim Il Sung's official visit to Moscow, his first in twenty-three years, North Korean public statements became much more friendly toward the Soviet Union.[14] South Korean observers, noting that Soviet Defense Minister Dimitri Ustinov had met with North Korean Defense Minister O Chin-u, speculated that Kim had received promises of military aid, perhaps MIG-23 aircraft. Mikhail Kapitsa, a Soviet vice minister of foreign affairs, spent two weeks in Pyongyang in November 1984, accompanied by a high-level military delegation headed by a colonel-general. According to Vasiliy Y. Matuzok, an intern at the Soviet Embassy in Pyongyang who defected across the DMZ during the Kapitsa visit, the delegation signed a military aid agreement with the North Korean authorities.

While Kapitsa was in Pyongyang, the first public report appeared that the North Koreans had acquired the SCUD, a surface-to-surface missile of 1950s vintage with a range of 96 to 162 miles, considerably greater than the range of the FROG missile that North Korea had possessed for years. Although very inaccurate, the SCUD, like the FROG, could be used for harassing Seoul. Libya, which has a supply of SCUDs, may have furnished the weapon rather than the Soviet Union. The security treaty between Libya and North Korea provides for supplying each other with weapons.[15] Early in 1986 North Korea reportedly began receiving SA-3 missiles to upgrade the air defense network of SA-2 missiles deployed many years earlier.

In 1985 the pace of military cooperation between Moscow and Pyongyang picked up. The two countries celebrated the fortieth anniversary of the Soviet victory over Germany in May 1945 by exchanging flights of fighter squadrons on goodwill visits. About the same time the first MIG-23 fighters began to appear in the North Korean airforce. More arrived later and South Korean officials predicted that North Korea probably would receive 35 to 50 of these long-desired aircraft. The Soviet decision to provide the North Koreans with MIG-23s may have been in part a reaction to the U.S. decision, announced in 1981, to sell 36 F-16s to South Korea, just as the provision of the SU-7s appears to have been in response to the arrival of F-4s in the South Korean airforce. The MIG-23 is less advanced than Soviet aircraft supplied to other Soviet allies and it is not a match for the F-16, but its arrival constitutes a significant modernization of the North Korean airforce.

To celebrate the fortieth anniversary of the liberation of Korea from Japan, three Soviet naval vessels headed by a guided-missile cruiser made an unprecedented port call at Wonsan. The Japanese press reported in August 1985 that small Soviet naval ships—under 1,000 tons—had made repeated port calls at Nampo, on Korea's west coast.[16] Meanwhile, a number of overflights of North Korean territory by Soviet military aircraft were detected.[17]

Relations between China and North Korea cooled somewhat in the late 1970s and early 1980s.[18] Nevertheless, both parties sought to bolster the important basic relationship between them by high-level visits back and forth. Kim Il Sung visited China in 1982 and 1984, and Kim Chong Il made a visit to China in 1983. Deng Xiaoping and Hu Yaobang visited North Korea in April 1982; Hu went again in May 1984 and May 1985. Other senior Chinese officials visiting North Korea included Premier Zhao Ziyang (1981), Defense Minister Geng Biao (1982), Politburo member Peng Zhen (1983), and Foreign Minister Wu Xueqian (1983). Their North Korean counterparts also visited China.

Senior military officials frequently accompanied Chinese and North Korean leaders and presumably had conversations with their military counterparts on security matters. For example, Politburo member Yang Shangkun, vice chairman of the Chinese Communist Party's Military Commission, accompanied Hu on his 1984 visit and Deputy Chief of Staff Xu Xin was with Hu both on that visit and in 1985.

In 1982 China provided North Korea with a number of A-5 aircraft (the Chinese version of the MIG-21) variously estimated by Western intelligence as between 20 and 40 planes.[19]

Chinese leaders have sought, especially after the Rangoon bombing, to assure the United States and Japan that the danger of conflict in Korea is low. Hu Yaobang, during his November 1983 visit to Tokyo, told Prime Minister Yasuhiro Nakasone that Kim Il Sung had declared in two recent meetings with Deng Xiaoping that North Korea had neither the intention nor the capability to attack South Korea.[20] Top Chinese leaders have given similar assurances to the United States. Chinese officials in private conversations with U.S. officials and scholars stress the obsolescence of North Korea's military equipment and express the view that U.S. and South Korean intelligence estimates exaggerate North Korean military strength.

Unconventional Warfare

Tension persisted along the DMZ during the first half of the 1980s, but no large-scale clashes occurred. A few officers and men from each side defected across the DMZ, despite minefields, watchtowers, electrified fences, and frequent patrols. The most spectacular defection was in November 1984 by the Soviet Embassy intern mentioned above, who burst out of a sightseeing group in the northern part of the security zone at Panmunjom and sprinted 100 yards to the South Korean side unscathed through a cross fire of bullets that killed two North Korean soldiers and one South Korean and wounded others. In February 1982 a North Korean pilot flew his Chinese-built MIG-19 type aircraft into South Korea, the first defector to bring a plane more advanced than the MIG-15.

Several times each year, South Korean forces intercepted North Korean agents attempting to slip into South Korea, either across the DMZ or, more often, from small, fast boats along the southern coast. A few were captured, most were killed. Some spy boats sunk by the South Korean navy were salvaged and displayed along with weapons and other equipment carried by agents. In April 1986, Pyongyang accused the South Korean navy of sinking a North Korean fishing boat, killing and injuring several fishermen. Defending the action in the Military Armistice Commission, the U.S. official charged that the boat, 3.5 kilometers south of the eastward extension of the Military Demarcation Line (MDL), fired first and that in the past the North Koreans had disguised spy boats as fishing boats.[21] Every month or two the Agency for National Security Planning (ANSP—the new name given the KCIA in 1980) announced the discovery of a North Korean spy ring and the arrest of its members. Most such spy rings were small, involving 1 to 6 persons, but one was said to have 29 members.[22] In 1980 Japanese police arrested members of a spy ring in Japan, charging them with sending spies into South Korea on behalf of Pyongyang.[23]

The opening of a sustained, multichannel, North-South dialogue late in 1984 had little apparent effect on espionage and counterespionage activities. The ANSP continued to report the arrest of North Korean spies; one case involved youthful South Koreans who were said to have been recruited in the United States and West Germany.[24] The South Korean navy sank a North Korean spy boat near Pusan in October 1985, the first such sinking since a similar boat was sunk, also near Pusan, in December 1973. The North Koreans rejected a protest made in the Military Armistice Commission by the South Koreans, dismissing the reported incident as a South Korean fabrication.[25] Shortly thereafter the North Koreans broadcast the unusual claim that they had captured a South Korean agent attempting to infiltrate North Korea.[26] The existence of a North-South dialogue may have helped to effect the release of a South Korean fishing boat seized by a North Korean gunboat, allegedly in North Korean waters, on October 6, 1985. The North Koreans used the Red Cross telephone channel to request information on the ship and its crew and, after holding them for twelve days, permitted them to return to South Korea aboard their ship.[27]

North Korean propaganda continued to call for revolution in South Korea. In August 1984 the *Nodong Sinmun* published an editorial celebrating the fifteenth anniversary of the founding of the RPR. It praised the "heroic underground anti-U.S. struggle" of the RPR and urged the South Korean revolutionaries to "more fiercely fan the flames of the democratic, antifascist struggle to eliminate the fascist, military dictatorial system of Chon Tu-hwan [Chun Doo Hwan], a colonial puppet for the U.S. imperialists."[28] Two obsequious letters to Kim Il Sung and Kim Chong Il, from "the RPR Central Committee" broadcast on the same day from North Korea and purporting to originate in Seoul, left no doubt of North Korea's intention to bring South Korea under Kim Il Sung's sway.[29] Reiterating its pledge of loyalty to Kim Il Sung, the RPR declared that "its existence cannot be thought of, and the victorious completion of the South Korean revolution cannot be expected, apart from the great leader and the immortal *chu che* idea." The RPR pledged to accelerate the introduction of Kimilsungism among its members and to "continue to be loyal to the great leader and the sagacious dear comrade leader, generation after generation for eternity." Again, on April 15, 1985, on the occasion of Kim Il Sung's seventy-third birthday, the RPR Central Committee pledged fealty to the great leader, "a matchless patriot, a lodestar of freedom and liberation, and the sun of mankind."[30]

South Korean propaganda did not appeal openly for North Korean residents to overthrow their rulers nor did it claim that a resistance organization dedicated to that purpose existed in North Korea. Pyongyang rarely announced the arrest of South Korean spies in tightly controlled North Korea, although it occasionally alleged that captured South Korean fishing boats had been bent on espionage. Nevertheless, certain actions taken by the South Korean government implied a South Korean intent to become dominant eventually throughout the Korean peninsula. For example, every other year since 1966 the government of South Korea appointed persons in South Korea born in cities and counties of North Korea as mayors and county chiefs of those places in order to "inspire the nation with hopes and aspirations for the recovery of lost territory." One of the military exercises conducted in the spring of 1985 was named Myolgong (destroy communism).[31]

The North Koreans did not limit themselves to propaganda attacks on Chun Doo Hwan, they tried to kill him. The first attempt was a bizarre plot to hire two Canadian adventurers to assassinate Chun in July 1981 while he played golf with President Ferdinand Marcos during a planned visit to the Philippines. The hired guns took the money from the North Koreans but did not carry out their part of the contract. A

Canadian court sentenced them to prison for fraud. The Royal Canadian
Mounted Police, who investigated the plot, said that the culprits had
been hired by James Choi, the son of a dissident South Korean general
living in Canada, and several North Koreans, all of whom fled to North
Korea before they could be arrested.[32]

A diatribe against Chun by the Voice of the Revolutionary Party for
Reunification in May 1983 warned that he did not have long to live.
"Traitor Chun Doo-hwan is a matchlessly outrageous, murderous devil
who exists only for the sake of the United States. He is a human butcher
and war maniac. . . . Our people will never leave traitor Chun Doo-
hwan intact. He will surely be executed by the people."[33]

On October 9, 1983, three North Korean army officers attempted to
carry out the execution at the Martyrs Mausoleum in Rangoon during
Chun's state visit to Burma. The bomb explosion they set off killed
seventeen members of Chun's party, including four cabinet ministers,
but failed to kill him because he arrived at the site later than planned.
After a careful and thorough investigation, the Burmese government
announced that it had established the North Korean government's
responsibility for the bombing and immediately broke diplomatic relations
with that government and withdrew recognition of it.[34]

This brutal act added to North Korea's international reputation for
reckless and abnormal behavior and had a profound effect on South
Korean leaders, especially the military. Although the government refrained
from military retaliation against North Korea, partly in response to U.S.
urging, the slaughter of their colleagues by North Korean agents deepened
the already intense hostility of senior government officials toward the
North Korean regime. The North Koreans' refusal to accept responsibility
for the action and their lame attempt to blame it on South Koreans was
infuriating. On the first anniversary of the bombing, President Chun
referred to the fury aroused in South Korea by this "treacherous, war-
like and uncivilized crime" and declared that only strength could tame
the "irrational and belligerent group" in the North and lead to peace
and unification.[35] The Rangoon bombing ensured that South Korean
officials would receive any ostensibly peaceful overtures by North Koreans
with extreme suspicion.

U.S. and South Korean officials speculated that the North Koreans'
principal objective in attempting to assassinate Chun was to create
political confusion in South Korea that they could exploit to improve
the prospects of revolution there. Chun's death would precipitate a
struggle for power within the military, as well as demands by politicians
and students for a civilian successor. Even though the North Koreans
probably expected another military man to emerge as the new leader,
the disorder, repression, and confusion of the process would serve North

Korean purposes. So also would the questionable legitimacy of a new leader.

A second purpose of the attempt on Chun probably was to disrupt his successful program to improve South Korea's international stature, particularly among the nonaligned nations. The prospect of his scheduled state visits to Burma, India, and Sri Lanka, must have been galling to Kim Il Sung. In addition, the concurrent hosting by Seoul of the Interparliamentary Union meeting seems to have created near-hysteria in Pyongyang at the possible attendance by representatives from the Soviet Union, Eastern European states, and many nonaligned countries.[36]

Resumption of the North-South dialogue in late 1984 did not bring to a halt the excoriation of Chun Doo Hwan and public appeals for revolutionary action in South Korea. In a lengthy commentary, the official party organ, *Nodong Sinmun*, condemned Chun's trip to the United States in April 1985 as "a dangerous conspiratorial conference between master and stooge" during which Chun fawned and cringed before U.S. officials.[37]

In August 1985 the purported revolutionary party in South Korea announced a change in its name from the Revolutionary Party for Reunification (RPR) to the Korean National Democratic Front (KNDF) and its broadcast arm, the Voice of the Revolutionary Party for Reunification to the Voice of National Salvation.[38] The Central Committee of the KNDF then issued a Declaration of Korean National Independence calling for the formation of a broad united front to expel from South Korea the "U.S. imperialist forces of aggression." The declaration called the working class "the decisive force that will determine the success or failure of the anti-U.S. struggle for independence," the peasants were termed "its reliable ally," and the youths and students were "the main force that will pioneer a breakthrough at the head of the struggle." The declaration, which described South Korea as "a complete colony of the United States," was couched to appeal to the various groups and individuals who resent aspects of the U.S. relationship with South Korea. These aspects include: support of the Chun government, U.S. operational control of South Korean forces, U.S. economic "domination" of South Korea, the influx of the "corrupt and depraved Yankee culture," and the responsibility for the perpetuation of the division of Korea.[39] The North Koreans clearly hope that by exploiting diverse nationalistic feelings they can encourage the formation of a unified opposition among South Koreans to the continued presence of U.S. forces in South Korea.

As the RPR had in 1984, its successor, the KNDF, in August 1985 sent fawning messages to Kim Il Sung and Kim Chong Il, this time celebrating the fortieth anniversary of national liberation. One message asserted that "the wall of toadyism serving the United States is collapsing;

an anti-U.S. sense of independence is being rapidly heightened; numerous patriotic struggle organizations are being formed; and the struggle against the U.S. imperialists and the nation-selling group by the people of all walks of life is violently developing." The other message looked forward to the day when "the dear comrade Kim Chong Il" will be "upheld in the reunified land without fail."[40] Such declarations reinforced the conviction in the minds of the South Korean leaders that the aim of North Korea is to bring South Korea under its sway and that the Democratic Confederal Republic of Koryo proposed by Kim Il Sung is merely a way station toward that objective. An article by North Korean Vice President Pak Song-chol in *Nodong Sinmun* was even more explicit: "The Korean revolution still has a long way to go and is full of trials. We should reunify the fatherland without fail, establish national sovereignty on the basis of the whole country, and establish a communist paradise in the land of the fatherland."[41]

To commemorate the fortieth anniversary of "the occupation of South Korea by the U.S. imperialist aggressor forces" on September 8, 1945, the KNDF broadcast a lengthy indictment of U.S. "crimes," calling on the people of South Korea to rally around "an anti-U.S. banner of independence" and ending with the demand: "Yankees go home!"[42]

The Resumption of North-South Dialogue

Soon after the assassination of Park Chung-hee in October 1979, the North Koreans proposed organizing a combined team for the 1980 Olympics and followed this up with a request to reopen the Seoul-Pyongyang telephone line. The South Koreans declined because the request was made by the Committee for the Peaceful Reunification of the Fatherland, not by officials of the SNCC or the Red Cross, for whose use the line had been opened.

Negotiations on Prime Ministers' Meeting

In January 1980 the North Koreans made a more significant move. A letter signed by North Korean Premier Yi Chong-ok and addressed to "Prime Minister Shin Yon-hwak, Republic of Korea" proposed a meeting between them and also a broad political conference, similar to those previously proposed by North Korea. Similar letters, signed by Kim Il, vice president of the DPRK and chairman of the Committee for the Peaceful Reunification of the Fatherland, went to ten others in South Korea, including Yi Hui-song, commander of the Martial Law Command, the three Kims, and other South Korean politicians and social leaders. Kim Il sent similar letters to ten Koreans resident abroad, all but one of them opponents of the Seoul government.

The South Korean government ignored the proposal for a political conference but responded positively to the North Korean suggestion of a prime ministers' meeting, attracted because the North Koreans for the first time had used the name "Republic of Korea" and had indicated a willingness to hold a formal meeting of high level officials of the two governments. Ten working-level meetings held at Panmunjom between February and August 1980, facilitated by the reopening of the Seoul-Pyongyang telephone line, failed to reach agreement on the agenda and procedural arrangements for a meeting of prime ministers. In September the North Koreans broke off both the working-level talks and the telephone connection.

The prevailing view in South Korea was that the North Koreans had made the proposal for a prime ministers' meeting in the hope of exploiting the uncertain political situation after Park's death. Pyongyang's renewed suggestion of a big political conference supported this view. Some observers believed, however, that North Korea was responding to increasing pressure to moderate its policy toward the South because of the growing economic gap between North and South, the approaching leadership transition in North Korea, and the implications for North Korea of the Soviet military occupation of Afghanistan and the Soviet-backed Vietnamese occupation of Kampuchea. They saw Pyongyang's willingness to consider formal meetings of high officials of the two governments as a significant modification of the North Korean position, even though efforts to reach agreement on the meeting failed.

As had happened on previous occasions, the confrontational aspect of North-South relations intruded on the dialogue. At the April 1 meeting the South Korean delegate complained vehemently about three armed incursions into ROK territory by North Korean agents during March. At the June 24 meeting the North Korean delegate sharply attacked the South Korean government for its suppression of the Kwangju uprising, and the South Korean delegate denounced the North Koreans for sending another spy boat into South Korean waters. In early August North Korean loudspeakers along the DMZ, which had remained silent since Park's assassination, loosed a barrage of appeals to the South Korean armed forces to mutiny and overthrow Chun Doo Hwan, who had just been inaugurated president. Long before the North Koreans broke off the working-level talks in September, the dialogue had degenerated into exchanges of heated and unproductive rhetoric.

The Democratic Confederal Republic of Koryo

In October 1980, in his speech to the Sixth KWP Congress, Kim Il Sung elaborated on his long-standing proposal for a confederation of the two Koreas.[43] Under this concept, the unified state, to be known as the Democratic Confederal Republic of Koryo (DCRK), would be governed by a "supreme national confederal assembly" with an equal number of representatives from North and South and some from overseas. This assembly, through its permanent "confederal standing committee" would make the basic decisions on "political affairs, national defense problems, foreign affairs, and other questions of common concern related to the interests of the country and the nation as a whole." Under the "guidance" of the confederal government, the "regional governments" of North and South would follow "independent" policies "within the limits consistent with the fundamental interests and demands of the whole nation." The confederal government of the DCRK would pursue the following policies.

1. It would adhere to a policy of neutrality and nonalignment.
2. It would effect democracy throughout the country, ensuring freedom of speech, the press, religion, assembly, and free travel throughout Korea.
3. It would bring about economic collaboration between North and South.
4. It would realize North-South cooperation in science, culture, and education.
5. It would restore transportation and communication between North and South.
6. It would see to stability of livelihood for the entire people.
7. It would organize a combined national army from the combined forces of North and South.
8. It would defend the interests of overseas Koreans.
9. It would coordinate the limited foreign relations of the two regional governments in a unified way.
10. It would serve as the only representative of the entire Korean nation in foreign relations, including membership in the United Nations and other international organizations. It would make the Korean peninsula a nuclear-free zone and prohibit the presence of foreign forces.

Kim Il Sung's proposal was not directed to the newly installed president of the ROK. On the contrary, Kim specified that "in order to achieve the independent, peaceful reunification it is imperative to eliminate military fascist rule and democratize society in South Korea. . . . The anti-communist law, national security law, and other fascist laws must be abolished and all the apparatuses of tyrannical rule be eliminated there." He excoriated the "military fascist blackguards" of South Korea for massacring thousands of their compatriots "under the manipulation and aegis of the United States." He proposed again negotiation with the United States on replacing the armistice with a peace agreement and called for the withdrawal of U.S. troops from South Korea as soon as possible.

South Korean Proposals, 1981–1982

South Korean leaders saw little new in Kim Il Sung's proposals, dismissing them as propaganda aimed at undermining the government of the ROK. Chun Doo Hwan decided to mount his own campaign on the unification issue to counter North Korean charges that the South Korean government was determined to perpetuate division. He transferred to the Ministry of Unification the offices and personnel of the former KCIA that had handled North-South negotiations and named Lee Bum Suk, an experienced and vigorous senior political figure as the minister. In January 1981 Chun proposed an exchange of visits between himself and Kim Il Sung in Seoul and Pyongyang, with no conditions attached. North Korean Vice President Kim Il promptly rejected the proposal, declaring that "Chun Doo Hwan is not a man worthy for us to do anything with."[44] Undeterred, Chun took advantage of his visit to the United States in January 1981 to discuss with UN Secretary-General Kurt Waldheim the desirability of the proposed exchange of visits and the advantages of the admission of both Koreas to the UN.

In June 1981 Chun inaugurated a nongovernmental Advisory Council on Peaceful Unification Policy with more than eight thousand members, which could serve as a counterpart of the Committee for Peaceful Reunification of the Fatherland in North Korea. In his speech inaugurating the committee, Chun reiterated his proposal for an exchange of visits with Kim Il Sung, adding that if visits to Seoul and Pyongyang were not feasible, he was prepared to meet Kim at Panmunjom or in a third country. He also called for athletic, cultural, academic, postal, and economic exchanges, leading to a complete opening of the two societies to each other. Two weeks later, the South Koreans proposed to North Korea the formation of a joint team for the 1984 Olympics in Los Angeles. In November 1981 Seoul proposed cooperation in the study of ancient Korean culture, including exchanges of exhibits of cultural artifacts, joint academic research, and joint sponsorship of Korean cultural exhibits to be sent abroad.

In President Chun's New Year's Policy statement of January 1982, South Korea for the first time made a detailed proposal for unification comparable to North Korea's confederation concept.[45] Chun proposed that the two Koreas organize a Consultative Conference for National Reunification to draft a constitution for a unified democratic republic of Korea. The draft constitution would be adopted by the voters throughout the country in a national referendum, after which a unified legislature and government would be established through general elections held in accordance with the constitution. As an interim arrangement, Chun proposed a seven-point Agreement on Basic Relations between the two Koreas.

1. Relations to be based on equality and reciprocity.
2. Both to abandon all forms of force and violence and settle issues between them peacefully through dialogue and negotiation.
3. Each to recognize the other's existing political order and social institutions and to not interfere in each other's internal affairs.
4. The armistice to continue in force while the two sides work out measures to ease tension and prevent war.
5. Progressive opening of each society to the other by family reunions, trade, transportation, sports, education, and in other ways.
6. Until unification achieved, each to respect the other's international agreements.
7. Each to appoint an envoy of cabinet rank to head a liaison mission resident in the capital city of the other.

In addition, Chun proposed an early meeting of cabinet-rank delegates to work out procedures for a North-South summit meeting.

North Korea promptly rejected Chun's proposals. A speech by Vice President Kim Il, chairman of the Committee for the Peaceful Reunification of the Fatherland, brushed them off as of no positive significance and insisted that the only realistic and feasible proposal was North Korea's proposal of a democratic confederal republic of Koryo. According to Kim Il, the first steps toward reunification must be the withdrawal of U.S. troops and the "democratization" of South Korea. He declared that they were willing to meet with the present leaders of South Korea if the latter would give up their two-Koreas policy, apologize for their crimes in massacring fellow countrymen, release political prisoners, and restore the freedom of political activities to those under the political ban.[46]

The negative response from North Korea did not deter the South Koreans from further initiatives. The Chun government apparently had decided to inundate Pyongyang with proposals for dialogue. In late January the head of the South Korean Red Cross urged the North Koreans to resume the Red Cross talks. In early February the Minister of Unification presented the North Koreans with a twenty-point package of proposals, including the opening of a highway between Seoul and Pyongyang, the opening of Inchon and Chinampo ports to trade between North and South, free press coverage of the other side by journalists of each side, the creation of joint fisheries zones and joint development of natural resources, the removal of all military facilities from the DMZ, and the discussion of arms control measures by military officers of both sides.[47]

The North Korean response was to reject all these proposals and to propose instead a conference of one hundred persons, fifty from each side, to discuss unification. Pyongyang obviously did not expect this proposal to be taken seriously by the South Korean government for it took it upon itself to name the South Korean participants in the proposed conference, including a number of individuals hostile to the Chun government in South Korea or resident abroad. The Minister of Unification then proposed high-level inter-Korean talks to discuss both President Chun's unification formula and the unification conference proposed by North Korea. The North Korean authorities did not respond directly, but the Voice of the Revolutionary Party for Reunification rejected the proposal in a radio broadcast.

Continued Stalemate—1983

During 1983 the South Korean authorities continued to call for a high-level dialogue between the two governments without conditions, expressing willingness to discuss all issues, including Kim Il Sung's confederal republic formula. The North Koreans showed no interest in meeting with representatives of the ROK government. Instead, the Korean Central News Agency (KCNA) broadcast a lengthy, propagandistic appeal, in the name of political parties in North Korea, for a conference of political parties and social organizations of the two Koreas to discuss the withdrawal of U.S. forces from South Korea.[48] In response, South Korea proposed a conference of government, political party, and social organization representatives to discuss a meeting of the top leaders of both sides and other unification issues.[49] In July 1983 the Central Committee of the Democratic Front for the Reunification of the Fatherland in Pyongyang sent letters to South Korean political parties and social organizations appealing to them to overthrow the "Chun Doo Hwan military fascist clique," democratize South Korea, and join hands with their brothers in the North to reunify the country in accordance with Kim Il Sung's proposal and to force the withdrawal of U.S. forces.

The proposals and counterproposals of 1983 continued the pattern established during the previous two years. The South Koreans stressed the need for high-level discussions between the two governments. The North Koreans refused to have anything to do with the Chun government, proposing instead large conferences of persons representing political and social groups from North and South, sometimes explicitly including avowed foes of the Chun government. Their propaganda persisted in condemning Chun in harsh terms. Both parties had presented elaborate proposals for unification. Pyongyang wanted its proposal adopted as a package, whereas Seoul emphasized the need for preliminary agreement on family reunions, trade, and other forms of interaction in order to break down mistrust and prepare the way for the negotiation of broad political arrangements.

Tripartite Talks Proposal

In 1984 North Korea dropped its obdurate refusal to deal with representatives of the South Korean government, and North-South dialogue reached a level of activity not seen since the early 1970s. The first move was an offer by Pyongyang to permit South Korea to participate "in an equal capacity" with the United States and North Korea in tripartite talks. The proposal, in the form of a letter addressed to the U.S. government and Congress, was adopted by a joint meeting of North Korea's Central People's Committee and the Standing Committee of the SPA. The letter was given to President Reagan on January 11 by Chinese Premier Zhao Ziyang during his visit to the United States. A separate letter, addressed to Prime Minister Chin Ui-chong from Premier Yi Chong-ok reached Seoul some days later by international airmail. Both texts had been broadcast by Pyongyang radio before delivery.

As formulated by Pyongyang, the tripartite talks would consist of two sets of negotiations, one between the United States and North Korea on a peace treaty to replace the armistice (including conditions for the withdrawal of U.S. forces), and one between South Korea and North Korea on a nonaggression pact and the reduction of armaments. Once these matters had been agreed upon, the two Koreas would hold a political consultative congress, composed of the authorities of North and South and persons from all walks of life, to work out arrangements for unification.[50]

The South Koreans reacted coldly to the North Korean proposal. Only three months had passed since the Rangoon bombing and their anger and grief were still fresh. They pointed to two messages agreeing to South Korean participation in tripartite talks passed by the North Koreans to the United States through Chinese channels in Peking in late 1983 as evidence of North Korean duplicity. One was passed on October 8, the day before the Rangoon bombing, the other on December 3, about the same time that the South Korean navy sank a North Korean spy ship and captured two agents off Pusan.

The South Koreans had never been enthusiastic about the tripartite format, which would enable North Korea to enter into official negotiations with the United States without any comparable action by the Soviets or Chinese toward South Korea. Park Chung-hee had agreed reluctantly to join Jimmy Carter in proposing a tripartite conference in order to ensure the suspension by the United States of troop withdrawals and with the expectation that North Korea would turn it down.

The conference proposed by the North Koreans in 1984 was not even a full-fledged tripartite conference, for South Korea was to be excluded from the critical negotiations on a peace treaty and the withdrawal of U.S. forces. This was clearly unacceptable to the South Korean government. Prime Minister Chin Ui-chong accordingly wrote to North Korean Premier Kang Song-san (who had succeeded Yi Chong-ok) decrying North Korea's refusal to admit to or apologize for the Rangoon bombing and stressing the urgent need for North-South dialogue.[51] Kang replied to Chin, regretting South Korea's rejection of the tripartite talks proposal and reiterating North Korea's long-standing position that only the United States was competent to conclude a peace treaty, as it was party to the armistice and held the supreme command of all forces in South Korea, including the ROK forces.[52] The United States did not flatly reject the trilateral talks concept, but made clear that it backed the South Korean appeal for bilateral talks and indicated that it would also welcome four-power talks, including China.[53]

Although Pyongyang formulated its proposal in a way that made it unattractive to the United States and South Korea, its willingness to contemplate negotiations with representatives of the Chun government was a significant moderation of the hard-line position maintained since Chun had become president. The decision to moderate that position probably was a response to a variety of pressures. Most important was the need to repair the damage done to North Korea's international image by the Rangoon affair. The tripartite talks proposal not only served to push Rangoon into the background, it also reduced the advantage Chun Doo Hwan derived from contrasting South Korea's willingness to have bilateral talks at any level with Kim Il Sung's refusal to have anything to do with his government. The need to placate the Chinese may also have been important. Only a few days after Deng Xiaoping himself had raised with U.S. Defense Secretary Caspar Weinberger the desirability of U.S. and Chinese cooperation in reducing tension in Korea, the North Koreans perpetrated the Rangoon atrocity, acutely embarrassing the Chinese leader. Moderation of policy toward South Korea also coincided with the greatly increased emphasis on foreign trade announced in January 1984. Trade prospects for North Korea would certainly be enhanced by a less provocative policy toward South Korea.

The failure to elicit a favorable response from the United States and South Korea did not discourage the North Koreans from continuing to publicize the tripartite talks proposal and to seek endorsements of it from friendly countries. The text of the proposal had painted in lurid colors the danger of nuclear war in Korea. The timing of its announcement enabled the North Koreans to contrast their call for peace negotiations with the annual Team Spirit exercise in South Korea, begun in early February. The exercise was pictured by the North Koreans as preparation for an attack on the North.

Bilateral Talks

Trilateral talks having failed to elicit a favorable response, the North Koreans turned to the bilateral North-South dialogue long advocated by the Chun government. On March 30, 1984, the chairman of the DPRK Olympic Committee sent a letter to the chairman of the ROK Olympic Committee unexpectedly proposing the formation of a joint North-South team to compete in the Los Angeles Olympics in July. The damanding and difficult task of organizing a joint team could hardly be accomplished in three months, and the South Koreans pointed out that North Korea had failed to respond to their proposal back in 1981 to form such a team for the Los Angeles Olympics. Nevertheless, delegates from the two Olympic Committees met three times at Panmunjom before the North Koreans refused to continue on the ground that South Korea had introduced political issues.

Chun Doo Hwan made the next move. In August at a press conference he again urged the North Koreans to join a North-South dialogue. He went on to offer North Korea "various technologies and commodities, free of charge, which would substantially contribute to improving the lives of our brethren there."[54] North Korea rejected this offer, but on September 8 took an action that resulted in breaking new ground in North-South relations. The DPRK Red Cross society offered to send to South Korea, which had just suffered a devastating flood, 50,000 bags of rice, 500,000 meters of fabrics, 100,000 tons of cement, and medical supplies as relief for flood victims.

South Korea had turned down similar offers by North Korea in the past. This time, however, the ROK Red Cross society accepted the offer, pointing out that the relief supplies were not needed—they had just declined aid proferred by the World Red Cross—but that they accepted the North Korean offer as a means of fostering "an atmosphere of harmony and mutual aid" between the North and South.[55] Negotiations over the means of delivery seemed on the verge of breaking down at times, but succeeded in the end through an unaccustomed willingness by both sides to make concessions. The rice, medical supplies, and fabrics were transferred to South Korean trucks at Panmunjom for the journey to Seoul, rather than exposing the local populace to the sight of a fleet of North Korean trucks entering the South Korean capital as the North Koreans had originally desired. The cement went by ship to Inchon and Pukpyong.

The transfer took place remarkably smoothly and with few hitches. A friendly atmosphere prevailed between the Red Cross personnel of the two sides supervising the shipment. North Korea took advantage of the propaganda opportunity to portray the South Korean people as poverty-stricken and enormously grateful to their better-off North Korean brethren and "the great leader" for their generous gift. South Koreans looked the gift horse in the mouth and commented on the low quality of the materials delivered. On the whole, however, both parties appeared gratified at the degree of cooperation achieved by North and South in carrying out this unprecedented operation.

The successful delivery of relief supplies opened the door to North-South talks on other subjects. From November 1984 through December 1985, representatives of the two Koreas held a dozen formal meetings, as well as a number of lower level meetings of working groups and liaison officers. The meetings dealt with four topics: reunions of separated families, economic cooperation, a conference of parliamentarians from each side, and the 1988 Olympics. Obstacles cropped up and delays occurred. The North Koreans postponed an economic meeting scheduled for December after the shoot-out between North Korean and South Korean soldiers provoked by the defection of the Soviet intern at Panmunjom. In January 1985 the North Koreans postponed both the economic and Red Cross talks scheduled for that month on the ground that the Team Spirit exercise, scheduled for February, March, and April, would spoil the atmosphere for dialogue. South Korea turned down a North Korean proposal for a meeting of deputy premiers to discuss the removal of this obstacle to the talks, and the dialogue remained suspended until May, after the Team Spirit exercise had ended.

Red Cross Talks

The talks on family reunions attracted the most attention, for they involved meetings of the two Red Cross delegations alternately in Seoul and Pyongyang and, for the first time ever, reunions of some separated family members with their relatives on the other side of the DMZ. The visits by the North Korean delegation to Seoul in May and December and of the South Korean delegation to Pyongyang in August received extensive media coverage, for each delegation of 14 members and 20 assistants traveled with 50 media representatives. Banquets and sightseeing for the visitors provided local color and opportunities for informal contacts. Minor differences arose over arrangements—the North Koreans for obvious reasons flatly refused to visit the stadium built for the 1988 Olympics and the South Koreans walked out of a gymnastics demonstration because of its military flavor and its tribute to Kim Il Sung—but on the whole the visits went smoothly.

The highlight of the year was the exchange of 151 persons from each side in September 1985, consisting of 50 members of separated families seeking their relatives, 50 folk art performers, 30 media representatives, and 21 support personnel. The South Korean Red Cross delegation had pressed for the family visitors to be allowed to see relatives in their hometowns, but the North Koreans insisted on limiting the visits to Seoul and Pyongyang. Both sides had difficulty in locating the relatives of the family visitors, and in the end only 30 of the North Koreans and 35 of the South Koreans actually met relatives during the visit. The sight of brothers and sisters, children and parents meeting tearfully for the first time in thirty-five years had a powerful emotional impact, demonstrating in human terms the tragedy of national division and the importance of dialogue.

Although only a tiny fraction of the estimated 5 million persons in South Korea who originated in North Korea met their relatives on the other side briefly in the September 1985 exchange of visits, that dramatic event was a significant advance over anything previously achieved in the Red Cross talks. Except for that success, however, the three formal talks produced little progress. As their first priority, the North Koreans wanted an agreement to permit family members from each side, certified by their respective Red Cross societies, to travel freely on the other side of the DMZ to seek out their relatives. The South Koreans preferred to reach agreement first on the procedures governing visits, including the inauguration of a Joint Committee and a Joint Panmunjom Project Office to negotiate and implement procedures for travel across the DMZ. They also wanted each side to establish Red Cross representative offices in each other's capital.

The North Koreans proposed that the Red Cross delegations travel to Seoul and Pyongyang by plane rather than by train, bus, and car. The South Koreans rejected the proposal, fearing that it might be exploited by North Korea for aerial surveillance. At the tenth full-dress meeting in Seoul in December 1985, the South Koreans proposed another exchange of family visits on the occasion of the lunar new year in February 1986. The North Koreans rejected the proposal, however, on the ground that it was a diversion from the main task of reaching agreement on "free visits" back and forth. All that could be agreed upon was to hold the eleventh full-dress meeting on February 26, 1986, in Pyongyang.

The media on both sides injected a pungent propaganda flavor into their coverage of the Red Cross encounters. Each stressed the reasonableness of its proposals and found evidence of insincerity in its rival's refusal to agree. Each discovered on the other side of the DMZ distressing sights that confirmed their downbeat image of the rival system. South Korean reporters described Pyongyang as a gray city, overflowing with statues and slogans honoring Kim Il Sung, where people on the streets were few and poorly dressed. Reports on the meetings between relatives focused on criticisms North Koreans made of religious belief in the South and their expressions of gratitude to Kim Il Sung for arranging the meeting. Critics of the North Korean folk art performances found them disappointing, influenced by the Soviet Union and China, and unrepresentative of the Korean national spirit. Commentators highlighted the differences between the two Koreas rather than what they had in common, and found little to praise in the strange land across the DMZ, despite the efforts of the hosts to show off their most impressive accomplishments.[56]

The North Korean media outdid the South Koreans in finding fault with the rival system. A Pyongyang domestic broadcast, entitled "74 Hours Across the Demarcation Line—A Land Which Is Suffocating Under the Foot of the U.S. Imperialists," related that reporters driving south from Panmunjom to Seoul were stared at by the "bloodthirsty eyes" of "U.S. imperialist aggressor wretches wearing helmets," and saw "offensive military installations for northward invasion" on every mountain ridge and in every valley.[57] A long three-part article in *Nodong Sinmun* criticized the arrangements made in Seoul for the relatives' reunion, charging that surveillance by security personnel prevented free conversation. "Everything we saw offended us during the visit," the article declared.[58] A female family visitor found Seoul "more deplorable than what she had heard about it," adding that "the attire and manner of women were so unseemly that they defied description."[59] North Korean visitors, claiming that they had been taken against their will to see the Lotte Department Store, reported that the goods there were for foreigners; the South Korean masses could only window shop, as they could not afford such things.[60] Air pollution in Seoul, caused by poorly equipped plants, military exercises, and the frequent use of tear gas, was suffocating.[61]

North Korean commentators reacted with outrage to South Korean criticisms that their folk art performance in Seoul departed from traditional Korean culture. On the contrary, they said, that performance was a brilliant *chu che* ray of light that thrilled the people of the South, who languished "amid the disgusting Western and Japanese culture." They chided the South Korean reporters who visited the North for having written propaganda attacks on North Korea at the behest of the South Korean government.[62]

The harshness of the reciprocal media attacks evoked by the Red Cross meetings suggests that the meetings may have driven the wedge deeper rather than eased the confrontation between the two Koreas. It reflects accurately the intensity of the suspicion and rivalry between them. Each wants to take maximum propaganda advantage of the dialogue and prevent, if possible, any gains by the other side.

Through the fog of propaganda, some favorable signs can be discerned. The exchange of famiy visitors and folk art troupes actually occurred, in spite of the dispute over the South Korean walkout from the militaristic gymnastic performance less than a month earlier. A substantial number of people have had a firsthand look at the land on the other side of the DMZ, and large numbers have seen the photographs and television shots brought back. The Red Cross delegations have become better acquainted with their opposition numbers through both formal and informal contacts. The head of the North Korean delegation even met at dinner five of his former classmates at a Seoul high school. The two sides have been more flexible than in the past, and neither has so far put forward patently unacceptable demands such as the North Korean demand in previous talks that South Korea must abrogate all anticommunist laws as a precondition for the exchange of families.

Economic Talks

The two Koreas held five sessions of economic talks at Panmunjom between November 1984 and November 1985. These talks, between delegations headed by government officials of vice ministerial rank, were important in demonstrating that the North Koreans would now deal officially with the government of South Korea. The chief North Korean delegate even brought a message to the first meeting from the North Korean vice premier expressing willingness to meet with South Korea's deputy prime minister. At the third meeting the South Koreans agreed to a North Korean proposal to form a North-South Joint Committee for Economic Cooperation. The committee would be headed by deputy prime ministers who would meet alternately in each capital.

The talks were serious in tone and largely free of the propaganda treatment by the media that characterized the Red Cross talks. The two sides agreed to open a telephone link exclusively for the economic talks. They exchanged lists of commodities that they were willing to trade and designated areas in which they were willing to undertake cooperative projects. Some overlap in the proposals indicated items on which early progress might be achieved, such as the expressed willingness of both sides to reopen the North-South railway and to open ports to the other side.

Early enthusiasm gave way to frustration as certain basic differences emerged and niggling over seemingly inconsequential issues delayed discussion of substance. The North Koreans took issue with aspects of South Korean proposals that seemed to them more appropriate to economic relations between separate states than to two parts of a single nation seeking unification. Hence, they gave priority to joint projects in such areas as mining and fisheries over trade. They showed no interest in a South Korean offer to purchase 300,000 tons of North Korean coal, as a pilot project to get economic interchange started. They insisted that raw materials should be exchanged for raw materials and manufactured goods for manufactured goods, rather than taking principally South Korean manufactures for North Korean raw materials, as the South Koreans initially proposed.

At the fifth meeting, presentation of substantive proposals gave way to argument over details. The negotiators disagreed on whether the three principles of national unification agreed on in 1972 should be included in the preamble or in a separate chapter of the economic agreement. They also disagreed on the title of the agreement. Should it be "Agreement on the Realization of Economic Cooperation and Exchange of Commodities between North and South and the Formation of a Joint Committee for North-South Economic Cooperation Chaired by Officials of Vice-Premier Level" or "Agreement on the Promotion of Exchange of Commodities and Economic Cooperation Between the North and South and Institution of a Joint Committee for North-South Economic Cooperation"?[63] Time ran out and further discussion of such critical issues had to be deferred to the next meeting, set for two months later.

The concrete nature of the proposals made, the serious attitudes of the negotiators, and the restrained treatment by the media suggest that both parties perceive advantages in pursuing some form of agreement on economic interaction. The tendency to quibble over minor points, however, presages a long and tortuous course of negotiations before any goods can actually be exchanged or any cooperative project can get underway. The two sides have already disagreed on what must be included in the basic agreement and what could be left to the Joint Committee to decide. Agreement will have to be reached at some level on a host of details: the organization, operation and places of meeting of the Joint Committee, goods to be exchanged, prices to be charged, currencies and accounting methods to be used, means of transport, the organization of cooperative projects, taxes to be applied, arrangements for the entry and exit of workers on cooperative projects, and many more.

Parliamentary Talks

In April 1985 the DPRK's Supreme People's Assembly addressed a letter to the "National Assembly, Republic of Korea." It pointed out that the vice premier meeting proposed earlier by North Korea to discuss easing the military confrontation had not been realized. The letter proposed either a joint session of the two parliamentary bodies or a meeting of delegates from each to discuss and agree on a joint declaration of nonaggression "to ease tension and improve North-South relations." After some delay due to the late opening of the newly elected National Assembly, the South Korean body replied, proposing a preliminary meeting of delegates from the two parliaments to discuss arrangements for a joint parliamentary meeting.

The North Koreans agreed, and in July 1985 five members from each legislative body and four assistants met at Panmunjom. The South Korean delegation, declaring that the negotiation of a nonaggression pact should be undertaken by the two governments, rather than by legislative bodies, proposed that the two parliaments agree on the formation of a "people's council of unification" to draft a unified constitution to be adopted by a free election throughout the country.[64] The North Koreans expressed willingness to accept as an agenda item the formation of a consultative body to draw up a unified constitution, but insisted that agreement on a nonaggression pact had to come first. A subsequent preliminary meeting in September failed to break the deadlock on the agenda. Despite pressure from the North Koreans for a third preliminary meeting, the South Koreans declined to set a date until after the fall session of the National Assembly recessed in late December.

In his speech to the SPA in April 1985 presenting the parliamentary talks proposal, Ho Tam, Politburo member and chairman of the Committee for the Peaceful Reunification of the Fatherland, expressly stated that the North Koreans regard the parliamentary talks as more important than the economic and Red Cross talks.[65] The parliamentary talks would provide the kind of forum frequently proposed in the past by Pyongyang, including, on the ROK side, delegates from both the government and the opposition. Parliamentary talks would also focus on a nonaggression pact, which Pyongyang closely associates with its primary objective—to bring about the withdrawal of U.S. forces from South Korea. Even though the difference between the two sides on the agenda is deep and unlikely to be resolved soon, the fact that members of the two parliaments met to discuss setting up parliamentary meetings on substantive issues was a notable advance by Seoul and Pyongyang toward accepting each other's legitimacy.

Talks on the Olympics

The fourth channel for North-South talks in 1984 and 1985 dealt with the 1988 Olympic Games. The North Koreans had been highly critical of the decision by the International Olympic Committee (IOC) to award the 1988 Olympic Games to Seoul. They had demanded that if the games were held in Korea at all, they should be divided equally between Seoul and Pyongyang. The chairman of the IOC, Juan Samaranch, saw no way consistent with the Olympic charter to divide the games equally between the two cities, but he invited representatives from both places to several meetings in Geneva. South Korea expressed willingness for some events to be held in Pyongyang, and as of mid-1986 Samaranch was seeking agreement between the two countries on which events should be held in North Korea (see Chapter 10).

Proposals Concerning the DMZ

On July 29, 1985, the North Korean representative in the Military Armistice Commission (MAC) proposed a drastic reduction in armed personnel stationed in the approximately 10-square-kilometer MAC Headquarters Area at Panmunjom, straddling the Military Demarcation Line. The proposal called for dismantling guardposts in the MAC Headquarters Area; removal from that area of all heavy and automatic weapons; reduction of security guards there from 65 to 20 on each side, to be armed only with handguns; and reduction of guards in the inner Joint Security Area around the Panmunjom conference site from 35 to 10, all to be unarmed. After considering the proposal for two months, the UN Command representative declined the proposal on the ground that the proposed arrangement would place the UN at a military disadvantage because of the geographical configuration of the area. In subsequent meetings the UN Command representative expressed willingness to reduce the arms carried by guards but only if agreement had been reached first on a system to verify compliance with this and other confidence-building measures.[66]

The unexpected North Korean proposal in the MAC may have been motivated primarily by a desire to prevent the kind of firefight that occurred when the Soviet defector dashed across the Military Demarcation Line in November 1984, as indicated in the text of the North Korean proposal.[67] It may also have been intended as a show of interest in confidence-building measures in the DMZ, which the UN Command had long urged and which Congressman Solarz had raised directly with Kim Il Sung in 1980. A standard U.S. response to Chinese efforts to persuade the United States to accept the tripartite talks proposal had been that one way the North Koreans could help reduce tension in

Korea would be to agree on confidence-building measures in the DMZ. The North Koreans may have concluded that showing interest in such measures would improve prospects for U.S. agreement on the tripartite talks.

Tripartite Military Talks

Early in 1986 the North Koreans again suspended the Red Cross, economic, and parliamentary talks as they had done in 1985 on the ground that the Team Spirit exercises spoiled the atmosphere for dialogue. They did not, however, resume the talks after the Team Spirit exercise ended, as they had done the previous year. Instead, they came up with a new proposal for tripartite talks. North Korean Defense Minister O Chin-u addressed letters to South Korean Defense Minister Lee Ki-baek and UN Commander General William J. Livsey asserting that military activities in South Korea had created a grave danger of nuclear war and had forced suspension of the North-South dialogue. He proposed talks among the three of them at Panmunjom on ways of easing tension, including halting military exercises, reducing forces and armaments, and observing the original provisions of the Armistice Agreement.[68]

A few days later the government of the DPRK issued a formal statement attacking the United States for introducing large numbers of nuclear weapons into South Korea and creating a serious threat of nuclear war there. The statement proposed, in connection with "the year of international peace," making the Korean peninsula a nuclear-free zone. It called on the United States to withdraw its nuclear weapons from Korea and pledged that the DPRK would not produce nuclear weapons, permit the establishment of foreign military bases on its territory, or allow the passage of foreign nuclear weapons through its territory. It offered to negotiate with the United States and South Korea the procedures for making Korea a nuclear-free zone.[69]

The United States and South Korea declined to enter into the proposed tripartite talks. The South Korean government denounced the tripartite military talks and nuclear-free zone proposals as propaganda ploys designed to shift the blame for tension on the peninsula away from North Korea. If North Korea genuinely desired peace and the easing of tension in Korea, the South Korean government declared, it would resume immediately the Red Cross, economic, and parliamentary talks and agree to a North-South summit meeting.[70]

Prospects

For more than twenty years the two Koreas concentrated exclusively on their military confrontation, totally rejected each other's legitimacy as governments, and had no contact whatsoever. Then, abruptly, in the early 1970s they began to talk to each other, less in the expectation of making genuine progress toward unification—their declared goal—than to gain advantage in their rivalry. The talks soon ground to a halt, primarily because North Korea saw no advantage in continuing, and both leaders again turned their full attention to the military buildup.

The 1980s have seen no letup in military preparations on either side. The Rangoon bombing greatly deepened hostility among South Koreans toward North Korea and intensified the suspicion with which they regarded North Korean overtures for dialogue. Despite this unpropitious atmosphere, the talks that began in 1984 surpassed the dialogue of the 1970s, both in variety of channels and in accomplishments.

Perhaps the most significant development was North Korea's willingness to deal officially with representatives of both the executive and legislative branches of the Chun Doo Hwan government. In tandem with the world community's increasing acceptance of the legitimacy of the two governments, the two Koreas were edging toward accepting each other's legitimacy. In January 1985, Chun Doo Hwan renewed his call for a face-to-face meeting with Kim Il Sung. Although not yet prepared to take this step, Kim stated in his New Year's address that if the North-South dialogue went well, a top-level meeting would become possible. Ho Tam reiterated this possibility in his April speech presenting the parliamentary talks proposal, a speech which referred to Chun as "South Korean President Chun Doo Hwan" and was remarkably free of the usual detraction of South Korea.[71] In late 1985 rumors abounded in South Korea that Ho Tam had secretly visited Seoul to confer with Chun Doo Hwan.

Schizophrenia was evident in the way the leaders of the two Koreas dealt with each other. On the one hand, they pursued dialogue, and their willingness to treat each other as legitimate interlocutors increased. On the other hand, they warned their people against the evil designs harbored by the other side. The report delivered by Vice Premier Chong Chun-ki to an October 1985 meeting commemorating the fifth anniversary of Kim Il Sung's proposal to found the Democratic Republic of Koryo serves as a good example of both attitudes incorporated into a single speech. Much of the speech was given over to denunciation of "the South Korean puppet clique" that "is running amok with provocative northward aggressive confrontation maneuvers" and gives "only lip service to the desire for dialogue and reunification." Nevertheless, Chong declared "we will make all possible efforts to make the current multifaceted North-South dialogues successful."[72] In South Korea Chun Doo Hwan alternated appeals for a higher level dialogue with warnings to the people to be alert to the military threat from the North.

Many officials in Seoul were convinced, like Chong Chun-ki, that their rivals gave only lip service to the dialogue. The dominant view among the military and officials of the Agency for National Security Planning (ANSP) was that North Korea's willingness to talk at that juncture was simply a cover for preparations to take over South Korea by force. In light of the military preparations and forward deployments in the North, the Rangoon atrocity, Pyongyang's encouragement of antigovernment violence in the South, and the derision of the South Korean government expressed in official North Korean publications, that view was difficult to refute.

Still, an influential minority in South Korea, particularly among intellectuals, although not excluding the possibility that the North Koreans would use force against the South if a suitable opportunity arose, argued that circumstances had compelled North Korea to take the dialogue seriously. They believed that the North Koreans needed substantive progress in the dialogue to impress favorably the United States and Japan, to expand foreign trade, to compete more effectively with South Korea in the international community, and to improve prospects for trilateral talks.

Those in South Korea who favor serious efforts to make progress in the dialogue, including President Chun himself, see important reasons for doing so. Perhaps the most important is the need for a peaceful atmosphere for the Olympic Games in 1988. Advocates of dialogue hope that substantive progress will reduce the risk that North Korea would try to disrupt the games by acts of violence. Keen public interest in the dialogue, especially in the family reunion talks, also acts as a stimulus to the government to keep the talks going. Chun's personal identification with the dialogue helps to assure popular acceptance of him as a leader so long as it seems to be moving ahead. Conversely, collapse of the dialogue, unless the onus could be placed indisputably on North Korea, would weaken Chun's political position. Thus, in spite of widespread cynicism concerning North Korea's motives in entering into the dialogue, the arguments for trying to press ahead with the talks are compelling.

Whether differences of opinion concerning the talks exist within the North Korean leadership cannot be determined. A case can be made that the schizophrenia shown by the media in its treatment of South Korea is evidence of conflicting views, but confirmation is lacking. A U.S. visitor to North Korea in the summer of 1985 was told by officials that they were seriously pursuing the dialogue and that they thought the South Koreans were also. The officials said that they had been surprised by the South Koreans' acceptance of the relief supplies and also by their agreement to a meeting of parliamentarians. They expressed optimism that progress would be made. However, when he visited

Pyongyang again after the talks had been suspended in the spring of 1986, he found their optimism replaced by pessimism.[73] A leading Chinese Korea-watcher had earlier described the opening of the dialogue as "a break-through" in North-South relations and was optimistic that progress would be made, even though the talks probably would move slowly and suffer occasional setbacks.[74]

The lengthy suspension of the talks in 1986 and North Korea's return to insistence on a tripartite format have reinforced the doubts of skeptics in South Korea concerning North Korean seriousness toward North-South dialogue. For its part, Pyongyang has clearly given precedence over the dialogue to the renewal of its efforts to compel the United States to enter into some form of official negotiation on the issue of the reduction and eventual withdrawal of U.S. forces. By linking their nuclear-free zone proposal to the UN proclamation of 1986 as a year of peace, they doubtless hoped to mobilize significant international support for their position.

The opposition political rallies and student violence in South Korea in the spring of 1986 may have been another factor causing the North Koreans to put off the resumption of North-South talks. They may have felt that resuming bilateral talks would strengthen the government's hand, whereas shifting to the U.S. and South Korean governments the onus of refusing to meet would strengthen resistance to the Chun government.

The hostility and wariness with which each Korea views the other remain the controlling elements in their relationship. By the nature of the profession, the military on each side will continue to grind out worst-case scenarios. And yet, despite the suspension of talks in 1986 and the uncertainty as to when they will resume, the divided Korea of the mid-1980s holds more promise of easing tensions than in any previous decade. Negotiators on both sides have shown greater flexibility and greater civility towards each other than in the past. Some family reunions have, for the first time, actually occurred. Pressures on the two governments, internal and external, seem more inclined to encourage than to discourage continuation of the dialogue.

When talks resume, as they must sooner or later, they are likely to develop a momentum of their own that would be difficult to halt or reverse. Each government has created units within its bureaucracy dedicated to planning for meetings and conducting negotiations. These officials will have a vested interest in having the talks continue, although their bureaucratic caution and fear of making an error will ensure endless wrangling over minor issues. Eventually, however, the two sides, in spite of their hostility and suspicion, may become locked into a process that will enable them to live more comfortably with each other.

Notes

1. Lack of reliable data makes difficult accurate estimates of North Korea's GNP and the proportion of GNP allocated to defense. Former U.S. ambassador to South Korea Richard L. Sneider gave an estimate of 15 to 20 percent of GNP for the late 1970s, see "Prospects for Korean Security," in Richard H. Solomon, ed., *Asian Security in the 1980s* (Santa Monica, Calif.: Rand Corporation, 1979), p. 115. Gregory F.T. Winn gives a broader spread, 15 to 25 percent, for that period reflecting uncertainties about the data; see "Riding the Tiger: Military Confrontation on the Korean Peninsula," in Kwak and others, *U.S. Korean Relations*, p. 269. Paul Wolfowitz, U.S. assistant secretary of state for East Asian and Pacific Affairs, in testimony before a Congressional committee, gave a figure of 20 to 25 percent for the past decade (*Korea Herald*, February 23, 1985). U.S. military commanders tend to cite the higher extreme: General Robert W. Sennewald, "at least 25 percent," (*Korea Herald*, October 9, 1983); Admiral William Crowe, Jr., "roughly 25 percent" (*Korea Herald*, March 2, 1985). Norman Levin of the Rand Corporation, after careful study of all available data, concluded in 1982 that the figure was "in the area of 20 percent" (*Korea Herald*, November 11, 1982).

2. According to the South Korean National Unification Board, South Korea's GNP in 1984 was 5.5 times that of North Korea, and military expenditures by the South were 1.2 times those of the North (*FBIS*, November 6, 1985, p. E2).

3. Testimony of James Kelley, deputy assistant secretary of defense, International Security Affairs (ISA), before Subcommittee on Asian and Pacific Affairs, House Foreign Affairs Committee, 99th Cong., 1st sess., March 5, 1985.

4. *Washington Post*, May 10, 1984.

5. *New York Times*, April 1, 1982; *Washington Post*, May 10, 1984.

6. *Washington Post*, January 13, 1981.

7. *Korea Herald*, February 3, 1981.

8. *Korea Herald*, November 18, 1983.

9. *Washington Post*, January 14, 1979.

10. *Korea Herald*, July 28, 1985.

11. A study by Norman Levin in 1982 expressed doubt that South Korea could catch up with North Korea militarily within five to seven years; see *Korea Herald*, November 11, 1982, and Norman D. Levin, *Management and Decision Making in the North Korean Economy* (Santa Monica, Calif.: Rand Corporation, February 1982), pp. 51–61. Defense Minister Yoon Sung-min predicted in 1983 that South Korea could catch up in 1990 if it continued to spend 6 percent of GNP on defense (*Korea Herald*, November 18, 1983). In an interview with Congressman Stephen J. Solarz in July 1980, Kim Yong-nam, then director of the International Department of the KWP, denied that North Korean forces were as large as the U.S. and South Korean estimates. He asserted North Korean forces were only between 350,000 and 400,000, but undercut his credibility by claiming that unlike U.S. and South Korean forces, the North Korean forces did not conduct maneuvers—they were too busy in the fields and on construction sites (*The Korean Conundrum*, p. 8).

12. *Korea Herald,* February 26, 1985.

13. *New York Times,* February 4, 1985; *Washington Post,* February 27, 1985.

14. See Chapter 8.

15. *Korea Herald,* November 29, 1984, quoted a statement by Zbigniew Brzezinski to JIJI Press. In early 1985 SCUD missiles, probably acquired by Iran from Libya, were fired at Iraqi cities (*New York Times,* March 20 and April 1, 1985).

16. *Yomiuri,* quoted in *Korea Herald,* August 27, 1985.

17. *Sankei,* quoted in *Korea Herald,* April 18, 1985.

18. See Chapter 8.

19. *Korea Herald,* September 19, 1982.

20. *Japan Times,* November 25, 1983.

21. *FBIS,* April 28, 1986, pp. D1–D5; *Korea Herald,* May 7, 1986.

22. *Korea Herald,* September 11, 1982.

23. *Japan Times Weekly,* May 3, 1980.

24. *Korea Herald,* September 11, 1985.

25. *Korea Herald,* October 22 and 29, 1985; *FBIS,* October 24, 1985, pp. D1–D2.

26. *FBIS,* October 28, 1985, pp. D3–D5.

27. *Korea Herald,* October 9, 1985; *FBIS,* November 15, 1985, p. D4; *FBIS,* November 18, 1985, p. D1.

28. *FBIS,* August 27, 1984, pp. D17–D19. Although North Korea first set up a subversive organization in South Korea in 1964, it dates the founding of the RPR in 1969, after the original organization had been rolled up by the KCIA.

29. *FBIS,* August 27, 1984, pp. D12–D14, D15–D16.

30. *FBIS,* April 18, 1985, pp. D4–D5.

31. *Korea Herald,* June 26, 1980; *FBIS,* May 13, 1985, p. D9.

32. *Korea Herald,* February 22, 27, 1982; *Washington Post,* February 18, 1984.

33. *FBIS,* May 16, 1983, pp. D8–D9.

34. *New York Times* and *Korea Herald,* November 5, 1983.

35. *Korea Herald,* October 10, 1984.

36. See Chapter 9.

37. *FBIS,* May 2, 1985, pp. D1–D5.

38. *FBIS,* August 8, 1985, pp. D2–D3. According to the *Chosun Ilbo,* the broadcasts originate in Haeju, Kwanghae Province, about 50 kilometers north of the DMZ (*FBIS,* August 12, 1985, p. E1).

39. *FBIS,* August 9, 1985, pp. D1–D8.

40. *FBIS,* August 27, 1985, pp. D9–D10, D12–D14.

41. *FBIS,* July 9, 1985, p. D8.

42. *FBIS,* September 17, 1985, pp. D1–D9.

43. *FBIS,* October 15, 1980. The section of the speech dealing with unification appears on pp. D1 to D15.

44. *New York Times,* January 20, 1981.

45. The full text of Chun's speech is carried in the *Korea Herald,* January 23, 1982.

46. *FBIS,* January 26, 1982.

47. *Korea Herald,* February 2, 1982.

48. *FBIS,* January 18, 1983, p. D1–D3; *Korea Herald,* January 20, 1983.

49. *Korea Herald,* February 2, 1983.

50. *FBIS,* January 11, 1984, pp. D6–D11.

51. *FBIS,* February 15, 1984, p. E1.

52. *FBIS,* March 7, 1984, pp. D1–D3.

53. For an official U.S. reaction, see testimony of John C. Monjo, deputy assistant secretary of state at a hearing before the Subcommittee on Asian and Pacific Affairs of the House Committee on Foreign Affairs, 98th Cong., 2d sess., March 20, 1984, pp. 67–77.

54. *Korea Herald,* August 23, 1984.

55. *FBIS,* September 14, 1984, p. E1–E2.

56. Examples of South Korea reporting on North Korea can be found in the *Korea Herald,* "Pyongyang streets, country eerily quiet" (August 28, 1985); "Seoul Red Cross Delegates Tour Downtown Pyongyang" (August 30, 1985); "A grim, repressed city, with surface modernity" (September 1, 1985); "North Korean citizens mobilized for propaganda" (September 3, 1985); "Abysmal South-North gap diminishes joy of family reunions" (September 25, 1985); "North Korean restrictions depress visitors" (September 26, 1985); "Pyongyang rife with propaganda, guile" (September 28, 1985); "'Paradise lost' in North Korean society" (September 29, 1985).

57. *FBIS,* October 2, 1985, pp. D1–D4.

58. *FBIS,* September 30, 1985, pp. D10–D13; October 1, 1985, pp. D14–D17; October 2, 1985, pp. D5–D7.

59. *FBIS,* September 30, 1985, p. D10.

60. *FBIS,* December 6, 1985, p. D8.

61. *FBIS,* December 6, 1985, p. D7.

62. *FBIS,* October 2, 1985, pp. D11–D12; October 4, 1985, pp. D2–D5.

63. *FBIS,* November 22, 1985, p. D1.

64. *FBIS,* July 23, 1985, pp. E1–E3.

65. *FBIS,* April 9, 1985, pp. D2–D10.

66. *Korea Herald,* May 30, 1986.

67. *FBIS,* July 29, 1985, pp. D1–D3.

68. *FBIS,* June 17, 1986, pp. D3–D6.

69. *FBIS,* June 23, 1986, pp. D1–D3.

70. *FBIS,* July 18, 1986, pp. E1–E2.

71. *FBIS,* April 9, 1985, p. D8. Note, however, Ho Tam's reversion to form in a *Nodong Sinmun* article of August 1985 in which he praised the "patriotic and just struggle to bury the fascist military dictatorship" in South Korea (*FBIS,* August 14, 1985, p. D15).

72. *FBIS,* October 17, 1985, pp. D19–D28.

73. Interviews, July 1985 and August 1986.

74. Interview, Peking, December 1984.

7

South Korea,
the United States,
and Japan

The dominant factor shaping the evolution of the two Koreas has been the global confrontation between the superpowers. The superpowers agreed on the division of the peninsula for the purpose of military occupation, and thereafter, as the cold war intensified, each became more determined to keep within its own camp the part of Korea that its forces had liberated. The Korean governing elite on each side had even stronger reason to cleave to its superpower sponsor. The desperate struggle for survival during the Korean War had instilled in them profound suspicion of each other and strengthened their determination to secure the dominant position in a reunified Korea. Their need for superpower support was greater than the superpowers' need of them, which placed them in a relatively weak bargaining position.

Big power relationships in East Asia have changed dramatically since the 1950s. The two-camp dichotomy of Korean War days has evolved into a four-power system in which Japan and China have prominent independent roles, a development that has significantly affected the positions and policies of the two Koreas.[1] Neither Japan nor China is in a position to replace a superpower as principal supporter of one of the Koreas, but both have supplemented superpower support in important ways. The dependence of the two Koreas on their principal sponsor has been thereby reduced somewhat, giving them greater freedom to maneuver.

The superpowers remain the principal military actors in the region. Here, as elsewhere in the world, their confrontation is constrained by a strong desire on both sides to avoid a direct military clash that could escalate into a nuclear war. Neither has used Korean territory as a strategic base for missiles or other armaments primarily intended to counter the other superpower.[7] U.S. forces in South Korea are armed, trained, and deployed to react to a North Korean attack. There is no Subic Bay or Yokosuka equipped to support U.S. regional military operations. The Soviet Union has no troops or bases in North Korea. Thus, the superpowers have excluded Korea from a direct military role in their strategic confrontation and have exhibited a common interest in preventing the renewal of large-scale conflict there.

Trends in big power relationships in East Asia have benefited the United States and, secondarily, South Korea, rather than the Soviet Union and North Korea. Most important was the Sino-Soviet split, which turned the Soviet Union and China from allies into adversaries. It also paved the way for the normalization of relations between the United States and China. Improved Sino-U.S. relations made possible the normalization of relations between Japan and China and eliminated the chronic friction between the United States and Japan over the China issue. The United States no longer viewed China as a military threat against which it deployed military forces in the western Pacific, but instead as a potential collaborator in containing Soviet military expansion.

Although the United States and China have remained allied to opposite sides in Korea and officially have endorsed the basic positions of their Korean allies, U.S. and Chinese views of Korea have drawn closer. Both see their interests served by stability and lowering of tension there. They have preferred the status quo to the risks and costs of any attempt to reunify Korea by force. The more important the relations between Washington and Peking have become, the greater their incentive for discouraging their Korean allies from actions that would damage those relations.

The alliance with Japan formed the foundation of the U.S. position in the western Pacific. With the passage of years and the rapid growth of the Japanese economy, the importance of the alliance has increased. Despite growing strains over trade issues, both countries value highly the strategic and economic benefits from the partnership. Attempts by the Soviet Union to compete with the United States for influence over Japan have had no significant impact. Moscow lacks a comparable ally in East Asia. Its relationship with Vietnam, although providing strategic advantages, is an economic burden and an obstacle to improving relations with China and the Association of Southeast Asian Nations (ASEAN).

The United States and Japan have common interests in the security, stability, and economic development of South Korea. Although they are to some extent competitors in trade and investment there, their policies in support of South Korea coincide closely. They are not rivals for influence over the government of the ROK, as the Soviet Union and China are in North Korea. And even though Korean animosity toward Japan, stemming from the colonial experience, has persisted, it has not prevented relations between Seoul and Tokyo from growing closer, despite frequent dire warnings by the Soviet Union and North Korea. Access to Japanese markets, capital, and technology has contributed importantly to South Korea's economic growth. U.S. encouragement of diplomatic, political, and economic ties between Seoul and Tokyo has helped to strengthen the position of the United States relative to the Soviet Union in Northeast Asia.

Trends in relations between the United States and China and Japan and China have also strengthened the U.S. position and have redounded to the benefit of South Korea. As Washington and Tokyo have become increasingly involved in Peking's economic modernization program, ties of various kinds have proliferated. Moscow has improved relations with the PRC somewhat, but the Chinese continue to view the Soviet Union as the principal long-term threat to their security and as much inferior to the United States and Japan in the ability to contribute to China's modernization. The evolving U.S.-China-Japan relationship tends to leave the Soviet Union odd man out in East Asia. The tri-power relationship also improves the atmosphere for the development of trade and other contacts between China and South Korea.

The one respect in which the Soviet Union has improved its position in East Asia over the past twenty years is in military strength.[3] Its combat divisions along the Chinese frontier have increased from 20 to more than 50. It has modernized its naval and air forces and has installed SS-20 intermediate range ballistic missiles within range of China and Japan. This military buildup has not, however, remedied the political and economic weakness of the Soviet position in the region. The principal effect of the buildup has been to increase U.S., Japanese, and Chinese concern over the threat to their interests posed by growing Soviet military power. The Reagan administration undertook a substantial improvement of U.S. sea and air forces in the western Pacific. Japan, although unwilling to strengthen its forces at the pace urged by the United States, has continued their expansion and modernization. The United States and China have exchanged military visits, have begun concrete discussions on ways to modernize Chinese weaponry and arms production, and have agreed on the sale of U.S. technology to improve the manufacture of artillery ammunition and to upgrade the performance of the F-8 fighter plane. South Korea, although not directly involved in the amassing of military strength to counter the Soviet Union, benefits indirectly from steps taken by the three big powers to counter a commonly perceived Soviet military threat.

The United States and South Korea

Relations between the United States and South Korea have expanded enormously during the thirty-some years since the Korean War. Security ties have dominated the relationship, but the relative importance of economic relations has steadily increased. Intercourse through tourism, educational and scientific exchanges, the immigration of Koreans into the United States, multiplying communication and transportation links, plus a host of other channels have drawn the two countries closer, doing much to overcome the physical distance separating them. The bond has proved durable, in spite of differences in national interests, cultures, and the asymmetry in size and power.[4]

Security Relations

The domination of the relationship by security ties is ironic, given U.S. willingness before 1950 to write off the Korean peninsula as of little strategic value. After the Korean War, the U.S. government justified economic and military aid to the ROK largely on national security grounds. These security concerns inhibited the United States from reacting as vigorously against human rights abuses in South Korea as it might otherwise have done.

For the United States, South Korea has been an important link in the global structure designed to contain the spread of Soviet influence. South Korea is particularly important to the defense of Japan, the keystone of the U.S. security system in the Pacific. The investment of lives and money during the Korean War created a stake in maintaining the alliance; the political cost to a U.S. leader of abandoning South Korea would be extremely high, especially after the failure in Vietnam. Moreover, U.S. behavior toward its commitment in Korea is viewed as a litmus test of the reliability of U.S. commitments elsewhere, particularly in Japan. The alarm in Japan at President Carter's decision without advance consultation to withdraw U.S. ground forces from South Korea testified to Japanese sensitivity.

The security interests of the ROK are local, not global like those of the United States. The two countries have agreed on the importance of deterring North Korea, an ally of the superpower rival of the United States, but do not always agree on the amount of U.S. or Korean resources that should be allocated to this objective rather than to U.S. objectives elsewhere. The ROK contributed forces to the U.S. war effort in Vietnam, an action highly valued by the United States, both for its military impact and its symbolic importance in internationalizing support for South Vietnam. Participation in Vietnam produced concrete benefits for South Korea in the form of foreign exchange and armaments, as well as served to bond the two allies more closely. Divergences in their interests regarding Vietnam became apparent, however, when the Koreans declined U.S. requests to increase their forces there on the ground that it would divert too many troops from their primary objective: the deterrence of North Korea.

The sharpest disputes between Washington and Seoul arose over U.S. decisions to withdraw forces from South Korea. Park Chung-hee was adamantly opposed to Richard Nixon's decision in 1970, pursuant to the Nixon Doctrine, to withdraw one of the two divisions stationed there, despite the offer of $1.5 billion over a five-year period to be used to modernize South Korean forces.[5] He was equally strongly opposed to Jimmy Carter's decision in 1977 to withdraw the remaining U.S. division. In both instances the decision was reached without advance consultation with the Korean government. The disputes reflected differing judgments of the North Korean threat and of the need for U.S. ground forces to deter a North Korean attack. Once the United States had made the decision, the South Korean government had no choice but to make the best of it. Nothing demonstrated more strikingly the unequal positions of the two allies.

As indicated above, the United States has not requested the use of South Korean territory for forces configured primarily to counter Soviet military power in the region. To do so would raise fresh issues. It could lead to Soviet use of North Korean territory for a comparable purpose and to demands by both Koreas for more advanced weapons in exchange for granting the use of their territory to serve superpower needs. Preventing the Soviet Union from utilizing the Korean peninsula for its strategic purposes is in itself an extremely important U.S. security objective. A heavily armed, unified Korea of 60 million people allied to the Soviet Union would radically alter the strategic balance in Northeast Asia.

Thus, there is a sizable, but not complete, overlap in the security interests of the United States and South Korea. So long as rivalry with the Soviet Union is the primary security interest of the United States and rivalry with North Korea is the primary security interest of South Korea, the need that the two allies feel for each other will remain strong. Security ties will continue to dominate their relationship.

Economic Relations

Until its economic takeoff in the mid-1960s, South Korea was a heavy economic burden for the United States, but the burden steadily diminished as the South Korean economy moved into its period of rapid economic growth. U.S. economic aid declined from a total of $2.6 billion in 1953–1961 to $1.7 billion in 1962–1969 and to $0.9 billion in 1970–1976, after which it was phased out.[6] The transformation of South Korea from the dependent "basket case" of the 1950s to the valued trading partner of the 1980s has been dramatic.

As of 1984 the ROK had become the seventh largest trading partner of the United States, with a two-way trade of $17 billion. It was the fourth most important market for U.S. agricultural products. The economies of the United States and South Korea are largely complementary. The U.S. advantages in natural resources, high technology, and capital are complemented by South Korea's educated, disciplined, relatively low-wage labor force and its middle level skills in labor and management. The United States has a comparative advantage in the production of foodstuffs, chemicals, aircraft, and sophisticated machinery. South Korea's advantages lie in textiles and electronic products, as well as certain types of ships and steel products.

The growing economic interdependence of the United States and South Korea has not been limited to trade. Banking relations are also important. In 1985 17 U.S. banks had branches in South Korea, more than one-third of the 45 foreign banks operating there. Six Korean banks had opened 17 branches in the United States.[7] From 1959 to 1984 U.S. banks supplied 26 percent of foreign loans provided to South Korea.[8] A Korean economist has estimated that U.S. banks in 1984 earned $1.2 billion in interest on such loans.[9]

U.S. equity investment in South Korea increased substantially in the 1980s, slightly exceeding investments by the Japanese during this period. The Japanese still led in total direct investment, with $814 million as of February 1985 or 51 percent of the total compared to the cumulative U.S. figure of $478 million or 29 percent.[10] In combined loans and equity investments, the United States has been the largest supplier of foreign capital. Equity investment by U.S. companies was a small fraction of their investment elsewhere in the world, but the trend has been sharply upward in recent years. A significant step in the internationalization of the world's automobile industry was General Motors' decision to invest in a joint venture with the Daewoo Corporation to produce subcompacts in Korea. Ford and Chrysler have also established links with Korean partners. The American Telephone and Telegraph Corporation owns 44 percent of Goldstar Semiconductor, Ltd., a leader in

South Korea's newly established semiconductor industry. Goldstar has become a supplier of chips to AT&T and other U.S. companies. Equity investment has not been one-way. From 1980 to 1984 Korean companies invested $52 million in the United States—including investments in a coal mine in Pennsylvania, a television plant in Alabama, and a high-tech firm in Silicon Valley, California.[11]

South Korea is an important member of the fast-growing group of Pacific Basin nations, which, in the aggregate, have become a more important trading partner for the United States than Western Europe. Thus, its economic importance to the United States transcends the bilateral relationship. South Korea's ties with Japan, the ASEAN, Australia, and recently even with the PRC, contribute significantly to the economic dynamism of the entire region.

The Washington-Seoul economic relationship, although beneficial in important ways to both parties, is far from equal. South Korea is the junior partner, much more dependent on economic relations with the United States than the United States is on South Korea. The United States is South Korea's most important trading partner, taking one-third or more of its exports and supplying about one-quarter of its imports. As indicated above, it has furnished one-fourth of South Korea's foreign bank loans and is second only to Japan in direct investment. Most of South Korea's technology has come from the United States and Japan in the form of licensing agreements, capital goods imports, direct foreign investment, and technical consultancies. In terms of value, Japan has supplied more, but the U.S. technology overall has been more capital-intensive, sophisticated, and complex.[12]

The economic relationship between Washington and Seoul has not been without problems. The prime difficulty has been the growing ability of South Korean manufacturers to undersell U.S. manufacturers in the U.S. market.[13] As early as 1963 the United States compelled South Korea to accept quantitative limits on the export of cotton textiles and garments to the United States. Subsequent agreements expanded the categories of textiles to which limits were applied. During the 1970s restraints were placed on the export of South Korean footwear and color television sets to the United States. Complaints by U.S. companies that Korean companies were receiving government subsidies on a number of other products or dumping them in the United States prompted investigations. Some of these cases were dismissed, others resulted in U.S. government administrative action.

The problems became more acute in the 1980s. Increasing competitiveness of South Korean manufacturers in the U.S. market coincided with growing concern in the United States at the soaring U.S. foreign trade deficit and rising unemployment in industries such as steel and

shoes, affected by large foreign imports. South Korea's shift from its
traditional deficit position in trade with the United States to a surplus
of $1.9 billion in 1983, $3.4 billion in 1984, and $4.2 billion in 1985,
deepened this concern. U.S. manufacturers filed dumping complaints
regarding imports of South Korean television sets, steel plate, tableware,
inner tubes, non-rubber footwear, and other products. The U.S. government urged the ROK to speed up its program to dismantle import
controls and reduce tariffs, thus opening its own market more widely
to U.S. exports. The United States also complained of stiff restrictions
on the operation of U.S. banks, insurance companies, and other service
industries in South Korea, as well as the lack of effective patent and
copyright laws. Some members of Congress urged the removal of South
Korea from the Generalized System of Preferences (GSP), under which
about 20 percent of its exports entered the United States duty-free.

The rising clamor in the United States for protectionist measures
alarmed the South Koreans. Although investigations in nearly half of
the 29 cases brought against Korean manufacturers between 1977 and
1984 found no dumping, subsidy, or injury to U.S. industry, ten were
found to justify the application of antidumping or countervailing duties
by the United States. As of mid-1985 several other cases were still under
investigation. The two countries also reached an agreement to limit steel
imports to 1.9 percent of the U.S. market. Up to this point the level of
South Korean trade with the United States had not been seriously
affected by protectionist actions. Few of the antidumping or countervailing
duties were high enough to exclude the Korean products; most of the
duties were less than two percent.[14]

During the autumn of 1985, friction over trade issues intensified. U.S.
manufacturers brought new complaints of dumping of South Korean
products. One dumping case, against Korean manufacturers of photo
albums, resulted in the application of an antidumping duty of 64 percent;
this provoked an uproar in Korea. Korean officials and businessmen
frequently cited this case as an example of excessive pressure by the
U.S. government. While responding to complaints by U.S. manufacturers
against Korean imports, the U.S. government was also pressing the ROK
to speed up the liberalization of its import market, to adopt measures
for the protection of intellectual property, and to allow U.S. insurance
companies to operate in South Korea. Koreans, feeling overwhelmed by
this succession of blows, complained that the U.S. giant was unfairly
punishing its small ally. Businessmen and officials, individuals who in
the past had been the most pro-American, became increasingly critical
of the United States. The government even threatened, as a retaliatory
measure, to shift some of its grain purchases from the United States to
other countries.

As the trade between the U.S. and South Korea grows, disputes over trade issues probably will become more frequent and intense, just as they have between the United States and Japan. The costs and benefits to the U.S. and South Korean economies of particular courses of action will be difficult to calculate in a period of rapid change. The questions facing the two nations includes: How much competitive pressure from Korean imports on particular sectors of U.S. industry should be accepted in order to give U.S. consumers continued access to inexpensive Korean products and to enable U.S. farmers and manufacturers to continue to sell to Korea large amounts of agricultural products, machinery, and aircraft? When U.S. multinationals combine their capital and technology in high technology areas such as the semiconductor industry with low Korean manufacturing costs in order to compete more effectively with Japan, how much risk do they take that the technology acquired by Korean companies will in the future make them potent competitors of U.S. companies? How rapidly must the Korean economy be opened to U.S. goods and services in order to diminish protectionist pressures in the United States? What will the impact be on Korean producers of such goods and services?

Although disputes over such issues will continue to produce strains in the relationship, the great and growing economic benefits to both parties will constrain them to find ways of managing the difficulties. South Korea's relatively small trade surplus with the United States in 1984 of $3.4 billion was a minor factor in the overall U.S. trade deficit of $123 billion, compared to surpluses of $10 billion for Taiwan and $37 billion for Japan. Reductions in the U.S. budget deficit and a further decline in the value of the U.S. dollar would ease tensions between Seoul and Washington over trade. The danger is that in the interim, emotional reactions on both sides will exaggerate basically manageable economic differences and turn them into serious political problems.

Political Relations

Relations between the United States and South Korea, although based predominantly on security interests and the mutual advantages of expanding trade and financial transactions, cannot be defined in these terms alone. The total relationship comprises also the perceptions that each government and people have of the other, the extent to which they cooperate in global policies, and the interactions of the two countries outside the realms of security and economic relations. This broad, encompassing variety of attitudes and actions is here termed political relations.

The most contentious issue in this political area has been the political system in South Korea. The restrictions on democratic freedoms imposed by South Korean leaders have placed a strain on relations between the two allies. The U.S. government has expressed support, in principle, for the evolution of South Korea into a more fully democratic country with fewer curbs on human rights. At the same time, it has recognized the importance of political stability to South Korea's security. Internal turmoil could be exploited by North Korea and make defense more difficult against a North Korean military attack. Concern for stability and the underlying security relationship has caused U.S. administrations to maintain fairly close relations with South Korean leaders who ruled with a firm hand, even when some of the measures they took to maintain themselves in power seemed excessive and perhaps in the long run counterproductive.

Official U.S. action to encourage progress toward democracy in South Korea has been hampered by the difficulty of judging the appropriate pace of progress for a country with South Korea's culture, political traditions, stage of economic and social development, and external threat. U.S. officials have differed among themselves on this question, as well as on the extent of the U.S. government's capability to influence domestic politics in South Korea and on the most effective ways of going about it. A marked decline in the U.S. government's influence over South Korea's domestic affairs since the days of large U.S. economic and military aid programs is evident. The Carter administration was more outspoken on issues of human rights and democratization than the Reagan administration, which favored quiet diplomatic efforts behind the scenes. But neither can claim dramatic successes. The one exception was the commutation of the death sentence for Kim Dae Jung in January 1981, a step that clearly had to be taken to enable Chun Doo Hwan to visit the United States at a politically crucial moment in his career.

U.S. government actions in recent years to further democracy in South Korea have been cautious and restrained. U.S. political leaders and officials have acted from a genuine conviction that orderly progress toward a more democratic system would produce more stable conditions than efforts to stifle progress. Nevertheless, they have been conscious of the limits of U.S. influence in this area and have wanted to avoid disturbing the close cooperation between the two countries in the security field. Some private U.S. citizens and members of Congress, impatient with the slow progress and frequent setbacks of the democratic movement in Korea, have urged the U.S. government to do more. They have argued that the presence of U.S. forces in South Korea and the U.S. commitment to the defense of the country imposed an obligation on the U.S. government to intervene in favor of those Koreans struggling to attain greater democracy or suffering deprivation of human rights. Not to intervene on behalf of these Koreans, they asserted, would be tantamount to U.S. intervention in support of the authoritarian government trying to suppress them.[15] A group of U.S. citizens, including two members of Congress, demonstrated their concern for the rights of the opposition in South Korea by accompanying Kim Dae Jung to Seoul in February 1985 to ensure his safe return from his two year sojourn in the United States.

In reacting to U.S. efforts to influence domestic politics in South Korea, Korean leaders have contended with conflicting pressures. They have given high priority to promoting good relations with the United States because of the vital need to maintain close and effective military cooperation, as well as to show North Korea and the people of South Korea that the U.S. defense commitment is firm and unwavering. They have used summit visits back and forth to demonstrate the warmth of U.S.-Korean relations and to obtain reaffirmations of the U.S. defense commitment at the highest level. Rhee visited the United States in 1954; Park in 1961, 1963, 1965, 1968, and 1969; and Chun in 1981 and 1985. Eisenhower, Johnson, Ford, Carter, and Reagan all visited Seoul. Korean leaders have benefited politically from the opportunity to demonstrate their close personal relationship with the president of the United States.

Despite their felt need for good relations with the United States, Korean leaders have at times ignored or resisted U.S. pressures in order to defend Korean national dignity and sovereignty or to pursue actions deemed essential to protect their own power position. They have resented attempts by the U.S. government or by individual U.S. citizens to promote democracy in Korea. These actions were often seen as meddlesome and destabilizing.

In the mid-1970s, U.S.-Korean relations suffered a severe strain from a clumsy attempt by the Korean government to cultivate support among members of Congress through financial contributions.[16] The influence-buying campaign, dubbed Koreagate by the U.S. press, grew out of the concern felt by Park Chung-hee and senior Korean officials that the Nixon Doctrine portended a serious weakening in U.S. backing of the ROK. Ironically, this effort to drum up support badly damaged the image of the ROK in the eyes of the U.S. public, as sensational press stories appeared day after day, some of them greatly exaggerating the extent of the operation and the involvement of members of Congress. The unpopularity of Sun Myung Moon's aggressively proselytizing Unification Church added to the unfavorable impression of South Korea that many U.S. citizens received during this period. So also did the increasingly repressive measures instituted by Park Chung-hee to maintain himself in power under the *yusin* constitution. These measures led Congressman Donald Fraser, chairman of the House Subcommittee on International Organizations, to hold a series of hearings at which witnesses decried human rights violations in South Korea. In public opinion polls taken in mid-1978, 73 percent of the respondents knew of Koreagate and 53 percent of those polled judged relations between the United States and South Korea to be only fair or poor, compared to 29 percent who said that they were good or excellent. Forty-seven percent of the respondents expected relations to stay about the same during the next few years, and 17 percent thought that they would get worse. Only 15 percent foresaw improvement.[17]

Two trends have been apparent for the past fifteen years or so among the Korean people. Economic development and the rising level of education have created a rapidly expanding middle class that favors orderly progress toward a more democratic system. At the same time, their sense of national pride and self-confidence has blossomed. They do not want South Korea to be pushed around by a big power. This complicates an assessment of the general attitude toward U.S. intervention in South Korea's political affairs. Many of those who favor more rapid liberalization of the political system believe that it should be brought about by Koreans themselves without outside interference. Others solicit U.S. help in promoting democracy, primarily by having the U.S. government refrain from actions showing support for the Chun Doo Hwan government. Kim Dae Jung has advocated a more activist policy for the United States; for example, he has suggested the U.S. could exert pressure for democratic reforms by granting or withholding trade and economic aid.[18]

Korean students share the ambivalence of the general public toward the relationship with the United States. Antagonism toward Chun Doo Hwan is widespread among students; they believe he came to power illegally, they blame him for the deaths at Kwangju, and they resent the restrictions on political activity imposed by his government. The students denounce the United States for supporting Chun. Some 60 students from leading universities occupied the U.S. Information Service (USIS) building in Seoul for four days in May 1985, demanding an official U.S. apology for having released from its operational command the Korean troops that suppressed the Kwangju uprising. Students briefly occupied the American Chamber of Commerce in Seoul and the American Cultural Center in Pusan, before being removed by police. Some students, attracted to dependency theory, condemn what they see as U.S. economic domination of South Korea. Others deplore the crowding out of traditional Korean culture by the influx of U.S. culture.

Yet the ambivalence is evident. Many students would welcome U.S. pressure on Chun Doo Hwan to allow a wider range of political activities. Students are among the most avid consumers of U.S. clothing styles, music, movies, and other manifestations of U.S. culture. Few students advocate the withdrawal of U.S. forces. Only a small radical fringe would sever all connections with the United States. Individuals of this persuasion carried out the arson against the U.S. cultural center in Pusan in 1982 and the bombing of the cultural centers in Kwangju and Taegu in 1983.

Koreans are in the process of redefining their relationship with the United States. They recognize their continuing need for a close security and economic relationship but seek to reconcile it with their pride in Korean culture and their consciousness of South Korea's growing power and world prestige. A woman professor, writing in the *Chosun Ilbo* after the student occupation of the USIS, stressed the great contribution made by the United States to South Korea's security and prosperity and the resultant pro-American feeling of the great majority of the Korean people. But she went on to say:

> When the government overemphasizes its close ties to the United States, when a dissident politician has Americans surround him for protection as he returns to the country, when Korean intellectuals bitterly criticize their own country in front of Americans or other foreigners, when even young Koreans who denounce foreign influence quote articles in foreign newspapers that they find favorable to them, Koreans in general feel a deep loss of self-respect. . . . While our respect for the United States as a fine and strong ally has not changed, we should long ago have discarded our emotional dependence on the United States.[19]

The heightened political activity in the spring of 1986 focused increasing attention on the role of the United States in South Korea. Demands for withdrawal of U.S. forces from South Korea were proclaimed more frequently and stridently by radical students at demonstrations. Opposition politicians criticized the May visit to Seoul by Secretary of State George Shultz for lending support to the Chun government rather than furthering the process of democratization in South Korea. Shultz met with Lee Min-woo, president of the NKDP, but declined to meet with Kim Young Sam or Kim Dae Jung. They in turn declined to meet with Assistant Secretary of State Gaston Sigur. The U.S. House of Representatives passed unanimously a resolution calling for rapid progress toward genuine democracy in South Korea and a companion resolution urging North Korea to accept cross-recognition and to cease its abuses of human rights. Political activity in South Korea attracted increased interest from the U.S. media, particularly when demonstrations ended in clashes between students and police.

Conclusion

The most striking feature of the U.S.-ROK relationship is its durability. The alliance, forged in the Korean War more than thirty years ago, has remained strong, despite the two countries' geographical separation, their differences in size and stage of economic development, and the acrimonious disputes they have had. Its strength is based on the compatability of the national interests of the two countries—security, economic, political, and diplomatic interests. In each of these areas there have been differences between the two governments, but the areas of compatability are more compelling than the differences.

The disputes tend to be about means, not ends. Both countries agree on the need to deter aggressive use of force by the Soviet Union or North Korea, but may differ on the best way to do so. Both agree in principle on the desirability of free enterprise economic systems and a minimum of restrictions on world trade, but often differ on specifics. Both agree in principle on the desirability of progress in South Korea and elsewhere toward more fully democratic systems, but may disagree on the appropriate pace and methods of change. The compatability of U.S. and South Korean global objectives make diplomatic cooperation relatively easy. In some areas, such as the Middle East, South Korea's diplomatic rivalry with North Korea may cause it to take steps not in accord with U.S. policies, such as carrying out construction projects in Libya or making gestures toward the Palestine Liberation Organization. But such differences have been few and not seriously divisive.

Over the years the U.S. stance, official and private, favoring evolution toward democracy has had an effect. The effect is palpable, although impossible to measure or document. The U.S. stance has strengthened moderates among Korean politicians, bureaucrats, academics, and businessmen and has tended to limit the extremism of hard-liners. Political opponents of the ruling elite, while expressing disappointment at the reluctance of the U.S. government to intervene more actively, have drawn encouragement from the support received from groups and individuals in the United States. A critical test for the political system in South Korea and U.S. policy toward it will come in the period from 1987 through 1988, the year of the Seoul Olympics and the scheduled change of presidents.

The overall political impact of the rapidly proliferating ties of many kinds between U.S. citizens and Koreans is difficult to evaluate. Korean emigration to the United States reached 30,000 to 40,000 a year in the 1980s, making Koreans the fastest growing ethnic body in the United States. Thousands of Korean students attend U.S. universities, and the upper ranks of the South Korean establishment—government, business, and academic—are dotted with thousands of returned students holding advanced degrees from U.S. institutions. Tens of thousands of U.S. military personnel have served in the U.S. forces in Korea. U.S. visitors to Korea for tourism, business, and other activities numbered 213,000 in 1984. Korean travelers to the United States numbered over 100,000, and this figure is certain to grow rapidly as the Korean community in the United States expands and increasing affluence enables more Koreans to visit.[20] Numerous ties have developed between U.S. church groups and the growing number of Christian churches in South Korea. Increased contact does not necessarily result in greater harmony between peoples, given the differences in culture and national interests; it can also create more scope for friction. So far, the growth in mutual understanding and appreciation between U.S. citizens and Koreans appears to have kept pace with the inevitable rise in friction.

The dominant characteristic of the U.S.–South Korean relationship has been the importance attached to it by the governments of each country and the consequent compulsion felt by government leaders on each side to manage problems in ways that preserve intact the vital underlying bond. The alliance with South Korea is analogous, on a smaller scale, to the U.S.-Japanese alliance. No matter how irritated or frustrated officials of either side become with the ally's behavior, they remain firmly convinced that for the sake of fundamental, long-term national interests, the alliance must be preserved. Official dedication to the relationship has remained remarkably constant, even when popular criticism of the ally was growing.[21] During Koreagate, for example, when emotions ran high among citizens of both countries, the two governments worked hard to find the mutually acceptable solutions that finally eased the crisis.

Popular U.S. perceptions of South Korea's importance to the United States have drawn closer to the official view of the U.S. government in recent years. From 1978 to 1984 respondents who regarded South Korea as "fairly important" or "very important" to the United States increased from 62 percent to 77 percent.[22] The importance of the United States to Koreans was demonstrated in a 1984 poll: 88 percent of the respondents thought that North Korea would almost surely launch a new invasion if U.S. forces were withdrawn, and 71 percent thought that South Korea could not defend itself without the participation of U.S. forces.[23]

Japan and South Korea

From the perspective of thirty-five years, four factors stand out as the primary determinants of the relationship between Japan and South Korea: the lasting effect of the colonial experience, the continuing dependence of both countries on the United States, the reciprocal benefits of economic exchange, and the dominance of a conservative ruling elite in both societies.[24]

The colonial experience left an enduring legacy of animosity toward Japan among Koreans and disdain of Koreans among Japanese. Since the early 1960s the governments of the two countries have recognized the overriding importance to their own national interests of cooperating with each other. But leaders attempting to cooperate have had to contend with undercurrents of hostility among the people, often whipped up and exploited by the political opposition for their own ends. Japanese discrimination against the 600,000 Korean residents of Japan who remained after the end of the colonial period has added irritants to the relationship. Feelings have moderated with the passage of time; South Korea's success in economic development; and the multiplication of official, business, and personal ties between Japan and South Korea. Nevertheless, Koreans remain highly sensitive to any real or imagined slight by the Japanese government or people.

Although the underlying negative feelings left over from the colonial period fueled highly visible disputes between Tokyo and Seoul, positive but less publicized legacies from the same period smoothed the way for cooperation. Japanese and Koreans knew each other better than they knew other foreigners. Large numbers of Koreans spoke Japanese. The familiarity of Korean industrialists with Japanese technology facilitated the acquisition of machinery from Japan and cooperation in joint ventures. Koreans resident in Japan served as middlemen between their compatriots in Korea and the Japanese.

The common dependence of Japan and Korea on the United States profoundly influenced their relations with each other. U.S. pressure on the two governments was a significant factor in bringing about the establishment of diplomatic relations in 1965. Thereafter, the value those governments placed on good relations with the United States for strategic and economic reasons, together with U.S. efforts to preserve harmony between its two allies, served to facilitate cooperation between them and moderate their conflicts of interest. Membership in the U.S.-led security system in the Western Pacific and in the global system of market economies, in which the United States also played a leading role, constrained them to harmonize their bilateral relations.

Economic relations between Japan and Korea had their roots in the connections established during the colonial period, but growth remained stunted until the establishment of diplomatic relations loosed a flow of official and private Japanese funds into South Korea. Japanese capital and technology made an important contribution to the rapid growth of South Korea's economy. For Japan, the bilateral relationship was less important than it was for South Korea, but by 1984 South Korea had become the second largest market for Japanese exports.

The dominance of Japan's conservative Liberal Democratic Party (LDP) in Japan's domestic politics throughout almost the entire postwar period facilitated cooperation between Japanese governments and the strongly anticommunist governments of South Korea. The Japanese Socialist Party (JSP), the chief opposition party in Japan, inclined toward North Korea. The outspoken preference of the JSP and many Japanese intellectuals for North Korea over South Korea provoked bitter anti-Japanese reactions in South Korea and greatly complicated the Japanese government's efforts to maintain good working relations with the South Korean government. Had the JSP been the dominant party, Japan's relations with both South Korea and the United States would have been radically different.

Establishing Relations

The negotiations over the establishment of diplomatic relations between Japan and the government administering the southern part of its former colony dealt with a number of thorny issues: a Japanese apology for the mistreatment of Koreans in the colonial period, the ROK's claim to be the legitimate government of all Korea, South Korean claims for losses under Japanese rule and Japanese counterclaims for Japanese property confiscated after World War II in Korea, fisheries rights, the legal status and treatment of Koreans in Japan, and conflicting claims over Dokto (Takeshima) Island.[25]

Negotiations began in 1951, breaking off and resuming several times during the decade, but making no significant progress. Neither government had the political will to resolve the contentious issues by making the difficult compromises needed. When Park Chung-hee came to power in 1961, he determined to push the negotiations to a successful conclusion. Park recognized that the establishment of diplomatic relations with Japan would give South Korea access to Japanese capital and technology, which was badly needed to carry forward his ambitious economic development plans. It would also reduce the ROK's economic dependence on the United States and improve its position in the diplomatic rivalry with North Korea. As a military man, concerned with the North Korean military threat, he saw the importance to South Korea's security of the greater freedom of action for the United States that diplomatic relations between Tokyo and Seoul would provide.

Park's desire to pursue seriously negotiations with Japan was matched by increased willingness on the part of the Japanese government to resolve this intractable problem. Japanese political leaders, notably Eisaku Sato, who became prime minister in 1964, were becoming increasingly conscious of the importance to Japan's security of a stable, economically healthy South Korea. They were also under considerable pressure from Japanese industrialists, who would benefit from the increased opportunities for trade and investment in South Korea, which would follow the establishment of diplomatic relations.

The agreements finally reached in June 1965 formally declared invalid the treaty of annexation of 1910 and earlier agreements between Japan and Korea. Foreign Minister Etsusaburo Shiina on a visit to Seoul expressed regret and deep reflection concerning the "unfortunate period" in the relations between Japan and Korea. Japan recognized the ROK as the only legitimate government in Korea, in accordance with the UN resolution of December 12, 1948. The Japanese government refused to accept the ROK's claim to jurisdiction over all of Korea, but declared that it would not establish diplomatic relations with the government of North Korea. On practical problems such as fisheries, Japan dealt with North Korea through unofficial organizations.

A compromise on conflicting monetary claims resulted in Japan's agreement to a $300 million grant plus $200 million in low interest government credits, and $300 million in commercial credits. Japan viewed these funds as economic cooperation, whereas the Koreans regarded them as compensation for Japan's past ill-treatment of Korea.

A long-standing dispute over fisheries had been a prime cause of trouble between Japan and Korea. In 1952 Syngman Rhee unilaterally reserved fishing within a line 50 to 60 miles off the coast of Korea for Korean fishermen. Japan refused to recognize the so-called Peace Line (or Rhee Line) and sought to provide protection for Japanese fishermen through the Maritime Security Agency. Nevertheless, the South Korean government between 1952 and 1964 seized 252 Japanese fishing boats and jailed 2,784 Japanese fishermen for trespassing within the line.[26] The 1965 agreement on fisheries allowed each country a 12-mile exclusive fishing zone off their coasts and jointly regulated zones elsewhere. In addition, Japan provided $120 million in commercial loans for the South Korean fishing industry.

In the agreement on the status of Koreans in Japan, all of those who had been in Japan prior to the end of World War II were granted permanent residence. Japan declined to give Koreans equal status with Japanese in such matters as education, health, and protection of livelihood, but agreed to give them "due consideration" in those matters. The agreement did not clarify the citizenship status of Koreans in Japan. The Japanese government registered those holding identification cards from the ROK mission in Japan as *Kankoku*, the South Korean name for Korea and the rest as *Chosen*, the North Korean name for Korea.

No agreement was reached on the ownership of Dokto (Takeshima), but the two countries agreed that any dispute between them would be settled by peaceful means.

The treaty negotiations aroused opposition in both Japan and Korea. The JSP, the Japanese Communist Party (JCP), and the Komeito charged that the Japanese government, by recognizing only the ROK and not the DPRK, was antagonizing the North Koreans. They held that Japan should either withhold recognition until Korea was unified or recognize both Korean governments. They also argued that establishing diplomatic relations with South Korea alone threatened to drag Japan into the military confrontation on the Korean peninsula, contrary to its peace constitution, and would complicate Japan's relations with China and the Soviet Union. Leftists in Japan denounced the increased Japanese economic involvement in South Korea that would follow the normalization agreement as capitalist aggression against the Korean people. The opposition raised a clamor in the media, but it lacked the political strength to overcome the LDP's determination to establish diplomatic relations with the ROK.

In Korea, opposition to the treaty negotiations was fiercer than in Japan. It fed on the underlying Korean distrust of the Japanese, which enabled opponents of the treaty to gain support for extreme and unrealistic demands and to denounce the government for accepting less. It also drew strength from the widespread antagonism to the Park Chung-hee government, whose legitimacy continued to be questioned, especially among students. Some Korean nationalists argued that normalization of relations with Japan by South Korea would be an obstacle to unification.

The treaty issue was ideally suited to exploitation by opposition politicians and students, who hoped to use it to bring down the government. Increasing resort to street demonstrations to oppose the treaty provoked violent clashes between demonstrators and riot police. At times the demonstrations became so large and violent that combat troops had to be called in to suppress them. During the ratification debate on the treaty in the National Assembly, a large number of opposition members resigned in protest at the government's tactics, opening the way for ratification of the treaty by National Assemblymen from the ruling party alone.

Security Relations

Japan and South Korea are linked for security purposes not by military ties between them but by the U.S. security commitment to both. Ever since the Korean War, when Japan served as a vital support area for U.S. forces in combat in Korea, the governments of all three countries have recognized that they have closely related security interests.

The security interests of the three countries, although related, are not identical. South Korea is obsessed with the threat from North Korea. South Koreans do not see the Soviet Union as a direct threat, but as a secondary adversary because of its support of North Korea and its confrontation with the United States. For Japan, the Soviet Union is the primary threat; the Japanese do not feel threatened by North Korea. Moreover, constitutional restrictions and deep differences among Japanese on the definition of Japan's security interests and ways of protecting them prevent any direct Japanese involvement in the defense of South Korea. U.S. security interests differ from those of both of its allies in its primary concern with the global confrontation with the Soviet Union. The priority given by the United States to military deployments in Northeast Asia depends on conditions elsewhere in the world and may differ considerably from its allies' views of the appropriate priorities. Despite these differences in the perception of their security interests, all three governments feel that the separate U.S. defense commitments to Japan and South Korea, now over thirty years old, continue to serve their interests well.

In 1969 Japanese Prime Minister Eisaku Sato publicly declared that "the security of the Republic of Korea was essential to Japan's own security." Sato also indicated that Japan would respond "positively and promptly" to a U.S. request to use its bases in Japan to defend South Korea against armed attack. In subsequent years the Japanese government's formulation of its concern for peace and stability in Korea underwent subtle changes on several occasions, drawing back from Sato's exclusive linkage of Japan's security to that of the ROK. The most recent formula was that used by Nakasone and Chun on the occasion of Chun's visit to Tokyo in 1984 in which they agreed that "the maintenance of peace and stability on the Korean peninsula is essential to those of East Asia, including Japan."[27]

The official Japanese attitude toward South Korea's security is compounded of (1) unwillingness to become directly involved militarily in Korea, (2) approval of the U.S. commitment to South Korea's defense and recognition of the importance of U.S. bases in Japan to carrying out that commitment, (3) willingness to contribute indirectly to South Korea's security through economic aid, and (4) a strong desire to see tension eased and the danger of conflict reduced by fruitful negotiations between the two Koreas.

Koreans have no desire to see Japan directly involved in the defense of South Korea. The sight of Japanese troops on Korean soil would bring back too many painful memories. Moreover, so long as U.S. forces are there, and the United States is committed to the defense of South Korea, Japanese forces are not needed. South Koreans have an uneasy feeling, however, that the United States may someday attempt to shift to Japan the burden of assisting in the defense of South Korea on the ground that U.S. military resources are stretched too thin throughout the world. Therefore, the U.S. government might contend that Japan, which would be more directly affected by a North Korean invasion of South Korea than the United States and has ample resources with which to increase its military capability, should take over from the United States this regional security responsibility. The alarm expressed in both South Korea and Japan over President Carter's plan to withdraw U.S. ground forces from South Korea arose in part from a suspicion that the withdrawal might be the first step in a scheme to substitute Japanese forces for U.S. forces.

Koreans are ambivalent about the strengthening of Japanese forces as urged by the United States. On the one hand, they recognize the need for an effective deterrent to growing Soviet military capabilities and the logic behind U.S. complaints that the United States is bearing too heavy a burden, while Japan is getting a free ride. On the other hand, they worry that a Japanese defense buildup might acquire a momentum of its own, again turning Japan into a powerful militarized nation, capable of threatening its neighbors.[28]

Given the sensitivities on both sides of the Tsushima Strait, the military forces of the two countries have been slow to develop the forms of cooperation that might, in principle, seem desirable in the light of their overlapping security interests. Cooperation has been limited to official visits back and forth, exchanges of intelligence, and, for the first time in 1985 and 1986, an exchange of port visits by naval vessels of the two countries.

North Korea, playing on the anti-Japanese feeling throughout Korea, stridently attacks port visits and other indications of military cooperation between South Korea and Japan as steps toward formal military ties that will create a triangular military alliance involving these countries and the United States and will lead to the stationing of Japanese forces in South Korea.[29] Such attacks by Pyongyang, though blatantly propagandistic, may help to perpetuate caution on Japan's part regarding military cooperation with South Korea. The Japanese government, as will be brought out in Chapter 11, wants to do all possible to promote an easing of tension between the two Koreas and is inclined to avoid actions that would diminish Japanese influence on North Korea in this regard.

Economic Relations

Since Japan and South Korea established diplomatic relations, trade between them has flourished, rising from $210 million in 1965 to more than $12 billion in 1984. Japan has been South Korea's principal supplier and the second largest market for its exports. South Korea has also been an important trading partner for Japan, although more as an export market than as a source of imports. In 1984 South Korea was the second most important buyer of Japanese goods, but ranked only ninth as a supplier, for it produced neither the advanced technology and surplus foodstuffs sold to Japan by the United States, nor the oil, coal, and iron ore bought by the Japanese in great quantities from Saudi Arabia, Indonesia, the United Arab Emirates, Australia, and other countries.

For years the South Koreans have complained about the large deficit in trade with Japan. Based to a great extent on the structure of the two economies and on firmly established ways of doing business, the deficit is difficult to reduce. Many Korean businessmen find Japan the most advantageous place to buy the machinery and intermediate goods essential to their manufacturing operations. Speed of delivery, advantageous terms, reliability of servicing, and Korean familiarity with the Japanese language give Japanese firms a marked advantage in the Korean market. On the export side, South Korean exporters, like those in other countries, have found the Japanese market for manufactured goods difficult to penetrate. Korean manufacturers of clothing and textiles, for example, have had to contend not only with increasing competition from lower-wage countries, but also with Japanese textile firms that have successfully defended themselves from low-wage foreign competition by technological advances. Occasional coups, such as the capture by South Korean steelmakers in 1983 of 70 percent (1.4 million tons) of the market for imported steel plate, have not been enough to prevent further increase in the trade deficit, which rose from $1.9 billion in 1982 to $2.8 billion in 1983 and $3.2 billion in 1984.[30]

Japan has been second only to the United States in providing the outside capital that has helped to stimulate South Korea's rapid economic growth. From 1959 through 1979 Japan supplied 19 percent of the public loans (U.S. 37 percent; international organizations, 38 percent), 18 percent of the private loans (U.S. 40 percent), and 64 percent of the direct investment (U.S. 23 percent).[31] Soon after Chun Doo Hwan took office, the South Korean government asked Japan for a loan of $10 billion, later reduced to $6 billion. Japan had been phasing out economic aid to South Korea, as the United States had done years earlier, on the ground that South Korea had advanced from the status of a less-developed country to that of a newly industrialized country. But Nakasone was convinced of the importance of cultivating good relations with South Korea for strategic, economic, and political reasons. One way of mitigating Korean dissatisfaction at the endemic large trade deficit with Japan and resentment that the Japanese defense burden as a proportion of GNP was only one-sixth of Korea's, was to continue to provide economic aid. Hence, shortly after Nakasone took office he brought to a conclusion long, drawn-out negotiations on the amount and terms of a loan by agreeing to provide $4 billion—$1.8 billion as a concessional loan over a seven-year period and the remainder in Export-Import Bank credits.[32]

Japanese equity investments in South Korea, although more numerous than those of the United States and larger in aggregate amount, have tended to be relatively small—under $1 million. Much of it has gone into the kind of labor-intensive industry in which Japanese factories are no longer competitive. Koreans have complained that such investments yield little in the way of technology transfer. Nevertheless, the investments have established a sizable network of links between Korean and Japanese businessmen who have a shared economic stake and hence a vested interest in promoting good relations between the two countries. Japanese direct investment slowed in the 1980s, and much of it went into hotels rather than factories, as rising wages in Korea's labor-intensive industries made them a less attractive investment than they had been earlier.[33]

As indicated above, Japan and the United States have been the principal sources of new technology for South Korean industry. As South Korean industry became more competitive with Japanese industry, particularly in steel and shipbuilding, Japanese industrialists became more cautious about transferring advanced technology to Korean firms. Mitsubishi hesitated at first to provide equipment for the second Pohang integrated steel complex, but rather than see the lucrative contract go to other suppliers, it agreed to cooperate in expanding the capacity of a potential competitor. Mitsubishi was responding to the complex interactions set in motion by technology transfer. Some sectors in Japan may suffer from the increased competition, but other sectors probably will benefit from South Korea's resultant enhanced capacity and need to acquire other Japanese goods. For example, in the South Korean shipbuilding industry, which has become highly competitive with Japan in certain types of ships, some 40 percent of ship construction value is said to consist of imported Japanese products that cannot be produced in South Korea.[34] The difficulty of calculating costs and benefits probably ensures a substantial flow of technology from Japan to South Korea, but also perpetuates Korean dissatisfaction with the quality and amount of such technology transfer.

In basic endowments Japan and South Korea are similar. Both lack natural resources and depend heavily on foreign trade to obtain the raw materials needed for industrial development. Both have well-educated, hard-working populations functioning in government guided, free enterprise economies, Japan has the advantages of an earlier start in industrialization and a home market four times the size of South Korea's. The similarity of the economies suggests competition rather than complementarity. In fact, however, the size of their trade demonstrates the existence of many sectors in which they meet each other's needs.

An unusual illustration of the capacity of Japan and the ROK to cooperate for economic purposes was the agreement signed in January 1974 on joint exploration and production of undersea oil in the continental shelf between Japan and South Korea. Rather than try to resolve a knotty dispute over the extent of each country's territorial sea, Tokyo and Seoul chose the pragmatic solution of conducting exploration and production jointly in areas where their claims overlapped. Costs and any oil produced were to be shared equally. The North Koreans excoriated the agreement as a sellout of national resources to foreigners, and the Chinese, who had made extensive claims to resources in the continental shelf, also objected. Ratification of the agreement was delayed until 1977, primarily out of concern for Chinese objections. As of mid-1985, joint Japanese–South Korean exploration had failed to locate commercial deposits of oil or gas, but the search continues.

Competition in the export of certain products will undoubtedly increase, as Korean industry becomes more advanced and sophisticated, but Japan's head start and innovative talent should keep it well in the lead. In the years ahead, the symbiotic relationship between the two economies probably will draw them even closer than in the past. Friction will continue to exist over the trade imbalance, along with Korean dissatisfaction with technology and capital transfer, but powerful business interests in both countries will work hard to prevent disputes from getting out of hand. Nevertheless, as in the past, heated rhetoric will sometimes exaggerate differences and obscure the great advantage to both countries of the deep and growing economic relationship.

Political Relations

The overriding importance of strategic and economic interests as defined by the conservative leaders of Japan and South Korea has bonded the two countries firmly together since 1965, despite a variety of shocks and strains that threatened relations. Management of the relationship has not been easy, however. In public opinion polls Koreans frequently placed Japan near the top of a list of least-liked countries and the Japanese did the same with South Korea. Both people reacted emotionally to political incidents, such as the abduction of Kim Dae Jung from a Tokyo hotel by KCIA agents or the assassination of President Park Chung-hee's wife by a Korean from Japan. Once derailed by an emotional outburst, relations were difficult to get back on track.

The governments sought to institutionalize ways of dealing with each other to promote closer relations. In 1967 they set up an annual ministerial conference, which proved useful for exchanging top-level views and for agreeing on the substantial Japanese government loans needed to further the ROK's ambitious economic development program. Leading businessmen from both countries met regularly in the Korea-Japan Economic Cooperation Committee. Japan-Korea Friendship Associations, set up in the 1970s to counter pro–North Korean activities in Japan, brought together prominent citizens in cities or prefectures, including Korean nationals in Japan, in meetings to demonstrate support for the ROK or in tours of South Korea. The Japan–South Korea Parliamentarians League provided a forum for legislators of the two countries to meet.

These well-intentioned efforts to promote good relations had to contend with the damaging effect on Japan–South Korean relations of domestic politics in each country. The Japanese opposition parties and certain individuals from non-mainstream factions of the LDP attacked the Japanese government's partiality for South Korea over North Korea. Some of them visited Pyongyang, where they were received by Kim Il Sung. They returned to Japan calling for an evenhanded Japanese policy toward Seoul and Pyongyang and expressing their support for Kim's views on Korean unification. The Japanese media, which tended to support opposition criticism of the government's policy on Korea, published a stream of articles painting an unflattering picture of corruption and repression in South Korea and accused Japanese businessmen of channeling funds secretly to South Korean politicians. From time to time the exasperated South Korean government shut down the branch offices of Japanese newspapers in South Korea and expelled their correspondents for what it described as distorted and biased reporting.[35] Most Japanese intellectuals were critical of the repressive measures adopted by Park Chung-hee to maintain his power under the *yusin* constitution.

Incidents that ignited hot disputes between Seoul and Tokyo illustrate the fragility of the relationship. The most serious of these, which plunged relations to their lowest point and forced the postponement of the annual ministerial conference, was the abduction of Kim Dae Jung in August 1973. The Japanese government regarded the Kim kidnapping as an affront to its sovereignty by a friendly government and demanded that South Korea cooperate in an investigation. The Koreans refused, denying any official involvement in the affair. Japanese articles and editorials critical of South Korea multiplied. Premier Kim Chong-pil traveled to Tokyo in late 1973 to offer to Japanese Prime Minister Kakuei Tanaka his government's regrets for the incident, but not until 1975, after further explanations by the South Korean government, was the incident officially laid to rest.

In the meantime, Koreans had been outraged by an attempted assassination of Park Chung-hee in August 1974 that killed his wife. The assassin was a Korean resident of Japan, who used a handgun stolen from a Japanese police box. The Korean government demanded an apology from the Japanese government for not controlling anti-ROK activities by Koreans in Japan and for failing to prevent the assassination. For years the South Korean government had complained that members of the Chosoren, the association of pro-Pyongyang Koreans in Japan, had been recruiting and training spies on behalf of North Korea and infiltrating them into South Korea. Some spy rings were discovered by the Japanese police, but others escaped detection until they were unmasked by the KCIA in South Korea.[36] Koreans accused the Japanese government of laxness in failing to prevent the use of its territory for espionage operations against a friendly neighbor. The Japanese government refused to accept responsibility for the assassination of Park Chung-hee's wife, and the Korean press reacted with bitter recriminations against the Japanese. Eventually, the dispute was resolved with U.S. help, and the Japanese government formally expressed regret for the incident.

The death sentence given Kim Dae Jung by a South Korean military court in September 1980 caused a furor in Japan. Kim's conviction was based in part on activities in Japan, thus violating the understanding reached between Japanese and Korean officials in 1973 that he would not be tried for such activities. Japanese Prime Minister Zenko Suzuki warned that economic aid to South Korea might be seriously restricted if Kim Dae Jung were executed. He also threatened that the government might be compelled by popular indignation to move closer to North Korea.[37] Seoul's government-controlled press harshly denounced Japan for interfering in South Korea's domestic affairs. In Tokyo the All-Japan Council of Transport Workers threatened to refuse to handle Korean goods, and in Yokohama 50 Japanese burst into the South Korean Consulate General demanding that Kim Dae Jung not be executed.[38] The South Korean government strongly protested the Japanese government's failure to provide adequate police protection. The rising tide of anger on both sides ebbed only after the commutation of Kim's death sentence in early 1981.

In 1982 an unwise move by Japan provoked the next tussle between Seoul and Tokyo. The Japanese Ministry of Education proposed to soften the textbook descriptions of Japan's overseas activities in the 1930s and 1940s in various ways, such as by using "advance" rather than "invasion" to describe Japan's military occupation of China and by characterizing the Korean demonstrations for independence as "riots." These proposed changes reflected rising nationalism in Japan, where the right wing of the LDP was riding high after an unexpected LDP election victory in 1980 that demoralized the opposition. But the Education Ministry's proposal struck sensitive nerves in China and Korea, where nationalistic feelings were also on the rise. The proposal brought a chorus of protest against Japan, not only from Chinese and Koreans but also from Southeast Asians whose countries had suffered Japanese military occupation.[39] The political maneuvering and diplomatic negotiations that eventually caused the Ministry of Education to back away from its proposal were particularly delicate with regard to South Korea, for the aggrieved South Korean reaction had angered Japanese right-wing advocates of textbook changes who were normally the staunchest supporters of the ROK. Even ancient history became an arena for confrontation between Japanese and Koreans. Nationalists attempting to portray the superiority of one people over the other sought evidence from a long-standing esoteric debate among historians and archaeologists over the extent of Korean influence on early Japan and a claim that Japan had dominated ancient Korean kingdoms.[40]

Yasuhiro Nakasone, who became prime minister in November 1982 soon after the resolution of the textbook issue, was determined to lift the sagging relations between Tokyo and Seoul. He put in a personal telephone call to Chun Doo Hwan soon after taking office and in January 1983 became the first Japanese prime minister to make an official working visit to Seoul, at which final agreement on Japan's $4 billion loan to South Korea was announced. Chun shared Nakasone's desire to improve relations between the two countries, and in September 1984 he made the first official visit of a South Korean premier to Tokyo. A notable feature of that visit was a state dinner at the Imperial Palace at which the Japanese emperor declared: "It is indeed regrettable that there was an unfortunate past between us for a period in this century and I believe that it should not be repeated again."[41] The Chun visit resolved no substantive issues, but it significantly improved the atmosphere between Tokyo and Seoul. Pyongyang, in a statement issued by a foreign ministry representative ridiculing the Japanese expression of regret as a "puppet farce" performed by a "fascist hooligan" and a "figurehead emperor," declared that "the Korean people still retain a legitimate national right to receive an apology from Japan."[42]

The Korean Minority in Japan

The Korean minority in Japan links Japan and Korea but also causes friction between them and serves as a battleground for the two Korean governments. Minority numbers have remained roughly constant for the past twenty years at about 600,000. Japanese society resists their assimilation, and the two Korean governments, for their own reasons, want them to retain their Korean nationality.

Koreans migrated to Japan during the colonial period looking for work. The majority were illiterate in both Korean and Japanese, and they took the lowest-paying, unskilled jobs. During World War II, the Japanese government brought in hundreds of thousands of Koreans to cope with a severe labor shortage, boosting the number of Koreans in Japan to a peak of 2.4 million in 1945.[43] Most of these returned to South Korea during the U.S. military occupation of both countries. Those who remained continued to occupy the lowest position on the social scale, looked down on by Japanese and discriminated against in education, employment, social welfare, and other respects.

Many Koreans took part in Japanese domestic politics as active supporters of the JCP until 1955 when, following instructions from Pyongyang, they cut their ties with the JCP and established a new organization, the Chosoren (General Federation of Korean Residents in Japan), dedicated to furthering the interests of the DPRK. Han Dok Su, founder of the Chosoren and still its chairman in 1985, developed the organization into an effective instrument of the DPRK in Japan, cooperating closely with the Japanese Socialist Party and other pro–North Korean left-wing groups and individuals.

In a farsighted move, Kim Il Sung made grants to Chosoren to set up a Korean-language school system, from elementary school through university levels. In these schools young Koreans were taught to regard North Korea as a paradise on earth and the DPRK as the legitimate representative of the Korean people. The DPRK took the view that Koreans were in Japan temporarily and would return to the fatherland after Korea's unification. Hence, it did not, like the ROK, press the Japanese government to grant permanent residence status to Koreans. Korean businessmen affiliated with Chosoren had the inside track in trade with North Korea, although they were expected in return to make contributions to the support of Chosoren and for the construction of "patriotic factories" in North Korea.

In 1958, when Syngman Rhee was refusing to repatriate Koreans from Japan until the Japanese government had agreed to compensate them for "forced labor" in Japan, Kim Il Sung magnanimously offered to pay for the repatriation of all Koreans who wanted to come and waived any claim for compensation. Despite irate protests from the Rhee government, Japanese Prime Minister Nobusuke Kishi accepted Kim Il Sung's proposal, and by December 1961, some 75,000 Koreans had left Japan for North Korea.[44] Thereafter, as news trickled back that conditions for repatriates were not as glowing as they had been painted, the outflow dwindled. By 1967 only 1,300 more had repatriated, and by 1980, only another 5,000 had left Japan.[45]

A rival of the Chosoren, the Mindan, composed mainly of conservative, middle-class businessmen, had been established in 1948, but the ROK was less prompt and astute than the DPRK in coming to the aid of its Korean adherents in Japan. By 1960 North Korea had sent Chosoren twelve times as much money as Mindan had received from the ROK. Chosoren operated 280 schools, whereas Mindan had only 50. Japanese government records show 444,586 Koreans had registered as citizens of North Korea and only 162,871 as citizens of South Korea.[46]

During the next twenty-five years, however, North Korean influence over Koreans in Japan waned, while South Korean influence grew. The government of South Korea gained a great advantage from the establishment of diplomatic relations in 1965, which gave it an official channel through which to promote the interests of Koreans in Japan. North Korea had to work through an unofficial organization. South Korea's economic achievements improved its image within the Korean community. Park Chung-hee substantially increased funds devoted to training teachers and supporting Korean schools in Japan. Gradually, left-wing dominance of the media in Japan declined, opening the way to more favorable treatment of South Korea and a more critical attitude toward North Korea.[47]

In 1975 Mindan began a program of inviting Chosoren members to visit the graves of their ancestors in South Korea during the *Hansik* holiday in April and the *Chusok* holiday in October, when Koreans traditionally make such visits. As nearly all of the first-generation Koreans in Japan originally came from South Korea, North Korea is not in a position to compete with this program. By 1984, 40,000 Chosoren-affiliated Koreans had visited South Korea, despite strenuous efforts by Chosoren officials to prevent them.[48] The program not only gave the visitors an opportunity to see relatives from whom they had long been separated, but also to contrast actual conditions in South Korea with those pictured in the propaganda disseminated by Chosoren.

The decline in Chosoren's influence resulted not only from the success of Mindan's home visit program, but also from several other factors. Pyongyang's default on its debts to creditors in Japan severely damaged its standing with Japanese business, including Chosoren-affiliated Korean businessmen. The shortage of foreign exchange seems to have affected North Korea's ability to support financially the Chosoren-supported Korean educational system in Japan. Remittances peaked at 3.7 billion yen in 1974, thereafter declining to 1 billion yen by 1977.[49] Pyongyang's refusal to allow any of the more than 6,000 Japanese wives of Korean citizens repatriated to North Korea since 1959 to visit relatives in Japan has created resentment. Many Koreans have concluded that the wives are kept from leaving in order to prevent them from revealing in Japan how bad conditions really are in North Korea.[50] The Rangoon incident and the North Korean government's clumsy attempt to blame it on South Korea further damaged the DPRK's prestige and credibility.

Discrimination against Koreans in Japan has been a chronic issue between the Japanese and South Korean governments. It is usually on the agenda of high level talks. The Japanese government has made significant concessions over the years, but important differences continue to exist. One of these concerns the requirement that long-term resident aliens in Japan must be fingerprinted every five years. Protesting that among Japanese only criminals are fingerprinted, the Korean community has fought for abolition of the practice, supported by the South Korean government. Many Japanese back the Koreans in their opposition to fingerprinting, and a significant number of Japanese municipal governments have declined to prosecute aliens who refuse fingerprinting.[51] The South Korean government, although officially calling for an end to alien fingerprinting, is of two minds, for the security authorities in Seoul would regret any weakening in the ability of the Japanese police to keep track of pro-Pyongyang Koreans in Japan. Discrimination against Koreans will undoubtedly continue, but, with the possible exception of the fingerprinting issue, it seems unlikely to produce major confrontations between the two governments.

Generational change within the Korean community is slowly diminishing the relevance of Chosoren and Mindan to the concerns of Koreans in Japan. The Japanese police estimated in 1984 that only 10 percent of the Koreans in Japan were associated with Chosoren and 15 percent with Mindan, the rest being unaffiliated.[52] Third generation Koreans, many of whom speak only Japanese, are more concerned with their personal future within Japanese society than with the struggle between the two governments in their ancestors' homeland. Chosoren and Mindan are having difficulty recruiting students for Korean schools because an education in Japanese schools promises a better future for young Koreans. Intermarriage with Japanese is increasing, and a recent change in Japanese law confers Japanese citizenship on children of Japanese mothers as well as Japanese fathers. Thus, the long-term trend is toward assimilation of the Korean community, for it is not being replenished with new immigrants from Korea. Full assimilation will take many decades, however, because of the persisting legal and social discrimination against Koreans. Meanwhile, the Korean minority will be a shrinking battleground for the two governments in Korea and a declining, although still significant source of friction, between Tokyo and the two Korean capitals.

Conclusion

Relations between Japan and South Korea have had their ups and downs, affected by changes in the international environment and the personal proclivities of Japanese and Korean leaders. The readiness of each people to think ill of the other created a dry brushland in which random incidents ignited conflagrations difficult to bring under control. Nevertheless, the overall trend has been toward closer and warmer relations. The era of Nakasone and Chun bears little resemblance to that of Kishi and Rhee.

A variety of factors have combined to produce this favorable trend. Support among the Japanese people for the U.S.-led security system has grown steadily and with it recognition of the importance of South Korea to Japan's security. The strength of the left wing in Japan has declined greatly, as evidenced by the weakening of the JSP and the emergence of a greater variety of views and increased independence of thought within the media. Reporting on the South Korean economy has broadened knowledge of and respect for South Korea's economic achievements. Travel to South Korea has given hundreds of thousands of Japanese tourists and businessmen an opportunity to experience personally South Korea's progress in modernization. At the same time, the Japanese image of North Korea has suffered from an increase in the publication of books and articles painting a drab picture of conditions there. Default on debts to businessmen in Japan and, above all, the Rangoon atrocity have seriously undermined the uncritical view many Japanese formerly took of North Korea.

Japanese condescension toward Koreans and Korean rancor toward Japanese probably will continue to exist for a long time among the general public. A U.S. journalist who has lived in both countries estimates that these feelings will persist for at least another generation.[53] In the opinion-influencing strata, however, signs of change are emerging: a Japanese journalist who speaks Korean, a few young Japanese scholars trained in Korean universities and specializing in Korean studies, the establishment of an association for Japanese studies in Seoul, meetings of Korean and Japanese scholars aimed at furthering understanding of each other's countries.[54] While erosion of prejudice pursues its slow course, the two governments will take the lead, as they have in the past, in keeping relations on an even keel. Barring an unlikely drastic change in the international environment, the strategic and economic interests of the two countries will continue to nudge them toward closer cooperation. The principal cloud on the horizon is the prospect of closer Japanese relations with North Korea, as the big powers expand cross-contacts with the two Koreas. That prospect and the South Korean reaction to it will be treated in Chapter 11.

Notes

1. For a discussion of the four-power system, see Ralph N. Clough, *East Asia and U.S. Security* (Washington, D.C.: Brookings Institution, 1975), Chapter 3, pp. 44–54. See also Donald A. Zagoria, "The Strategic Environment in East Asia," in Donald A. Zagoria, ed., *Soviet Policy in East Asia* (New Haven, Conn.: Yale University Press, 1982), pp. 1–28.

2. Harry Gelman and Norman D. Levin, *The Future of Soviet–North Korean Relations* (Santa Monica, Calif.: Rand Corporation, 1984), pp. 49–50.

3. Paul F. Langer, "Soviet Military Power in Asia," in Zagoria, *Soviet Policy in East Asia*, pp. 255–282.

4. Three useful collections of essays on U.S.-Korean relations appeared in commemoration of the centennial of the establishment of diplomatic relations between Seoul and Washington in 1882: Youngnok Koo and Dae-Sook Suh, eds., *Korea and the United States: A Century of Cooperation* (Honolulu: University of Hawaii Press, 1984); Tae-Hwan Kwak, John Chay, Soon Sung Cho and Shannon McCune, eds., *U.S.-Korean Relations, 1882–1982* (Seoul: Kyungnam University Press, 1982); Sung-joo Han, ed., *After One Hundred Years: Continuity and Change in Korean-American Relations* (Seoul: Asiatic Research Center, Korea University, 1982).

5. Robert Boettcher, *Gifts of Deceit: Sun Myung Moon, Tongsun Park and the Korean Scandal* (New York: Holt, Rinehart and Winston, 1980), pp. 86–95.

6. Mason and others, *Economic and Social Modernization*, p. 182.

7. *Korea Herald*, June 15, 1985.

8. Republic of Korea, International Economic Policy Council, *Korea's Economic Policy Reform* (Seoul, March 1985), p. 15.

9. Duk-Choong Kim, "Prospects for Korean-American Economic Cooperation in the 1980s" (unpublished paper, April 1985), p. 8.

10. Ibid., p. 14.

11. Ibid., p. 16.

12. Kim Linsu, "Technological Transfer and Foreign Investment," in Thomas Stern, ed., *Korea's Economy*, vol. 1, no. 1 (Washington, D.C.: Korea Economic Institute, April 1985), p. 24.

13. John S. Odell, "Growing Trade and Growing Conflict Between the Republic of Korea and the United States," in Karl Moscowitz, *From Patron to Partner: The Development of U.S.-Korean Business and Trade Relations* (Lexington, Mass.: D. C. Heath & Co., 1984), pp. 123–148.

14. U.S. Department of Commerce (unpublished document, March 7, 1985), pp. 1–2.

15. Hearing, House Committee on Foreign Affairs (Subcommittee on Asian and Pacific Affairs), 99th Cong., 1st sess., March 11, 1985, pp. 357–358.

16. Boettcher, *Gifts of Deceit*, contains a detailed account of this affair. See also the many reports of Congressional hearings on Korean affairs between 1976 and 1978 listed on pp. 351–352 of his book, and Chae-Jin Lee and Hideo Sato, *U.S. Policy Toward Japan and Korea* (New York: Praeger, 1982), pp. 73–94.

17. William Watts, George R. Packard, Ralph N. Clough, and Robert B. Oxnam, *Japan, Korea and China: American Perspectives and Policies* (Lexington, Mass.: D. C. Heath & Co., 1979), pp. 90–91.

18. Kim Dae Jung, "The Korean Peninsula: Peace, Reunification and the Role of the United States" (May 1, 1984), in *Kim Dae Jung in Armerica*, 2d ed. (Alexandria, Va.: Korean Institute of Human Rights, undated), p. 73.

19. Oh Jeung-ja, "What Is America to Us Koreans?" *Korea Herald*, June 11, 1985.

20. *Korea Herald*, November 9 and December 3, 1985.

21. Donald C. Hellman discusses the gap between official and popular perceptions of South Korea in the United States in "The American Perception of Korea: 1945–1982," in Koo and Suh, *Korea and the United States*, pp. 77–88.

22. *Gallup Report International*, vol. 2, no. 3 (Princeton, N.J.: Gallup Organization, Inc., June 1984), pp. 7–8.

23. Poll conducted by *Kyunghyang Sinmun*, *Korea Herald*, July 2, 1985, p. 3.

24. For a recent, comprehensive survey of Japan's relations with South Korea, see Chong-Sik Lee, *Japan and Korea: The Political Dimension* (Stanford, Calif.: Hoover Institution Press, 1985).

25. Kwan Bong Kim analyzes the negotiations between Japan and South Korea and the internal political struggle over the treaty in *The Korea-Japan Treaty Crisis and the Instability of The Korean Political System* (New York: Praeger, 1971). See also Lee, *Japan and Korea*, Chapter 3.

26. Kwan Bong Kim, *The Korea-Japan Treaty Crisis*, pp. 60–61.

27. *FBIS*, September 10, 1984, p. C14.

28. For a thoughtful presentation of Korean misgivings concerning Japanese rearmament, see Han Sung-joo, "Memories of Conflicts Past," in *Far Eastern Economic Review*, November 26, 1982, pp. 34–35.

29. *FBIS*, June 17, 1985, pp. D5–D7.

30. World Bank, *Korea: Development in a Global Context* (Washington, D.C., 1984), p. 5. International Monetary Fund, *Direction of Trade Statistics Yearbook, 1984* (Washington, D.C., undated), pp. 248–250.

31. *Handbook of Korea*, 4th ed. (Seoul: Korean Overseas Information Service, Ministry of Culture and Information, 1982), p. 475.

32. These loan negotiations were complicated by injudicious hard-sell tactics by the Koreans, an unsuccessful attempt by the Koreans to have the loans accepted by the Japanese as partial compensation for South Korea's contribution to Japan's security, and Japanese indignation at Kim Dae Jung's death sentence. See Lee, *Japan and Korea*, Chapter 5.

33. *Far Eastern Economic Review*, February 16, 1984, p. 66.

34. Japanese official, interview, Seoul, November 1984.

35. See, for example, *FBIS*, January 10, 1979, p. E1 concerning the expulsion of the *Mainichi* correspondent, and *Korea Herald*, July 5, 1980, reporting the closing down of the branch offices of the *Asahi* and *JIJI* Press.

36. For some examples, see *Korea Herald*, April 29, 1980; April 10, 1981; June 17, 1981; November 7, 1981; and November 14, 1982.

37. *Washington Post*, September 23, 1980; November 27, 1980.

38. New York Times, November 30, 1980, Washington Post, December 6, 1980.
39. Washington Post, August 24, 1982; New York Times, August 29, 1982.
40. Lee, Japan and Korea, pp. 151–163.
41. Korea Herald, September 8, 1984.
42. FBIS, September 12, 1984, D15–D16.
43. Richard H. Mitchell, The Korean Minority in Japan (Berkeley: University of California Press, 1967), p. 76.
44. Ibid., p. 154.
45. Korea Herald, June 28, 1980.
46. Mitchell, The Korean Minority in Japan, pp. 129, 131.
47. Far Eastern Economic Review, May 26, 1978, pp. 69–72. See also Shun Den, "Political Organizations of ROK and Korean Residents in Japan," JIYU, December 1978, trans. in U.S. Embassy, Tokyo, Summaries of Selected Magazines, December 1978, pp. 11–20.
48. Korea Herald, March 29, 1984.
49. Shun Den, "Political Organizations of ROK and Korean Residents in Japan," p. 15. According to Pyongyang radio, 91 installments totaling 35,347,682,033 yen had been remitted to Chosoren for educational purposes by February 1984, the latest installment amounting to 364,755,000 yen (FBIS, February 15, 1984, p. E3).
50. Korea Herald, May 23 and May 25, 1985.
51. New York Times, May 14, 1985; Korea Herald, May 16, 1985.
52. Interview with U.S. Embassy officer, Tokyo, December 1984.
53. Herman Pevner, writing in the Korea Herald, October 19 and October 20, 1984.
54. Papers presented at one such meeting were published in Bae Ho Hahn and Tadashi Yamamoto, eds., Korea and Japan: A New Dialogue Across the Channel (Seoul: Asiatic Research Center, 1978).

8

North Korea, the Soviet Union, and China

As South Korea depended on the United States and Japan, so North Korea depended on the Soviet Union and China for help in achieving its objectives: survival as a state, economic development, military modernization, and ultimately, the reunification of Korea on its own terms. The quarrel between its two allies placed Pyongyang in a difficult position. Kim Il Sung knew that he needed support from both and that he could not afford, therefore, to throw North Korea's full weight behind one of them. He signed mutual assistance treaties with both in 1961. He maneuvered between them, backing Moscow on some issues and Peking on others, seeking to stake out an independent position that would enable him to extract as much support as possible from each.

Kim's bargaining power was relatively weak, for he needed the support of the Soviet Union and China more than they needed his. The picture sometimes drawn of North Korea playing one ally off against the other to maximize its gains from each fails to take account of the weakness of North Korea's position. Given the pressures that Moscow and Peking were capable of exerting by withholding support, North Korea had to be more concerned with minimizing losses than with maximizing gains.[1]

The Soviet Union and North Korea

Inextricably bound together by geography and history, the Soviet Union and North Korea have been uncomfortable bedfellows. The Soviet Union wants a friendly neighbor on its southern flank, and the importance of North Korea has increased since the Soviet break with China. The growing power of the U.S.-Japan security alliance and the beginning of

U.S. military cooperation with China has augmented the strategic importance of North Korea to the Soviet Union. For North Korea the Soviet Union has been the sole source of advanced weapons and the ultimate guarantor of its security in the face of the threat from the United States and South Korea.

Common strategic concerns have not ensured smooth cooperation. Relations between the two countries have generally been cool and sometimes severely strained. Moscow found Pyongyang to be a fractious and unruly ally, often pursuing domestic and foreign policies sharply at odds with those desired by its patron. The North Koreans resented Soviet attempts to interfere in their internal politics and to dictate their foreign policy. The Soviets could not be relied on to back Kim Il Sung in achieving his chief objectives: maintaining himself and his son in power, maximizing North Korea's freedom of action, and unifying Korea on his terms. The North Koreans saw the Soviet Union as niggardly in extending military and economic aid, whereas the Soviets regarded the North Koreans as excessively demanding and ungrateful. The two countries often disagreed on policy toward the United States. The North Koreans at times charged the Soviets with being overly cautious, even pusillanimous, in facing up to the United States; the Soviets feared that Kim Il Sung's belligerent and sometimes reckless behavior might draw them into an unwanted confrontation with the United States. Particularly disturbing to the Soviets were the occasions on which the North Koreans backed the Chinese in the ongoing struggle between Moscow and Peking. To a limited extent China provided North Korea with an alternative supporter and therefore diminished the leverage that the Soviet Union might otherwise have been able to exert on Pyongyang.

Despite the ups and downs in the relationship, the Soviet–North Korean alliance has lasted. Each country needed the other and would not permit relations to deteriorate beyond a certain point. North Korea, however, needs the Soviet Union much more than the Soviet Union needs North Korea, making the relationship an unequal one, somewhat comparable to that between the United States and South Korea.

Strategic Relations

The principal strategic function of North Korea for the Soviet Union has been to deny to a potential enemy the part of Korea adjoining Soviet territory.[2] Although the land border is only 12 miles long, enemy use of North Korean airfields and ports and the basing of medium-range missiles on North Korean territory would pose a serious threat to Vladivostok, the principal Soviet naval base in the Pacific. Of course, the Soviet–North Korean alliance could become the basis for the use of North Korean territory by Soviet forces, not just for the denial of that territory to an adversary. Access to North Korea's ice-free ports, in particular, would substantially increase the flexibility of Soviet naval forces. However, since the withdrawal of Chinese forces from North Korea in 1958, Kim Il Sung has firmly opposed as a matter of principle the stationing of foreign forces in any country. To permit the basing of Soviet forces in North Korea would not only antagonize the Chinese and inhibit Pyongyang's freedom of action, but would undercut the effort it has made to mobilize support throughout the world for the withdrawal of U.S. forces from South Korea. A Soviet military presence would also in all probability lead to the upgrading of U.S. forces in South Korea to serve as a counterweight to Soviet forces in North Korea, not just as a counter to North Korean forces.

When Stalin backed Kim Il Sung's attempt in 1950 to unify Korea by force, he presumably believed that a unified Korea would be a compliant ally, a valuable adjunct to the PRC, at that time newly linked to the Soviet Union by a thirty-year treaty of alliance. The experience of the past thirty years, however, must have caused the Soviets to question whether a united Korea would serve Soviet interests. If Kim Il Sung often defied Soviet wishes when North Korea was struggling against a more populous South Korea firmly backed by the United States, could Moscow count on the leader of a unified Korea to be a dependable Soviet ally? A unified Korea of 60 million people, highly industrialized and well armed, would have much more freedom of choice than North Korea has today. The probability would be high that it would gravitate into the orbit of the United States and Japan, particularly if the current trend of increasing cooperation of these two countries with China were to continue into the future.

Thus, Soviet failure to exhibit enthusiasm for unifying Korea is not surprising. Officially, the Soviet government gives rhetorical support to Kim Il Sung's proposals for peaceful unification, but privately Soviet officials and scholars see little prospect of Korea's unification in the foreseeable future. They criticize Kim's position as unrealistic and express the view that peaceful coexistence between the two Koreas on the pattern of the two Germanies would serve Soviet interests better than the present state of tense military confrontation. The Soviets have shown restraint in supplying Kim Il Sung with advanced weapons not only because of the costs and risks for the Soviet Union that would result from an adventuristic assault on South Korea, but because even if Kim were successful, the Soviets would have no assurance that his success would benefit the Soviet Union. Moscow has done what has been necessary to maintain significant influence and safeguard its basic interest in retaining North Korea as a buffer state on its border, but little more.

North Korea has had little choice but to rely on the Soviet Union as its principal source of economic and military aid and as the guarantor of its survival in the face of the combined power of South Korea and the United States. This dependency has bred frustration and resentment. Infuriated by Soviet meddling in North Korea's domestic politics in the 1950s and earlier, Kim Il Sung sought to reduce his country's strategic dependence by building a self-reliant industrial base and an armaments industry. He achieved only partial success. Lacking a design capability, the North Korean armaments industry remained dependent on the Soviets for technology needed to build new weapons, which the Soviets were slow to provide. When they did provide the technology for a later model weapon, such as the T-62 tank which North Korea began to turn out in the mid-1970s, the weapon was already obsolescent.

Overflights by Soviet aircraft, exchanges of military visits, and the Soviet decision to provide MIG-23s and SA-3s to North Korea after years of withholding them, were aspects of a general improvement in relations between Moscow and Pyongyang during 1984 and 1985. This upturn in their relationship will be discussed more fully below. The military actions served to remind South Korea and the United States that the Soviet Union continued to have a strategic stake in North Korea, whatever the past differences between the two countries. Even so, the Soviets did not appear to be departing from their practice of offering North Korea only limited and cautious military support.

Economic Relations

North Korea is not an important trading partner for the Soviet Union, although its proximity to the Soviet Far East makes it a useful supplier of products such as cement to that region. The volume of trade is small, and its value declined from 1.5 percent of total Soviet foreign trade in 1969 to 0.46 percent in 1983.[3] Two-way trade of 587 million rubles in 1983 made North Korea a minor trading partner for the Soviet Union, as compared to the $14 billion two-way trade between the United States and South Korea and South Korea's ranking as the seventh most important trading partner of the United States.

During most of the period since the Korean War, the Soviet Union shipped more to North Korea than it received in return, the difference being financed with Soviet grants and loans. Grants were large during the reconstruction period after the Korean War, but during the 1960s and 1970s, loans replaced grants. North Korea had difficulty in repaying loans in accordance with agreed schedules. The Soviet Union wrote off some loans and rescheduled payments on others. In 1970, in order to provide greater assurance that loans would be repaid, the two countries signed agreements whereby North Korea would pay for factories furnished by the Soviet Union by exporting to the Soviet Union a specified proportion of the products of such factories. Some of these agreements did not work out as planned and had to be cancelled. Indeed, a detailed analysis of Soviet credit arrangements with North Korea concluded that none of these arrangements was carried out as originally agreed; agreements reached had to be renegotiated repeatedly to change the list of projects to be carried out or to reschedule payments.[4]

Economic relations between the Soviet Union and North Korea reached a critical stage in 1976 and 1977, marked by acrimonious disputes between them. Trade had declined substantially from the high level of 1971 and 1972, the drop in North Korean imports of Soviet plants and machinery being particularly steep. Pyongyang's cumulative indebtedness had risen rapidly between 1968 and 1977 until it exceeded $900 million.[5] North Korea was faced with Soviet pressures to reduce its indebtedness at the very time that it had been forced to default on payments to Western creditors. Moscow showed no inclination to help Pyongyang pay off its hard currency debt.[6] North Korea had to tighten its belt and accept the prospect of a less forthcoming attitude on the part of its Soviet ally in providing raw materials and capital goods for the seven-year plan launched in 1978.

Differences over economic issues had plagued Soviet–North Korean relations from the outset. North Korea's refusal to join the Soviet-dominated international economic organization, Council for Mutual Economic Assistance (CMEA), limited Soviet influence over the North Korean economy. Kim Il Sung's rejection of Soviet advice on economic policy in the mid-1950s, at a time when economic growth was heavily dependent on Soviet grants, demonstrated a stubborn determination to go his own way. So did Kim's failure to follow the Soviet line against China in the early 1960s, despite the pressure that Moscow applied by withholding economic aid. Thus, not only did Pyongyang perform poorly in purely economic terms in meeting the commitments made in trade agreements, but the political payoff to the Soviet Union for being the leading supplier of raw materials and capital goods for North Korea's economic construction was disappointing. In economic terms, North Korea has clearly been more of a burden than an asset. Moscow has had to pay for the strategic and political advantages of maintaining minimal influence in Pyongyang.

In the late 1970s the Soviets demanded and received better performance from North Korea in the repayment of debts. Each year from 1978 to 1983 (with the exception of 1981) North Korean exports to the Soviet Union exceeded its imports.[7] The Soviets also benefited from North Korea's agreement to the use of Najin port in the extreme northeastern part of Korea as a transshipment point for goods sent on by rail to the Soviet Union. This helped ease the congestion in Soviet Pacific ports. Soviet vessels entering the port increased from 250 in 1975 to 450 in 1978. The ships carried 900,000 tons of cargo that year, which included industrial plant facilities, cement, crude oil, and cotton. A protocol signed in December 1978 provided for Soviet assistance in expanding Najin's port facilities.[8]

In 1984 Soviet–North Korean relations showed marked improvement, highlighted by Kim Il Sung's visit to Moscow and Eastern Europe, his first official visit to the Soviet Union since 1961. The improvement continued into 1985. Observers speculated that Kim obtained promises from Moscow of increased economic aid, but in private comments Soviet officials and scholars indicated that the promised aid was not large. Most significant was Moscow's agreement to assist in the construction of North Korea's first nuclear power plant. In any case, after Kim's visit the North Korean press stressed the primary importance of expanding economic relations with socialist countries. The North Koreans publicly acknowledged that economic cooperation with socialist countries had made great contributions to the North Korean economy. They reduced emphasis on economic self-reliance and on economic relations with the Third World.

If Soviet–North Korean economic relations have been, for the Soviet Union, primarily an instrument for maintaining minimal political influence in Pyongyang, for North Korea they have been vital to its economic growth and weapons production. Nevertheless, Kim Il Sung has striven over the years with some success to reduce his nation's dependence on its economic links with Moscow. As a percentage of total foreign trade, North Korea's trade with the Soviet Union declined from 80 percent in 1955 to 25 percent in 1978, recovering to 30 percent by 1984. This reversal of the long-term trend may have resulted from giving socialist countries pride of place in North Korea's drive to increase foreign trade begun in 1984.

Pyongyang's rhetorical enthusiasm for maintaining its principal trade ties with the Soviet Union and other socialist countries contrasts sharply with its tentativeness toward expanding trade with capitalist countries. In an interview with the Japanese magazine SEKAI in June 1985, Kim Il Sung said that many offers had been received from abroad in response to the joint venture law promulgated in September 1984, but in the same interview he declared: "We will never introduce foreign capital. . . . We will not become a country burdened with $50 billion in debt like South Korea." He went on to explain that the extraction and sale abroad of the abundant nonferrous metals in North Korea would provide enough funds for "stable growth step-by-step" to fulfill the new economic plan then being drawn up. Kim's remarks did not suggest any revo- lutionary moves, either with respect to foreign trade or in economic development generally, where he placed emphasis on the familiar bot- tleneck sectors of the mining industry, energy, and the railroads.[9] The intractability of the hard currency debt problem and the reluctance to open North Korean society to the extent that would be required to develop internationally competitive manufactures may have compelled the North Koreans to conclude that they had no feasible alternative but to continue and perhaps to increase their economic dependence on the Soviet Union. Keeping North Korea predominantly within the economic orbit of the Soviet Union and other Communist countries would also limit the opportunities for North Koreans to make invidious comparisons of life in North Korea with that in capitalist states.

Political Relations

In the three decades since North Korea recovered from the devastation of the Korean War with Soviet and Chinese help, relations between Moscow and Pyongyang have gone through two cycles of decline and recovery. Because Soviet–North Korean relations generally were in decline when Chinese–North Korean relations were good and vice versa, analysts have tended to explain these swings in terms of the Sino-Soviet dispute. The differences between Moscow and Peking did indeed have a strong influence on Pyongyang's behavior, but they fall short of providing a full explanation. The reality is much more complicated. Bilateral military and economic relations, Moscow's attitudes toward Pyongyang's goals and policies on the Korean peninsula, and basic differences of approach toward various international trends and events, particularly those in- volving the United States, all affected the state of the overall relationship.

Soviet–North Korean relations sank into their deepest trough in the early 1960s. From 1959 through 1961, as the Sino-Soviet dispute heated up and came increasingly into the open, Kim Il Sung maintained a careful public neutrality. By then, however, he already had reason to distrust the Soviets because of their attempts to meddle in North Korea's domestic politics, their denunciation of the personality cult, and the unfairness of their trade policy. The Soviets' abrupt cancellation of aid agreements with China and the overnight withdrawal of their technical experts and blueprints from China in 1960 provided an example of the harsh punishment Moscow would visit on dissenters. Despite this warning and the economic pressure that Khrushchev was beginning to apply to North Korea in 1962, Kim tilted toward China rather than the Soviet Union in the Sino-Indian border clash. He openly sided with the Chinese in attacking the "modern revisionists" for backing down in the Cuban missile crisis and appeasing "American imperialism."

The arrogance of the Soviets in resorting to crude pressures to impose their views on fellow Communist parties was deeply resented in both Peking and Pyongyang. But the most compelling reason for them to make common cause against Moscow was the failure of the Soviets to take a stronger stand against the United States. For them the United States was the enemy that prevented them from achieving their cherished respective goals of unification. The Chinese felt that the Soviets had let them down in the 1958 confrontation with the United States over the offshore islands. The compromise struck by the Soviets over Cuba doubtless raised questions in the minds of both Chinese and North Koreans as to how far they could depend on Soviet support against the United States. Both attacked the U.S.-Soviet nuclear test-ban treaty signed in 1963 as an attempt by the two big powers to monopolize nuclear weapons. During 1963 and 1964 North Korean attacks on the Soviet Union steadily mounted, and Khrushchev retaliated by cutting off military aid and most economic aid. North Korea accused the Soviets of arrogance, of attempting to exclude China from the socialist camp, of scheming to overthrow the leadership of fraternal parties, of using economic aid to interfere in the domestic politics of other countries, of unilaterally suspending economic aid, and of charging higher than world prices for its products and paying less than world prices for products bought from others.[10]

By late 1964 both the Soviets and the North Koreans recognized that they had allowed relations to deteriorate too far. Khrushchev's ouster provided an opportunity to reverse the trend. The new Soviet premier, Alexei Kosygin, headed a high-level delegation to Pyongyang in February 1965 to repair relations. Thereafter, the Soviets resumed military and economic aid to North Korea, and the North Koreans ended their harsh attacks on the Soviet Union. Trade grew steadily and large amounts of military equipment arrived. Soviet–North Korean relations never again dropped to the low point they had reached in the 1962 through 1964 period. North Korea followed an independent policy, criticizing Moscow or Peking according to its judgment of its own national interests. For example, it endorsed the Soviet demand for united action by the socialist countries in support of Vietnam, which the PRC opposed. When Pyongyang did criticize the Soviet Union, it couched its criticisms in milder language than in the past, and Moscow showed greater tolerance of its wayward ally. The improvement in Soviet–North Korean relations in the mid-1960s contributed to some extent to growing strains in Chinese–North Korean relations, although the principal cause was the fanaticism that gripped China during the Cultural Revolution.

During the 1970s, Soviet–North Korean relations worsened again, but the two countries did not engage in a shouting match as they had in the 1960s. The cooling of relations could be discerned in the military, economic, and political fields. The most obvious indication of differences was Soviet withholding from North Korea of weapons that it provided to other friendly countries. Not only were the Soviets dissatisfied with Pyongyang's unwillingness to follow Soviet guidance, but they were concerned that Kim Il Sung's belligerent and provocative behavior toward South Korea and the United States, such as the assassination attempt on Park Chung-hee, the commando raids, the digging of tunnels, the capture of the *Pueblo*, the shooting down of the EC-121 reconnaissance aircraft, and the ax murder of two U.S officers in the DMZ, risked dragging the Soviet Union without warning and against its will into a direct military conflict with the United States. The Soviets demonstrated their disapproval by withholding rhetorical support for any of these provocative actions and, in the EC-121 case, cooperating with the United States in searching for survivors. The Soviets may have felt that their rather generous supply of weapons in the late 1960s had encouraged the reckless behavior of the North Koreans and that it would be against Soviet interests to modernize Kim Il Sung's military capability.

Soviet–North Korean differences over economic issues in the mid-1970s discussed above, added to Pyongyang's unhappiness with Moscow's failure to provide modern weapons. The strains in the relationship were clearly reflected in the relative coolness of the language each used about the other, the low level of official visitors back and forth, and open differences on certain issues. The contrast with the distinctly warmer relationship between China and North Korea during this period was readily apparent.

Particularly disturbing to Pyongyang was Moscow's disinclination to give enthusiastic backing to North Korean policies aimed at unifying Korea. Although Soviet official statements nominally expressed support for Kim Il Sung's proposals on unification, the Soviets indicated in a variety of ways that they did not take them seriously. The Soviet Union did not, like the PRC, declare that the DPRK was the sole legitimate sovereign Korean state. On the contrary, it referred publicly to "both Korean states." A Soviet commentary in 1972 warmly welcomed the opening of talks between the two Koreas, stating that "both sides have many problems to solve if they want to remove the old obstacles in order to bring the two sides together. This can only be done if the two parties take realistic attitudes and show goodwill." The commentator underlined this evenhanded approach by referring approvingly to the precedent of East and West Germany.[11]

Kim took umbrage at any attempt to liken the situation of the two Koreas to that of the two Germanys. During the visit of Erich Honecker, chairman of the German Democratic Republic in 1977, Kim devoted a long section of his speech to emphasizing the differences between the two divided countries. Germany, he said, had attacked its neighbors in the past and might do so again if unified, whereas Korea had never attacked anyone and was divided only because half of its territory was occupied by an imperialist power. A united Korea would threaten no one. In private conversations, Soviet officials and scholars criticized Kim's reunification policy as unrealistic. They expressed the view that a relationship between the two Koreas similar to that of the two Germanys would be more stable than the present tense confrontation and therefore would be in the interests of the two Koreas as well as the big powers.[12]

Through 1978 Soviet–North Korean relations continued their steady decline. Pyongyang published Chinese attacks on the Soviet Union. It criticized Moscow's protégé, Cuba, and refused to participate in the World Festival of Youth in Havana in July 1978. It frequently denounced "dominationism" in contexts where it was clearly aimed at the Soviet Union, as in Foreign Minister Ho Tam's speech to the nonaligned conference in Belgrade in July 1978. At the celebration of the thirtieth anniversary of the DPRK in September 1978, the Soviet Union was represented by N. M. Matchanov, vice president of the Supreme Soviet, who was listed number eighty among the guests and was not received by Kim Il Sung. On the other hand, the Chinese representative, senior Vice Premier Deng Xiaoping, was listed number three and was warmly received by Kim. Pyongyang parted company with Moscow most decisively over the Vietnamese invasion of Kampuchea, which the North Korean's denounced as "outrageous" and "a crude violation of the publicly recognized international law."[13]

Although North Korea tilted markedly toward China in the 1970s, it was careful to hold open the possibility of an improvement in its relations with the Soviet Union. It did not criticize the Soviets for backing Vietnamese aggression. It neither condemned nor praised the Chinese military punishment of Vietnam in February 1979; it simply omitted mention of it in the media. It did not join in China's bitter condemnation of the Soviet invasion of Afghanistan. As in the case of the Chinese military attack on Vietnam, the North Korean media did not report it. Initially, North Korea showed reluctance to endorse the Babrak Karmal regime established by the Soviets in Kabul, but before long they established diplomatic relations with it.

Despite Kim Il Sung's distaste for Soviet policies toward Vietnam and Afghanistan, North Korea began in 1979 and 1980 to make cautious overtures to the Soviet Union signaling a desire for improved bilateral relations. These pro-Soviet gestures coincided with evidence of strain in Pyongyang-Peking relations. The Soviets showed little inclination to respond to Pyongyang's signals until after Brezhnev's death in December

1982, when scattered signs of responsiveness began to appear from Moscow. In April 1983 the North Korean civil airline opened a once-a-week round-trip flight from Pyongyang to Moscow, adding to the existing twice-weekly Moscow service by Aeroflot and the once or twice weekly service to Khabarovsk by both Soviet and North Korean aircraft.

Two incidents in 1983 provided occasions for the Soviet Union and the DPRK to stand shoulder to shoulder in the face of worldwide condemnation of their behavior. When the Soviets shot down the KAL plane, the North Koreans unaccountably delayed three weeks before commenting publicly, but when they did they endorsed the Soviet version of the incident, placing blame on the United States. The following month, when much of the world censured North Korea for the brutal Rangoon bombing, the Soviets published the North Korean defense and ignored the official Burmese account. Moscow's one-sided support of North Korea contrasted with China's evenhanded publication without comment of both the Burmese and North Korean versions of the incident.

Upturn in Relations, 1984–1986

It was Kim Il Sung's trip to the Soviet Union and Eastern Europe, however, that was the real turning point in Soviet–North Korean relations. In 1975, when Kim had visited Peking, the Soviets had discouraged a visit to Moscow. Thus, the fact that an official visit took place, after a lapse of twenty-three years, was in itself evidence of improved relations.[14] In April 1984, when Kim was on the verge of departing for Moscow, he commented to a visiting TASS delegation on the coincidence of views between the Soviet Union and North Korea. He praised TASS for the many articles it had published denouncing moves to form a U.S.-Japan-South Korea military alliance, which he said coincided precisely with his views. He added that his government attached great importance to the comrades-in-arms relationship between the DPRK and the Soviet Union and declared that any differences between them were "trifling matters" that could not obstruct improvement of relations.[15] The concern shown by the Soviets on a matter of overriding importance to the North Koreans, that is, U.S.-Japan-South Korean military relations (a concern not shown by the Chinese media), probably was a primary factor in Pyongyang's decision to try to reverse the deterioration in North Korean–Soviet relations that had occurred in the 1970s.

Kim's sojourn in Moscow did not produce any immediately visible dividends for him. His reception there was correct, but relatively low key, without the fanfare that accompanied his visits to China. The Soviets were less willing than the Chinese to pander to Kim's inflated sense of self-importance. Observers noted that the Soviets did not endorse Kim's tripartite talks proposal, and that no agreements on military or economic aid were announced. Soviet officials privately said later that general agreements had been reached on these subjects and also on an increase from about 100 to 700 in the number of North Korean students that could be accepted in the Soviet Union.[16] The appearance of the MIG-23s in the North Korean airforce a year later suggested that an agreement in principle on this matter had been reached by Kim and his Soviet hosts.

Immediately after Kim's return, the treatment of the Soviet Union in the North Korean media changed in striking fashion. Emphasis on the nonaligned movement and economic relations with developing countries declined steeply, to be replaced by articles extolling the "indestructible friendship and unity" between North Korea and the socialist countries and placing particular stress on economic, scientific, and technical cooperation as a means of accelerating "socialist construction" in the DPRK.[17]

The most remarkable change in North Korea's posture toward the Soviet Union was a newfound willingness to pay tribute to the Soviet role in defeating Japan and liberating Korea. For years the North Koreans had infuriated the Soviets by attributing the liberation of Korea exclusively to the glorious exploits of the Korean People's Revolutionary Army led by Kim Il Sung. On Liberation Day (August 15) 1984, however, a *Nodong Sinmun* editorial declared that the annihilation of Japanese imperialist aggressors by the Soviet Union "opened a decisively favorable phase in our people's struggle for the liberation of the fatherland. . . . Our people always remember the liberator's role of the Soviet Union which helped the cause of the liberation of the fatherland at the cost of its blood."[18] Through this candid acknowledgement of Soviet wartime help and later expressions of gratitude for Soviet economic aid, the North Koreans sought to remove a serious cause of irritation in their relations with Moscow.

Although the Soviet media were less forthcoming than those of North Korea in extolling the bonds between Moscow and Pyongyang, high level visits by Soviet officials demonstrated Soviet willingness to reciprocate friendly North Korean overtures. Deputy Foreign Minister Mikhail Kapitsa led a delegation to Pyongyang for two weeks in November 1984 to negotiate an agreement on border trade. He was accompanied by a military delegation headed by a colonel-general. In April 1985 Foreign Minister Kim Yong-nam made an official visit to Moscow, where he was received by Mikhail S. Gorbachev, general secretary of the Central Committee of the Communist Party Soviet Union (CPSU), and signed the previously negotiated agreement on border trade and a consular agreement. In the joint communique on the visit, the Soviets expressed support of the principal North Korean unification proposals, called on the United States to withdraw its forces from South Korea, and declared its opposition to U.S. and South Korean efforts to bring about cross-recognition or the admission of both Koreas to the United Nations.

The Soviets and North Koreans celebrated Liberation Day 1985—the fortieth anniversary—with unprecedented fanfare. No less than twenty Soviet delegations arrived, the most senior headed by Politburo member G. Aliyev, first deputy chairman of the USSR Council of Ministers, and the second by Marshal V. I. Petrov, first deputy minister of defense. Among the other delegations were those representing the Ministry of Interior, the Ministry of Civil Aviation, the State Commission for Science and Technology, the Soviet Trade Unions, the Lenin Young Communist League, the Soviet Women's Committee, and the Soviet Film Committee. All delegation heads were received by Kim Il Sung. Three Soviet warships, headed by the flagship *Tallin* with the first deputy commander of the Soviet Pacific Fleet aboard, called at Wonsan. An exchange of fulsome speeches lauded the friendship of the two peoples, including a speech by Vice President Yi Chong-ok celebrating the renovation of the 95-foot Liberation Obelisk erected to honor the sacrifices of the Soviet armed forces in the liberation of Korea.

A similar, somewhat lower key celebration occurred in July 1986 on the occasion of the twenty-fifth anniversary of the Soviet–North Korean treaty of mutual assistance. Air units of the two countries exchanged visits; ships of the Soviet Pacific Fleet called at Wonsan; and ships of the North Korean navy, in the first such visit ever to a foreign port, cruised to Vladivostok. Admiral V. V. Sidorov, commander of the Pacific Fleet, declared that the Soviet fleet was ready to launch joint operations with North Korea in case of emergency.[19] The celebration of the signing of the similar Chinese–North Korean treaty also received high level attention, but did not include an exchange of visits by military units.

The Soviets demonstrated willingness to send higher level visitors to Pyongyang than in the past. In January 1986, Eduard Shevardnadze made the first visit to Pyongyang by a Soviet foreign minister. During a visit to Moscow in December 1985 by North Korean Premier Kang Song-san, the Soviets agreed in principle that Premier Nikolai Ryzhkov would make a return visit.

Kim's un-Marxist plan to pass the mantle of leadership to his son posed a delicate problem for the Soviets. They were slower than the Chinese in publicly acknowledging Kim Chong Il's importance. By 1984, however, they were toasting his health and delivering gifts to him. Kapitsa called on him during his Pyongyang visit. In April 1986 a North Korean official told Japanese journalists that Kim Chong Il had been invited to visit the Soviet Union.[20] Privately, Soviet scholars and officials disparaged the concept of dynastic succession, but conceded that if Kim Chong Il should, in fact, succeed, the Soviet government would, of course, have to deal with him. Soviet specialists differed as to whether Kim Chong Il would be able to maintain his hold on power once his father was gone.

Why did Soviet–North Korean relations improve so dramatically during 1984 through 1986 after a decade in the doldrums? Clearly, both parties had reasons for desiring a closer relationship, but North Korea's motivations, given its degree of dependence on the Soviet Union, are easier to discern than those of the Soviets.

Trends in Chinese policy must have disturbed Kim Il Sung. From the signing of the Sino-Japanese peace treaty in 1978 and the normalization of relations between Peking and Washington in 1979, Chinese and North Korean policies toward these two big powers increasingly diverged. China's relations with the United States and Japan grew closer. Top-level visits occurred, trade expanded, and relations of various kinds multiplied. Probably most troubling to North Korea were the growing military relationships between the United States and China and visits back and forth by the Chinese and Japanese military. At the same time, China was expanding its contacts and trade with South Korea. As in the past when China's policies ran counter to those of North Korea, the North Koreans showed their displeasure by seeking better relations with Moscow. Moreover, while a warming trend was underway between Washington and Peking in 1984 through 1986, U.S. relations with the Soviet Union were at a low ebb. The Soviets were vigorously attacking U.S.-Japan-South Korea military cooperation; the Chinese were not. Drawing closer to Moscow under these circumstances was more congenial to Pyongyang than drawing closer to Peking.

More basic and important than the China factor, however, in Pyongyang's desire for better relations with Moscow, were military and economic needs. With the South Korean air force scheduled to receive F-16s in 1986, the North Korean air force must have felt more keenly than ever the lack of a more advanced aircraft than the MIG-21. Moscow's willingness to provide MIG-23s and the closer relations demonstrated by Soviet port visits, overflights, and rhetoric praising past military cooperation all would help to counter the increase that Pyongyang perceived in U.S.-Chinese-Japanese-South Korean military cooperation. In the economic areas, North Korea's efforts to diversify its trading relationships by expanding trade with Western Europe, Japan, and Third World countries had not been very successful; consequently, in their new policy intended to sharply increase foreign trade, the North Koreans turned back to their traditional reliance on the Soviet Union as their primary trading partner. Whether the Soviets will be more forthcoming than in the recent past is uncertain, but Pyongyang's more friendly posture toward the Soviets is clearly based in part on the hope that they will.

The Soviet decision to improve relations with Pyongyang during this period cannot be ascribed persuasively to rivalry with Peking over influence in Pyongyang. The Soviets had not taken vigorous action to try to reverse the pro-China tilt that North Korea had maintained throughout the 1970s. On the contrary, Soviet behavior toward North Korea over the years and private comments by Soviet officials and scholars suggested that the Soviet Union was prepared to concede to the Chinese a closer relationship with the North Koreans so long as it did not threaten the Soviet's fundamental strategic stake in North Korea.

A more probable reason for desiring a closer relationship with North Korea is Soviet concern over what it saw as an emerging U.S.-Japan-China entente. Although the Chinese had backed away from the concept of a united front against the Soviet Union that they had advocated so stridently in 1978 and 1979 and had embarked on a gradual improvement of state-to-state relations with the Soviet Union, the pace of that improvement was far outdistanced by the growing interaction of China with the United States and Japan. The beginning of military cooperation between the United States and China, even though so far of little significance in enhancing China's military power, alarmed the Soviets, as it did the North Koreans, because it could foreshadow far more extensive cooperation among the three powers in the future.

A related Soviet concern was the danger of being excluded from diplomatic activity relating to Northeast Asia in general and Korea in particular. Soviet unwillingness to endorse the North Korean proposal for tripartite talks involving the United States and the two Koreas was a manifestation of this concern. The North Korean choice of the Chinese rather than the Soviets to convey the tripartite talks proposal to the United States, the U.S. counterproposal of a four-power conference including China but not the Soviet Union, and the reported Chinese offer of Peking as the venue for tripartite talks all constituted an exclusion of the Soviet Union from decisionmaking important to its national interests in Northeast Asia. This exclusion the Soviets could not accept. The Soviets may have felt that a more active involvement in North Korea was necessary in order to keep their hand in.

A common speculation in South Korea, suggested by the port visits by the Soviet navy, was that the Soviets had received basing rights in North Korea in exchange for the provision of MIG-23s and other Soviet actions establishing a closer relationship with Pyongyang. As of mid-1986, however, there was no evidence that Kim Il Sung had abandoned his principled opposition to the stationing of foreign forces on Korean territory. The principal military gain for the Soviet Union was the right to overfly North Korea in order to shorten the distance to bases in Vietnam and to improve intelligence on the activities of U.S. and Chinese forces in the region.

From a broader perspective, the Soviet decision to improve relations with North Korea, like the steps taken to ease tension with China, seems to be part of a Soviet strategy aimed at strengthening its position throughout the Asian-Pacific region. During the 1970s, when the United States was withdrawing forces from Vietnam, and reducing its military presence in East Asia, relations with North Korea could be given a low priority by the Soviet Union. The adoption of a more activist policy there and elsewhere in the region may be intended to offset the strengthening of the U.S. position that has occurred during the 1980s. General Secretary Mikhail Gorbachev outlined the diplomatic and economic elements of this new strategy in his speech of July 28, 1986, in Vladivostok.

Conclusion

Strategic needs, as perceived by Moscow and Pyongyang, have provided the glue that held the two countries together, despite the many policy differences that have plagued their relations over the years. The prominence of the military in the warming of relations that occurred in 1984 and 1985 indicated that strategic considerations were at least as important as in the past and perhaps becoming more important. They will continue to be the fundamental factor in the relationship so long as rivalry between the United States and the Soviet Union remains active and the confrontation between the two Koreas persists.

The importance of future economic ties between the two is somewhat less predictable than their strategic links. The complementarity of the two economies and the probability that the manufactured goods that each sells to the other will be difficult to sell for hard currency on the international market makes it likely that trade between the two will continue to constitute a substantial proportion of North Korea's foreign trade, probably not less than 25 to 30 percent.

The Soviet decision to pay greater attention to the importance of its ties with North Korea probably is an element in a broader policy of seeking a larger role for the Soviet Union in the Pacific. It complements the improvement of state-to-state relations between the Soviet Union and China that has been underway since 1982. The easing of Sino-Soviet confrontation diminishes the intensity of Sino-Soviet rivalry for influence on Pyongyang, which, in turn, reduces Pyongyang's leverage on its two allies, mitigating their concern that contacts with Seoul will be used by their rival to do them harm in Pyongyang.

South Korean officials and analysts frequently express the view that the Soviet Union has an interest in maintaining a high degree of tension between the two Koreas. Some have even advanced the hypothesis that Moscow would see its interests served by open conflict between Pyongyang and Seoul because of the damage to Washington-Peking relations that would result. Some Chinese officials and scholars also express doubts that the Soviets favor stability in Korea.

Soviet behavior in recent years offers little support for the theory that Moscow favors violence in Korea. Soviet failure to endorse North Korean acts of violence against South Korea or against U.S. forces and Soviet restraint in providing advanced weapons are persuasive evidence that the Soviets have not encouraged resort to violence. The immediate involvement of U.S forces in any open conflict would confront the Soviet Union with serious dangers and difficult choices. Consequently, although the Soviets may find useful a level of tension sufficient to remind the North Koreans of their dependence on the Soviet Union, they seem unlikely to favor high tension that could explode into open conflict.

Although the Soviets give rhetorical backing to North Korea's unification proposals, their policies and private comments indicate that they see no prospect of early unification. They seem content to live with two Koreas indefinitely. They also appear confident that their lead over the Chinese in industrial and military technology will continue to afford them influence in Pyongyang that the Chinese will be unable to challenge. The increased attention that the Soviets have given North Korea since 1984 probably resulted in part from a determination to be favorably positioned during the succession process and to strengthen the Soviet claim to inclusion in any big power negotiations over Korea.

The North Koreans, losing ground in the economic and diplomatic competition with South Korea and unable to make radical reforms in their economy so as to diversify their foreign trade, probably will remain heavily dependent on the Soviet Union for advanced technology and weapons. The unequal relationship will produce friction, as it has in the past, but reciprocal need will keep the two together. The Chinese connection will continue to give North Korea more maneuverability than if it were solely dependent on the Soviet Union. An increase in Soviet contacts with South Korea, as Seoul becomes an increasingly active player in international affairs, will add to strains between Moscow and Pyongyang, as will be discussed in Chapter 11.

China and North Korea

Sino-Soviet rivalry has forced North Korea's relations with the two big powers into a seesaw pattern—when relations with one are up, relations with the other are down. The metaphor is imprecise, however, for the distance each rises and falls is not equal, and over the years the Chinese–North Korean relationship has been markedly friendlier than that between Pyongyang and Moscow.[21]

The reasons why the Chinese get along better with the North Koreans than the Soviets do are geopolitical, historical, and cultural. The location of Korea next to China's industrial heartland makes it more important strategically to China than to the Soviet Union. Hence, Chinese troops, not Soviet troops, intervened in the Korean War to preserve a Communist buffer state between its territory and the U.S. sphere of influence. Blood shed by Chinese in that war made their relationship with North Korea qualitatively different from that of the Soviets.

For centuries Korea lay within the orbit of Chinese political and cultural influence, which instilled in the Koreans ways of thinking and social behavior more akin to Chinese than to Russian thought and behavior. Moreover, as developing countries, China and North Korea have more in common with each other than with the relatively advanced industrial society of the Soviet Union. Both have been heavily dependent militarily and economically on the Soviet Union. China broke away from that dependency; North Korea has struggled to break free, but has not yet succeeded. Both countries have suffered Soviet interference in their domestic politics and have been the objects of crude Soviet pressures aimed at forcing changes in their foreign policies. Both are divided countries and share the view that the United States is the main obstacle to their unification.

Personal factors have also contributed to the affinity of the Chinese with North Koreans. The leaders in China and North Korea came from the revolutionary generation, which gave them different domestic and world outlooks from those of the postrevolutionary leaders of the Soviet Union. Kim Il Sung spent his formative years in China as a student and as a guerrilla leader under Chinese Communist commanders. His fluency in the Chinese language and his long association with the Chinese makes him more comfortable with them than with the Soviets.

Despite all that China and North Korea have in common, their relationship has not been free from friction, and in the mid-1960s it suffered severe strain. Differences have arisen for a variety of reasons: chiefly, North Korea's unwillingness to give China unqualified support in the Sino-Soviet dispute; China's rapprochement with North Korea's chief adversaries, the United States and Japan; and China's contacts with South Korea. A basic problem is the disparity in size and global influence between the two countries. Kim Il Sung has been outspoken in his opposition to "big power chauvinism" on the part of either of his giant Communist neighbors. North Korea has been a touchy and difficult partner for the Chinese as well as the Soviets, but the Chinese have been more sensitive to the feelings of the North Koreans than the Soviets and willing to go to greater lengths to please them.

Security Relations

The decision by the year-old People's Republic of China to intervene militarily in Korea in 1950, even though it was ill-prepared to do so, demonstrated the high strategic importance the Chinese attached to the Korean peninsula. Nineteen years earlier the Japanese had used Korea as a base from which to invade Manchuria. When the• United States ordered the Seventh Fleet to prevent the PRC from taking Taiwan and Chinese warnings through diplomatic channels failed to prevent the United States from sending its forces up to the Yalu River, the Chinese acted decisively to prevent the establishment of a hostile, U.S.-dominated regime just south of their border.

The Chinese already had more intimate ties with North Korea's armed forces than the Soviets had. The all-Korean Sixth Army, which had fought for years as part of Lin Piao's Fourth Field Army and had participated in its victorious march all the way from Manchuria to Hainan Island, provided a large proportion of the North Korean army's most experienced fighters. The majority of the officers in the army had fought in the Chinese civil war. Although many of these Chinese-oriented officers and men were killed during the Korean War and their leaders were pushed aside by Kim Il Sung in favor of his Kapsan comrades, they provided links with the Chinese forces that had come to North Korea's rescue.

The Chinese kept their forces in Korea until 1958, long enough to allow the North Korean economy and armed forces to recover from the war and to satisfy themselves that the armistice would hold. Removal of their forces eliminated any temptation they might have felt to use them to influence domestic affairs in North Korea. The Chinese withdrawal also placed Kim Il Sung in a position to stress *chu che* and to demand the withdrawal of U.S. forces from South Korea. Of course, Peking permanently stationed a substantial number of forces not far away in Manchuria, where they could be sent quickly back across the Yalu should they be needed. In July 1961 Kim Il Sung signed a mutual security treaty in Peking, a month after signing a similar treaty in Moscow. It is the only security treaty that China has with any country.

The Cultural Revolution in China caused a precipitous decline in Chinese–North Korean relations in the late 1960s, the political aspects of which will be discussed below. From the security viewpoint, the most serious development was rising tension over a boundary dispute.

According to a North Korean embassy official in New Delhi, China claimed one hundred square miles of Korean territory near Mt. Paektu, the mountain on the border of China and Korea, which the North Koreans regard as sacred territory because of Kim Il Sung's early guerrilla activities in that area. The dispute even led to military clashes along the border in 1967, 1968, and 1969.[22]

Through the 1950s the Chinese had seen the main threat to their security interest in Korea as coming from the United States. The emergence of the Sino-Soviet dispute, however, created a new threat—that North Korea might become, as Mongolia has, an exclusive ally of the Soviet Union and hostile to China. The military clash between Chinese and Soviet forces on the Amur River in 1969 highlighted the danger. If Soviet forces should ever obtain bases in North Korean territory, the difficulty of defending China from Soviet attack would be magnified. In the late 1970s the Chinese began to view the Soviet objective as the military encirclement of China through the strengthening of forces along the Sino-Soviet frontier; the military occupation of Afghanistan; the close Soviet military relationship with India; and the alliance with Vietnam, which dominated Laos and Kampuchea and provided military bases to the Soviet Union. From this perspective, Soviet success in alienating North Korea from China would forge a critical link in the almost complete chain of encirclement.

Still another potential threat had emerged in 1969. The Nixon Doctrine called on U.S. allies to assume more of the burden of their own defense. When Japanese Prime Minister Eisaku Sato declared in the Nixon-Sato communique that the security of the Republic of Korea was essential to Japan's own security, the Chinese feared that the United States intended to turn the defense of South Korea over to Japan. Faced with threats to interests in Korea from two directions when Peking's own relations with Pyongyang were at an all-time low, the PRC despatched Premier Zhou Enlai to Pyongyang in April 1970 to restore good relations. This he did, in part, by joining with Kim Il Sung in roundly denouncing "the revival of Japanese militarism," a subject on which both countries had strong feelings.

Although committed like the Soviets to help defend North Korea, the Chinese have not been in a position to compete with the Soviets in providing military equipment. When Khrushchev cut off Pyongyang's military aid in the early 1960s, the Chinese, having recently been cut off by the Soviets themselves, could not fill the gap. Later, as their own military production capability improved, they began to furnish Chinese-made copies of Soviet 1950s generation weapons, such as the T-59 tank (Soviet T-54) and the MIG-19 fighter. After 1973, when the large flow of Soviet arms provided from 1965 on declined, Chinese shipments increased. In some years the shipments exceeded the military equipment supplied by the Soviets.[23] In 1982, following Kim Il Sung's visit to China, the PRC sent to North Korea a substantial number (variously reported as from 20 to 40) of its most advanced aircraft, the A-5 fighter (Soviet MIG-21).

China's policy toward Korea in the mid-1980s is consistent with its overall security policy. That policy seems based on the following assumptions:

- that the Soviet Union is the principal threat to China's security;
- that an early military conflict with the USSR is unlikely;
- that China does not, therefore, need a crash program to strengthen its military forces; it requires a fairly long period of peace, during which it can modernize its industrial base and become self-sufficient in the design and production of advanced weapons; and,
- that the principal sources of the science and technology needed to modernize China are Japan, the United States, and Western Europe.[24]

The Chinese are seeking through diplomacy to soften their differences with the Soviet Union. Although the Soviets have given little indication that they will modify the policies that gave rise to Chinese fear of encirclement, they have shown willingness to improve bilateral relations with China. In turn, the Chinese have abandoned the strident confrontational posture that they took in 1978 through 1980.

With respect to Korea, the Chinese have expressed the view that the risk of conflict there is low. They have repeatedly told U.S. and Japanese officials at high levels that their talks with Kim Il Sung and their knowledge of North Korea convinces them that Kim has no intention of attacking South Korea. They argue that the United States overestimates the strength of North Korea's armed forces, equipped as they are with obsolescent weapons. They emphasize the importance that they attach to stability in Korea and their strong support for the North-South talks as a means of lowering tension. Since the early 1980s the Chinese have become increasingly active and involved in promoting negotiations over Korea, both the North-South talks and the tripartite talks.

China's reasons for wanting stability in Korea are obvious. A military conflict there would draw them in as North Korea's ally and would severely damage their important relations with the United States and Japan. Soviet influence in North Korea would increase, as only the Soviets could supply modern weapons. Should the North Koreans succeed in unifying Korea by military force, the unified state might then be drawn into the Soviet orbit. The Chinese publicly endorse Kim Il Sung's unification proposals, but stress that unification must take place peacefully.

Privately, Chinese officials and scholars see little prospect for early unification, and China's increasing contacts with South Korea, which will be discussed in Chapter 11, suggest that the Chinese might even prefer a stable divided Korea to a strong unified Korea that could, like Vietnam, ally itself with Moscow.

Economic Relations

China has come closer to rivaling the Soviet Union as an economic collaborator of North Korea than as a provider of weapons, despite its relative weakness in economic power. One estimate, based on South Korean sources, credits China with providing slightly more nonmilitary assistance than the Soviet Union did during the period 1945 through 1978.[25]

During the Korean War China made grants and loans to North Korea in the form of food, clothing, and other daily necessities and waived repayment of the loans after the war was over. Chinese troops then provided badly needed labor to repair war-damaged bridges, reservoirs, dikes, roads, and railways. To assist further in reconstruction during the period 1954 through 1957, the Chinese made a grant of $320 million, supplying coal, cloth, cotton, grain, building materials, fishing boats, locomotives, railway cars, textile machinery, and paper.[26] Trade between the two countries rose rapidly during the reconstruction period. By 1957 trade with China constituted 27 percent of North Korea's total foreign trade.

Quantitative information on China's trade with North Korea during the 1960s is sketchy, but reports of agreements on loans, trade, maritime transport, scientific and technical cooperation, and railway cooperation indicate that economic interaction between the two countries expanded further. The timing of the agreements suggests that the Chinese took advantage of the strain in Soviet–North Korean relations in the early 1960s to lend a helping hand to Pyongyang, although they were not in a position to replace the Soviet Union as a source of heavy industrial plants and complex machinery. During the Cultural Revolution in China, particularly in 1967 and 1968 when Chinese–North Korean relations reached their nadir, economic activity fell off. By 1970, when political relations had been restored to normal, trade between China and North Korea reached $100 million, a modest increase of about 60 percent over the thirteen years from 1957. At this point, trade between the Soviet Union and North Korea, which had been rising rapidly since 1967, had become 40 percent of North Korea's total trade, while trade with China was only 13 percent.[27]

During the 1970s, China's trade with North Korea increased steadily, both in absolute terms and relative to Soviet–North Korean trade. The absolute figure, showing a more than fourfold growth from 1970 to 1978, is overstated, because it reflects the global inflation of prices that occurred during that period, set off by the sudden jump in oil prices. Nevertheless, the growth was substantial, and by 1978 trade with China constituted 20 percent of North Korea's total trade, as compared to the Soviet Union's share of 25 percent.[28] Growth in Soviet–North Korean trade had been held down by Moscow's unwillingness to go on extending large credits and its insistence that Pyongyang make payments on the credits previously extended, as discussed earlier. North Korea's indebtedness to China probably was smaller than that to the Soviet Union, and there are indications that China was a more lenient creditor. In 1984, coincident with North Korea's renewed emphasis on trade with the Soviet bloc, its trade with the Soviet Union increased to 30 percent of total trade, while trade with China, North Korea's second most important trading partner, remained at 20 percent.[29]

China's contribution to North Korea's industrialization consisted mainly of assistance in building light industry, although the Chinese also aided in the construction of cement plants and the Supung and Unbong hydroelectric power stations (the output of which China shares), as well as helping in the expansion and improvement of North Korea's railway system. The Chinese trained North Korean technicians in China and sent their technicians to assist the North Koreans in various fields. One of the most important contributions was in easing North Korea's dependence on Soviet petroleum products. The Chinese completed a pipeline to the Korean border in 1976 and assisted the North Koreans in building the Ponghwa petroleum refinery, the second stage of which was completed in 1980. China reportedly offered North Korea a relatively low "friendship price" for oil at a time when the market price was rising rapidly and the Soviets demanded an increase in the price of their oil.[30] During the early 1980s the value of China's exports of petroleum and petroleum products constituted two-fifths to three-fifths of China's total exports to North Korea.

To some extent China's economic system has served as a model for North Korea. Both countries mobilized thousands of workers to construct by hand labor large-scale public projects, such as irrigation works. In the late 1950s and again in the 1980s, when the Chinese made major changes in their Soviet-style system, the North Koreans emulated some of the Chinese innovations. The Chollima campaign inaugurated in 1958 was clearly modeled on China's Great Leap Forward, although it was less extreme and hence inflicted less damage on the economy. For example, although the North Koreans consolidated collective farms into large units during this period, these never attained the size of a Chinese commune. They averaged only three hundred households, about the size of a Soviet *kolkhoz*. After the fall of the Gang of Four, the Chinese decried the Great Leap Forward as having been a serious error, but the North Koreans continued to praise their Chollima campaign.

During the 1980s, particularly after Kim Il Sung's visit to China in 1982 when Deng Xiaoping gave him a personally conducted tour of Sichuan, China's pathbreaking province for economic reform, the North Koreans have shown interest in several of China's economic policies. They were attracted to the increased production of consumer goods, the stress on foreign trade, the special economic zones, and the joint venture law aimed at attracting foreign investment. During former prime minister Zenko Suzuki's visit to China in October 1984, Deng urged investment by Japanese companies in North Korea.[31] The North Koreans are unlikely to move as far or as fast as the Chinese have in opening their economy to foreign trade and investment, for reasons given in Chapter 5, but as of late 1985 the trend in that direction continued.

In 1983 Peking and Pyongyang signed an agreement allowing the Chinese to use the east coast port of Chongjin as a transshipment point for goods sent on to China by rail—the counterpart of the agreement allowing the Soviets to use Najin. Transit goods increased from 34,000 tons in 1983 to 60,000–70,000 tons in 1984, a substantial increase, although far short of the 200,000-ton target for 1984 given by a Korean official to Hu Yaobang during the latter's visit to Chongjin. A Chinese official visiting Japan said that Chongjin's port facilities were poor and that the Chinese would help in improving them.[32]

By the 1980s Chinese global foreign aid had declined to a trickle. China no longer undertook showy but expensive projects such as the Tanzam railway. The Chinese apparently had learned that the political payoff for giving large amounts of economic aid was meager and that the attempt to compete with developed nations in this activity was a costly luxury for a country as poor as China. Visits to Peking by senior North Korean officials in the 1980s produced no evidence of substantial Chinese economic aid. Chinese Premier Zhao Ziyang, at a banquet for North Korean Premier Kang Song-san in Peking in August 1984, praised North Korea for attaining the status of "a socialist country with modernized industry and agriculture and with developed science and culture." Kang, who had come to Peking accompanied by the ministers of coal, railways, and light industry, all problem areas for North Korea, praised China and North Korea for "helping each other," but went on to assert that North Korea was "vigorously advancing, demonstrating the spirit of self-reliance and arduous struggle."[33]

Political Relations, 1960–1980

Like North Korea's relations with the Soviet Union, its relations with China have passed through cycles of improvement and deterioration, relations with one country being the obverse of relations with the other. From an attempt at neutrality in the emerging Sino-Soviet dispute from 1959 through 1961, North Korea swung to the Chinese side in the early 1960s, fell out with China during the late 1960s, and resumed close relations with Peking in the 1970s, when relations with Moscow cooled. Evidence of strain in Chinese–North Korean relations in the early 1980s was followed by a decided warming of Soviet–North Korean relations beginning in 1984. The cyclical swings in Chinese–North Korean relations were most extreme and apparent in the 1960s, readily discerned but less advertised in the 1970s, and blurred and subject to contradictory evidence in the 1980s.

During the first pro-Chinese period, the North Koreans were drawn to the Chinese side by a similarity in world outlook and a shared resentment of Soviet pressure. Peking and Pyongyang endorsed each other's territorial claims and took a more militant attitude toward the United States than Moscow did, rejecting Khrushchev's policy of peaceful coexistence with the United States. Both disagreed with Khrushchev's attack on Stalin and Stalin's cult of personality. North Korea took the Chinese side at international meetings of Communist parties and firmly backed China against India from the beginning of their border dispute in 1959. During the border clash of 1962, North Korea denounced "Indian aggression" and gave full support to China. The North Koreans broke openly with the Soviets over the Cuban missile crisis, joining the Chinese in public attacks on "modern revisionism." For the next two years, Pyongyang agreed with Peking on all major issues in the Sino-Soviet dispute. Frequent high-level visits took place back and forth. In June 1963, Liu Shaoqi, chairman of the PRC, and Choe Yong-gon, chairman of the Supreme People's Assembly of the DPRK, condemned "modern revisionism" in a joint communique issued during Choe's visit to Peking.

Khrushchev's ouster in 1964 and Kim Il Sung's decision to repair relations with the Soviet Union caused an immediate cooling of relations with China. The North Koreans moderated their warnings against "modern revisionism" and did not pick up the Chinese slur on the Brezhnev-Kosygin policies as being "Khrushchevism without Khrushchev." Instead, the North Koreans began to attack "dogmatism" and "left opportunism," the code words in the Communist world for China's policies during the Cultural Revolution. Pyongyang took issue with Peking in 1966, siding with the Soviet Union and the Japanese Communist Party on the question of united action in support of North Vietnam.

As domestic violence increased in China and the Chinese became more intemperate in their propaganda attacks on other countries— Communist, capitalist, and neutralist alike—Pyongyang distanced itself further. In an ostensible attack on Trotskyism in September 1966, the

North Koreans expressed their distaste for Mao's encouragement of Red Guard violence and his thesis that repeated revolutions were needed in socialist countries. At a KWP conference in October of the same year, Kim Il Sung criticized the Chinese for intervening in the internal affairs of the KWP and the Japanese Communist Party. In China, Red Guard posters and pamphlets alleged that uprisings against Kim Il Sung had occurred in North Korea and belittled him as a "fat revisionist."[34] The irritated North Koreans reacted by mistreating visiting Chinese in Pyongyang and hotly denying the Red Guard allegations of political disturbances in their country. As the propaganda war heated up, high level visits between Peking and Pyongyang dropped off and economic and cultural exchanges declined.

Despite the severe strain on Chinese–North Korean relations, the North Koreans did not swing all the way to the Soviet side. They refrained from explicit public attacks naming China and declined to attend the Budapest conference of 1968, organized by the Soviet Union to gain backing from the Communist parties of the world for the Soviet position in the Sino-Soviet dispute. Kim Il Sung, particularly in his speech to the KWP party conference in October 1966, stressed the independence of North Korea's foreign policy and criticized attempts by "great power chauvinists" to dictate the policies of smaller Communist countries. North Korean statements warned against both revisionism and dogmatism.[35] The Soviets were more tolerant of North Korean deviation than they had been in the early 1960s, continuing economic and military aid in spite of Kim Il Sung's unwillingness to back them all the way.

By 1969 the military had restored order in China and the stage was set for an improvement in Sino–North Korean relations. As discussed in the preceding section, signs of strain in Soviet–North Korean relations began to appear in 1968 and 1969. North Korea took a neutral position on the Sino-Soviet border dispute in 1969 and refused, along with China, to attend the subsequent Moscow conference of world Communist parties. Evidence of improving relations with China was the arrival in Peking of Choe Yong-gon, chairman of the Supreme People's Assembly, heading up a North Korean delegation to celebrate the PRC's twentieth anniversary in October 1969. Premier Zhou Enlai met him at the airport, and the North Koreans were listed first among visiting delegations. Zhou Enlai's own trip to Pyongyang in April 1970 underlined the restoration of friendly relations between the two countries.

From the early 1970s up to 1978 and 1979, relations between China and North Korea remained cordial, despite the shock dealt to Pyongyang by China's abrupt change in policy toward the United States and its establishment of diplomatic relations with Japan. The Chinese appear to have done their best to ease North Korean apprehensions by sending a high level delegation to Pyongyang just before the announcement of the forthcoming Nixon visit and, later in 1971, by signing agreements with visiting North Korean delegations to provide Chinese economic and military aid.

The most impressive confirmation of the warmth of Chinese–North Korean relations during the 1970s was Kim Il Sung's nine-day visit to China in April 1975, just before the fall of Saigon. The Chinese gave him an elaborate reception, and he spent much time with Deng Xiaoping, including a trip to Nanjing, renewing a personal relationship that was to become a crucial link between the two countries after Deng emerged as China's paramount leader in 1977. Although Kim failed to obtain a Chinese endorsement of the threats that he uttered against South Korea on this occasion, he did obtain Chinese recognition of the DPRK as "the sole legal sovereign state of the Korean nation."[36]

Twists and Turns, 1980–1985

Toward the end of the 1970s analysts watching for telltale signs in the form of the language used and the treatment accorded on ceremonial occasions began to see indications of friction between Peking and Pyongyang.[37] Chinese policies were diverging in important respects from those of North Korea. The North Koreans also probably were disturbed by China's large-scale military incursion into Vietnam.[38] Internally, the Chinese began to downgrade the role of Mao Zedong in the history of the PRC and to attack the cult of personality. Externally, China signed a friendship treaty with Japan in 1978 and normalized relations with the United States in 1979. Deng Xiaoping's warmly received visit to the United States, the euphoric welcome accorded normalization in both the United States and China, and the rapid expansion of interchange between the two countries must have particularly worried Kim Il Sung. In his report to the Sixth Party Congress in October 1980, Kim issued a warning clearly aimed at China against making unprincipled compromises with the imperialists.[39]

The Chinese acted vigorously to check the downturn in their relations with North Korea. Premier Hua Guofeng visited Pyongyang in May 1978 and Deng Xiaoping, then vice premier, in September. Zhou Enlai's widow, Deng Yingchao, a Politburo member, visited Pyongyang in 1979, and another Politburo member, Li Xiannian, in 1980. In 1981, reacting to protests from the North Koreans, the Chinese cut back sharply on trade with South Korea, which had surged in 1980. The years 1981 and 1982 brought a procession of high-level Chinese to Pyongyang, beginning with Premier Zhao Ziyang in December 1981. Deng Xiaoping and Hu

Yaobang made a secret visit to Pyongyang in late April 1982, which permitted them to offer their congratulations to Kim Il Sung on his seventieth birthday—an extremely important anniversary in both Chinese and Korean tradition—without becoming involved in the unrestrained public adulation of Kim that occurred during the official celebration of the birthday a few days before. Three additional Politburo members made separate visits to North Korea during 1982: Xi Zhongxun; Defense Minister Geng Biao; and Chen Muhua, minister of foreign economic relations.

The most important visit during 1982, however, was Kim Il Sung's seven-day trip to China. He was welcomed at the Peking railway station by most of China's top leaders. Deng Xiaoping devoted four days to escorting him personally on a tour of Sichuan Province; Hu Yaobang accompanied him from Chengdu to Xian and back to Peking. Speeches on various formal occasions lauding Chinese-Korean friendship were unusually effusive.

In their efforts to cement bilateral relations and to counter the effects of differences on foreign policy issues with North Korea, the Chinese have courted Kim Chong Il, the heir apparent. They have done so despite their own public criticism of the concentration of power in the hands of an individual and private comment by Chinese officials and scholars denigrating the Kim cult and the plan for succession by Kim's son.[40] As early as 1981 Chinese officials were beginning to toast the health of "comrade Kim Chong Il," along with that of his father. In 1983 Kim Chong Il made a ten-day unofficial trip to China during which he was received at the highest levels of the Chinese Communist Party. Hu Yaobang, recalling the visit in a later speech, said that Kim had had "an emotional reunion" with members of the standing committee of the Chinese Communist Politburo. He added that he himself had accompanied Kim to Chengdu and Nanjing, and Hu Qili, a member of the secretariat of the Central Committee, had escorted him to Shanghai and Hangzhou.[41]

In September 1983, Politburo member Peng Zhen headed a delegation to celebrate the thirty-fifth anniversary of the founding of the KWP. Kim Chong Il accompanied the delegation to Wonsan, where Hu Qili spoke, crediting Kim with personally arranging the delegation's visit. Lengthy films of Kim's visit to China and Peng's visit to North Korea broadcast over Chinese and North Korean television showed that each government had made elaborate arrangements to honor the visiting dignitary. Kim Il Sung saw the Peng Zhen delegation twice, on one occasion paying Peng the signal honor of calling on him at the guest house. Exchanges of delegations of all kinds between China and North Korea doubled from one hundred in 1981 to two hundred in 1983.[42]

Chinese–North Korean relations received a jolt in October 1983, when North Korean agents carried out the terrorist bombing in Rangoon. In late September Deng Xiaoping had raised the subject of Korea with visiting U.S. Defense Secretary Caspar Weinberger, suggesting that the United States and China both should work to ease tension on the Korean peninsula. The day before the Rangoon bombing, the Chinese received a message from the North Koreans to pass to the United States, stating for the first time that they were prepared to take part in trilateral talks in which South Korea would be a full participant. The bombing of which the Chinese clearly had no advance warning blasted the possibility of talks and embarrassed Deng himself. According to reports circulating in the diplomatic corps in Peking, Deng refused for weeks afterward to see any North Korean. A year later Deng acknowledged to Japanese visitors that China did not agree with some North Korean policies.[43] In public reporting on the bombing the Chinese did not, like the Soviets, accept the North Korean version. Instead, they were scrupulously neutral, publishing the Burmese government's account and the North Korean version side by side in the *People's Daily*, using precisely the same number of Chinese characters in each account. They cut out the more belligerent portions of the North Korean statement, including the allegation that the South Koreans were responsible for the incident.

The Chinese did not, however, allow their anger at North Korean behavior to divert them from pursuing their efforts to promote an easing of tension in Korea, which they considered to be in China's interest. In January 1984, Premier Zhao Ziyang passed to President Ronald Reagan in Washington Pyongyang's formal proposal for tripartite talks. The Chinese continued throughout 1984 and 1985 in their public statements and in private talks with Americans to express their support for trilateral talks and for the North-South talks that began in the autumn of 1984. The willingness of Chinese officials to become actively involved in promoting stability in Korea was a remarkable change from their attitude before 1983, when it was difficult for U.S. officials and scholars to engage them in serious discussions of Korean affairs. The Chinese also showed declining sensitivity to having contacts and trade with South Korea, a matter that will be discussed in detail in Chapter 11.

The parade of high level visitors between Peking and Pyongyang continued into 1984 and 1985. North Korean Foreign Minister Kim Yong-nam visited Peking in February 1984. Hu Yaobang went to Pyongyang in early May 1984, just after President Reagan's visit to China and just before Kim Il Sung departed for Moscow. Premier Kang Song-san visited Peking in August, and Kim Il Sung himself made a quick "unofficial" visit to Peking in late November of the same year. Hu Yaobang traveled to the border town of Sinuiju in May 1985 for a two-

day unofficial visit, where he conferred with Kim Il Sung, Kim Chong
Il, and Defense Minister O Chin-u.

Foreign Minister Kim Yong-nam eloquently likened North Korea's
relationship with China to "eternally beautiful roses." It is a relationship,
he said, "unlike any that exists between any other two countries on
this earth. It is a particularly close one, characterized by profound
mutual trust and great emotional warmth." In the same interview in
the summer of 1985, a year after the marked warming of relations
between Moscow and Pyongyang had begun, Kim referred to those
relations as "basically friendly."[44]

Chinese diplomats and scholars for the most part professed to be
unworried about the improvement of relations between Pyongyang and
Moscow. They stressed the traditionally close and friendly Chinese–
North Korean relations. By mid-1986, however, some were privately
expressing concern with the expansion of military relations between the
Soviet Union and North Korea, particularly the long-term implications
for Chinese security of Soviet overflights of North Korea.[45]

Conclusion

China, except during the aberration of the Cultural Revolution, has
demonstrated a firm commitment to good relations with North Korea.
Its fundamental strategic interests require a friendly state across the
Yalu.

China has geographical, cultural, and historical advantages over the
Soviet Union in maintaining close relations with North Korea, but the
Chinese have not simply relied on these advantages; they have worked
hard at cultivating warm relations. Doing so has not always been easy,
for North Korean pride and sensitivity to real or imagined big power
pressures have made them prickly partners. Nevertheless, the Chinese
have prepared elaborate receptions for Kim Il Sung and Kim Chong Il,
sent frequent high-level delegations to Pyongyang, and entertained a
large number of delegations from North Korea. Unable to compete with
the Soviets in supplying advanced military equipment and industrial
technology, they have sought to compensate by cordial treatment of
North Koreans, particularly Kim Il Sung and Kim Chong Il.

China's interest in stability in Korea, as demonstrated during 1984
and 1985 by its active encouragement of North-South dialogue and
trilateral talks, grows out of its desire for a prolonged period of stability
in the region, during which it can pursue undistracted its modernization
goals. Conflict in Korea that would make China an adversary of the
United States and Japan would severely set back that effort.

Although the Chinese have been more forthcoming than the Soviets
in endorsing North Korean positions and proposals, they, too, appear

to regard early unification as unlikely. Since 1983 they have surpassed the Soviets in contacts with South Korea. Trade with South Korea in 1985 approached the level of Chinese trade with North Korea. Various incidents involving Chinese ships and aircraft compelled China to negotiate with South Korea. Contacts with South Korea have the additional advantage for China of causing friction between South Korea and Taiwan, arousing fears in Taiwan that South Korea and China will eventually establish diplomatic relations, isolating Taiwan further. The Chinese seem to be taking the long view of their interests in the Korean peninsula, encouraging North-South talks in the hope that lowered tension will permit China to have growing interchange with both Koreas.

Notes

1. For more detailed analyses of Soviet–North Korean relations, see Scalapino and Lee, *Communism in Korea*; Chin O. Chung, *Pyongyang Between Peking and Moscow*; Donald S. Zagoria, "North Korea Between Moscow and Beijing," in Scalapino and Kim, *North Korea Today*; Helen Louise Hunter, "The Myth of Equidistance," in Kwak, Patterson, and Olsen, *The Two Koreas in World Politics*; Wayne Kiyosaki, *North Korea's Foreign Relations: The Politics of Accommodation, 1945–1975*; Harry Gelman and Norman D. Levin, *The Future of Soviet–North Korean Relations*; and Ralph N. Clough, "The Soviet Union and the Two Koreas," in Donald A. Zagoria, *Soviet Policy in East Asia*.

2. Note statement of Colonel General T. F. Shtikov, head of the Soviet delegation on the U.S.-Soviet Joint Commission on March 20, 1946: "The Soviet Union has a keen interest in Korea being a true democratic and independent country, friendly to the Soviet Union, so that in the future it will not become a base for an attack on the Soviet Union" (*FRUS 1946*, vol. 8, p. 653).

3. Gelman and Levin, p. 12.

4. George Ginsburgs, "Soviet Development Grants and Aid to North Korea, 1945–1980," *Asia Pacific Community*, no. 18 (Fall 1982):58.

5. Clough, "The Soviet Union and the Two Koreas," p. 182.

6. Ibid., p. 184, n. 16.

7. Gelman and Levin, p. 12.

8. *Far Eastern Economic Review, Asia 1980 Yearbook* (Hong Kong, 1980), p. 211, quoting Soviet broadcasts.

9. *FBIS*, July 15, 1985, pp. D13–D14.

10. North Korea published its harshest and most specific condemnations of the Soviet Union in two long editorials in the *Nodong Sinmun* in October 1963 and September 1964. See excerpts in Chung, *Pyongyang Between Peking and Moscow*, pp. 88–90 and 102–103.

11. Commentary by Ligonov in *Foreign Broadcast Information Services, Daily Report Soviet Union*, November 22, 1972, pp. C2–C3.

12. Interviews with the author in Soviet Union and United States, 1983–1984.

13. *FBIS*, January 12, 1979, pp. D1–D3.

14. In a conversation with a U.S. scholar in July 1985, Foreign Minister Kim Yong-nam indicated that Kim Il Sung had visited the Soviet Union in 1968—a visit not previously announced. See *Journal of Northeast Asian Studies* 4, no. 3 (Fall 1985).67.

15. *FBIS*, April 10, 1984, pp. D5–D9.

16. Conversations by the author with Soviet officials, 1984–1985.

17. *Nodong Sinmun* editorial, July 1, 1984 (*FBIS*, July 3, 1984, pp. D1–D5). See also *FBIS*, August 20, 1984, pp. D11–D14, and article in *Kulloja* (*FBIS*, September 18, 1984, pp. D15–D21).

18. *FBIS*, August 16, 1984, p. D5.

19. *Korea Herald*, July 13, 1986.

20. *Korea Herald*, April 23, 1986.

21. Gelman and Levin, p. 2; Adrian Buzo, "The Gap Between Lips and Teeth," *Far Eastern Economic Review*, April 7, 1983, pp. 32–34; Hunter, "North Korea and the Myth of Equidistance," pp. 195–209.

22. Chung, *Pyongyang Between Peking and Moscow*, pp. 120, 130; Hunter, "North Korea and the Myth of Equidistance," pp. 198–199.

23. Hunter, "North Korea and the Myth of Equidistance," p. 201; Clough, "The Soviet Union and the Two Koreas," p. 185; Chung, *Pyongyang Between Peking and Moscow*, p. 145. Data on the relative size of Soviet and Chinese military shipments to North Korea are scarce. The series published by the U.S. Arms Control and Disarmament Agency entitled *World Military Expenditures and Arms Transfers* (Washington, D.C., published periodically) contains figures on Soviet and Chinese arms transfers to North Korea, but they do not show trends year by year because figures for a number of years are bulked together.

24. For a recent sophisticated analysis of China's defense policy see Paul H.B. Godwin, "The Chinese Defense Establishment in Transition," in A. Doak Barnett and Ralph N. Clough, eds., *Modernizing China: Post-Mao Reform and Development* (Boulder, Colo.: Westview Press, 1985).

25. Bunge, *North Korea*, p. 255.

26. Chung, *Pyongyang Between Peking and Moscow*, pp. 18–19.

27. Gelman and Levin, p. 11.

28. Ibid., p. 11.

29. *China Newsletter*, no. 57 (July–August 1985) (Tokyo: Japan External Trade Organization):8.

30. Chung, *Pyongyang Between Peking and Moscow*, p. 145.

31. *Korea Herald*, October 25, 1984.

32. *Foreign Broadcast Information Services, Daily Report, China*, May 10, 1984, p. D4; *Korea Herald*, July 4, 1985.

33. *FBIS*, August 8, 1984, pp. D4, D7.

34. Chung, *Pyongyang Between Peking and Moscow*, pp. 128–130.

35. *Foreign Broadcast Information Services, Daily Report, Far East*, October 12, 1966, supp., p. 11.

36. *Peking Review*, 18 (May 2, 1975): 9.

37. See Clough, "The Soviet Union and the Two Koreas," pp. 190–191, and Zagoria, "North Korea Between Moscow and Beijing," pp. 359–362.

38. When Congressman Stephen Solarz in July 1980 asked Kim Il Sung his view of the Vietnamese invasion of Kampuchea and the Soviet military occupation of Afghanistan, his reply was that just as he was opposed to the presence of U.S. forces in South Korea, he was also opposed to foreign forces in other countries; all of these matters should be settled by peaceful negotiation. The North Korean press did not criticize the Chinese attack on Vietnam, neither did it express approval; it simply did not report it.

39. *FBIS,* October 15, 1980, p. D14.

40. As part of the process of downgrading Mao Zedong, an article in *Hongchi,* the CCP's theoretical journal, condemned the concentration of power in the hands of a single individual *(Beijing Review,* November 3, 1980, pp. 15–17). The condemnation was applied explicitly to the North Korean scheme for dynastic succession in an article in a Hong Kong journal associated with Deng Xiaoping supporters in Peking *(Zheng Ming,* November 1, 1980, in *Foreign Broadcast Information Services, Daily Report, PRC,* November 21, 1980, p. U1). In private comments to the author and other U.S. citizens, Chinese officials and scholars make no secret of their disapprobation of the cult of personality and dynastic succession in North Korea, but they usually add that China cannot interfere in these domestic affairs.

41. *FBIS,* May 7, 1984, p. D11.

42. *FBIS,* May 7, 1984, p. D12.

43. *Korea Herald,* October 12, 1984.

44. Interview with the U.S. scholar, Young C. Kim, in July 1985; see *Journal of Northeast Asian Studies* 4, no. 3 (Fall 1985):67–69.

45. *Korea Herald,* July 6, 1986, quoting the Japanese Kyodo News Service.

9

Diplomatic Competition

The primary arena for international competition between the two Koreas has been in their relations with the four big powers. These have been the relations that counted, in terms of security, economic development, and diplomatic support. Relations with all the other countries of the world have been of secondary importance. Yet, with each passing decade, rivalry between Seoul and Pyongyang in this secondary arena has become more intense and important.

The ultimate goal for each Korean government has been its recognition by the world as the sole legitimate government of Korea. They have seen the contest as a zero-sum game, in which gains by one meant losses for the other. The diplomatic battle has been fought in the United Nations in the nonaligned movement, and in other international organizations. Each has sought to gain diplomatic recognition from as many countries as possible and to block recognition of the other. They have used many tactics in the struggle: obtaining diplomatic support from the big powers; stressing their credentials as anticommunist, socialist, or Third World governments; offering support on issues dear to the hearts of courted countries; providing economic and military assistance; training Third World students and technicians; inviting foreign leaders on red carpet visits; sending top officials on visits abroad; and, in some instances, threatening reprisals should a country establish official relations with the rival Korean government.

The long, drawn-out struggle to gain exclusive recognition and to prevent the world community from recognizing the rival government has proved a losing battle for both. Paradoxically, the stepped-up activities aimed at gaining support for one at the expense of the other have only served to demonstrate that both deserve recognition. Preventing recognition of either has become increasingly difficult. Nations in growing numbers are establishing diplomatic relations with both. The community of nations is overcoming the political inhibitions that have prevented universal recognition of both Korean governments and is adjusting gradually to the reality that both qualify to be treated as full-fledged members of the international system.

Rivalry in the United Nations

During its early years, as a virtual ward of the UN, the ROK held a substantial advantage over the DPRK in establishing its legitimacy in the community of nations. The UN had observed the elections that established the ROK government, had attested to the validity of those elections, and had declared the ROK government to be "a lawful government" over that part of Korea to which the UN Temporary Commission had had access.[1] The UN had thus "placed its stamp of legal validity on the Republic of Korea" and had given the ROK "the promise of moral support."[2] Although the UN carefully limited its endorsement of the ROK to that part of Korea over which it had "effective control and jurisdiction," the ROK government used the UN cachet to support its claim to be the legitimate government of all Korea, as the UN, denied access to the territory controlled by the DPRK, had given its government no endorsement.

The UN also created a UN Commission on Korea with a mandate to lend its good offices to bring about the unification of Korea and the further development of representative government there, as well as to observe the withdrawal of foreign forces. The Commission duly reported the withdrawal of U.S. forces in June 1949 and the Soviet announcement that Soviet forces had withdrawn from North Korea in December 1948, although the Commission was unable to verify the Soviet withdrawal. The Commission also warned of an increase in border clashes, and in October 1949 it was given the further authority to observe and report developments that might lead to conflict.

Thus, when the Korean War broke out, the UN had been involved in Korea for several years and had representatives resident in and reporting from South Korea. The UN Security Council, in the absence of the Soviet representative, acted promptly on hearing of the invasion of South Korea. The council called for the withdrawal of North Korean forces, recommended that UN members aid the ROK to repel the attack, and set up a UN Command under a U.S. officer to command the forces contributed by 16 UN members to assist the ROK.

In October 1950, as UN forces advanced toward the Yalu, the UN established a UN Commission for the Unification and Rehabilitation of Korea (UNCURK) to supersede the existing UN Commission on Korea and "to represent the United Nations in bringing about the establishment of a unified, independent and democratic government of all Korea."[3] Subsequent resolutions of the UN General Assembly dealt with Chinese aggression in Korea, called for an embargo by all states of the supply of war materials to North Korea and the PRC, and made provision for handling the POW question in the armistice negotiations. In August 1953, the UN General Assembly welcomed the armistice and the decision to hold a political conference on Korea, recommending that the states contributing forces to the UN Command participate in that conference.[4]

When the Korean War ended, the ROK, then less than five years old, had acquired a favored position in the eyes of a majority of UN members as a victim of aggression defended by the UN itself. The DPRK, on the other hand, was seen by many as an outlaw state that had flouted the civilized norms of international conduct. The memory of the Korean War strongly affected the behavior of UN members toward Korean issues during the 1950s.

A basic issue was the membership of the two Koreas in international organizations, particularly the UN itself. Already, in January 1949, the ROK had applied for UN membership, supported by nine members of the Security Council, but the Soviet Union vetoed its application. When the DPRK applied, the Security Council refused even to refer the application to the membership committee. The ROK did gain membership in 1949 in the World Health Organization (WHO) and the Food and Agriculture Organization (FAO), as well as an associate membership in the Economic Commission for Asia and the Far East.

In 1956 the General Assembly passed a resolution requesting the Security Council to reconsider the ROK's application for membership, sponsored by the United States and others, which argued that the ROK had a special claim to membership because it had been established under the auspices of the UN. The Soviet Union again vetoed the application in the Security Council. Moscow countered in 1956 and again in 1958 with proposals that both Koreas be admitted to the UN simultaneously. The Soviets argued that the admission of both Koreas would place them on an equal footing and promote their unification. The Soviet spokesperson pointed out that two separate states existed with two different social and economic systems and that both had international recognition. The United States and a majority of other members opposed the Soviet proposals on the grounds that North Korea was not a peace-loving state, it had been guilty of aggression, it had violated the Armistice Agreement, and it refused to recognize the competence of the UN to deal with the Korean question.[5]

Even though the ROK could not gain entry into the UN because of the Soviet Union's veto power, it received special attention from the world organization. UNCURK continued to function in South Korea, submitting annual reports to the UN on the situation in the Korean peninsula. The UN Command submitted annual reports to the Security Council on matters relating to the Armistice Agreement. The United Nations Korean Reconstruction Agency (UNKRA), established in 1950 during the Korean War, received contributions from UN members to be used to reconstruct facilities destroyed or damaged during the war. By the time that agency was phased out in 1959, it had expended $149 million for this purpose.[6]

By 1960 the ROK had joined a number of additional international organizations affiliated with the United Nations, including UNESCO, the International Telecommunication Union (ITU), the Universal Postal Union (UPU), the International Atomic Energy Agency (IAEA), the International Civil Aviation Organization (ICAO), the World Meteorological Organization (WMO), the World Bank, and the International Monetary Fund (IMF). It had made token contributions to the UN's Expanded Program for Technical Assistance, the UN High Commissioner for Refugees, and the UN International Children's Emergency Fund.

During the 1960s, the UN General Assembly debated the Korean question nearly every year. The majority of members, aligned with the United States on this matter, regularly invited the ROK to participate in the debate—without a vote—and rejected Soviet bloc efforts to invite a North Korean representative on the ground that North Korea refused to acknowledge the authority of the UN to deal with the Korean question. The General Assembly also repeatedly voted down Soviet bloc resolutions calling for the withdrawal of UN forces from South Korea and the dissolution of UNCURK. Resolutions reaffirming the UN objective of bringing about a unified, independent, and democratic Korea and extending the mission of UNCURK, regularly received the support of a majority of UN members. In the debate, the United States and its supporters urged the holding of elections throughout Korea under UN supervision, which the Soviet bloc opposed on the ground that participation in the Korean War had deprived the UN of authority to deal fairly with the Korean question.

The United Nations served as a channel for informing member nations of the upsurge in violence perpetrated by North Korea along the DMZ and through infiltration of South Korea during 1967 to 1969.[7] Details of these incidents, as reported by the UN Command, were circulated to UN members in official Security Council documents.[8]

By 1970 UN consideration of the Korean issue had become predictable, routine, and unproductive. Memories of the Korean War had faded. The large number of newly independent developing countries recently admitted to the UN were much more concerned with general Third World issues than with the stale debate on Korea. U.S. influence on the voting behavior of member nations had declined, as evidenced by its inability to prevent the expulsion of its ally, the Republic of China, in 1971. Consequently, when the two Koreas began for the first time to open direct bilateral contacts in 1971 and 1972, members of the UN General Assembly readily agreed to forgo the debate on Korea during those two years.

The year 1973 was a crucial turning point. The General Assembly for the first time invited representatives from both Koreas to attend the debate and voted to dissolve UNCURK. The DPRK, after a severe struggle, won admission to the WHO, its first such success in a UN-affiliated organization. North Korea promptly opened permanent observer missions in Geneva and New York. Park Chung-hee, bowing to reality, abandoned the effort to exclude the DPRK from the UN. In June 1973 he announced a new policy, withdrawing opposition to the simultaneous admission of both Koreas to the UN, as an interim measure pending unification. Park was reacting, not just to the DPRK's recent gains in the international arena, but to sweeping changes in the international system and in the UN itself that facilitated such gains. Concluding that the cold war had ended, Park declared that the world had "embarked on a new era of peaceful coexistence, based on the status quo, through the balance of power among the major Powers." In this changed climate he offered to open the ROK's door to Communist states "on the basis of the principles of reciprocity and equality." He also expressed doubt that Korea's unification could be attained "within a short period of time."[9]

Prime Minister Kim Chong-pil predicted that the new policy would lead to intensified international competition with North Korea. He told the press

> Under our foreign policy on peaceful unification, there will be a new level of diplomatic competition with the north, on various international occasions and in various international places. There will be economic competition. In the United Nations or in other international organizations, there will be competition between us and the north. We must win all these competitions. Only when we win, will North Korea understand us. Only when we win will North Korea awaken and show sincerity in the dialogue. Only when we win, will the road to unification be shortened.[10]

Pyongyang denounced Park's proposal for both Koreas to enter the UN as a device to perpetuate division, refusing to enter the UN except as part of a single Confederal Republic of Koryo. This reversal of Pyongyang's position since the Soviet proposals in the 1950s for the simultaneous admission of the two Koreas reflected gains made by North Korea in securing international recognition and Kim Il Sung's confidence that trends favored the DPRK. The advantage held by the ROK in the UN when the DPRK was recognized by few states outside the Soviet bloc had been significantly reduced. Despite its refusal to be seated in the United Nations alongside South Korea, Pyongyang redoubled its efforts to gain admission to other international organizations affiliated with the UN. By 1979 it had become a fellow member with South Korea not only of the World Health Organization, but also of the Food and Agriculture Organization, the International Atomic Energy Agency, the International Civil Aviation Organization, the International Telecommunication Union, the United Nations Committee for Trade and Development, the Universal Postal Union, and UNESCO. The DPRK explained its willingness to enter these organizations together with the ROK on the ground that their function was to promote international technical and practical cooperation, whereas entry of the two Koreas into the United Nations, a world political body, would constitute public recognition of the existence of two Korean states.[11]

In 1973, encouraged by its successes in the international arena, including recognition by many Third World countries and even by several NATO countries, North Korea and its supporters went on the attack in the UN in an effort to secure UN backing for North Korean objectives in Korea, primarily the dissolution of the UN Command and the withdrawal of U.S. forces. The United States and China, engaged in improving their bilateral relations, wished to avoid a confrontation in the UN on the Korean issue. Consequently, they worked out a compromise arrangement in behind-the-scenes negotiations, resulting in a General Assembly consensus statement simply expressing hope that the two Koreas would continue their dialogue and widen exchanges so as to expedite reunification.

In 1974 North Korea and its supporters returned to the attack. The growing influence of Third World states in the United Nations and North Korea's own diplomatic successes[12] created a favorable climate for Pyongyang's efforts. Also, the Chinese were more cautious than the year before, having been the target of barbs from the Soviets for collaborating with the United States. As in previous years, the main objective of the pro-DPRK resolution was to place the General Assembly on record as favoring the dissolution of the UN Command and the withdrawal of foreign forces, the presence of which was attacked as an obstacle to dialogue and unification. ROK backers, in order to draw greater support, presented a resolution assenting to consideration by the Security Council of the dissolution of the UN Command *in conjunction with appropriate arrangements to maintain the Armistice Agreement.* This time the pro-DPRK resolution barely lost by a tie vote: 48 to 48 with 38 abstentions. The General Assembly adopted the pro-ROK resolution by 61 to 43 with 31 abstentions.[13]

In 1975 the contention between the two Koreas in the United Nations reached a climax. The United States made a new proposal aimed at strengthening the U.S.-ROK position by implicitly acknowledging the growing sentiment in the United Nations for abolishing the UN Command. The United States declared its readiness, in consultation with the ROK, to terminate the UN Command by January 1, 1976, appointing U.S. and ROK officers as successors in command to ensure the enforcement of the Armistice Agreement, provided that the Korean People's Army and the Chinese People's Volunteers, as signatories to the Armistice Agreement, agreed that it would remain in force. Based on this new position, the pro-ROK resolution called for continuing North-South dialogue and for negotiations among the parties concerned to replace the armistice with new arrangements so that the UN Command could be dissolved. The General Assembly passed this resolution by a vote of 59 to 51 with 29 abstentions.

The pro-DPRK resolution in 1975 as usual called for the dissolution of the UN Command and the withdrawal of foreign forces. In addition, the resolution urged "the real parties" to the Armistice Agreement (meaning the United States and North Korea) to replace it with a peace treaty between them. The General Assembly passed this resolution by a vote of 54 to 43 with 42 abstentions.[14]

Thus, the two resolutions stood in stark contradiction to each other. Ignoring the contradiction, Pyongyang hailed the passage of the pro-DPRK resolution as "a great turning point in the history of the United Nations . . . an epochal event which broke down the old pattern in the United Nations in which the United States would rig up illegal 'resolutions' on the Korean question at will annually during the past 30 years by setting its handraising machine in motion, and adopted a fair decision on the Korean question for the first time."[15] Since that time, the North Koreans have cited that resolution repeatedly as evidence that the United Nations supports the DPRK position on Korea.

The year 1975 proved to be the apogee of North Korean success in the United Nations. The following year both DPRK and ROK backers requested inclusion of Korean items on the agenda of the General Assembly, but just before the session opened, the sponsors of the pro-DPRK item withdrew it and ROK supporters followed suit. Presumably, North Korea and its backers concluded that support for a pro-DPRK resolution in the UN had not increased and might even have declined. The 1975 test had shown the two Koreas to be so evenly balanced that eking out another slight victory over the opponent was not worth the diplomatic effort required. Many UN members were tired of having to line up each year in a purely symbolic nose count on a Korean issue that was of little interest to them and which produced no significant change in Korea. Consequently, the Korean question lay dormant in the UN from 1975 to 1983. Rivalry deteriorated into a meaningless contest to see which Korea could persuade the most countries to include a favorably phrased reference to the Korean issue in its annual address to the UN General Assembly.[16]

In 1983 two events in rapid succession brought Korea into the headlines and produced debate in the United Nations—the shooting down of a Korean Air Lines plane by a Soviet fighter in September and the assassination in Rangoon of 17 senior Korean officials by North Korean agents in October. ROK Ambassador Kim Kyung-won spoke during the Security Council debate on the KAL incident, a tragic event that attracted worldwide attention and much sympathy for South Korea. The dignified and restrained handling of the issue by South Korean representatives made a favorable impression on many UN delegates. North Korean representatives remained silent and inactive.

The Rangoon bombing received attention from the UN General Assembly's Sixth Committee (legal affairs) in the course of a debate on international terrorism. The Burmese representative declared that investigation had "established conclusively that the perpetrators of the bomb attack were North Koreans who acted under instructions of [their] government." Forty-five countries condemned the action in their speeches, and none of North Korea's allies spoke in its defense.[17]

The two Koreas have reached an impasse in the UN Security Council and the UN General Assembly; utilizing those organizations to the advantage of either is difficult. North Korea, with the cooperation of the Soviet Union and China, can block the admission to the United Nations of both Koreas or of South Korea alone. South Korea with the cooperation of the United States, can prevent the Security Council from dissolving the UN Command and ending the Armistice Agreement. Even the passage by the UN General Assembly of purely symbolic resolutions favoring North or South Korea has lost its value, now that the two sides are so evenly balanced. Both Koreas assiduously cultivate relations with UN members to prevent an adverse shift in the balance, but if no substantial change in the balance occurs, neither seems likely to seek UN action on the central issues in Korea.

Several years ago the ROK mission in New York for the first time began to speak on issues before UN committees, particularly on economic questions. Although members of observer missions cannot vote, they can speak before committees with the concurrence of the committee chairman. The issues are often technical and speeches have to be prepared by experts in Seoul. The ROK mission has adopted a low-key approach, striking a reasonable and constructive note. The ROK mission spoke in committees eight times in 1983 and more frequently in 1984 and 1985. The DPRK mission has not attempted to compete in this form of activity, although whenever they learn that a South Korean is to speak, they attend to listen and take notes. In general, members of the DPRK mission are less active than the South Korean diplomats and have less contact with other UN missions.

The DPRK diplomats in New York have been admitted to the United States exclusively to carry out their official functions at the United Nations. Strictly speaking, they have no authority to have contacts with U.S. citizens outside the United Nations other than those essential to functioning in New York. Nevertheless, as the only North Korean officials resident in the United States, they do see news correspondents and private U.S. citizens. Through UN channels they issue press releases from time to time, which are typically so turgidly propagandistic as to attract little press attention. Lacking diplomatic relations with the United States, they are greatly disadvantaged compared to the South Koreans, who have a large consulate general in New York in addition to their UN Observer Mission. South Korea also has an embassy in Washington and consulates in various U.S. cities. But South Korean diplomats point out that North Korea gains an advantage over South Korea through its UN connections by having been able to establish official missions in several countries with which it lacks diplomatic relations, including not only its mission in New York, but also its missions accredited to UNESCO in Paris and the UN Food and Agriculture Organization in Rome. As no UN organizations are based in Soviet bloc countries or China, the ROK has no comparable opportunity to establish official missions in any of those countries.

In April 1986 the two Koreas moved a step closer to membership in the United Nations. Both were admitted to the UN Asia Group, consisting of 44 Asian countries, one of five unofficial regional groupings established to facilitate the exchange of views on UN matters. South Korea had long sought membership in this group, but North Korea had opposed it. Once North Korea withdrew its opposition, both Koreas were admitted by unanimous vote, including the favorable votes of Communist states in Asia such as China, Mongolia, and Vietnam.[18] South Korea, working doggedly to win international support for the admission of both Koreas to the UN, in May 1986 obtained an endorsement from Jaime de Pinies, president of the UN General Assembly, and from the leaders of the seven major industrial nations at their summit meeting in Tokyo.

During the 1980s competition in gaining admission to specialized agencies of the United Nations continued. As of 1984, South Korea belonged to 14 of the 15 such organizations. North Korea was a member of 9.[19] In 1986 it was admitted to the tenth—the International Maritime Organization—which entitled it to set up a permanent resident mission in London.[20]

A form of competition that will probably increase and may help to force a change in North Korean policy toward South Korea is the hosting of meetings of UN-affiliated organizations. South Korea has hosted meetings sponsored by the FAO, WHO, and UNESCO.[21] ROK policy, in line with UN requirements, is to admit the delegation of any member nation desiring to attend, including that of North Korea. The North Koreans have refused to admit South Korean delegations; consequently, the FAO and the UN Development Program (UNDP) rejected North Korea as the venue for a study tour and regional consultations on the achievement of stable high yields of paddy rice that had been scheduled there for 1982.[22]

North Korea held a nine-day WHO Southeast Asia Regional Conference on Primary Health Care in September 1983, which was not officially sponsored by the WHO. Although billed as a Southeast Asian Regional Conference, the only delegates from that region listed by the Pyongyang media as attending were from Indonesia and Thailand. The rest of the delegates came from countries outside Southeast Asia, including the PRC, Yugoslavia, India, Sri Lanka, Afghanistan, Malta, the Maldives, and Jamaica.[23] The lengthy conference received much attention from the North Korean media.[24]

Both Koreas have received assistance from the UNDP, which has official representatives stationed in each country to supervise the programs. In 1983 the UNDP approved for the first time an integrated "country program" for North Korea, funded by an $18.4 million allocation. South Korea was awarded a $15.7 million program. The funds go primarily for technical training to upgrade science, industry, agriculture, transport and communications, and natural resources development.[25] In 1985 the ROK was elected as one of three members representing Asia on the governing council of the UNDP, along with Indonesia and Kuwait.

Diplomatic Recognition

Despite its sponsorship by the United Nations, the ROK had won diplomatic recognition from only six countries when the Korean War broke out: the United States, the Republic of China, the United Kingdom, France, the Philippines, and Spain. The DPRK had established diplomatic relations with twelve countries, all members of the Soviet bloc, including the People's Republic of China, which recognized Pyongyang immediately after announcing the establishment of its government in October 1949.

No countries recognized either Korea during the Korean War or the three years immediately thereafter. From 1956 through 1959 the ROK picked up recognition from South Vietnam, Italy, West Germany, Turkey, Thailand, Norway, Sweden, Denmark, and Brazil. The DPRK gained no additional diplomatic relationships during the 1950s, although it stepped up activities in the Third World, exchanging visitors, signing trade agreements, and attending Afro-Asian conferences, thus laying the foundation for advances in diplomatic relationships during the 1960s.[26] At the end of the 1950s, the ROK held a small lead over the DPRK in diplomatic relationships, its partners coming mainly from NATO and from among Asian countries close to the United States, whereas the DPRK's partners came exclusively from the Soviet bloc, except for Yugoslavia, which had broken with the Soviet Union in 1948.

Diplomatic competition gathered speed during the 1960s. The ROK took an impressive lead, establishing diplomatic relations with 30 countries in 1962 alone. By 1969 it had relations with 79 countries; the DPRK lagged with only 34. South Korea's strong position in the United Nations in the 1960s and its gratifying success in rapidly expanding its diplomatic relationships led it to adopt its own version of the Hallstein Doctrine.[27] In 1965 it broke the relations it had had since 1962 with Congo (Brazzaville) because that country established relations with Pyongyang. By 1969, however, Seoul had second thoughts as to the wisdom of that policy. When North Korea established relations with Chad, with which South Korea had maintained relations since 1961, Seoul decided against breaking off. The door was opened for countries to have relations with both Koreas, and many soon followed Chad's example.

The 1970s were notable for the diplomatic successes of North Korea. The changed international climate noted by Park Chung-hee in announcing South Korea's new foreign policy favored Pyongyang's drive for recognition. So did the 1972 announcement that North and South Korea were seeking reunification through dialogue. North Korea's increasingly active and skillful diplomacy in the 1970s added 65 countries to its list of diplomatic partners.

South Korea had some success in establishing relations with newly independent countries and with countries that had previously recognized only North Korea. But a reverse current set in. Seven countries broke relations with South Korea: South Vietnam, Benin, Rwanda, Togo, Kampuchea, Afghanistan, and Laos; three broke with North Korea: Argentina, Chile, and Australia. In some instances, as with South Vietnam, Afghanistan, and Chile, changes of government were responsible; in others, governments responded to North Korea's diplomatic tactics. In the Australian case, North Korea took the initiative to withdraw its mission. By 1980 the gap between the two Koreas had narrowed substantially. South Korea had diplomatic relations with 112 countries and North Korea with 100. Neither Korea had much success in trying to check the trend toward dual recognition. Sixty-one countries had diplomatic relations with both Seoul and Pyongyang.[28] The community of nations had opted decisively for the acceptance of both Koreas as legitimate, independent states.

The struggle continued into the 1980s. By October 1985 the scorecard stood at 118 countries that had diplomatic relations with the ROK, 101 with the DPRK, and 67 with both. The trend toward dual recognition continued but slowed, as countries that had maintained relations with both broke with one or the other. The ROK lost Rwanda and Lesotho, while the DPRK lost Burma, the Comoro Islands, Costa Rica, and Western Samoa, all as a result of the Rangoon bombing.[29]

Aside from the four big powers, each Korea has had a core group of supporters with which it has maintained diplomatic relations for twenty or thirty years and which have eschewed relations with its rival. Pyongyang's core group consists of the Soviet Union's East European allies, and Mongolia, Vietnam, and Cuba. Seoul has been unable to break into this solid phalanx. South Korea's core group, the members of NATO, has proved less solid. Four of them established diplomatic relations with North Korea during the 1970s: Norway, Denmark, Iceland, and Portugal. Since 1975 the North Koreans have made no further inroads, although France seemed about to take the step when the socialist government of François Mitterand took power. Mitterand, on a visit to Pyongyang in 1981 as head of the Socialist Party before becoming president of France, had said that he favored recognition. South Korea let it be known that a large contract for a nuclear plant then under negotiation with a French company would be dropped and other French economic interests would suffer if France were to establish diplomatic relations with North Korea. The French government did not do so, but in December 1984 it authorized North Korea to upgrade the status of its trade mission in Paris to that of "general delegation," the status granted to representatives of the Canadian province of Quebec and the Palestine Liberation Organization (PLO). The secretary general of the French foreign ministry stated that it was not good to isolate North Korea from the rest of the world.[30]

In Europe, the Asian-Pacific region, the Middle East, and North Africa the two Koreas have almost equal numbers of diplomatic partners. In sub-Saharan Africa North Korea holds a significant lead, with 39 states to South Korea's 30. The reverse is true in the Americas, where South Korea has relations with 28 states to North Korea's 10.

South Korea took an early lead in Africa with its active diplomacy of the 1960s, but during the 1970s most of the states that had relations with South Korea established them also with North Korea. A few broke relations with South Korea upon establishing them with its rival: Rwanda, Togo, Benin, Lesotho, and the Seychelles. But South Korea gained ground in establishing relations with states that had recognized only North Korea: the Comoro Islands,[31] Equatorial Guinea, Guinea, Guinea-Bissau, and Nigeria.

North Korea has had difficulty breaking into the Americas, where its only early success was with Cuba in 1960. Venezuela (1974) and Mexico (1980) are the only large countries with which it has relations, although it once had diplomatic missions in Argentina and Chile, both of which broke relations in the 1970s. It established relations with the Sandinista government of Nicaragua in 1979.

The factors that determine whether a country establishes relations with North or South Korea or with both are many, and they interact in a complex fashion. They include the ideological bias of governments, their links with the United States or the Soviet Union, personal ties between leaders, domestic politics, military and economic aid, the diplomatic skill or lack of it on the part of the Korean governments, and the perceived trend in world affairs.

Ideology was a decisive factor in the early years, when many nations chose sides in the cold war between the Communist bloc and the free world. But by the 1970s, the intensity of ideological conviction had waned and barriers between Communist and noncommunist countries had weakened. Newly independent countries multiplied, many without clear-cut ideological leanings and more interested in demonstrating their independence and in obtaining help from both noncommunist and Communist nations than in adhering to one camp or the other. Ideology declined as a criterion for recognizing Seoul or Pyongyang, although it still determines the choice of Communist states, not one of which has recognized South Korea. Certain radical governments heavily dependent on the Soviet Union, such as Syria, Angola, and South Yemen, also refuse to recognize the ROK. Some strongly anticommunist states, such as Saudi Arabia, Morocco, and Paraguay, reject relations with North Korea on ideological grounds, but most governments in recent years have based their decisions on other factors.

Domestic politics sometimes decides the diplomatic orientation of a government toward Korea. For example, the advent of right-wing General Augusto Pinochet in Chile led to the severance of diplomatic relations with North Korea, whereas the overthrow of Anastasio Somoza by the Sandinistas resulted in the establishment of diplomatic relations between Nicaragua and North Korea.

Military aid can be decisive. North Korea's despatch of MIG-21 pilots to fly for Egypt during the 1973 war with Israel earned Anwar Sadat's deep gratitude.[32] North Korea also supplied Egypt with small arms and parts for Soviet-made equipment after Sadat had expelled Soviet military advisers. Gratitude for past aid and a desire to maintain access to North Korean military assistance may explain why Sadat's successor, Hosni Mubarak, a former defense minister, has rejected South Korea's request to upgrade consular relations with Egypt to the level of diplomatic relations.

Economic power was instrumental in helping South Korea to establish diplomatic relations with Libya, an improbable occurrence in the light of Libya's radical policies and its close relations with the Soviet Union. North Korea had established diplomatic relations with Libya in 1973. In the mid-1970s South Korean construction companies, which had an impressive record of accomplishment elsewhere in the Arab world, began to win construction contracts in the Libyan government's massive modernization program, financed by its oil revenues. South Korean construction workers in Libya soon began to outnumber those from North Korea. In 1978 Seoul opened a Consulate General in Tripoli. By 1980 South Korean construction contracts in Libya exceeded $1.4 billion, and 3,502 workers from South Korea were there compared to 1,500 North Koreans.[33]

Contacts between Libya and the small Moslem community in Korea[34] also contributed to the warming relations between Seoul and Tripoli. Mohamed Ahmad Al-Sherrif, secretary-general of the Islamic Call Society of Libya, visiting South Korea in 1980 to participate in the dedication of the Pusan Mosque and Islamic Center and the ground-breaking ceremony for the Korean Islamic University, declared that the establishment of diplomatic relations between Libya and the ROK would be no problem.[35] They were established in 1980, and in 1981 Libya opened a People's Bureau, the equivalent of an embassy, in Seoul.

The two Koreas have competed intensively in receiving high-level foreign visitors and sending official delegations to foreign countries, as well as in propaganda aimed at impressing foreigners with the progress of their society and the rightness of their cause. North Korean propaganda has suffered from heavy-handedness, as for example by the purchase of space in Western newspapers to carry speeches by Kim Il Sung in fine print. That practice seems to have been abandoned several years ago, at least in the United States, and signs of greater sophistication have appeared. Nevertheless, the required infusion of praise for Kim Il Sung and Kim Chong Il and the *chu che* philosophy places a heavy burden on North Korean propagandists. A full-page advertisement in the *New York Times* in 1985 plugging a biography of Kim Chong Il demonstrated that old habits die hard.

In receiving and sending delegations, the two Koreas are probably more evenly matched than in propaganda skills, although the impact of such visits is difficult to measure and evaluate. In the early 1970s North Korea gained an advantage from the sharp increase in Chinese invitations to prominent foreign leaders. As Pyongyang is only a two-hour flight from Peking, the North Koreans were able to persuade many to add a day or two in North Korea to their itinerary.[36] Both Koreas are considerably more advanced than many of the Third World countries whose leaders they seek to impress. Seoul is more lively, dynamic, and modern than Pyongyang, yet the North Korean capital is impressive with its quiet elegance and orderliness. To some Third World leaders it may seem a more suitable model for their countries than the hurly-burly of Seoul, with its swarming population of nine million. Certain authoritarian leaders also admire Kim Il Sung's political skill in running his country. At least one trip to Pyongyang, that of the president of Togo in 1974, paid immediate dividends for North Korea. Within a few days after his return to Lomé, he notified the South Korean Embassy that Togo was breaking relations with the ROK because of the presence of U.S. troops there. A more persuasive reason may have been the promise by North Korea of $15 million for the construction of a massive party building and the training of party cadres.[37]

Premiers, foreign ministers, and other high officials from the two Koreas had ranged the world seeking support, but trips abroad by Kim Il Sung were rare, and by Park Chung-hee infrequent. Kim's only trips outside the Soviet bloc or China were to Indonesia in 1964; to Yugoslavia, Romania, Mauritania, Bulgaria, and Algeria in 1975; and to Tito's funeral in Belgrade in 1980. Kim was inhibited from traveling abroad by his well-known dislike of flying. He made his 1984 trip to the Soviet Union and Eastern Europe entirely by rail, taking 47 days for the trip. Park's travels abroad consisted mainly of five trips to the United States.

When Chun Doo Hwan came to power in South Korea in 1980, he stressed delegation diplomacy at the level of head of state. He visited the United States in February 1981 at the beginning of the Reagan administration. He followed this up by a tour of the five member states of the Association of Southeast Asian Nations in June 1981 and a trip to four African states and Canada in 1982. He was on a trip to Burma, India, Sri Lanka, Australia, and New Zealand, in October 1983 when it was interrupted by the Rangoon bombing. He took with him on these trips a large entourage of economic officials and businessmen, stressing the importance of South Korea's economic power in cementing relations with the countries visited. The inroads being made into the Third World by these trips and North Korea's difficulty in competing at the head of state level may have been a consideration in reaching the decision to send assassins to Rangoon. In 1985 Chun made a precedent-setting official visit to Tokyo, in return for a visit to Seoul the year before by Prime Minister Nakasone.

Maladroitness by its diplomats has marred North Korea's image. The most bizarre and widely publicized cases were the expulsions of North Korean diplomats from Sweden, Norway, Denmark, and Finland in 1976 for abusing diplomatic privileges by smuggling and selling liquor, cigarettes, and hashish. Puzzled observers speculated that the diplomats had been ordered to raise money in this way because of the severe shortage of foreign exchange that had caused North Korea to default the year before on the repayment of large foreign currency debts.[38]

In October 1975 the entire diplomatic staff of the North Korean Embassy in Australia decamped abruptly, without informing the Foreign Ministry. The North Koreans in a subsequent note accused the Australians of having taken "an unfriendly attitude" toward North Korea, an apparent reference to the Australian vote in the UN for a pro–South Korean resolution and abstention on a pro–North Korean resolution. A week later Australian diplomats in Pyonyang were asked to leave, accused of conducting subversive activities against the DPRK.[39] In 1982 the Colombian government asked the North Korean deputy foreign minister and three assistants to leave the country because they had arrived without a visa.[40] In 1983 two North Korean diplomats were expelled from Pakistan for trying to smuggle in 4,592 wristwatches, and a North Korean diplomat in India was forced to leave for having attempted to smuggle in wristwatches and diamonds.[41] In 1986 a North Korean diplomat fled Nepal after $22,000 in gold and 1,800 wristwatches found in his baggage had been seized.[42]

In some Third World countries, Pyongyang's diplomacy has met setbacks because North Korea has promoted revolution against the ruling government. The most blatant example occurred in Sri Lanka. The government of Mrs. Sirimavo Bandaranaike recognized North Korea shortly after coming into office in 1970. The North Korean mission arrived in September. Six months later the ambassador and his entire staff were on their way home, expelled for having provided funds and training in guerrilla warfare to members of the People's Liberation Front, then engaged in a campaign of violence against the government. Diplomatic relations between Sri Lanka and North Korea remained suspended from 1971 to 1975.[43] The Mexican government in 1971 arrested 20 members of a revolutionary organization said to have been trained in North Korea.[44] In 1977 the Nepalese government asked the North Korean mission to stop flooding that small country with propaganda attacking the United States and South Korea, which was being churned out in such quantities that rural mail carriers complained of the weight they had to carry over mountain trails.[45]

The Nonaligned Movement

During the 1970s and 1980s North Korea has used the nonaligned movement to support its claim to be the only legitimate government in Korea, just as South Korea used the UN during the 1950s and 1960s. The ROK, although not a member of the UN, regularly participated in the debate on the Korean issue, while the DPRK was on the outside, looking in. In the nonaligned movement, their positions were reversed. The outsider, unable to participate directly, was forced to rely on friendly countries inside the organization to look out for its interests.

The nonaligned movement lacks the universality, the elaborate formal structure, and the prestige of the UN. It has nothing comparable to the specialized agencies of the UN from which many Third World countries gain practical benefits. Still, with a membership of one hundred governments meeting regularly at foreign minister and summit levels, its deliberations and decisions attract considerable attention, especially in the Third World. Member states do not have to line up and vote on issues as they do in the UN. Formal statements issued by nonaligned conferences aim at representing a consensus of members' views, but members disagreeing with parts of consensus statements customarily submit their own statements of reservations.

North Korea became a member of the nonaligned movement at the conference of foreign ministers in Lima, Peru, in 1975, along with North Vietnam and the Palestine Liberation Organization. South Korea, which had also applied for membership, was rejected. In 1979, at the sixth nonaligned summit conference in Havana, Cuba, the DPRK was one of 36 countries named to the coordinating bureau of the nonaligned movement.

Pyongyang's chief objective at nonaligned conferences has been to secure acceptance of resolutions attacking the United States and South Korea that can be cited as evidence of broad international support for its position. The year after entering the nonaligned group, North Korea sent a delegation of more than one hundred, headed by Premier Pak Song-chol, to the fifth summit conference in Colombo, Sri Lanka. The North Koreans attracted undesired attention when the Sri Lankan government ordered their naval vessel in the harbor to close down its elaborate radio facilities, said to be capable of monitoring the messages of other delegations, and refused to allow the landing of large wooden crates, contents undisclosed.[46] News of the ax-murder of two U.S. officers in the DMZ, which arrived in the middle of the conference, also evoked critical comment.

Despite these complications, the North Koreans won acceptance of a strongly worded resolution condemning "imperialist maneuvers for aggression against Korea." The resolution declared: "Today the imperialists have turned South Korea into a military base for aggression and a base for nuclear attack . . . and have created a threat of aggression against the Democratic People's Republic of Korea."[47] Many countries objected to the resolution during the debate, and 24 submitted formal written reservations.[48]

The objections to the pro-Pyongyang resolution at Colombo were precursors of the increasing opposition the North Koreans were to encounter at subsequent nonaligned conferences. The foreign ministers meeting at Belgrade in 1978 and the summit meeting in Havana in 1979 both called for the withdrawal of foreign forces from Korea, the dismantling of foreign bases there, and the replacement of the Armistice Agreement with a peace treaty, but in more moderate language than used in the Colombo resolution. At the 1981 foreign ministers conference in New Delhi, the prospect of a divisive debate and uncertain outcome caused the North Koreans to withdraw their proposal on the Korean issue. The nonaligned summit in New Delhi in 1983 expressed only a bland "hope that the fulfillment of the Korean people's desire for peaceful reunification would be enhanced by the withdrawal of all foreign troops from the area."[49]

The declining willingness of the nonaligned group to endorse hard-hitting pro-Pyongyang resolutions arose in part from the deep differences that had developed within the group over other issues. The Cuban attempt in 1979 to draw the group closer to the Soviet Union, for example, split it into sharply contending factions.[50] The Vietnamese invasion of Kampuchea, the Soviet occupation of Afghanistan, and the Iran-Iraq War caused endless wrangling. These more immediate and demanding issues pushed Korea into the background. In this contentious atmosphere, few countries wished to become involved in further argument on Korea, which for most of them was a remote and unpressing matter.

Gains made by the ROK in its relations with Third World countries strengthened the bloc of nations unwilling to see the nonaligned group used to promote the interests of North Korea at the expense of South Korea. From 1981 on, Chun Doo Hwan's repeated calls for bilateral talks between the two Koreas made more persuasive the argument used by governments friendly to South Korea that the two Koreas should be encouraged to resolve their problems through North-South dialogue, without outside interference.[51]

Despite the weaknesses and divisions that afflict the nonaligned movement, the North Koreans have made it central to their view of the world, describing it as "an independent political force which has the lofty aim of resolutely rejecting the great powers moves to divide the world into blocs and spheres of influence, of opposing all sorts of aggression and interference, subjugation and inequality, defending the sovereignty of each country and nation, and safeguarding world peace and security."[52] It is "a progressive movement against any form of domination and subjugation and for independence; it is a mighty revolutionary force of our times which is opposed to imperialism. Only when this movement is expanded and developed can imperialist aggression and intervention be frustrated successfully and all international problems be solved in conformity with the demands and interests of the peoples of the newly emerging countries."[53]

North Korea's goals for the nonaligned movement can be condensed into two words: *independence* and *unity*. Third World nations should strive for independence from any form of domination by the superpowers, but they can be successful only by combining their strength. Hence, North Korea repeatedly appeals to members of the nonaligned movement to put aside their quarrels, negotiate solutions to their differences, and form a united front against those who would dominate them.[54] In Kim Il Sung's view, conflict between members of the nonaligned movement is instigated by "the dominating forces," which "are working slyly to alienate and egg nations of the newly emerging forces on to fight each other and to fish in troubled waters."[55]

The North Korean vision of the correct road to victory for the nonaligned movement is linked closely with the *chu che* idea and the policy objective of expelling U.S. forces from South Korea. In Pyongyang's view, true national independence, in both political and economic terms, must be based on *chu che*. In other words, self-reliance and independence also demands the withdrawal of foreign forces and bases from all countries, including, of course, South Korea.[56] Thus, the North Koreans visualize the nonaligned movement not only as a forum in which to highlight South Korea's political isolation in the Third World, but also as a mechanism for creating pressure on the United States to withdraw its forces from South Korea.

Barred from hosting UN conferences so long as it refuses to admit delegates from South Korea, North Korea has turned to hosting conferences of the nonaligned movement. In 1981 Pyongyang held a nonaligned nations conference on food production and in 1984 a meeting of irrigation experts, attended by representatives from some forty countries and from the Group of 77 and the Food and Agriculture Organization. A more ambitious effort was the First Conference of Ministers of Education and Culture of the Nonaligned and Other Developing Countries held in Pyongyang in September 1983, attended by representatives from 56 countries. The conference adopted a declaration setting out many bona fide educational goals, but mixed in highly political statements, such as an appeal for measures to check the infiltration of imperialist ideas and attitudes and a condemnation of "all attempts by imperialists, old and new colonialists, racists, Zionists, and all hues of dominationists to violate the sovereignty and dignity of other nations."

An action program adopted by the conference revealed North Korea's intention to expand its influence in the nonaligned movement. The program contained

- an offer by North Korea to host in 1984 or 1985 a seminar on experience gained in anti-illiteracy and school enrollment programs;
- a recommendation to establish in Pyongyang a museum of national musical instruments;
- a recommendation for a biennial or triennial film festival of nonaligned and developing countries, the first to be held in Pyongyang in 1985 or 1986; and
- a recommendation that the first art festival of nonaligned and developing nations be held in Pyongyang in 1986 or 1987.

The conference asked the DPRK to submit the declaration and action program to the nonaligned foreign ministers conference and to the twenty-second general conference of UNESCO.[57]

The nonaligned foreign ministers conference at Luanda, Angola, in September 1985 welcomed the North Korean offer to hold a film festival and a symposium on anti-illiteracy and school enrollment programs in 1986. It also approved a North Korean proposal to hold meetings of high-ranking sports officials and of experts on pisciculture.[58]

North Korea appears to have chosen the nonaligned movement as the principal arena in which to pursue heightened world recognition through hosting international conferences, an arena in which the issue of South Korean participation does not arise. It seems an inadequate response to the holding of the Interparliamentary Union (IPU) conference in Seoul in 1983, the World Bank/IMF annual meeting in 1985, the Asian Games in 1986, and the plan to host the Olympic Games in 1988. Pyongyang will be unable to gain the worldwide recognition that Seoul is attaining until it is willing, as Seoul is, to admit its rival to meetings on its home turf.

The Interparliamentary Union

The two Koreas have pursued their intense rivalry in still another world forum, the IPU, an international organization composed of members of the legislative bodies from 98 nations. Their rivalry in this body had been relatively low-key and little noticed until the IPU annual conference held in Rome in September 1982 chose Seoul as host for the seventieth annual meeting in October 1983.[59] Alarmed at the potential boost to the ROK's stature and claim to legitimacy that would result from hosting this prestigious conference, especially if delegations from the Soviet bloc and the Third World were to attend in large numbers, North Korea immediately launched a campaign to have the venue changed.

The North Koreans focused their efforts on the meeting of the IPU's Parliamentary Council in Helsinki in April 1983, at which the venue for the fall meeting could be reconsidered. The North Korean ambassador to Finland, in a desperate effort to get the Rome decision reversed, offered $5,000 to the Finnish president of the IPU, for which the Finnish government declared him persona non grata and sent him packing. During the conference North Korean diplomats waked delegates up early in the morning to urge them to vote against Seoul. One delegate, who had opposed a conference in Seoul, was so annoyed by the early morning North Korean call that he changed his mind. In the vote the delegates confirmed the decision to hold the conference in Seoul.[60]

Having failed to prevent the conference from being held in Seoul, the North Koreans began a massive diplomatic and propaganda campaign to persuade delegates from Soviet bloc and nonaligned countries not to attend. The task was difficult, as IPU delegates are legislators, not government officials, and in many countries are not barred from attending conferences simply because of the lack of diplomatic relations with the host country. Numerous legislators whose countries did not have diplomatic relations with Cuba and East Germany had attended previous IPU conferences in Havana and East Berlin. Veteran parliamentarians had made friends with IPU delegates from other countries and found the annual get-togethers worthwhile and enjoyable. Others were interested in seeing Seoul.

As the time for the meeting approached, North Korean propaganda on the subject became increasingly shrill. A letter from the Central Committee of the Revolutionary Party for Reunification to political parties and legislative bodies around the world urged delegates to stay away from South Korea, "a U.S. colony and military base, where human rights are brutally suppressed and where the people unanimously oppose the IPU meeting." The letter continued: "If the representatives of national assemblies of the IPU members nations, despite our opposition, come to Seoul, where the South Korean people's deep-rooted indignation and grudge against the U.S. imperialists and their stooges are burning, they will undoubtedly court the enmity of the South Korean people."[61]

A broadcast by the Voice of the Revolutionary Party for Reunification on September 17 revealed the deep anxiety felt in Pyongyang at the possible appearance of Soviet bloc and nonaligned delegates in Seoul. Denouncing the meeting, the broadcast declared: "The United States and its stooges are trying to cook up two Koreas by distorting the fact that South Korea is a colony of the United States rather than an independent state. They act as if there were two states on the Korean peninsula by dragging into Seoul the representatives of the parliaments of the socialist and nonaligned countries which do not recognize South Korea as an independent state under the pretext of an international meeting."[62] In a special article the *Nodong Sinmun* protested: "South Korea is a U.S. colony, which is not a suitable place for the parliamentary delegations of socialist countries to visit, and the Chon Tu-Hwan [Chun Doo Hwan] ring, who are the worst tyrants in the world, are not men of reason to sit and talk to." Anyone going to South Korea would involve himself in the U.S. two-Koreas plot, the article continued, and assist those pursuing perpetual Korean division, "regardless of one's subjective intention."[63]

North Korea's dire warnings probably would not have deterred the delegates of some socialist countries from attending the IPU conference in Seoul, had the Soviets not shot down a Korean Air Lines plane on September 1, causing an outburst of hostility toward the Soviets among the people of South Korea. Pio-Carlo Terenzio, secretary-general of the IPU said that Hungary and Mongolia had submitted applications to attend before the KAL incident and that the Soviet Union and other East European countries seemed to have planned to participate.[64] Sixty-seven member countries did attend, including many from the nonaligned group. The IPU conference adopted a resolution proposed by the Swiss delegation condemning the Soviet Union for shooting down the KAL plane and calling on the ICAO for measures to enhance the safety of civil aircraft. North Korea's *Nodong Sinmun* crowed that the refusal of more than thirty nations to attend the conference, including all the socialist states, had foiled "the U.S. imperialist plot to get the South Korean puppet clique recognized as an independent state."[65] The South Koreans, although disappointed that circumstances beyond their control had prevented them from gaining maximum advantage from the conference, were gratified at the boost to the ROK's prestige from successfully hosting so large and prominent an international gathering.

World Bank and International Monetary Fund

In October 1985, Seoul hosted another large international gathering, the annual meeting of the boards of governors of the World Bank and the International Monetary Fund. Some 7,000 persons, including officials of the Bank and Fund, central bankers, finance ministers and officials, private bankers, and journalists attended the meeting. Most of the 148 member countries of the two organizations sent representatives. The meeting gave the ROK a chance to demonstrate that it possessed the physical facilities and organizational skills to host world-class events. A variety of guided tours gave the visitors, many of whom had not visited South Korea before, an impression of the country.

The meeting attracted representatives from thirty nonaligned and Communist states that had no diplomatic relations with the ROK. China sent a 22-member delegation, and delegations from Hungary, Laos, and Yugoslavia were also present. The absence of representatives of the Soviet Union and most East European countries, which do not belong to the World Bank or the IMF, somewhat curtailed the benefits accruing to Seoul, but hosting a meeting of the most prestigious and influential of global economic organizations added to South Korea's stature in the world community.

Meeting of Textile Exporters

In September 1985 the ROK organized a workshop to combat protectionism in the textile trade and to seek cooperative action to oppose renewal of the multifiber arrangement that expires in 1986. Representatives from 24 textile exporting developing countries attended. All except China were countries with market economies.

Arms Sales and Training

North Korea began on a very small scale during the 1960s to use military assistance to enhance its influence with Third World countries, expanding such activity substantially in the 1970s. It sent military personnel abroad to provide military training and, in a few countries, to operate military equipment or to serve as bodyguard to the ruler. It brought foreign military personnel to North Korea for training. According to a South Korean source, from 1966 through 1981 North Korea sent 5,500 military instructors abroad and trained 6,110 foreign military personnel in North Korea.[66] The International Institute of Strategic Studies reported that as of 1985 North Korea had 300 military personnel in Iran, 1,000 in Angola, 100 in Madagascar, 40 in Seychelles, 20 in Uganda, and unspecified numbers in seven other African countries.[67] It provided military equipment, occasionally gratis, but as its military production capability grew, it increasingly sold weapons for cash.

Some thirty countries have received military assistance from North Korea.[68] About half of these have diplomatic relations with North Korea only, but the others have diplomatic relations with both Koreas. Armaments supplied include small arms and ammunition, antiaircraft guns, artillery, mortars, machine guns, and patrol boats. Zaire, Zimbabwe, and Iran reportedly received tanks. Madagascar acquired several MIG-17 aircraft on loan, together with North Korean pilots, but as of 1983 these were said to be no longer operational.[69] The amounts of arms supplied to most of these countries were small—only Egypt, Zaire, Zimbabwe, and Iran received substantial amounts.

North Korea has learned that gains in political influence from military assistance are uncertain. Aid to Egypt still provides a diplomatic payoff, as indicated above. But Pyongyang's largest assistance program, arms sales and training for Iran, caused Iraq to break diplomatic relations in 1980. That diplomatic loss has been offset to some extent by Iran's willingness to pay for arms in oil or hard currency, thus easing Pyongyang's severe foreign exchange shortage to the extent of $800 million in 1982 alone, according to one estimate. North Korea shipped to Iran 150 T-62 tanks, 400 artillery pieces, 1,000 mortars, 600 antiaircraft machine guns, and 12,000 smaller weapons.[70] In addition to what North Korea has earned from sales to Iran, it may also have received some form of compensation, tangible or intangible, for providing a cover for shipment to Iran of Chinese-built F-6 fighters (based on the Soviet MIG-19) and T-59 tanks, allowing the Chinese to deny any transfer of arms from China to Iran.[71] Despite its wartime dependence on arms from North Korea, Iran has not broken relations with South Korea.

Pyongyang made sizable arms deliveries to Zaire in 1975, including patrol boats, artillery, and small arms, together with instructors, but the following year Zaire expelled the instructors, putting an end to the North Korean military aid program in that country.[72] Beginning in 1982, North Korea sent 500 to 700 military training personnel to Uganda to assist the government in counterinsurgency operations. When General Tito Okello replaced Milton Obote as chief of state in August 1985, he sent the North Korean trainers home.[73] In 1985 diplomatic sources in Zaire asserted that 3,000 North Korean troops and 1,000 advisers were stationed in Angola. That report and a similar one carried in the Japanese daily, *Sankei Shimbun*, citing rebel statements to a U.S. Congressional source, were flatly denied by the North Koreans, who declared that North Korea had only civilian experts in Angola.[74]

In 1981, ten months after Zimbabwe's prime minister, Robert Mugabe, visited Pyongyang, 100 North Korean instructors arrived in Salisbury to begin the training of an elite brigade, recruited from Mugabe's Shona tribe. North Korea donated $13 million in military equipment for the brigade, including T-54 tanks, armored personnel carriers, artillery, and trucks. Three years later the North Korean instructors had departed, after the brigade had been accused of committing many atrocities in a counterinsurgency campaign. British instructors took over the training of the brigade from the North Koreans, whose training methods and behavior had become a target of criticism.[75] Termination of this training program did not end the military relationship between North Korea and Zimbabwe. A "friendship delegation" from the Zimbabwe defense ministry, headed by the permanent secretary of the ministry, visited Pyongyang in April 1984, and 20 North Korean armored troop carriers worth about $3 million arrived in Zimbabwe in February 1985 accompanied by 6 North Korean instructors to train the Zimbabwean army in their use.[76] The instructors returned home in March 1986, having completed the training project.[77]

North Korea has a special military relationship with Libya, the only country aside from the Soviet Union and China with which it has a mutual defense treaty. The treaty, signed on November 2, 1982, during a visit to Pyongyang by Libyan leader Muammer el-Qaddafi, states that "if either of the contracting parties is subject to a threat or aggression by imperialists and their minions, the other party shall in every way render military and material support, regarding this as a threat or aggression against itself."[78] The treaty, rooted in the common hostility of both nations toward the United States, probably has more symbolic than practical meaning. It may be intended in part to mitigate the affront to North Korea represented by Libya's establishment of diplomatic relations with the ROK and its large contracts with South Korean construction companies. The treaty calls on each party to "strive to supply the other party with weapons not possessed by it." The Soviet-built SCUD missiles that appeared in North Korea in 1984 may have been provided by Libya.

North Korea has also employed military aid as an instrument for extending its influence in the western hemisphere. The North Korean ambassador in Managua received a decoration from the Sandinista government in September 1985 for military assistance rendered.[79] Provision of North Korean military equipment to the government of Grenada was forestalled by the U.S. invasion of that country.[80] In 1986 North Korea sold 100,000 automatic rifles to Cuba and was negotiating the sale of 10,000 to Peru.[81]

In the late 1970s and early 1980s, South Korea became a major Third World arms exporter, surpassing North Korea in the value of arms sold.

Data compiled by the U.S. Arms Control and Disarmament Agency lists South Korea as having exported $2.38 billion in armaments between 1975 and 1983, compared to North Korea's $2.16 billion. South Korea had become the second largest Third World arms exporter, well behind China, but ahead of North Korea, Israel, and Brazil.[82] All of these countries were minor suppliers compared to the United States and the Soviet Union or even the principal European arms producers, such as France and Britain. During 1983 and the first eleven months of 1984, South Korea's armaments exports were principally to the Middle East ($140 million), Latin America ($130 million), and Asia ($110 million), with negligible amounts sold in Africa ($2 million) and Europe ($1.4 million).[83]

South Korea had become one of the world's most competitive exporters of infantry munitions and weapons and light naval vessels. Its products were of good quality and relatively inexpensive. Most were based on U.S. designs and therefore readily assimilated by the armed forces of the many countries supplied mainly by the United States. The South Korean arms industry had developed to the point where it badly needed export markets in order to maintain production. From 1980 to 1984 six defense contractors went bankrupt, and the industry as a whole was operating at only 52 percent of capacity in 1984. Consequently, the ROK had adopted an active arms export strategy.

In order to obtain the U.S. technology on which the South Korean arms industry was heavily dependent, the government had to agree not to export some types of weapons without U.S. concurrence. Concurrence proved difficult to obtain in many cases, for the United States applied its own policy criteria to the decision whether to approve a sale of arms to a particular country, and also took into account the potential competitive impact on the U.S. defense industry. It approved only 3 percent of the $55.4 million in sales requested by South Korea in 1981 and 1982, 8 percent of the $49 million requested in 1983, and 2.8 percent of the $31 million requested in 1984.[84] This severe constraint on expanding sales of weapons based on U.S. technology caused growing friction between the two governments and led the South Koreans to seek technology elsewhere. They acquired Italian technology to produce armored personnel carriers and British technology for naval vessels. Whether the Soviets applied restraints on the export of North Korean weapons based on Soviet technology is unknown.

Conclusion

Rivalry between the two Koreas has caused each to work indefatigably to expand its own official ties throughout the world and to prevent its rival from doing the same. Each has succeeded in establishing diplomatic relations with a large number of countries, but has had little success in isolating its rival. The world community has accepted the legitimacy of both governments and the number of countries maintaining diplomatic relations with both Seoul and Pyongyang has steadily increased. As of 1985, Seoul had a small lead in the number of countries from which it had gained diplomatic recognition, but being ahead in this race was no longer of great importance. The important fact was that both had long ago earned the right to be treated as independent members of the international community. Attempts to stigmatize either as illegitimate carried little weight.

Since 1973 South Korea had abandoned the effort to exclude North Korea from the United Nations. Only North Korea's refusal to accept dual representation for Korea has prevented the two Koreas from entering the UN as separate states, following the precedent of the two Germanys. The impasse cannot be broken until North Korea changes its position. In the meantime, the UN provides an opportunity for the observer missions of the two Koreas to have informal diplomatic contacts with representatives of states with which they do not have diplomatic relations. Moreover, since North Korea could not keep South Korea out of the specialized agencies of the UN, it too has entered most of them. Thus, these organizations provide additional arenas for participation by the two Koreas in international activities.

In those countries giving heavy emphasis to antiimperialist ideology, especially in Africa, North Korea has benefited from its similar ideological stance. South Korea has had difficulty in developing relations with many of these countries because of its close identification with the United States and the presence of U.S. forces in its territory. The importance of ideology in determining the international orientation of countries has been on the decline, however, making South Korea's pragmatic approach more effective. Although still excluded from the nonaligned group of nations, it has increased its influence among individual members of that group, making the group less receptive to North Korean attempts to exploit it.

South Korea's strength resides in its more powerful economy and its long experience of participation in a wide variety of private international organizations and activities, which will be discussed in the next chapter. It has much in common with other developing nations and at times joins them in opposing the policies of the industrialized states, as in convening a meeting of textile exporting countries to oppose protectionism. South Korea has a readier entrée than North Korea has into most countries outside the Communist states and the more Marxist-inclined of the Third World countries. In the years ahead it will probably maintain its substantial lead over North Korea in international relationships and activities.

Notes

1. Resolution 195 (III) of the UN General Assembly (UNGA), December 12, 1948. For text see Leland M. Goodrich, *Korea: A Study of U.S. Policy in the United Nations* (New York: Council on Foreign Relations, 1956), pp. 217–219.

2. Goodrich, *Korea*, p. 69.

3. Resolution 376 (V) of the UNGA, October 7, 1950. Goodrich, *Korea*, pp. 223–226.

4. Goodrich, *Korea*, pp. 226–234.

5. *Yearbook of the United Nations, 1956* (New York: Columbia University Press, in cooperation with the United Nations, 1957), pp. 110–113; *Yearbook of the United Nations, 1958* (New York: Columbia University, 1959), pp. 104–105; *Yearbook of the United Nations, 1959* (New York: Columbia University, 1960), p. 71.

6. *Yearbook of the United Nations, 1959*, p. 74.

7. See Chapter 4.

8. See Security Council documents S/8217, November 2, 1967; S/8366, January 27, 1968; and S/9198, May 8, 1969.

9. Park Chung Hee, *The Special Statement Regarding Foreign Policy for Peace and Unification* (Seoul, June 23, 1973).

10. *FBIS*, June 26, 1973, p. E4.

11. *Government Memorandum of the DPRK on the Korean issue in the UNGA*, in *FBIS*, no. 197, supp. 38, October 11, 1973, p. 28.

12. In 1973, 1974, and 1975 North Korea established diplomatic relations with 23 Third World countries in addition to Finland, Sweden, Norway, Denmark, Iceland, Australia, Austria, and Switzerland. See Koh, *The Foreign Policy Systems of North and South Korea*, p. 11.

13. *Yearbook of the United Nations, 1974* (New York: Office of Public Information, United Nations, 1976), pp. 173–180.

14. *Yearbook of the United Nations, 1975* (New York: Office of Public Information, United Nations, 1978), pp. 193–204.

15. "Statement of the Government of the 'Democratic People's Republic of Korea,'" in *On the Question of Korea* (Pyongyang: Foreign Languages Publishing House, 1976), p. 310, quoted in Samuel S. Kim, "Pyongyang, the Third World, and Global Politics," in Tae-Hwan Kwak, Wayne Patterson, and Edward A. Olsen, *The Two Koreas in World Politics*, p. 72.

16. According to the ROK foreign ministry, of 45 countries making keynote speeches at the 1985 General Assembly, 26 spoke in favor of the ROK, 14 spoke in favor of the DPRK, and 5 were neutral (*Korea Herald*, October 6, 1985).

17. *Washington Post*, December 9, 1983.

18. *Korea Herald*, April 5, 1986.

19. *Korea Herald*, August 14, 1984; Prime Minister Lho Shin Yong's address to the UN, October 21, 1985 (*Korea Herald*, October 22, 1985).

20. *FBIS*, May 23, 1986, p. E1.

21. See list of UN-sponsored meetings, Appendix 2.

22. *Korea Herald*, September 1, 1982.

23. According to a South Korean diplomat, delegates agreeing to attend received free plane tickets from the North Korean government.

24. *FBIS*, September 20, 1983, pp. D3–D8.

25. *Far Eastern Economic Review*, March 3, 1983, p. 84.

26. See John Chay, "North Korea: Relations with the Third World," in Park and Kim, *The Politics of North Korea*, pp. 264–265.

27. A policy, named for West German Foreign Minister Walter Hallstein, to refuse to have diplomatic relations with any state establishing relations with East Germany.

28. U.S. Department of State, Bureau of Intelligence and Research, Report No. 1373, *Diplomatic Relations of Republic of Korea (ROK) and the Democratic People's Republic of Korea (DPRK)*, May 9, 1980.

29. Lesotho restored diplomatic relations with the ROK in February 1986 after a military coup displaced the pro-Pyongyang prime minister.

30. *Korea Herald*, November 25 and December 30, 1984.

31. The Comoro Islands broke relations with North Korea in 1983 as a result of the Rangoon incident.

32. See statement by Muhammad Hasan Muhammad al-Tuhami, vice prime minister and special envoy of President Sadat, in Pyongyang, February 10, 1978 (*FBIS*, February 10, 1978, p. D1).

33. *Korea Herald*, January 6, 1981.

34. Islam was introduced into Korea by Turkish troops during the Korean War. As of 1982 there were about 20,000 Moslems in Korea and mosques in Seoul, Pusan, and Kwangju. See *A Handbook of Korea*, 4th ed. (Seoul: Korean Overseas Information Service, Ministry of Culture and Information, 1982), p. 210.

35. *Korea Herald*, September 14, 1980.

36. For example in 1974 the heads of state of Senegal, Algeria, Togo, Mauritania, and Zaire all visited North Korea in connection with their visits to Peking. In 1976 the heads of state of Benin, Malagasy, Botswana, and Mali made similar visits. See Sang-Seek Park, "North Korea's Policy Toward the Third World," in Scalapino and Kim, *North Korea Today*, p. 325.

37. Interview with South Korean diplomat, December 1983.

38. *Washington Post*, October 22 and 31, 1976.

39. *FBIS*, November 3, 1975, p. D11; November 6, 1975, p. D1.

40. *Korea Herald*, February 19, 1982.

41. *Korea Herald*, May 20, June 17, and August 5, 1983.

42. *Korea Herald*, February 4, and 6, 1986.

43. *Washington Post*, April 17, 1971.

44. Jae Kyu Park, "North Korea's Policy Toward the Third World: The Military Dimension," in Kwak, Patterson, and Olsen, *The Two Koreas in World Politics*, p. 97.

45. *Far Eastern Economic Review*, July 22, 1977, p. 26.

46. *New York Times*, August 18, 1976.

47. *Washington Post*, August 20, 1976.

48. Samuel S. Kim, "Pyongyang, the Third World, and Global Politics," p. 77.

49. *Korea Times*, March 12, 1983.

50. Samuel S. Kim, "Pyongyang, the Third World, and Global Politics," p. 78.

51. See interview with Ambassador Yun Suk-heun, ROK permanent observer to the UN, *Korea Herald*, March 13, 1981.

52. *Communiqué on the Joint Meeting of the Political Committee of the Central Committee of the Workers' Party of Korea and the Central People's Committee of the Democratic People's Republic of Korea* (Pyongyang, June 1980), p. 2.

53. Kim Il Sung's speech to the Sixth KWP Congress, October 10, 1980 (*FBIS*, October 15, 1980, p. D14).

54. See, for example, Foreign Minister Ho Tam's speech to the nonaligned foreign ministers conference at Belgrade in July 1978 (*FBIS*, July 31, 1978, pp. D1–D6).

55. Kim Il Sung's speech to the Sixth KWP Congress (*FBIS*, October 15, 1980, p. D13). In North Korean rhetoric, the term "dominating forces" refers to any country outside the nonaligned movement that seeks to dominate a member of that movement by force or by more subtle means. When used together with "imperialists," as in the formula "imperialists and dominationists," the terms generally refer to the United States and the Soviet Union.

56. North Korea explicitly opposed the invasion of Kampuchea by Vietnamese forces. Although it has not publicly criticized the Soviet military occupation of Afghanistan, its opposition is implicit in its condemnation of such behavior by the superpowers. See Chapter 8.

57. *FBIS*, October 5, 1983, pp. D12–D19.

58. *FBIS*, September 13, 1985, p. D11.

59. According to a South Korean diplomat, the ROK had not planned in advance to propose Seoul as the venue for the next meeting and had done no advance lobbying. Consequently, the North Koreans were caught by surprise. They tried desperately to get the decision postponed, but failed.

60. *Korea Herald*, April 28 and 30, 1983. The North Korean ambassador, in a public statement on his departure defending his action, claimed that it was an ancient custom in his country to give friends presents on their birthdays, but the Finnish government apparently thought that $5,000 was too generous. In an ironic footnote to this episode, Johannes Virolainen, speaker of the Finnish parliament and target of the bribe offer, lost his seat in an election and therefore had to resign his position as IPU president just before the April IPU meeting (*Korea Herald*, April 21, 1983).

61. *FBIS*, July 28, 1983, pp. D11–D14.

62. *FBIS*, September 19, 1983, pp. D7–D8.

63. *FBIS*, September 20, 1983, p. D7.

64. *Korea Herald*, October 4, 1983. An officer of the U.S. Embassy in Moscow told me that the embassy believed the Soviets would have gone, had the KAL incident not occurred.

65. *FBIS*, October 4, 1983, pp. D1–D5.

66. Jae Kyu Park, "North Korea's Policy Toward the Third World: The Military Dimension," pp. 94–95.

67. International Institute for Strategic Studies, *Military Balance, 1985–1986* (London: International Institute for Strategic Studies, Autumn 1985), p. 127.

68. See table, Appendix 3.

69. *New York Times*, June 12, 1983.

70. *New York Times*, December 19, 1982, quoting U.S. Defense department analysts. *The Wall Street Journal*, May 2, 1984, quotes estimates of North Korea's foreign exchange earnings from arms sales to Iran ranging from "hundreds of millions" to $3 billion annually. These estimates are much higher than those of the U.S. Arms Control and Disarmament Agency, which lists North Korea's total arms exports for 1981 at $612 million and for 1982 at $650 million; see *World Military Expenditures and Arms Transfers, 1985* (Washington, D.C.: U.S. Arms Control and Disarmament Agency, August 1985), p. 111.

71. *Washington Post*, April 3, 1984.

72. *Korea Herald*, November 12, 1983.

73. *Korea Herald*, July 31, 1985; *FBIS*, August 29, 1985, p. D9.

74. *Korea Herald*, July 12, 1985; *FBIS*, July 11, 1985, p. D1, and July 30, 1985, p. D6.

75. *New York Times*, March 6, 1983, and May 1, 1984.

76. *FBIS*, April 27, 1984, p. D13; *Korea Herald*, February 26, 1985.

77. *Korea Herald*, March 11, 1986.

78. *Far Eastern Economic Review*, December 3, 1982.

79. *New York Times*, October 27, 1985.

80. *Korea Herald*, January 8, 1984.

81. *Korea Herald*, March 14 and 23, 1986.

82. U.S. Arms Control and Disarmament Agency, *World Military Expenditures and Arms Transfers, 1985*, pp. 89–130.

83. Chung-in Moon and Kwang Il Baek, "Loyalty, Voice or Exit? The U.S. Third-Country Arms Sales Regulation and ROK Countervailing Strategies," in *Journal of Northeast Asian Studies* 4, no. 1 (Spring 1985):27.

84. Ibid., p. 33.

10

Beyond Diplomacy

The intense international rivalry between the two Koreas has extended far beyond the realm of formal diplomacy. Their efforts to achieve wider recognition of their legitimacy and to gain greater international support for their positions in the North-South confrontation have given a political tinge to almost all of their relations with foreign countries. Even the ostensibly nonpolitical sports arena has become highly politicized since South Korea won the right to host the Asian Games in 1986 and the Olympic Games in 1988. South Korea's larger and more dynamic economy and the openness of its society to ouside contacts have given it a great advantage in making itself known through a wide variety of mainly private channels. North Korea has been handicapped in developing a broad range of contacts by its reclusiveness and its obsession with ideology.

The Economic Sphere

South Koreans speak with great confidence of their large and growing economic lead over North Korea, particularly in foreign trade. In 1984 South Korea's external trade reached $60 billion, compared to North Korea's $2.7 billion.[1] The disparity in trade, large as it is, falls far short of reflecting the difference in trade-related contacts abroad. South Korea's export-led economy has demanded the aggressive pursuit of foreign markets. Exporters have welcomed droves of foreign buyers to help their factories turn out internationally competitive products and have sent many of their own people abroad to push sales, study markets, and learn foreign manufacturing techniques. This process has created an immense network of relationships between South Korea and the outside world. North Korea, instead of looking outward for ways to promote economic development, has been one of the most inward-looking of nations. It has traded principally with the Soviet bloc and China, exporting mainly primary products. Such trade, carried on pursuant to agreements negotiated by government officials on each side, has minimized the need for personal contacts between North Koreans and outsiders. It is a trading process well-suited to protecting the people of North Korea from undesired outside influences, but ill-suited to making the people and products of North Korea widely known throughout the world.

South Korea has cultivated foreign economic contacts not only through trade, but also through a variety of other activities: construction contracts, investment, shipping and air transport, fisheries, training of foreign students, and sending skilled labor abroad. North Korea has engaged in similar activities, but on a much smaller scale and its activities have received much less worldwide publicity than those of South Korea.

Construction Contracts

During the past twenty years South Korean construction firms have become known throughout the world for the low cost, speed, and reliability of their work. Overseas construction began in 1965 with a highway project in Thailand, followed by various projects in Vietnam, financed by the United States. In the late 1970s, taking advantage of the construction boom in the oil-rich Middle Eastern states, South Korea's overseas construction took off. By 1980 its construction firms were second only to the United States in the volume of orders received worldwide. Construction orders reached a peak in 1981 of $13.7 billion, after which they declined as oil prices fell, dropping to about $6 billion in 1984.[2]

All has not been rosy in the overseas construction business, particularly since the pool of funds in the main arena, the Middle East, began to contract. Cutthroat competition and delays in receiving payment brought losses to some South Korean companies and forced many of the smaller firms to withdraw from the bidding. Saudi Arabia, the largest user of foreign construction firms, began to divert an increasing share of contracts to Saudi companies. Despite these difficulties, South Korean construction firms, after a period of regrouping, remain among the leading contenders in that highly competitive market.[3]

Overseas construction created for South Korea an exceptional number and variety of connections with foreign countries, far outstripping those developed by North Korea from similar activities. North Korea has yet to gain a foothold in anticommunist Saudi Arabia's huge construction market, whereas it has been surpassed by South Korean firms in Libya, where they are building cement, power, and desalination plants. In 1983 Dong Ah Construction won a $3.3 billion contract to build two concrete

pipe plants, lay 1,900 kilometers of underground water pipe, and build
1,700 kilometers of road in Libya's massive project to bring water from
the interior to the coastal region.[4] South Korean construction projects
in Libya not only have exceeded those of North Korea in size and
numbers of Koreans employed, but also in technological sophistication.

International connections developed through construction contracts
have not been limited to the contacts with the country where the work
is being performed. Often they involved collaboration with construction
firms of other countries. For example, Dong Ah Construction learned
of the Libyan project from the U.S. firm that designed it, Brown and
Root, with which Dong Ah had worked earlier. Another U.S. firm, Price
Brothers Company, is providing technical assistance in the construction
of the cement pipe factories. At least ten Austrian firms have engaged
in third-country projects with Korean firms, including the construction
of a rolling mill in Libya.[5] South Korean construction firms have
continually upgraded their technical expertise through working with
technologically more advanced U.S. and West European companies.
Another channel for foreign contacts has been the employment of
increasing numbers of foreign laborers by Korean firms as the cost of
Korean labor rose. In 1983 South Korean companies may have employed
as many as 50,000 nationals from Southeast Asian countries on their
overseas construction contracts, together with 170,000 Koreans.[6]

Investment

Another means through which South Koreans have expanded their
international connections is equity investment abroad. Such investments
began in 1968 and by the middle of 1985 totalled $458 million.[7] Although
the amount is not large compared to the foreign investments of major
industrial nations, the willingness of a substantial number of firms to
risk capital in direct investments abroad reflects an increasingly sophisticated understanding of world economic conditions and growing
confidence in the ability of Koreans to establish productive working
relationships with foreign countries. The government has encouraged
foreign investment, especially in mining and oil drilling, by making
available investment loans through the Export-Import Bank, the Korean
Mining Promotion Corporation, and the Oil Development Fund, as well
as by granting tax advantages and providing foreign investment insurance.

Most South Korean investment has gone to North America, Australia,
and Southeast Asia, with smaller amounts in the Middle East, Central
and South America, and Africa. Nearly half of the total amount invested
is in mining and forestry projects. These include iron ore and coal
production in Australia, coal projects in the United States and Canada,

and forest products in Indonesia. A South Korean firm, KODECO, in a joint venture with Indonesia's state-run Pertamina, discovered offshore oil and gas in commercial quantitites; the first oil shipment from this deposit arrived in Korea in 1984. Four other South Korean firms, in a joint venture with a U.S. firm, are engaged in offshore drilling in North Yemen. South Korean petrochemical firms have entered into joint ventures in Saudi Arabia and Indonesia to produce chemicals and fertilizer. South Korean manufacturers of color television sets, threatened by protectionist measures, have established wholly owned subsidiaries to manufacture these products in the United States, Portugal, and West Germany.

International Economic Organizations

South Korea's extensive involvement in world trade (it was ranked twelfth in exports and fourteenth in imports in 1984) has led to its participation in a wide array of international economic organizations.

An example is the World Trade Centers Association, which South Korea joined in 1972. In 1976 Seoul hosted the General Assembly of this organization, attended by 100 delegates from 40 countries. In 1981 South Korean delegates attended the General Assembly held in Moscow, together with over 200 participants from 30 countries. North Korea was not a member of this organization and did not participate in the Moscow conference.[8]

In March 1985 Seoul hosted the annual conference of the International Chamber of Commerce, attended by some 250 business leaders from 40 countries. In April of the same year, the Pacific Economic Cooperation Conference met in Seoul to continue its ongoing discussion of economic cooperation in the Pacific region, participated in by national committees from 14 member countries composed of representatives from government, business, and academia. In September 1985, 400 insurance experts from 20 countries met in Seoul at the 12th Pacific Insurance Conference. In April 1984 South Korea was represented at the Washington meeting of the Confederation of International Contracting Associations (CICA), which has 54 member countries. A number of South Korean construction firms have been admitted to the International Construction Group, affiliated with the CICA.

The examples mentioned are only a few of the many international economic organizations in which South Koreans participate. North Korea belongs to few such organizations, but its participation probably will increase as it strives to enlarge its trade. For example, in September 1985 Pyongyang held a seminar on aviation and engineering insurance attended by companies belonging to the Federation of Afro-Asian Insurers and Reinsurers, as well as by representatives from nonmember companies in West Germany, Belgium, France, Britain, Italy, the Soviet Union, and Eastern European countries. Altogether 23 nations were represented at the seminar.[9]

Fisheries

South Korea's distant-water fishing fleet, ranging throughout the oceans of the world, has been an important means of developing links with other nations. From 1971 through 1980, South Korea ranked third among distant-water fishing nations, after Japan and the Soviet Union, in the total tonnage of fish caught in distant waters and home waters combined. In 1985 it had 650 fishing vessels, of which 290 operated in the Pacific Ocean, 230 in the Atlantic Ocean, and 130 in the Indian Ocean. Overseas fishing bases included Capetown (South Africa), Karachi (Pakistan), Wellington (New Zealand), Las Palmas (Morocco), Quboos (Oman), Ensenada (United States), and Port of Spain (Suriname).[10]

During the past ten years, South Korean vessels have been excluded from many of their customary distant-water fishing grounds, as state after state proclaimed a 200-mile exclusive fishing zone in its coastal waters, an action accepted in international law by the 1982 UN Law of the Sea Convention. In order to continue fishing in such waters, South Korea had to negotiate fisheries agreements with the coastal states, which specified the conditions for the operation of Korean fishing vessels in these areas and the fees to be paid for the privilege. In 1983 the ROK paid $22 million for fishing rights, about $10 million of this going to the United States. It has formal fishing agreements with a dozen nations and has reached informal temporary arrangements with 15 others.

In order to facilitate entry into foreign fishing zones, South Korea has entered into 15 joint venture projects, mostly with U.S. companies. To smooth relations with developing countries, it has offered training and has donated vessels and equipment to some countries, including the Maldives, the Ivory Coast, and Kiribati. One hundred nineteen fishermen from 38 countries have received training in South Korea's fishery institutes.[11] Under a joint venture arrangement with an Argentine firm, 122 fishing households were to emigrate to Argentina by 1987 to fish in Argentine waters.

Thus, the far-flung operations of South Korea's fishing fleet have provided another means for the state to make itself known throughout the world. Since the widespread adoption of exclusive 200-mile fishing zones, its distant-water fisheries have become less profitable. The catch has declined and fees have cut into the profits. The foreigner's impression of South Korea may not be uniformly favorable when, for example, the occasional Korean fishing boat is caught fishing in prohibited waters or negotiators cannot agree on the fee for fishing privileges. Nevertheless, the scope of South Korea's distant-water fisheries operations gives it a distinct advantage over North Korea in establishing itself as a well-known actor in the world community.

North Korea fishes intensively in nearby waters, but does not have a distant-water fishing fleet. In 1983 it ranked thirteenth among the nations of the world in total catch, with 1,600,000 metric tons, whereas the ROK ranked eighth with 2,400,387.[12] North Korea's principal fishing ground is the East Sea of Korea where it operates "tens of thousands" of fishing vessels, including factory ships, refrigerator ships, and trawlers up to 3,750 tons.[13] It has drawn on its fisheries expertise to cement relations with at least one Third World country, Ethiopia, where it agreed to help design and build fishing boats.[14]

Economic Aid, Training, and Study Abroad

The Koreas have competed for influence on developing countries by extending relatively small amounts of grant and loan aid. Lack of data makes comparison of the two programs difficult. In 1978 South Korea programmed $1.5 million in grant aid in the form of commodities, such as automobiles and marine engines, to countries in Asia, Africa, Latin America, and the Middle East. The government planned to increase such aid to $10 million by 1983.[15] North Korean aid during the 1970s and early 1980s went to 23 countries, mostly in Africa and often in the form of loans at low or no interest. The North Koreans specialized in labor-intensive projects providing immediate benefits to people, such as irrigation works, rice-processing mills, rural housing, health clinics, civic centers, gymnasiums, and light industrial plants. They also made some cash grants and gifts of relief goods to disaster victims.[16] Some small countries took advantage of the competition between Seoul and Pyongyang in order to extort aid from both in exchange for diplomatic recognition. Some South Korean diplomats grumbled that being squeezed this way by tiny states cost more than it was worth.

Countries short of particular kinds of skilled labor hired large numbers of Koreans, mainly from South Korea. In addition to the South Koreans working on construction projects in the Middle East, more than 700 South Korean nurses worked in hospitals in Saudi Arabia until a dispute about overtime pay in early 1983 caused some of them to leave.[17] In the early 1970s about 12,000 Korean nurses went to West Germany to relieve a severe shortage there, but several thousand of these had to return home in the late 1970s, as more German nurses became available.[18] In 1978 South Korean doctors, nurses, and tae kwon do instructors were working in Libya. Nearly 30,000 Korean seamen were working on foreign flag carriers in 1984.[19]

South Korea added to the reputation of its skilled labor by winning in the International Youth Skill Olympics year after year. In this contest teams of skilled workers compete in activities such as carpentry, plumbing, television repair, pipe-laying, welding, machine designing, lathe operation, and gold and silver craftsmanship. At the 28th annual competition in Osaka in October 1985, the Korean team took first place for the sixth year in a row, beating second-place Japan, which had dominated this competition in the 1960s and 1970s, and third-place Switzerland. No Communist countries participated in this event.[20]

Little information is available on North Koreans working abroad. They are probably much fewer in number than the South Koreans, partly because of a shortage of labor in North Korea and partly because of Pyongyang's disinclination to expose many of its people to conditions abroad. The largest numbers probably are in Libya, working on construction projects, and in the Soviet Far East, engaged in lumbering. Pyongyang has sent technical advisers to various small projects in African states and has exchanged mining engineers with Indonesia.

Another area in which the two Koreas compete is in the exchange of persons for training and education. Both have been active in inviting trainees from Third World countries for training in Korea and in sending specialists to conduct training abroad.

Third World trainees have studied in South Korea under a variety of programs. In 1983 alone, some 800 persons from nearly 80 countries received some form of training. The state-operated Agricultural Development Corporation, which also provides technical assistance and consulting services abroad, by 1984 had trained 379 agricultural technicians from 46 countries and had given 970 government officials and others from 21 countries tours of agricultural development projects in South Korea.[21] The ROK has also trained large numbers in industrial technology, including shipbuilding, construction, heavy industry, and energy. In addition to those trainees funded by the South Korean government, others have received training in programs funded by their own governments, by the United Nations, and by private Korean firms. An example of the latter was the training of 220 Libyans by Hyundai Engineering and Construction Company to operate a power and desalinization plant under construction by that company. Training was to take place in both South Korea and Libya between 1984 and 1987.[22]

In an unusual and extensive program the West German government has aided vocational and technical training in South Korea since 1962, contributing funds and technical specialists to establish and operate the Korean-German Vocational Training Institute in Pusan and 14 other vocational training institutes throughout the country. Bonn also provided funds and teachers for the Changwon Industrial Masters' College, established in 1979. In addition, several hundred skilled workers and vocational training institute teachers have gone through training courses in Germany.[23]

A different form of interaction was the International Development Exchange Program inaugurated in 1982 by the Korean Development Institute. This program arranged forums in Seoul at which officials and experts from developing countries and Korea presented papers and exchanged views. Examples were the forum on Economic Development and Development Strategy held in 1983 and attended by representatives from 11 African countries and the forum on Industrialization and Rural-Urban Linkages, which drew participants from 20 Latin American and Asian countries.[24]

In addition to those foreigners who visit South Korea for technical training or exchanges of view on economic development, activities that are conducted in a foreign language, usually English, a handful of foreigners go to Korea to study Korean language and culture. The reverse flow—Koreans who go abroad for their education—is enormous. In 1984 more than 20,000 persons from South Korea were studying in 48 foreign countries, about half of them in the United States.

Data are lacking on the numbers of Third World technicians brought to North Korea for training or trained by North Korean experts in their own countries. The paucity of reports on such activities in the Pyongyang media, including the principal propaganda monthly printed in English, *Korea Today*, suggests that the numbers are not large. A small number of scholars from the Soviet Union, China, and East European countries are known to have studied the Korean language in Pyongyang. The North Koreans have also sent small numbers of students to the Soviet Union, China, Guyana, and some Eastern European countries. The numbers cannot be more than a small fraction of the number of South Koreans studying abroad, considering that North Korean students in the Soviet Union only recently increased from below 100 to 700.

Transportation, Tourism, and Conventions

Indices of North Korea's limited interchange of goods and persons with the outside world are the small size of its merchant fleet and international airline compared to those of South Korea. North Korea in 1984 had 700,000 tons of oceangoing cargo ships, compared to South Korea's 7.3 million tons. The South Korean merchant fleet carried 46 percent of outgoing and incoming freight, while North Korea's carried only 21 percent.[25]

The contrast between the two Koreas in international air travel is even greater than in ocean shipping. Korean Air, the South Korean international air carrier, is the eighth largest in the world. It operates 38 aircraft, more than two-thirds of them the wide-bodied Boeing 747s, DC-10s, and A-300 Airbuses. It flies to 30 cities in 20 countries, including Tokyo, Los Angeles, New York, Hong Kong, Bangkok, Colombo, Jidda, Paris, Amsterdam, and Zurich. In 1980 it carried nearly 3 million passengers on its international routes. It also transported over 200,000 tons of cargo, mostly on international routes. Kimpo International Airport at Seoul has the capacity to handle 4.8 million passengers annually, and it is being expanded so as to be able to handle 9 million by the 1988 Olympic Games.[26] Seven foreign airlines fly to South Korea, and 36 maintain offices or sales agents in Seoul.

Until 1977 North Korea's civil air fleet consisted entirely of propeller-driven aircraft. In the late 1970s it acquired three Soviet TU-154 jet aircraft and has used an IL-62 four-engine jet to bring visitors in for special events.[27] The only regular international flights flown by North Korea are to Moscow, Peking, and Khabarovsk. In 1980 the North Korean airline flew once a week to Peking and the Chinese Aviation Administration of China (CAAC) flew once a week to Pyongyang. Only two foreign airlines offered service to Pyongyang: CAAC and Aeroflot. The North Koreans often brought in high-level visitors by charter flights. Presumably, the civil air agreements signed with Kampuchea and Libya in 1977 and 1978 specified the reciprocal arrangements for such charter flights. The Kampuchean government with which that agreement was signed no longer exists in Pnom Penh, and no regular service has been established between Libya and North Korea by the airline of either country. No figures are available on the number of passengers carried annually by North Korean airlines on international flights or on the number of passengers using Pyongyang's airport. But given the small number of planes and routes and the infrequency of service, the figures must be very small. Those who have seen Pyongyang's airport remark on the small scale of the terminal and the absence of the bustle of people associated with modern-day airports.

The quietness of Pyongyang's airport in contrast to the milling crowds at Kimpo is related in part to the absence of any large-scale tourist travel to North Korea. Groups of Soviet and East European tourists do visit the scenic spots in North Korea, but the total numbers cannot be large, or they would quickly overflow the few hotels and restaurants available. They could equal only a tiny fraction of the 1.4 million foreigners who visited South Korea in 1985.

South Korea has courted foreign tourists for years as a means of earning foreign exchange and of making Korea better known in the world. Tourist trade brought in an estimated $704 million in the first eleven months of 1985.[28] The Korea National Tourism Corporation has offices in the United States, Europe, and elsewhere dedicated to boosting tourist travel. In 1983 Seoul hosted 3,000 delegates attending the 53d congress of the American Society of Travel Agents at a six-day meeting largely devoted to promoting tourism in Korea. Delegates to the congress came from more than one hundred countries, including four Eastern European states. By a cruel irony, the congress took place less than a month after the Soviets had shot down the KAL civil airliner with tourists aboard.

In a rare public reference to tourism in North Korea, an English language broadcast of the Korean Central News Agency in July 1986 predicted (without giving any numbers) that tourist visits in 1986 would be twice those of 1985. The report stated that the visitors would come from socialist countries, and from Finland, Britain, West Germany, Hong Kong, and elsewhere. It added that airport capacity was to be markedly increased, that additional hotels would be built in Pyongyang, and that "tourist hotels with tens of thousands of beds" would appear in Wonsan.[29]

An increase in tourism on a significant scale would require substantial expenditures for new hotels, tourist buses, restaurants, training of interpreters, and the expansion of money-changing services. It would also require a great increase in air service to and from Pyongyang, including flights by additional foreign airlines. Local handicrafts or other products that tourists might like to buy would have to be developed and produced in quantity.[30] Most difficult of all, the North Koreans would have to overcome their fear of allowing foreigners to wander about unescorted. All this would require a radical change in the mind-set of North Korea's leaders, but without it they are ceding to South Korea without a contest one of the most effective ways of making their country known abroad.

Since 1981 when Seoul was selected as the site for the 1988 Olympic Games, South Korea has hosted international gatherings in increasing numbers. Including sports events, which will be discussed below, some 95 international meetings of all kinds drew 20,000 foreign visitors in 1985, including the World Bank/IMF meeting, the 22d general assembly of the Asian-Pacific Broadcasting Union, and the World Leasing Association's general assembly. Among events scheduled for 1986 were the 11th Asian-Pacific Labor Ministers' Conference and the 31st Asian-Pacific Film Festival.[31] The additional hotels and other facilities being built in preparation for the Asian Games and the Olympic Games augmented Seoul's capability for hosting international conferences. The city was increasingly being recognized around the world as a suitable place for international organizations to hold their meetings.

Pyongyang is handicapped as an international convention center, as it is for tourism, by the shortage of first-class hotels and restaurants and by the difficulty of access by air. North Korea tried but failed to get Pyongyang selected for the 1986 summit conference of the nonaligned nations. International conferences in Pyongyang have been almost exclusively those organized by North Korea itself to advance its political purposes. In order to compete effectively with Seoul as an international conference center, the North Koreans would not only have to greatly improve Pyongyang's facilities, but also drop their opposition to the participation of South Korean delegations in such meetings. Otherwise, North Koreans will rule Pyongyang out as a conference site for the large number of world and regional organizations to which South Koreans belong.

Politics and Ideology

An activity monopolized by North Korea is the organization of groups abroad dedicated to promoting its ideology and its position on unification. South Korea has utilized the usual tools of national promotion: newsletters; a weekly magazine, *Korea Newsreview;* and glossy brochures on the occasion of President Chun Doo Hwan's visits abroad. The *Korea Herald*, an English-language daily newspaper comes out in a U.S. edition.

North Korean counterparts include a monthly magazine, *Korea Today,* and the English-language *Pyongyang Times.* But North Korea goes beyond such public relations activities in establishing and publicizing groups abroad that express support for Kim Il Sung's proposals on unification and the *chu che* philosophy.

The campaign to demonstrate widespread foreign support for North Korea's position on unification began with a World Conference for the Independent and Peaceful Reunification of Korea, held in Brussels in February 1978. The conference, said to have been attended by 170 persons from 68 countries, had the declared aim of arousing world public opinion, "notably the public opinion of West European and North American countries which are not well informed of the Korean question," to the tragic situation of divided Korea. It adopted a series of resolutions in support of the North Korean position, reiterating the standard demand for the withdrawal of U.S. forces and the conclusion of a peace treaty between Pyongyang and Washington, denouncing the South Korean government, and expressing support for "the patriotic struggle of the South Korean people for democratic freedom." The organizing committee for the conference despatched a letter to Kim Il Sung reporting on its accomplishments and sent letters to various heads of state and government transmitting copies of the resolutions.[32]

Beyond Diplomacy

Many of those who attended the conference were members of Communist parties in various countries or representatives of Communist-dominated organizations, such as the World Peace Council and the World Federation of Trade Unions. Among the noncommunists who attended was Hideo Den, at that time director of the international department of the Japanese Socialist Party.

The Brussels conference resulted in the formation of an International Liaison Committee for the Independent and Peaceful Reunification of Korea with a permanent secretariat in Paris. The committee held an initial conference in Algiers in June 1977 and a second conference in Paris in May 1978. The latter produced a lengthy white paper in support of North Korea's position. In November 1978 a Second World Conference for the Reunification of Korea was held in Tokyo, reportedly attended by 504 delegates from 60 countries and 12 international organizations, which adopted a resolution supporting the North Korean position on reunification.[33] In 1979 the International Liaison Committee launched a signature campaign in support of North Korea and claimed that by November of that year it had collected 580 million signatures.[34]

The International Liaison Committee has continued to function over the years, modifying its activities to suit the latest developments. For example, in March 1984 it sponsored an international conference in support of Pyongyang's tripartite talks proposal. In March 1985 it joined with the World Peace Council to cosponsor in Paris an "emergency international conference for removing the danger of war and achieving peace in Korea and her peaceful reunification," attended by representatives of some 25 mainly Communist-dominated international organizations. In October 1985, Kim Il Sung received an 8-member delegation of the International Liaison Committee, including Guy Dupre, its secretary-general; Stanley Faulkner, chairman of the U.S. Lawyers' Committee on Korea; and Alfonso Gianni, Communist member of the Italian parliament and one of the leaders of the Italian Committee for Supporting the Reunification of Korea. In Tokyo in December 1985, 900 persons attended the fourth national meeting of the movement to support Korean reunification. Among those attending were Makoto Ishikawa, vice chairman of the International Liaison Committee; Han Dok Su, the chairman of Chosoren; and Akira Iwai, the chairman of the Japanese Committee for Supporting the Independent and Peaceful Reunification of Korea.[35]

Promotion of support for North Korea's position on reunification is closely linked with international front organizations engaged in promoting other causes espoused by the Soviet Union and its Communist allies. The many *chu che* study groups established in various countries, on the other hand, are a uniquely North Korean enterprise, probably disdained by orthodox Marxist-Leninists. For example, a Marxist from

Sierra Leone, who had been one of the founders of the Sierra Leone–North Korea Friendship Society in 1969 and had attended a two-month course in Pyongyang on the *chu che* idea in 1981, later wrote in the Sierra Leone newspaper, *The New Citizen*, that *chu che* was not a scientific doctrine and was unsuited to Africa.[36] Meetings of *chu che* study groups, especially in Japan, and visits to Pyongyang by leaders of such groups are reported regularly in the Pyongyang media. North Korea claims to have a combined total of 1,500 *chu che* study groups, solidarity committees for Korean reunification, and friendship associations in 118 countries.

North Korea has made a special effort to influence foreign media. The most ambitious and expensive affair was hosting the World Conference of Journalists against Imperialism and for Friendship and Peace in July 1983. The 169 delegations from 118 countries and 17 international organizations included delegations from the Soviet Union, the United States, China, Japan, and a large number of Third World countries. The conference predictably demanded that the United States stop military exercises in Korea, withdraw its troops and nuclear weapons, dismantle military bases, turn the Korean peninsula into a nonnuclear zone, and replace the armistice with a peace treaty.[37]

In August–September 1984 North Korea invited journalists from 14 Third World countries to a three-week training course. In January 1985 it announced the establishment of a permanent International Journalists Training Center, where it held the first training course for four weeks in May–June. Most of the 39 participants came from Africa, with a sprinkling from the Middle East, Asia, and Latin America. According to the Pyongyang media, the participants wrote Kim Chong Il that they were deeply impressed with the greatness of the *chu che* idea that they had learned about in the course.[38]

Not all who attended Third World journalists' conferences in Pyongyang were favorably impressed. An Egyptian journalist, writing in the weekly, *Rose el Youssef*, complained that he and his colleagues were the only genuine journalists in the group. He found that the conference consisted of lectures on *chu che* and speeches lauding the North Korean leadership read by certain foreign participants but written for them by the North Koreans. He declined a request by the North Koreans to write a poem to present to Kim Il Sung.[39]

The North Koreans have enlisted a number of foreign authors to sing the praises of Kim Il Sung and Kim Chong Il in books and poems published in foreign languages. Examples are *Juche Korea* by a Japanese writer (in Japanese), *The Sun of the World* by a Syrian (in Arabic), and *Juche Korea* by a Tanzanian (in English). *Korea Today* regularly carries sycophantic poems by foreign writers, nearly all from Third World countries, but at least one European, a Finn, also has been published.[40]

Attempts to obtain favorable publicity in Western Europe and the United States have not been very successful. North Korean officials have expressed disappointment with the accounts written by Western correspondents admitted to North Korea. A television film shown by a Swedish journalist after a visit to North Korea was harshly attacked as "an intolerable provocation against the Korean people and an outright insult to our country."[41] For a time, Pyongyang resorted to buying space in major Western newspapers to publish in fine print lengthy speeches by Kim Il Sung. The few readers who noticed them reacted more with amusement than admiration. A full-page advertisement in the *New York Times* in October 1985 announced that "Korea has given birth to one more hero" and plugged a new biography of Kim Chong Il as "The book you have been waiting for—now on sale—a must."[42]

How effective North Korea's organizational and public relations activities abroad are in gaining sympathy and support for its cause is difficult to judge. They certainly have made its concerns better known among the foreign Communist and left-wing activists who have participated. Whether they have much impact beyond these limited circles is doubtful. Such conferences, declarations, and study groups in support of North Korea are rarely mentioned in the major news media of the countries where meetings were held. Some Third World countries, particularly the smaller African countries, may be more easily impressed, especially if the organizational and public relations activities are complemented by economic or military aid programs and a judicious selection of persons to visit North Korea.

Sports

In the modern era competition in sporting events has become one of the chief methods by which nations vie for attention and prestige. With the advent of worldwide television hookups, major world athletic events, such as the Olympic Games and World Cup soccer matches, attract millions of viewers. Inevitably, the international rivalry between the two Koreas has come to include sports. When the International Olympic Committee chose Seoul as the site for the 1988 games, competition intensified.

Evolution of Sports Competition

During the 1960s and early 1970s, sports were a minor element in North-South rivalry. The two Koreas took part in relatively few international events. North Korean athletes competed mainly with those from other Communist countries. South Koreans occasionally entered matches in Eastern Europe, for example, the World Women's Basketball Tournament in Prague in 1965 and the World Table Tennis Championship in Ljubljana, Yugoslavia, in the same year. Few Korean athletes were up to international standards, and neither Seoul nor Pyongyang was prepared to host world tournaments.

After 1973, when South Korea announced that it was prepared to open its doors to nonhostile Communist states, sports exchanges began to take on greater political significance. Some sports organizations and facilities in South Korea had developed sufficiently so that Seoul could host world championships. When it did so, it extended invitations to North Korea, the Soviet Union and Eastern European states. North Korea feared that participation in sports events in Seoul by Communist states, which had no diplomatic relations with Seoul, would add to South Korea's prestige and strengthen its claim to legitimacy. Consequently, Pyongyang refused to participate in sports events in Seoul and put pressure on other Communist states to follow its example. As a result, Communist states turned down several invitations from South Korea.

As South Korea became more active in the sports world and hosted more important international events, refusal by Communist states to participate began to exact a price. Their athletes were forced to forgo competing in such important contests in Seoul as the 42d World Shooting Championship in October 1978 in which 1,300 contestants from 71 nations took part, and the 8th World Women's Basketball Championship in May 1979. Moreover, their willingness to inject political criteria into decisions on sports participation made the world athletic community less inclined to choose their nationals to serve on governing bodies of athletic federations. The general assembly of the International Shooting Union barred from its leadership nationals of those countries that had refused to go to Seoul: the Soviet Union, Romania, Yugoslavia, East Germany, and Poland.[43]

In 1979 Pyongyang had its first opportunity to host an important international athletic event, the 35th World Table Tennis Championships. It delayed inviting South Korea until two months before the tournament, when it suddenly proposed that the two Koreas form a joint team. After four meetings the two sides were unable to reach agreement on a joint team, and it became clear that Pyongyang did not intend to admit to separate South Korean team. The South Korean team traveled to Geneva to apply for visas and for passage to Pyongyang on the charter flight arranged by North Korea for foreign athletes, but they were refused visas. The South Koreans urged the United States not to participate, but the U.S. team, already en route to Pyongyang before the final rejection of South Korea was evident, was unwilling to withdraw at the last moment.

Thus, the two Koreas had adopted radically different policies toward sports events held in the rival capital. South Korea welcomed all comers, including North Korea and the Communist states. It had no objection to the United States and other friendly countries competing in events in Pyongyang, so long as it was not excluded. North Korea not only refused to admit South Korean teams but urged Communist countries to stay away from Seoul.

Pyongyang's monopolistic attitude toward the hosting of world sports championships in Korea worked to its disadvantage. Since 1979 it has not been chosen again as the venue for a major world sports championship. Its lack of popularity can be accounted for only in part by the fact that it has been less active in world athletic competition than South Korea. Its known unwillingness to admit South Korean teams practically ruled it out as a host for games sponsored by organizations to which South Korea belonged. Moreover, few sports figures were impressed by North Korean allegations that the "fascist and dictatorial rule" in South Korea and "the military rackets launched almost daily" made Seoul an unsuitable locale for athletic competitions.[44] During the 1980s the Communist countries were no longer willing to pay the price of staying away from competition in Seoul. Their athletes, including some from the Soviet Union and China, began to show up at contests there.

As sports rivalry between the two Koreas intensified, they took part with increasing frequency in competitions around the world. East European countries, even though declining until the 1980s to compete in Seoul, did not hesitate to invite South Korean athletes to contests that they sponsored. South Korean teams appeared at the 18th World Gymnastics Competition in Sofia in 1974, the summer Universiad at Bucharest in 1981, the Women's World Handball Championships at Budapest in 1982, the World Amateur Baseball Championship at Havana in 1984, and at a number of other contests in Eastern Europe. The North Koreans did not send a team to the 1981 Universiad at Bucharest, offering the curious excuse that its college students were too busy taking examinations.

Although no matches between North Korean and South Korean teams took place in Korea, they found themselves pitted against each other with increasing frequency at matches abroad as their participation in international sports increased. In such matches the players battled with heightened emotion and determination. As early as 1974 North Korea bested South Korea in gymnastics at the Asian Games in Tehran, at which North Korea came in third and South Korea fourth. In 1976 the two Koreas clashed for the first time in soccer, at the 18th Asian Youth

Soccer Championship in Bangkok. When the North Korean team blanked South Korea 1–0 and tied with Iran for the gold medal, Pyongyang radio proudly reported that its players had fought "a powerful ideology battle, fighting spirit battle, speed battle, and technique battle."[45]

Competition in table tennis was particularly spirited, perhaps because the South Koreans, feeling that they had been unfairly excluded from the competition in Pyongyang in 1979, redoubled their efforts to excel. The South Korean women's team won first place at the 5th World Collegiate Table Tennis Championships in Gdansk, Poland, in September 1984, but the North Koreans beat the South Koreans at the 7th Asian Table Tennis Championships in October. At the 38th World Table Tennis Championships at Gothenburg, Sweden, in April 1985, both the South Korean men's and women's teams lost to the North Koreans. A North Korean sports official said that his country had made table tennis a "strategic sport" in which 100,000 members of table tennis clubs throughout the country competed annually in regional and national championships in order to qualify to represent North Korea in international meets.[46] In the world rankings announced by the International Table Tennis Federation in May 1985, individual South Korean men and women players ranked higher than the North Koreans, although all the Koreans were outranked by the world champion Chinese men and women players.[47]

South Korean participation in international athletics increased rapidly in the 1980s, and South Korean athletes were establishing themselves as formidable competitors in some sports. In 1983 South Korean wrestlers won gold medals at the Espoirs Freestyle Wrestling Championships in Los Angeles and the World Junior Amateur Wrestling Championships at Oak Lawn. At the World Cup Amateur Boxing Championships in Rome in 1983, a South Korean light flyweight boxer beat a Soviet boxer to take a gold medal. As might have been expected, the South Korean team came in first in its native sport at the 6th World Tae kwon do Championships in Copenhagen in 1983. In other notable wins, two South Korean women took first and second place in the 32d World Archery Championships in Long Beach in 1983, and the South Koreans won the women's singles, the men's doubles, and the mixed doubles at the Asian Amateur Tennis Championships in Hong Kong in the same year.

The North Koreans were also stepping up their sports activities, sponsoring international contests in 1981 and 1982 for a small number of countries in marathon, table tennis, boxing, gymnastics and soccer. They sent boxers, wrestlers, weightlifters, shooters, table tennis, and volleyball players to 42 events in 16 countries in 1982. South Korean teams or individual athletes took part in 381 events abroad that year.[48]

In November 1984, a North Korean athlete won three gold medals at the 16th Asian Weightlifting Championships in Tabriz, and in October 1985 at Melbourne the North Korean women's volleyball team qualified for the World Volleyball Championships. The North Koreans carried off several gold, silver, and bronze medals at the 13th Universiad in Kobe, Japan, in September 1985. In order to transport their athletes to the Universiad, the North Koreans for the first time received permission from the Japanese government to fly a charter aircraft into Japan.

A comparative study by the National Unification Board of sports activities of the two Koreas in 1984 concluded that North Korean athletes were superior in gymnastics, men's shooting, skating, and women's medium-range track events. South Koreans, according to the study, had the edge in basketball, volleyball, tennis, boxing, swimming, judo, wrestling, and archery; the two were about equal in soccer, table tennis, weightlifting, and boat racing.[49]

Nineteen eighty-five was a banner year for Seoul in hosting international sports meets, as South Korean sports officials and athletes sought to gain experience in preparation for the 1986 Asian Games and the 1988 Olympics. Seoul hosted the 7th World Tae kwon do Championships, the Asian Youth Gymnastics Competition, the World Target Archery Championships, the World Judo Championships, and the 4th World Cup Amateur Boxing Championships. Communist countries no longer held back. Soviet and East German boxers carried off half a dozen gold medals. The judo competition attracted contestants from the Soviet Union and seven East European countries. The Chinese swept the Asian Youth Gymnastics meet, with 16 gold medals to one each for South Korea and Japan. South Korea retained its first place in team standings in Tae kwon do. In addition to these major events, South Korea hosted a dozen lesser international sports competitions, including handball, field hockey, cycling, yachting, bowling, and horse jumping. The most exciting and gratifying sports event for the year was the soccer victory over Japan in November 1985, qualifying the South Korean team to play with 23 other teams in the World Cup finals in Mexico in 1986. In the less prestigious sport of basketball, the South Korean team edged out the Malaysians to qualify along with China and the Philippines to represent Asia in the World Cup finals in Spain in September 1986.

Asian Games

Next to the Olympic Games, the Asian Games are the most prestigious athletic event in which the two Koreas compete. South Korea first entered the games in 1954, and both have participated since at least the Tehran games in 1974. The energy that they poured into sports and the importance that they attached to winning made their participation in the 9th Asian Games in New Delhi in 1982 a climactic confrontation.

The two Koreas placed among the five most powerful sports nations in Asia, well behind China, the winner of the games, and Japan, the runner-up, but ahead of India, the host country. South Korea, which entered 20 of the 21 events, won decisively over North Korea, which entered only 15. South Korea won 93 medals (28 gold, 28 silver, and 37 bronze) compared to North Korea's 57 (17 gold, 19 silver, and 21 bronze).[50]

North Korea incurred worldwide notoriety for an incident during a soccer match, which detracted from its relatively impressive performance at the games. Infuriated by the Thai referee's penalty call against them in a match with Kuwait, North Korean players and officials dashed onto the field to beat up the hapless referee, who suffered head and arm injuries and had to be rescued by the Indian police. For this display of bad manners, the Asian Football Federation and the Federation of International Football Associations barred North Korea for two years from participating in officially sanctioned soccer matches throughout the world.

Both Koreas bid to host the 10th Asian Games in 1986, along with Iraq. Iraq withdrew its bid because of the war with Iran, leaving Seoul and Pyongyang as the only bidders. Since Seoul had already been chosen as the site for the 1988 Olympics, the South Korean government gave high-level consideration to conceding the Asian Games to Pyongyang, as a means of opening North Korea to the outside world and lessening its hostility to Seoul's hosting of the Olympic Games. President Chun decided against this course of action, however, and Seoul, which had campaigned vigorously to be chosen, easily won the balloting at the Asian Games Federation meeting.

Both Koreas took part in the first Winter Asian Games held in Sapporo, Japan, in March 1986. Japan dominated the small field of seven countries, taking over half of the medals, including 83 percent of the gold medals. China was second with 21 medals, South Korea third with 18, and North Korea fourth with 8. The two Koreas battled head to head in two ice hockey matches, both won by South Korea.

The Asian Games, viewed by South Koreans as a dress rehearsal for the 1988 Olympic Games, took place in Seoul in September and October 1986. More than 4,800 athletes from 27 Asian countries competed. China, ignoring North Korea's charge that the South Koreans were exploiting the games for "impure political aims," sent a 514-member delegation to the event by special plane direct from Peking. The Chinese retained their title of Asian Games champions. The South Koreans surprised everyone by taking second place, soundly beating the third-place Japanese. North Korea did not publicly criticize China for taking part in the games, but condemned South Korea for using the games to perpetuate the division of the country. The South Koreans, encouraged by the successful staging of the games and by the performance of their athletes, redoubled their efforts to prepare for the Olympics.

Olympic Games

South Korea first competed in the Olympic Games in London in 1946, and thirty years later at the 1976 games in Montreal a South Korean wrestler won his country's first gold medal. North Korean Olympic athletes contended with those from South Korea as long ago as the Winter Olympics in Innsbruck in 1964.

In 1981, when the International Olympic Committee (IOC) chose Seoul as the site for the 1988 Olympics, the games took on a transcendent political importance for the two Koreas. For South Korea it was a tremendous boost to national pride and an unparalleled opportunity to make a favorable impression on thousands of foreign visitors and millions of television viewers around the world. For North Korea it was another device for South Korea to attract Communist and Third World visitors in furtherance of its "plot to create two Koreas."

North Korea's protests attracted little attention until the back-to-back politically motivated boycotts of the Moscow Olympics in 1980 and the Los Angeles Olympics in 1984 raised the possibility that the Communist countries might heed Pyongyang's appeals and stay away from the Seoul Olympics, thus threatening the future of the Olympic movement. Articles began to appear in the Soviet press questioning the choice of Seoul and calling for a change of venue.[51] The North Korean premier, Kang Song-san, applauding a letter from Fidel Castro to the president of the IOC criticizing the choice of Seoul, urged the IOC not to proceed with holding the Olympics in this "dangerous hotbed of a new war," a place where human rights "are wantonly trampled underfoot." The chairman of the DPRK Olympic Committee addressed a long letter to the chairman of the IOC reiterating Kang's denunciations of Seoul and adding that South Korea's anticommunist national security law made the country unsafe for players and officials from Communist and socialist countries. He stated they would stay away, thus causing another divided Olympic Games. He opposed holding the games in either Seoul or Pyongyang.[52]

Despite Pyongyang's determined opposition to holding the Olympics in Seoul and mutterings elsewhere in the Communist world, the IOC held firm. At a general meeting in Mexico City in November 1984 the Association of National Olympic Committees unanimously adopted a Mexico Declaration urging all members to participate in the 1988

Olympics.[53] The Soviet and North Korean delegations present did not speak against it. An extraordinary session of the IOC in December 1984, convened to consider sanctions against countries boycotting future Olympics, formally backed the selection of Seoul for the 1988 games. The president of the IOC, Juan Antonio Samaranch, responded to the letter from the chairman of the DPRK Olympic Committee assuring him that he had no fears for the safety of athletes in Seoul.

Having failed to persuade the IOC to change the venue of the 1988 Olympics, North Korea adopted a new tack. In July 1985, Chong Chun-ki, vice premier of the DPRK, proposed that the 1988 Olympics be divided between Seoul and Pyongyang, each hosting half of the events, and that the two Koreas field a single team. The games would be called the "Korea Olympiad" or the "Pyongyang-Seoul, Korea Olympiad." South Korea rejected the proposal for cohosting the Olympics as contrary to the Olympic charter, a position upheld by Samaranch, who declared that the games had been awarded to Seoul and would be held in Seoul. Both the South Koreans and Samaranch expressed willingness, however, for some events to be held in Pyongyang.

They offered to permit North Korea to host the table tennis and archery events and one of the four groups in the soccer competition. In addition, the 100-kilometer cycle road race would start in the North and finish in Seoul. In return, North Korea would drop other demands and agree to permit "all members of the Olympic family," including reporters, to enter North Korea. As of mid-1986, North Korea had neither accepted nor flatly rejected this proposal.

In April 1986 the Association of National Olympic Committees held its fifth General Assembly in Seoul, with a record attendance of 152 national Olympic committees, including representatives from the Soviet Union, Eastern European countries, and China. Among the few countries failing to attend were North Korea and Cuba.

North Korea's response to this display of support for the Seoul Olympics was to host the second conference of ministers and sports officials from nonaligned countries in July 1986. Representatives from 53 countries and national liberation movements attended the conference, which was addressed by Kim Il Sung. Among the resolutions adopted by the conference was one expressing firm support for the cohosting of the 1988 Olympics by Seoul and Pyongyang.

With the Seoul Olympics still two years away, none of the Communist countries had made firm commitment that they would participate. Samaranch stated after a meeting of sports ministers of 12 Communist countries in Hanoi in November 1985 that they would declare their intentions six months before the games, when the IOC sent out formal invitations. In the meantime, indications were mounting that they would participate, particularly because increasing numbers of athletes from the Soviet Union, China, and Eastern Europe had made an appearance at international sports events in South Korea.

Conclusion

The two Koreas are not far apart in the extent of their official international activities and relationships, as shown in the previous chapter. South Korea is ahead, but its lead is lessened by its exclusion from the nonaligned group of nations. In the unofficial international activities and relations discussed in this chapter, however, South Korea's open society and export-oriented economy have given it an enormous lead over North Korea.

In the competition between the two Koreas for formal recognition, which must by definition be fought out in the realm of official relationships, how important is South Korea's lead in unofficial activities? What is the link between the two realms? Some South Korean diplomats, preoccupied with their mission of protecting and expanding the ROK's official relations, brush aside unofficial activities as not contributing decisively to the accomplishment of their mission. They worry about their total official exclusion from Communist countries, while North Korean diplomats have succeeded in penetrating the NATO group. They dislike being on the outside looking in when the foreign ministers or heads of state of the nonaligned group get together.

Yet it would be a mistake to underestimate the long-term influence of South Korea's widespread and growing unofficial activities and relationships on the official behavior of nations toward it. In some cases, notably in Libya and the Sudan, South Korean economic power paved the way for official recognition. Even more persuasive evidence of the importance of South Korea's unofficial international activities is the alarm and opposition that some of them provoke in Pyongyang. The North Koreans patently fear that South Korea's exchange of persons with Communist and Third World countries, particularly the attendance of individuals from those states at prestigious international events in Seoul, adds to the ROK's prestige, strengthens its claims to legitimacy, and increases the risk that those states may eventually establish diplomatic relations with the ROK.

Pyongyang is caught in a dilemma. It cannot prevent South Korea from expanding unofficial relations, even with Communist countries. Its only choice is to compete by expanding its own activities abroad, but it is starting far behind in most fields. Moreover, the expansion of activities abroad entails the inescapable risk of contaminating its rigidly

controlled society with foreign ideas and even setting in motion currents
that in the long run could change the nature of that society.

Notes

1. Republic of Korea, National Unification Board, *A Comparative Study of the
South and North Korean Economies* (Seoul, 1986), p. 73.

2. *Korea Herald*, July 20, 1984; December 8, 1984.

3. *Far Eastern Economic Review*, "Asian Contractors Learn the Hard Way
. . . ," ad. supp. to May 26, 1983, issue; and June 2, 1983, pp. 78, 80.

4. *Korea Herald*, November 8, 1983.

5. *Korea Herald*, February 19, 1981.

6. *Far Eastern Economic Review*, June 2, 1983, p. 78.

7. *Korea Herald*, July 27, 1985.

8. *Korea Herald*, July 5, 1981.

9. *FBIS*, September 30, 1985, p. D17.

10. Seo Hang Lee, "Distant-Water Fishing Nations' Response to Extended
Fisheries Jurisdiction: The Experience of South Korea," *Marine Policy Reports*,
vol. 6, no. 5, May 1984 (College of Marine Studies, University of Delaware),
p. 2; *Korea Herald*, January 16, 1985.

11. Lee, "Distant-Water Fishing Nations'," p. 3; *Korea Herald*, January 16,
1985.

12. UN Food and Agriculture Organization, *Yearbook of Fishery Statistics*, vol.
56 (1983), p. 77. North Korean statistics on the production of fisheries products
run much higher because they include freshwater fish, seaweed, shellfish, laver,
and fish cultivated in shallow saltwater. Pyongyang's target for 1990 for all
types of fishery products is 5 million tons.

13. *Pyongyang Times*, September 21, 1985, p. 3.

14. *Korea Herald*, August 2, 1984.

15. *FBIS*, January 16, 1978, p. E5.

16. Sang-Seek Park, "North Korea's Policy Toward the Third World," in
Scalapino and Kim, *North Korea Today*, pp. 325–326.

17. *Korea Herald*, February 19, 1984; April 19, 1985.

18. *Washington Post*, September 24, 1978 (*Parade* section, p. 12).

19. *Korea Herald*, June 2, 1985.

20. *Korea Herald*, October 29, 1985.

21. *Korea Herald*, October 29, 1983; February 27, 1985.

22. *Korea Herald*, August 9, 1984.

23. *Korea Herald*, March 28, 1980.

24. *Korea Herald*, October 11, 1984; February 28, 1985.

25. Republic of Korea, National Unification Board, *A Comparative Study of
the South and North Korean Economies*, p. 69.

26. *Handbook of Korea*, 4th ed. (Seoul: Korean Information Service, Ministry
of Culture and Information, 1982), pp. 639–640.

27. Bunge, *North Korea*, pp. 127–128.

28. *Korea Herald*, December 21, 1985.

29. *FBIS,* July 29, 1986, p. D14.

30. A Korean-American visiting Pyongyang in 1981 pointed out to the North Koreans that the large pots for sale in the hotel were unlikely to be bought by air travelers. They would have to develop more portable souvenirs.

31. *Korea Herald,* June 6, 1985; January 1, 1986.

32. *FBIS,* March 8, 1977, pp. D1–D5.

33. *FBIS,* December 6, 1978, pp. D4–D7.

34. *FBIS,* November 7, 1979, p. D3.

35. *FBIS,* December 11, 1985, pp. D4–D6.

36. "Juche Idea is Unsuitable for Africans," *Vantage Point* (Seoul: Naewoe Press), vol. 8, no. 4, April 1985, pp. 13–17.

37. *FBIS,* July 11, 1983, pp. D3–D13.

38. *Vantage Point,* Vol. 8, no. 7, July 1985, pp. 23–24.

39. *Korea Herald,* July 5, 1985.

40. *Vantage Point,* vol. 8, no. 6, June 1985, pp. 12–18.

41. *FBIS,* March 21, 1978, pp. D13–D14.

42. *New York Times,* October 8, 1985.

43. *FBIS,* January 15, 1979, p. D3; October 3, 1978, p. E5.

44. *FBIS,* March 21, 1978, p. D2.

45. *FBIS,* May 14, 1976, p. D6.

46. *Korea Herald,* April 9, 1985.

47. *Korea Herald,* June 23, 1985.

48. *Korea Herald,* March 8, 1983.

49. *Korea Herald,* March 10, 1984.

50. *Korea Newsreview,* December 11, 1982, p. 25.

51. *FBIS,* November 5, 1984, p. D10.

52. *FBIS,* December 10, 1984, pp. D1–D3; December 17, 1984, pp. D1–D3.

53. *Korea Herald,* November 11, 1984.

11

Toward Cross-recognition: The Soviet Union, China, and Japan

During the 1950s and 1960s the ideological battlelines observed by the two Koreas in their rivalry for international recognition were clear-cut, precluding initiatives by South Korea to seek relations with China or the Soviet Union or by North Korea to seek relations with the United States. The ROK had stringent anticommunist laws forbidding its citizens to have any intercourse with Communist states. It joined with the United States to battle communism in Vietnam. It viewed the Soviet Union and China as enemies who backed North Korea in its plan to conquer the South, just as they supported the spread of Communist domination in Indochina. It saw itself and the United States as staunch allies in the struggle to prevent Communist expansion.

North Korea likewise saw the world in black and white terms, with the United States as the imperialist enemy blocking the reunification of Korea by Kim Il Sung or even as harboring designs to back a South Korean military attack on the North. The capture of the *Pueblo* and the shooting down of the EC-121 demonstrated the intensity of the hostility felt by North Korea toward the United States.

The sudden change in U.S. relations with China in 1971 and 1972 and steps taken by the United States and the Soviet Union to promote detente between them shot holes in the certainties upon which Seoul and Pyongyang had based their policies. A reappraisal was called for, if not of strategy, at least of tactics. They opened talks with each other and began to reconsider their policies toward each other's allies.

South Korea moved first, announcing in 1971 its willingness to have diplomatic relations with the Soviet Union and the PRC if they ceased "hostile activities," recognized the sovereignty of the ROK, and stopped aid to North Korea. In 1973 Park Chung-hee dropped South Korea's objection to the membership of both Koreas in the United Nations, declared that the ROK would open its door to all nations on the basis of reciprocity and equality, and urged "countries whose ideologies and social institutions are different from ours to open their doors likewise to us."[1] In 1974 North Korea's Supreme People's Assembly sent a letter to the U.S. Congress proposing the negotiation of a peace treaty between Pyongyang and Washington to replace the Armistice Agreement. The United States did not respond to the North Korean initiative, but declared its support for the admission of both Koreas to the United Nations and expressed its willingness to improve relations with the DPRK if its allies would take similar action toward the ROK.

Japan's relations with the two Koreas differed from those of the other big powers. History, Japanese domestic politics, and the presence of a large Korean minority in Japan caused the Japanese government to permit more unofficial intercourse with North Korea than the Soviet Union and China had with South Korea or the United States had with North Korea. Japan's policy toward official relations, however, closely followed that of the United States, supporting the dual entry of the Koreas into the UN and rejecting diplomatic relations with North Korea until the Soviet Union and China took similar action toward South Korea.

For the past ten years no change has occurred in the policies of the big powers toward establishing diplomatic relations with the rival of their Korean ally. The United States and Japan have continued to favor the South Korean position, which has come to be known as "cross-recognition" of the two Koreas by all four big powers. North Korea has repeatedly condemned cross-recognition as a plot devised by the United States to perpetuate the division of Korea. The Soviet Union and China, without much enthusiasm, have backed North Korea's position.

Both Seoul and Pyongyang have been extremely sensitive to the slightest move by one of their allies that could be interpreted as a step toward diplomatic recognition. They would prefer that no contact whatsoever take place between a big power ally and the rival Korean state. Recognizing the impossibility of totally preventing such contact, they have done their best to keep it to a minimum. Each has also striven to develop contacts with its rival's allies.

During the past ten years as the two Koreas expanded their international activities, preventing big power allies from having contact with the rival became more difficult. The big powers were increasingly reluctant to curtail the participation of their citizens in international activities because their Korean ally disapproved. "Cross-contacts" between the big powers and the part of Korea with which they had no diplomatic relations continually increased.

In the cross-contacts game South Korea had a substantial advantage. It had a big lead in the number of international activities in which its citizens participated alongside Soviets and Chinese, compared with those which brought U.S. citizens, Japanese, and North Koreans together. North Korea's unwillingness to admit South Koreans to events in Pyongyang barred it from hosting many events that would attract U.S. citizens and Japanese. The looseness of control by the U.S. and Japanese governments over the travel of their nationals compared to the controls exercised by the Soviet Union and China made it easier for U.S. citizens and Japanese to respond to North Korean invitations to visit than for Soviets and Chinese to respond to such invitations from South Korea. Significant numbers of Japanese traveled to North Korea and smaller numbers of North Koreans to Japan, but very few U.S. citizens went to North Korea, and hardly any North Koreans visited the United States. The DPRK lacked an effective strategy for utilizing cross-contacts to promote its interests in the United States.

The expansion of cross-contacts does not lead inevitably to cross-recognition. Diplomatic relations can be withheld for political reasons even from countries with which another country has extensive trade and other relations, as the United States and Japan have amply demonstrated in respect to Taiwan. But the situation of the two Koreas differs basically from that of the PRC and Taiwan. Neither Korea has been able to prevent the other from establishing diplomatic relations with a majority of the nations of the world, and 67 countries maintain diplomatic relations with both. In this situation, in which the world community increasingly accepts the legitimacy of both Korean governments and they play increasingly important international roles, the expansion of cross-contacts by the big powers strengthens the case for cross-recognition.

Soviet Contacts with South Korea

Since the announcement of its willingness to establish relations with Communist countries, South Korea has shown a keen interest in making contacts with the Soviet Union. Moscow did not reciprocate the public statements by South Korean officials expressing a desire to promote relations, but in 1973 it began quietly admitting South Korean visitors to the Soviet Union. A South Korean businessman was allowed to visit Leningrad with a tour group, and a playwright attended a conference of the International Theater Institute in Moscow. Later that year a South

Korean team took part in the World Universiad in Moscow, despite vehement protests from North Korea. ROK diplomats sought informal opportunities to converse with Soviet diplomats. In 1975 a South Korean wrestling team took part in an international meet in Minsk, and a weightlifting team competed at a match in Moscow. The South Korean press prominently reported each of these infrequent contacts, treating them as evidence of improvement in South Korean-Soviet relations.

The public reports of contacts between South Korea and the Soviet Union afforded an opportunity for the Chinese media to take swipes at the Soviets. The Xinhua News Agency accused "Soviet social-imperialism" of "intensifying its collusion with the Pak Chong-hui [Park Chung-hee] clique."[2] In order to defend its reputation in Pyongyang, TASS denounced as a "dastardly act of the Pak Chong-hui clique to mislead world public opinion" a statement made by a South Korean businessman, based on a conversation with a Soviet trade official in London, that the prospect for direct trade between South Korea and the Soviet Union was bright.[3] Moscow also struck back at Peking, alleging that it had signed a deal with Seoul for the sale of 1,000 tons of red peppers, which provoked a heated denial from Xinhua citing additional examples of "open and secret collusion between Soviet social-imperialism and the South Korean puppet Pak Chong-hui clique."[4]

Protests from Pyongyang and accusations from Peking did not deter Moscow from continuing to admit South Koreans to international events in the Soviet Union. Several attended the meeting in Moscow of the World Federation of United Nations Associations in 1975. In 1977 the Soviets issued a visa to the South Korean ambassador to France to attend a UNESCO conference in Tbilisi, the first South Korean official to be admitted. The following year the South Korean Minister of Health and his delegation attended a WHO conference in Alma Ata, accompanied by two South Korean journalists. In reporting the meeting, the local newspaper, the *Kazakhstanskaya Pravda*, referred to the "Republic of Korea" by name.[5] According to a Soviet scholar, the North Koreans were "very angry" at the Soviets for having admitted this South Korean cabinet minister.[6]

In April 1978, a Korean Air Lines plane on a polar flight from Paris to Seoul went off course and deeply penetrated Soviet airspace south of Murmansk, where it was fired on by Soviet fighters and forced to land. Two passengers were killed and ten wounded. The Soviets allowed the passengers to leave promptly and returned the crew within ten days. President Park expressed "profound gratitude" to the Soviet authorities for the prompt return of the passengers and crew.

The plane incident had no noticeable detrimental effect on contacts between the Soviet Union and South Korea, which continued to increase from 1979 to 1983. During 1979 South Koreans attended Moscow conferences of the Ice Hockey Federation, the International Sports Reporters Federation, the Association of International Press Services, and the International Political Science Association. Sixteen South Korean scholars attended this last event. South Koreans, including two government officials, also participated in the conference of the International Social Security Association in Tashkent.

The South Korean media publicized with alacrity each contact with the Soviet Union, no matter how slight. Two Soviet consular officials had only to appear in the crowd at a South Korean trade exhibit in Kingston, Jamaica, to attract the attention of Seoul's Haptong News Agency. Soviet scholars privately deplored this passion to publicize, which caused friction with Pyongyang and provided grist for Peking's anti-Soviet propaganda mill. The Chinese kept their own skirts clean by refusing to admit South Koreans to international events in China, even at the cost of forgoing at least one important athletic contest as a result.[7] In spite of North Korean and Chinese criticism, Soviet contacts continued. South Koreans attended the Pacific Science Conference in Khabarovsk in 1980 and the World Trade Center Association convention in Moscow in 1981.

Soviet–South Korean contacts during this first decade were one-way. South Koreans attended athletic meets and conferences in the Soviet Union, but no Soviets visited Seoul. Hosting international events was important to the Soviets. They were unwilling to follow the Chinese practice of forgoing such events in order to avoid offending Pyongyang. Declining to send representatives to world events held in Seoul was easier, but, as discussed in the previous chapter, the political cost of nonparticipation began to rise in the late 1970s, as Seoul with increasing frequency became the site of important world gatherings. Finally, in October 1982 the taboo was broken. Three TASS reporters attended a meeting in Seoul of the Organization of Asia-Pacific News Agencies. They were said by a South Korean journalist to have been received along with other participants by President Chun, a meeting that the local press was forbidden to report.[8] About the same time a Soviet official from the Cultural Preservations Bureau attended a conference in Seoul. This new departure in Soviet policy toward South Korea elicited strong criticism of the Soviet Union in a Tokyo-based North Korean organ, *People's Korea*.[9] Nevertheless, in March 1983, two Soviet officials took part in an international conference on agriculture in Seoul.

Trade and Communication

Trade was another form of contact with the Soviet Union eagerly sought by the South Koreans, once they decided to open their door to nonhostile Communist countries. The Soviets refused direct trade, which would have required negotiations with South Korea by Soviet officials, but a small indirect trade gradually developed. Some South Korean exports reached the Soviet Union via intermediaries in Western Europe. Soviet timber from Vladivostok reached South Korea in Japanese ships. Finland became an increasingly important European transshipment point. In a visit to Helsinki in May 1979, Foreign Minister Park Tong-jin reached agreement with the Finnish government that both governments would assist private businessmen in exporting South Korean products to the Soviet Union and Eastern Europe. Indirect trade was estimated at about $20 million in 1978, with Moscow importing electronic goods, textiles, and machinery and exporting coal and timber.[10]

The South Koreans have made some progress in developing transportation and communication links with the Soviet Union. The Soviets rejected requests from South Korea that its ships be admitted to Soviet Far Eastern ports, but since 1977 South Korean goods have been shipped on third-country vessels to those ports for transshipment to Europe on the Trans-Siberian Railway.

A Japanese company served as the relay link for the first telephone call from Seoul to Moscow in September 1978. In October 1979, by agreement between the South Korean and British governments, a permanent link via London was established for telephone calls between South Korea and the Soviet Union.

Shootdown of KAL Plane

The burgeoning contacts between the Soviet Union and South Korea halted abruptly in September 1983 when a Soviet fighter shot down a Korean Air Lines plane with the loss of 269 lives. President Chun Doo Hwan condemned the action as "an utterly inhuman act" and demanded an apology. The Soviets refused to accept responsibility for the disaster, and a sense of outrage and frustration boiled up among the South Koreans.

The air tragedy occurred at a most inopportune point in the development of contacts between the Soviet Union and South Korea. As recounted in Chapter 9, the Soviet Union seemed on the brink of ignoring Pyongyang's strident warnings and sending a delegation to the Interparliamentary Union conference in Seoul. Tension between the Soviet Union and South Korea ruled out Soviet participation, despite assurances by the ROK government that it would guarantee the safety of the Soviet visitors.

When the loss of the KAL airliner occurred, South Korea had been preparing to take part in a number of events in the Soviet Union. A delegation enroute to Tashkent to attend a UNESCO conference turned back midway. South Korean sports associations cancelled plans to participate in wrestling, judo, and weightlifting championships in the Soviet Union in September and October and a fencing championship in April 1984. Within a few months after the plane incident, however, the government and ruling party had declared their intention to continue energetically to pursue Nordpolitik, South Korea's counterpart of West Germany's Ostpolitik, which aimed at enhancing ties with the Soviet Union and China and ultimately establishing diplomatic relations with those countries. As a policy booklet issued by the DJP noted, the airplane incident demonstrated the necessity of having official relations with the Soviet Union and China.[11] Therefore, despite Moscow's continued refusal to apologize for shooting down the KAL plane and to pay compensation to the victim's families, South Korea dropped its self-imposed ban on contacts in August 1984 and sent two representatives to an international geological conference in Moscow. The South Koreans also invited a Soviet representative to the opening of the Olympic stadium in September. The Soviet official did not attend, but representatives from China, Hungary, and Romania did.

South Korea's desire for the participation of the Soviet Union and East European countries in the 1988 Olympics provided a strong motivation for restoring sports exchanges with the Soviets. Moscow's questioning of Seoul's suitability as an Olympic site created troubling uncertainties for the South Koreans. During 1985, however, Soviet criticism declined and comments by Soviet sports figures increasingly suggested the probability of Soviet participation.

A more concrete indication of Soviet intentions was the procession of Soviet athletes and sports officials to South Korea. In March 1985 12 Soviet skaters, accompanied by 2 Soviet officials, took part in exhibition performances by an international troupe in Seoul and Taegu. The Soviet vice president of the International Volleyball Federation arrived in May to inspect Seoul's Olympic facilities. The Soviet president of the International Gymnastic Federation, arriving in Seoul in August, told reporters that Soviet athletes were training earnestly to prepare for the Seoul Olympics. During 1985 Soviet teams competed in world championships in Seoul in archery, women's junior handball, men's volleyball, boxing, and judo. A South Korean team competed in the World Youth Modern Pentathlon in Moscow in September 1985. Sports exchanges were back on course.

Significance of Contacts

The contacts between Soviets and South Koreans reviewed above fall far short of constituting an ineluctable trend toward the establishment of diplomatic relations. Nevertheless, they have gathered momentum in response to South Korea's growing importance in world affairs, and the trend cannot easily be reversed.

A powerful motivation for increased contacts with South Koreans is Moscow's determination to play a greater role in Asian-Pacific affairs. South Korea's weight in the region is growing. It is a member of the principal regional organizations and of world organizations active in the region. If the Soviets wish to become more active here, as suggested by Foreign Minister Shevardnadze's visit to Tokyo in January 1986, their officials cannot avoid increasing contacts with South Korean officials.

Scholarly interest in South Korea in the Soviet Union is growing. Opportunities for Soviet scholars to meet and converse in depth with South Korean scholars at international conferences are increasing. One Soviet scholar, who participated with South Korean scholars in a multinational study group in Tokyo in the late 1970s on the Pacific Basin concept, was advised by the authorities in Moscow that it would be "premature" for him to attend the next meeting of the group, which was to be in Seoul.[12] In the 1980s scholarly meetings in South Korea are unlikely to remain forbidden to Soviet scholars, now that the bars have fallen for athletes.

The improvement of Soviet relations with North Korea since 1984 probably has made contacts between the Soviet Union and South Korea easier. Pyongyang's increased military and economic dependence on the Soviet Union diminishes the effect of North Korean complaints about Soviet dalliance with South Korea. So also does the expansion of China's intercourse with that country. China for a long time lagged behind the Soviet Union in its contacts with the ROK, but it has now surged ahead. The Chinese continue to cultivate good relations with North Korea, but they are willing to take greater risks than in the past in their development of contacts with South Korea. Both Moscow and Peking seem to have given up the practice of seeking to gain a few debating points in Pyongyang by attacking its rival's "collusion" with South Korea. They have apparently decided that the pot calling the kettle black achieves little.

Opportunities for trade with South Korea will be difficult for the Soviet Union to ignore. A more active Soviet role in East Asia implies a growing economy and expanding trade for the Soviet Far East. South Korea has much to offer. Indirect trade through Japanese middlemen can, of course, be increased, but at some point the Soviets may decide to seek the economies of cutting out the middleman.

Chinese Contacts with South Korea

China was much slower than the Soviet Union to develop contacts with South Korea. During most of the 1970s the Chinese were too preoccupied with the internal political struggle to contemplate modifying the policy of refusing such contacts. Only after 1978 when Deng Xiaoping's pragmatic open-door policy began to take effect, did a change in Chinese policy become possible. Even then old habits died hard. The shock of Soviet-Vietnamese collaboration in Indochina impressed on the Chinese the importance of clinging to North Korea to frustrate Soviet encirclement of China. In order to avoid offending the North Koreans by inviting South Korean teams to participate in international sports events in China, they gave up the right to host a hockey match in 1978 and a soccer championship in 1979. When Pyongyang protested the development of a sizable trade between China and South Korea in 1980 and 1981, the Chinese cut it back sharply in 1982.

The South Koreans were as eager to develop contacts with China as the Chinese were reluctant to respond. The same historical and cultural factors that made the Chinese more comfortable partners than the Soviets for the North Koreans also affected the South Koreans. Moreover, they were attracted by the potential market for South Korean products offered by China's open-door economic policy and the ease of making deals unobtrusively in Hong Kong. The Chinese were not averse to selective quiet contacts that served their interests, so long as these did not stir up the North Koreans. But the South Koreans had a tendency to publicize the contacts, just as they had done with the Soviets.[13]

A fortuitous happening broke the logjam on open contacts between Peking and Seoul. The hijacking of a Chinese civil aircraft to South Korea in May 1983 brought an official Chinese delegation quickly to Seoul to negotiate the return of the plane, passengers, and crew. Thereafter, sports exchanges and attendance at international meetings in each other's countries began and soon surpassed Soviet–South Korean contacts, which were also increasing during this period.

Trade

The existence of trade between China and South Korea first came to public notice in 1979 when a U.S. correspondent reported that South Korea was negotiating the purchase of Chinese coal through intermediaries in Hong Kong.[14] By 1981 coal to fuel South Korean cement plants was arriving in Chinese ships at a port north of Pohang on South Korea's east coast. The Chinese crew was not allowed ashore. U.S. officials in Seoul estimated that bilateral trade, including indirect trade via Hong Kong, amounted to hundreds of millions of dollars. Besides coal, the Chinese exported textile yarns, fabrics, and raw silk. They imported television sets, electronic components, polyester fiber, and petrochemical intermediates. A few Chinese officials even visited Seoul clandestinely to work out the detail of shipments.[15] The trade between

China and South Korea was an open secret among foreign businessmen in Peking, who said that manifests covering the exports showed destinations other than South Korea so that the Chinese could deny that trade was occurring.[16]

Trade dropped sharply in 1982 in response to North Korean protests. Chinese customs began to ban products with South Korean labels. A U.S. citizen operating a joint venture in China was able to import via Japan machinery parts from its principal Far Eastern plant in South Korea, but when a shipment labeled "made in the ROK" slipped through by accident, the factory in China incurred a heavy fine.[17] Chinese exports to South Korea, however, continued to grow.

After the cooperation between Peking and Seoul in resolving the hijacking problem in May 1983, which in retrospect proved to be a watershed in China's willingness to deal with South Koreans, trade between the two countries again flourished. It probably was facilitated by the decentralization of foreign trade under China's open-door economic policy. This decentralization reduced the control of the central government over trade with South Korea in favor of trade arranged by factories under provincial or municipal direction.

During 1984 trade-related contacts proliferated. In July 1984 both the South Korean and Chinese delegations to a multifiber arrangements meeting in Geneva joined with delegations of other textile-exporting countries in establishing an international textiles and clothing bureau in Karachi. This bureau promoted cooperation in resisting protectionism by the advanced industrial countries. Part of the growing trade between China and South Korea was handled by the Hong Kong offices of Japanese trading companies, but the South Korean conglomerates increasingly established their own subsidiaries in Hong Kong to do business with China. A senior South Korean official stated privately that representatives of the conglomerates were going into China to discuss possible projects with Chinese officials.[18] The Chinese gave them visas on separate sheets of paper. Some of the direct trade between China and South Korea was carried in third-country vessels, some in ships owned by South Koreans but flying Liberian or Panamanian flags.

During 1985 trade between China and South Korea became more regularized and more difficult to conceal, although South Korean officials, acceding to Peking's desire to avoid attracting attention to the trade, declined to discuss it with the press. Accurate figures on the size of the trade were difficult to obtain. Perhaps half of it passed through Hong Kong, the remainder shipped direct or via Japan and other transshipment points. Estimates of total two-way trade through all channels for 1984 were in the $700 to $800 million range.[19] In early 1985 trade declined, as the Chinese, alarmed by the rapid depletion of their foreign exchange reserves, cut back on foreign purchases. However, Chinese exports to South Korea continued to rise, and total trade for the year may have reached close to $1 billion.[20]

Complementarity between the Chinese and South Korean economies made the two countries natural trading partners. The first shipment of Chinese crude oil reached South Korea in 1984. China supplied increasing amounts of cotton yarn to South Korean textile mills, and Chinese corn began to cut into the South Korean market for U.S. corn. The U.S. Department of Agriculture expected that corn shipments from China would meet one-fourth of South Korea's needs for this grain in 1985. Kia, South Korea's third largest auto maker, received 250 inquiries from 6 Chinese provinces and shipped 50 sample vans and trucks there. Company officials were discussing with the Chinese the possibility of a joint venture auto assembly plant in China.[21] Some South Korean refrigerators were shipped to China in knockdown form and assembled by a factory in Fujian.[22]

Enthusiasm for trade with China ran high among South Korean businessmen. Some sent Hong Kong Chinese or Korean-Americans to negotiate with Chinese officials for them, but others went to China themselves to do business, including Kim Woo Chung, chairman of the Daewoo group. Responding to the rising interest in China, the Federation of Korean Industries published a research report on the Chinese economy, discussing the potential for trade between China and South Korea. The Chinese Committee for the Promotion of International Trade invited Hong Kong branches of South Korean companies to participate in a trade fair in Peking in November 1985.

Incidents

The proximity of China and South Korea not only facilitated trade, it made unavoidable incidents involving nationals of both countries, which the two governments had to resolve. Lacking the diplomatic and consular relations that governments normally rely on to work out such matters, the PRC and the ROK found other ways to handle them. Arms-length, indirect contact between officials of the two countries had disadvantages, and when the need was important and urgent enough, as in the hijacking incident of May 1983, the Chinese did not hesitate to negotiate directly with South Korean officials.

Problems between China and South Korea arose over fisheries in the Yellow Sea, an area fished intensively by fishermen of both countries. The absence of diplomatic relations made impossible official negotiations to settle conflicting claims to fishing grounds, and clashes occurred between Chinese and South Korean fishermen, especially during 1976 and 1977. The Chinese accused the South Korean fishermen of intruding into their territorial waters and damaging Chinese fishing nets, while the South Koreans accused the Chinese of harassing their fishing boats on the high seas. The Chinese occasionally seized alleged intruding boats. On other occasions the Chinese attacked South Korean boats, seized and destroyed their fishing gear, and carried off their crews.

The South Korean Foreign Ministry appealed in vain to the Chinese to negotiate differences over fisheries. The South Korean fishing industry lacked even a private agreement with China, such as Japanese politicians have negotiated with North Korea on behalf of the Japanese fishing industry. Nevertheless, the tension between Chinese and South Korean fishermen on the Yellow Sea has subsided since the confrontations of 1976 and 1977. The Chinese repatriate South Korean fishermen who fall into their hands. Understandings now even permit Chinese fishermen to seek shelter from the weather in South Korean ports. Fifteen hundred did so in 1982, compared to 800 in 1981.[23] A procedure exists whereby Chinese fishermen shipwrecked on the South Korean coast are returned by South Korea without publicity to Chinese authorities in Hong Kong.[24]

A potentially more dangerous difference between China and South Korea in the Yellow Sea relates to their overlapping claims to undersea oil deposits. The Chinese objected to concessions granted by the ROK to foreign oil companies permitting them to drill in an area that had not been delimited by international agreement. The prompt South Korean offer to negotiate such an agreement brought no response from China. Chinese fishing boats harassed seismic survey vessels operating about halfway between China and South Korea. When Gulf Oil began to drill in this area in 1973, the Chinese Foreign Ministry denounced the action, and a Chinese gunboat hovered menacingly in the vicinity of the drilling operation. No oil was found in the two holes drilled, and the U.S. State Department discouraged Gulf Oil from continuing to drill in a disputed area.[25] Since that time neither China nor South Korea has attempted to drill there, but the conflicting claims remain unsettled.

A hijacking incident on May 5, 1983, resulted in a breakthrough in South Korea's relations with China. Six hijackers, hoping to defect to Taiwan, seized control of a Chinese civil aircraft bound from Shenyang to Shanghai with 97 Chinese and 3 Japanese passengers aboard and forced it to land in South Korea. This was not a matter that could be hushed up and handled quietly behind the scenes. The Chinese, abandoning their usual reserve, immediately cabled the ROK requesting permission to send a negotiating team to Seoul. Two days later a Chinese Boeing 707 landed at Kimpo Airport carrying Shen Tu, director-general of the Civil Aviation Administration of China (CAAC), as head of a 10-member delegation to negotiate the return of the passengers, crew, and aircraft. Also aboard was a crew to fly back the hijacked plane. The South Korean authorities were delighted with this fortuitous opportunity to engage in official negotiations with the PRC and made the most of it. The government announced that it would handle the incident in accordance with the Convention for the Suppression of Unlawful Seizure of Aircraft of which both the ROK and the PRC were signatories.

Three days of negotiations produced a formal memorandum, signed by Shen Tu in his capacity as director-general of the Civil Aviation Administration of the People's Republic of China and by Gong Romyung, assistant minister of foreign affairs of the Republic of Korea. For the first time the two governments signed an official agreement, according each other tacit recognition. The Chinese had resisted doing so, but eventually yielded to South Korean insistence. In the memorandum Shen Tu expressed his appreciation to the Koreans for the "speedy and appropriate measures" taken for the safety of the aircraft and the well-being of the crew and passengers, as well as for the medical care given to two crew members shot by the hijackers. Looking to the future, the memorandum declared: "Both sides have expressed their hope to maintain the spirit of cooperation, which was amply manifested in handling the incident, in future case [sic] of emergency which may involve the two sides."[26]

While the negotiations were going on, the Koreans lodged the Chinese passengers in a first-class hotel, wined and dined them, took them on sightseeing tours of Seoul (including a shopping arcade and an electronics plant), and presented them with gifts. The passengers and crew returned to China on the CAAC 707 five days after the hijacking, together with the negotiating delegation.

The chief difference between China and South Korea during the negotiations had been the Chinese demand for the extradition of the hijackers to China. The South Koreans refused this demand, declaring that the hijackers would be tried in a South Korean court for their crime, a course of action permitted under the Convention. The Republic of China, with which the ROK had diplomatic relations, pressed vigorously to have the "freedom seekers" sent immediately to Taiwan, but the South Korean government rejected this demand also. The hijackers were sentenced to jail terms of four to six years. After they had served about fifteen months of their terms, the government, citing humanitarian considerations, deported them to Taiwan, where they received a tumultuous welcome. The foreign ministry of the PRC, expressing "regret and anger" over the action, accused the Korean authorities of violating international treaties on air piracy "in conspiracy with Taiwan."[27]

Although the Chinese felt that South Korea's treatment of the hijackers left something to be desired, their negotiations with the South Koreans had been businesslike, reasonably expeditious, and had achieved their principal goals: the prompt return of the passengers, crew, and aircraft. South Korea's imprisonment of the hijackers for more than a year, rather than permitting them to leave immediately for Taiwan, showed sensitivity to Peking's concern and created friction between Seoul and Taipei, which Peking no doubt regarded with satisfaction. The experience demonstrated the need to be able to deal officially with South Korea when the need arose and showed that it was possible to do so.

China's readiness to send officials to Seoul to negotiate must have nettled the North Koreans. China and South Korea presumably could have conducted their negotiations on neutral ground such as Tokyo, where both had embassies, even though the process would have been less efficient there. An unheralded five-day visit to Pyongyang shortly after the hijacking incident by the Chinese foreign minister, Wu Xueqian, probably was at least in part for the purpose of assuaging North Korean concern.

Another type of air incident between China and South Korea, requiring different handling, was the defection to South Korea of Chinese pilots with their planes. Two civilian flyers in a small plane flew to South Korea in 1961, and an air force pilot defected in October 1982. Another air force pilot came over in 1983 and one in 1985. The PRC routinely demanded the return of the pilot and aircraft. The ROK invariably honored the pilot's request to be sent to Taiwan, where he received a hero's welcome, a large reward in gold, and appointment to the Republic of China's air force. The South Koreans also kept the planes, which were similar to Chinese-built aircraft flown by North Korea and therefore of technical value to the ROK.

Through 1982 the Chinese version of the Soviet MIG-19 was the most advanced aircraft flown to South Korea, but in August 1983 a Chinese test pilot brought in an F-7, the Chinese version of the Soviet MIG-21. In August 1985 a B-5 light bomber, a modification of the Soviet IL-28, crash-landed in South Korea with three military personnel aboard. The crash killed the navigator and a Korean farmer and badly injured the pilot. The pilot requested political asylum, but the radioman, who was unhurt, asked to return to China. The Chinese foreign ministry issued a low-key statement through the New China News Agency (NCNA), expressing hope that the South Korean authorities would return the plane and crew as soon as possible. The South Korean government announced that the pilot would be sent to Taiwan when his injuries had healed. Three weeks after the crash it sent the radioman back to China via Hong Kong carrying the ashes of the deceased navigator.[28] Neither government revealed how the arrangements had been worked out, but an exchange of messages probably took place between the

NCNA office in Hong Kong and the South Korean Consulate General there.

Before the crash landing of the B-5 occurred, the Chinese and South Koreans had resolved through their officials in Hong Kong a bizarre incident involving a Chinese torpedo boat. While the gunboat was engaged in maneuvers in the Yellow Sea with other ships in March 1985, a quarrel broke out in which 6 of the 19 crew members were shot and killed and two wounded. The boat became disabled and drifted into South Korean territorial waters, where a South Korean fishing boat, attracted by its distress flares, towed it to a nearby island. Three Chinese naval ships entered South Korean waters searching for the missing torpedo boat, but withdrew after being warned off by ships of the South Korean navy. The following day South Korea strongly protested the intrusion into its territorial waters through its consul general in Hong Kong, demanding an apology and an assurance against the recurrence of such behavior. The foreign ministry in Peking issued a mild public statement, admitting that Chinese naval ships had "inadvertently" entered South Korean waters, but said that they had withdrawn as soon as they had realized their mistake. The statement appealed for South Korean cooperation in returning the ship and crew.

Rumors spread that the mutineers had tried to defect to Taiwan. The ambassador from the Republic of China tried to interview the crew, but was refused permission. The South Korean government issued a statement to the effect that the fighting had broken out over personal differences between crew members, not from political motives, implying that the question of political asylum would not arise.

Within a few days the matter had been resolved. A memorandum addressed to the "Consul General of the Republic of Korea in Hong Kong" signed by the deputy director for diplomatic affairs of NCNA's Hong Kong office and authorized by the foreign ministry in Peking apologized for the intrusion, said that the PRC would make efforts to prevent future violations of territorial waters and would take the necessary action against those responsible. The memorandum expressed appreciation for the decision by the South Korean authorities to return the boat and crew.[29]

Seven days after the incident began, the torpedo boat with the bodies of the dead crew members aboard was towed by a South Korean coast guard vessel, accompanied by a flotilla of coast guard and navy ships, to a rendezvous point halfway between South Korea and China where it was met by ships of the Chinese navy. The chief of staff of the Chinese navy's North Fleet accepted on behalf of the PRC the torpedo boat, the bodies, and the 13 surviving members of the crew. The meeting was cordial, marked by smiles, handshakes, and gifts of liquor and cigarettes from the Chinese to the Korean hotel employees, hospital staff, and others who had looked after the Chinese sailors.[30]

Thus, an incident that began with a tense confrontation between the PRC and ROK navies was amicably resolved. The two governments had devised a procedure for expeditiously and effectively negotiating with each other through Hong Kong. The ROK took the precaution of transmitting its original protest through the United States as well as to Chinese officials in Hong Kong, but the United States bowed out as the two governments began to deal with each other directly. Foreign Minister Wu Xueqian later told Susumu Nikaido, vice president of Japan's LDP, that he was much pleased with the quick and amicable settlement of the incident.[31] In Taipei, however, demonstrators pelted the South Korean Embassy with eggs and tomatoes to show their displeasure at Seoul's decision to return the boat and crew to the PRC.

Shortly after the torpedo boat incident had been resolved, another maritime incident involving South Korea and China occurred. On April 18, 1985, a 10,000-ton Chinese freighter struck and sank a South Korean fishing boat with the loss of all 12 fishermen aboard. Negotiations again were conducted in Hong Kong, with a legal adviser to South Korea's Fisheries Administration representing the owners of the lost vessel and the families of the deceased. The director of the Shanghai Ocean Transport Corporation was the principal on the Chinese side. After twelve days of negotiations, the Chinese agreed to pay $470,000 as compensation for the loss of the boat and the death of the fishermen. In September 1985 the Chinese shipping corporation remitted the money through the Korea Exchange Bank's branch in Hong Kong.[32]

These various sea and air incidents brought home to the Chinese the need to be able to conduct prompt and direct negotiations with the ROK. A neighbor as close, active, and important as South Korea could not be ignored. China probably would have responded years ago to the ROK's unconcealed desire for formal diplomatic relations had it not been constrained by rivalry with the Soviet Union for influence in Pyongyang. Another constraint was the problem of Taiwan. China's willingness to have diplomatic relations with both Korean governments, that is, the acceptance of "two Koreas," might be regarded in some countries as strengthening the case for "two Chinas." Firmly backing both one Korea and one China involved no such ambivalence or double standard. On the other hand, compelling the ROK to choose between Peking and Taipei would undoubtedly result in the severance of diplomatic relations between Seoul and Taipei, thus furthering the important PRC effort to isolate Taiwan in the world community.

Although not an adequate substitute for diplomatic relations, the usefulness of Hong Kong as a locale for both official negotiations and unofficial contacts was becoming increasingly apparent. The PRC's senior representative in Hong Kong headed the NCNA office, and the senior South Korean representative was a consul general. As neither had diplomatic status, their contacts were free of the symbolism that would attach to negotiations between diplomatic missions of the two countries in Tokyo or elsewhere. Moreover, the PRC representative, Xu Jiatun, was far more than a news agency director. A member of the Central Committee of the Chinese Communist Party, he was the resident representative of the central government in Hong Kong. As such, he constituted a high level channel for communications to and from Peking in official negotiations between the Chinese and South Koreans. For unofficial contacts, Hong Kong was ideal. South Korean bankers and businessmen could meet regularly and unobtrusively with their Chinese counterparts and could even slip across the border when necessary in order to meet with higher level Chinese officials.

Conferences and Other Contacts

The PRC began much later than the Soviet Union to admit South Koreans to China or to allow its own nationals to go to South Korea. So rare were such contacts that a Chinese who stopped overnight in Seoul enroute from Los Angeles to Hong Kong on a Korean Air Lines plane in 1974 was written up in the South Korean press as the first holder of a PRC passport to be admitted to the ROK. Unlike the Soviets, Chinese diplomats abroad declined to engage in social conversations with South Korean diplomats. A South Korean who served as ambassador to Bonn and Ottawa in the 1970s said that the PRC Embassy was the only mission that returned unopened newsletters sent by the ROK Embassy to the diplomatic corps.

The South Korean government had made it clear since 1973 that it was prepared to develop relations with the PRC. After the United States in December 1978 announced agreement on normalizing relations with the PRC, the South Koreans stepped up their overtures, seeking trade, cultural, and sports contacts that might pave the way to eventual diplomatic relations.[33] Except for trade, where the benefits to China were too great to resist, the PRC turned a deaf ear to South Korean proposals.

Eventually, as had happened a decade before with the Soviet Union, the desire to host prestigious international events forced the Chinese to drop their ban on admitting South Koreans. The matter came to a head in the spring of 1983, after the PRC had refused to allow South Korean delegates to attend conferences in China of UN organizations to which South Korea belonged. The ROK protested strongly to the UN secretariat, which warned the Chinese that to host future conferences of UN organizations they would have to agree to admit delegates from all member countries. The PRC yielded and in August 1983 for the first time admitted a South Korean official. He was from the National Institute of Fishery Promotion and entered China to attend an FAO-sponsored conference in Wuxi. Once the door had been opened, other South Koreans followed. In October 1983 two South Korean officials took part in a conference of the International Telecommunications Union in Shanghai, and two South Korean professors attended a training course in Dalian sponsored by the International Maritime Organization and the UN Development Program.

During 1984 the PRC's guidelines for admitting South Koreans to international events in China broadened to include meetings not sponsored by the United Nations, such as athletic competitions. Such visits were still few, but the principle had been established. Ji Pengfei, a member of the Chinese State Council, declared in a statement broadcast over Peking radio that China would not conclude bilateral relations with South Korea, but that it would continue to admit South Koreans to international conferences in China in accordance with international practice.[34] In September 1984 China lifted the taboo on Chinese participation in international conferences in South Korea with the arrival in Seoul of a 12-member delegation to the conference of the Olympic Council of Asia. In November a four-member delegation headed by the deputy director of the department of external affairs of the Post and Telecommunication Ministry took part in the general assembly of the Asia Pacific Telecommunity. In October 1985 a large Chinese delegation attended the World Bank/IMF conference.

In December 1984 a Chinese scholar specializing in Korean affairs spelled out China's policy toward attending conferences in South Korea: (1) Chinese would attend conferences in Seoul sponsored by international organizations to which China belonged; (2) Chinese would not attend conferences in Seoul sponsored solely by South Korean organizations or by international organizations of which China was not a member; (3) individual Chinese would not accept invitations to visit South Korea nor would individual South Koreans be invited to visit China. With respect to this last point, however, he added that if the dialogue between the two Koreas progressed well, such visits would become possible. He also remarked that opportunities for Chinese scholars to meet and talk at length with South Korean scholars at conferences in third countries were increasing rapidly.[35]

Exchanges continued during 1985, including the attendance of two South Korean foreign ministry officials at a UN seminar on the question of Palestine in Peking in April. Two other South Korean officials attended a Peking conference, also in April, on women, population, and devel-

opment sponsored by the UN Fund for Population Activities. Except
for the increasing number of sports exchanges discussed below, the visits
of Chinese and South Koreans remained few. South Koreans were not
invited to an Asia-Pacific meeting of young people in May 1985 to
celebrate international youth year, but did send three persons representing
Buddhist and Christian organizations to the World Conference on Religion
and Peace held in Peking in June 1986. The previous week five Chinese
attended the third Asian Conference on Religion and Peace in Seoul.[36]

Koreans Resident in China

A special channel for promoting exchange of visits between China
and South Korea developed from the presence in Northeast China of
the largest community of persons of Korean origin outside of Korea,
estimated to number as many as 1.8 million. About 40 percent of them
live in the Yanbian Korean Autonomous District in Jilin Province,
bordering North Korea and the Soviet Union, where they constitute 40
percent of the population.[37] Most of the rest live elsewhere in Jilin
Province or in Heilongjiang and Liaoning Provinces. In Yanbian Korean
is still spoken, even among third or fourth generation Koreans, and
Korean customs have been preserved. Required courses in Yanbian
University are taught in both Chinese and Korean. Korean is the primary
language of instruction in the most prestigious middle school in Yanbian,
the First Yanbian Middle School in Yanji, capital city of the Yanbian
District.[38]

Many of the Koreans in northeast China came originally from South
Korea and some still have relatives there. Beginning in 1978 the Chinese
government allowed persons of Korean origin in China to visit their
relatives in South Korea. Through April 1984, 194 of them did so.[39]
Some of them remained in South Korea, but most returned to China
after visits of as long as six months.

Beginning in 1984, visits by South Koreans to their relatives in China
became possible. Japanese Prime Minister Yasuhiro Nakasone raised the
subject on behalf of the ROK with Chinese Premier Zhao Ziyang during
his visit to Peking in March 1984. Zhao told Nakasone that the PRC
would admit South Koreans to visit their relatives, as well as continue
to allow persons of Korean origin in China to visit their relatives in
South Korea.[40] Shortly after the Nakasone visit, the Korean Red Cross
Society wrote to the Red Cross Society of China proposing a meeting
to discuss cooperation of the two societies in facilitating such visits back
and forth. The Chinese Red Cross Society apparently did not respond
to this proposal, but the South Korean Red Cross has continued its
efforts to collect data on separated families and to facilitate their reunion.

The foreign ministry reported that as of the end of August 1984, 255 Koreans had come from China, 152 of them on temporary visits to relatives and 103 to settle permanently.[41]

Several Korean-American scholars who grew up in Northeast China have visited Yanbian and have been active in promoting contacts between the people of that region and Koreans in South Korea and the United States. In November 1984 the chief administrator of the Yanbian District visited Los Angeles at the head of a 5-member economic observation mission. His delegation was welcomed by the large Korean-American community in Los Angeles, and he pledged to cooperate in arranging reunions between Korean family members in China and those in the United States. The president of Yanbian University visited several U.S. universities in 1984, and in 1985 Yanbian University signed an academic exchange agreement with the University of Kansas.[42]

In July 1985 a native of northeast China, Dr. Hyun Bong-hok, director of the department of pathology at the Muehlenberg Hospital in New Jersey and the author of a book on Koreans in the PRC, announced the establishment of a U.S.-China Korean Friendship Association for the purpose of promoting scholarly, cultural, and economic exchanges between Korean-Americans and Korean-Chinese. He said that an associate professor of pathology in the Yanbian Medical School, the first Korean-Chinese to come to the United States to do research, had arrived the previous month.[43] A Korean-American professor at the University of California, Berkeley, made a two-week visit to the Korean Studies Institute in Jilin and the Korean Studies Institute at Yanbian University. Thus, Korean-Americans, who have readier access to China than South Koreans, have begun to serve as an important link between South Korea and the Korean minority in China.

Yanbian's links with adjacent North Korea are more numerous than those with South Korea, although the latter are growing. Publications, films, and radio and television broadcasts from North Korea are readily available in Yanbian. Cultural exchange programs are active. Some teachers in Yanbian received their training in North Korea. Koreans in Yanbian visit their relatives in North Korea with travel permits issued by local governments, and some North Koreans visit Yanbian. During 1985 an estimated 150 persons a day crossed the Tumen Bridge between Yanbian and North Korea.

Radio Seoul, particularly its music programs, has an audience in Yanbian. Tapes of popular South Korean songs are also available. Yanbian University has several thousand books from South Korea. Scholars met by visiting Korean-Americans were eager to obtain books in their fields from South Korea. They complained that books from North Korea were shallow in scholarly content and full of political propaganda. Works by

South Korean writers have begun to appear in both Chinese-language and Korean-language publications in Northeast China.[44]

Some Chinese Koreans have relations in North Korea, some in South Korea. Visits to North Korea have given some Chinese-Koreans the impression that the standard of living in North Korea is lower in some respects than their own. Only within the past few years has information begun to trickle in concerning the higher living standard in South Korea. As the flow of information increases, the desire to correspond with relatives in South Korea, to visit them, or even to move there is likely to grow. North Korea will find it difficult to counter through its official propaganda outlets the credible eyewitness accounts of South Korea passed on by friends or relatives.

Sports

Until 1984 the Chinese adhered strictly to a policy of not inviting South Korean athletes to international meets in China and not sending Chinese athletes to compete in South Korea. As early as 1975, when the Second Asian Field and Track Meet was held in Seoul, the South Koreans invited the Chinese. South Korean sports officials sought in other ways to develop connections with China, but without success. Chinese and South Korean athletes occasionally played each other at international championships in other countries, but not on each other's soil. As mentioned above, the Chinese were prepared to forgo hosting international meets in China when it was necessary in order to avoid inviting South Koreans.

By 1984, as had happened earlier with the Soviet Union, sports had become an important way for China to promote its national prestige. Giving up the chance to host prestigious events became increasingly costly. Moreover, by this time China had been forced to negotiate directly with South Korea over the hijacking incident and compelled to admit South Koreans to UN-sponsored events in China. Admitting South Korean athletes to China and sending its own to South Korea occasionally could not greatly increase North Korea's displeasure over its dealing with South Korea, especially when the Soviet Union was doing the same.

The Davis Cup Eastern Zone quarterfinal in March 1984 provided the occasion for dropping the PRC's ban on sport exchanges with South Korea. Perhaps out of deference to Pyongyang's feelings, the match was held in Kunming, in southwest China, about as far as possible from North Korea. The Chinese press was silent on the meet, except for an inconspicuous item reporting the Chinese team's 4–1 victory. In Seoul, on the contrary, the press trumpeted the news on the front page,

complete with pictures. Furthermore, South Korean commentators hastened to point out the parallel between the "tennis diplomacy" between
China and South Korea and the "ping-pong diplomacy" of 1971 that
had foreshadowed the opening of relations between China and the
United States.

A few days after the Kunming breakthrough, a senior Chinese official,
Ye Fei, one of twenty vice chairmen of the National People's Congress,
was quoted as saying in Tokyo that China would take part in international
sports competitions, cultural events, and meetings in South Korea.[45]
The new policy quickly produced results. In April 1984, Chinese men's
and women's basketball teams arrived in Seoul to compete in the Eighth
Asian Junior Basketball Championships. This competition had a political
spin-off for the PRC in the form of friction between Seoul and Taipei.
The South Koreans, wary of disrupting their newly established sports
exchanges with the PRC, insisted on applying to teams from Taiwan
the Olympic formula, that is, referring to those teams as "Chinese-
Taipei" and requiring them to use their Olympic flag and song instead
of their national flag and anthem. The Republic of China withdrew its
teams, protesting bitterly that the Olympic formula was inappropriate
for a competition in a state with which it had diplomatic relations.

Other sports exchanges followed. Chinese swimmers won decisively
over the second-place Japanese at the Second Asian Swimming Championships in Seoul in April. The South Korean women's basketball team
narrowly defeated the Chinese to win the 10th Asian Women's Basketball
Championship in Shanghai in October 1984. The South Koreans flew
their own national flag at the game, which was televised throughout
China. The Chinese admitted 10 Korean correspondents to cover the
match and opened a direct telephone connection with Seoul for their
use, perhaps in reciprocation of South Korea's opening of a direct
telephone link to Shanghai the month before for the use of Chinese
delegates to the Olympic Council of Asia meeting in Seoul. The Chinese
sent representatives to meetings in Seoul of the Asian Basketball Confederation and the Asia Sports Press Union. South Korean delegates,
accompanied by two reporters, attended the meeting of the Asian Football
Confederation in Guangzhou, along with delegates from North Korea.
Delegates from both Koreas also took part in a meeting of the Asian
Pacific and Oceania Sports Assembly in Peking.

During 1985 sport exchanges gathered momentum. The deputy prime
minister of the ROK reported to the National Assembly that Korean
athletes took part in 19 sports events in China during the year and
that Chinese athletes had come to South Korea for 10 events.[46] At the
17th Asian Weightlifting Championships in Hangzhou in April, won by
China, South Korea placed second and North Korea placed fourth. South

Korean divers took part in the 4th World Cup International Diving Championship in Shanghai, and a Chinese men's handball team competed in the preliminary round of the 11th World Men's Handball Championships in Seoul. These growing sports exchanges increased the probability that China would compete in the 1986 Asian Games to defend the title it had won in New Delhi in 1982.

Transportation

Confrontation and rivalry between the two Koreas has prevented agreement on overflights of Korea by commercial aircraft that would substantially shorten the flying time between Japan and China. In 1980 the president of the International Civil Aviation Organization sounded out China, Japan, and the two Koreas on the possiblity of opening two new routes: Tokyo-Seoul-Peking and Tokyo-Pyongyang-Shenyang-Peking. Japan and South Korea favored the proposal, but North Korea opposed it on the ground that establishment of two routes would solidify the division of Korea. North Korea wanted a single route across its territory, which South Korea opposed.

In 1983 aviation officials from China, Japan, and South Korea, meeting in Singapore, agreed on an arrangement permitting flights between Tokyo and Shanghai to cut across the southern part of the ROK's flight information region (FIR) south of Cheju-do Island instead of flying farther south to skirt the FIR entirely. The shortcut saves about half an hour flying time. Flights on the new route began in August 1983. Flight control in Shanghai does not communicate directly with its counterpart in Taegu, South Korea, but goes through the Japanese flight control center in Fukue.[47] In October 1984 the South Korean government for the first time authorized a foreign airline, Swissair, to fly a charter flight from Zurich through Peking to Seoul.

In 1985 China and South Korea, for the first time since 1949, opened parcel post service between them via Hong Kong, supplementing the mail service that had been available for some time. Families with relatives in northeast China promptly took advantage of the new service to exchange packages back and forth.

Trends in Chinese Contacts

Contacts between China and South Korea have increased at a remarkable pace since 1983, when the Chinese lifted the nearly total ban (except for trade) that had previously existed. The proximity of the two countries, the complementarity of their economies, their easy access to each other through Hong Kong, and the participation of both in the proliferating network of Asian-Pacific organizations of all kinds have made this trend inevitable.

The decline in North Korea's ability to prevent China from expanding contacts with South Korea can be explained in large part by the increasingly important roles played by China and South Korea in the world, in everything from trade to athletics. Peking is no longer willing to refrain from useful international activities in order to avoid irritating North Korea. The North Koreans have been compelled to acquiesce in a level of contacts between China and South Korea that would have been hard to imagine a few years ago, almost seeming to give their blessing to such contacts by appearing alongside South Koreans at meetings and sports events in China.

As of mid-1986, the trend appears irreversible. How fast it will move and the form it will take depend on complex calculations of national interest, involving not only China and the two Koreas, but the Soviet Union, Japan, and the United States. These complexities will be discussed at the end of this chapter and in Chapter 12.

Japanese Contacts with North Korea

For a variety of reasons, Japan's contacts with North Korea have been more numerous and have had more obvious political implications than the contacts between the United States and North Korea or those of China and the Soviet Union with South Korea. Familiarity with Korea acquired during the colonial period gave the Japanese greater access to both Koreas than the nationals of other countries had. The large Korean minority in Japan, cultivated effectively by North Korea from the 1950s on, became in important link between Japan and North Korea. Japan's heavier dependence than the great continental powers on foreign trade created significant pressures among Japanese businessmen for trade with North Korea. Disputes between Japan and North Korea regarding access to fishing waters required contacts to resolve. Finally, contacts with North Korea seemed necessary to many Japanese as a means of promoting North-South dialogue and a lowering of tension in the Korean peninsula.

Before 1965 Japan had diplomatic relations with neither part of Korea and carried on trade and unofficial contacts with both. Even so, Japan's relationship with the United States, the dominance of the Japanese government by conservative politicians, and the relatively greater opportunities for trade in the South tilted Japan's policy markedly toward South Korea. Nevertheless, substantial contacts with North Korea developed during this period, including those related to trade and to the repatriation of Koreans from Japan to North Korea managed by the Red

Cross Societies of the two countries in accordance with the agreement reached in 1959.

A new period began with the establishment of diplomatic relations between Japan and the ROK in 1965. Japan formally recognized the government of the ROK as the only legitimate government in Korea, in accordance with the UN resolution establishing the ROK, but made clear that it did not recognize ROK jurisdiction over North Korea. Prime Minister Eisaku Sato, while declaring that Japan would not establish diplomatic relations with North Korea, indicated that contacts with it on economic, cultural, and humanitarian matters would be continued. Trade with South Korea between 1965 and 1970 surged, stimulated by the establishment of diplomatic relations and the influx of Japanese capital. Trade between Japan and North Korea also increased, but at a much slower pace.

In the first half of the 1970s, the Japanese showed an unprecedented interest in expanding contacts with North Korea, brought on by changes in the international situation. Announcement of the Nixon Doctrine, the withdrawal of a U.S. division from South Korea, the opening of relations between the United States and China, and the pursuit of detente between Washington and Moscow cast a new light on the situation in Northeast Asia. The two Koreas responded to this radical change by opening a dialogue with each other. Japanese politicians and businessmen, feeling that these developments required a new policy toward Korea, hastened to devise ways of expanding contacts with North Korea. Concern that the United States, which had abruptly changed its policy toward China without consulting Japan, might do the same toward North Korea, imparted a sense of urgency to their activities.

Expansion of contacts with North Korea was only one manifestation of the notable shift in Japan's policy toward Korea during this period. The government of Prime Minister Sato (1964–1972) had vigorously cultivated relations with South Korea and strictly limited contacts with North Korea, even to the extent of causing cancellation of a machinery plant sale to North Korea by refusing entry to North Korean technicians in response to South Korean pressure. In the Nixon-Sato communique Sato had declared that "the security of the Republic of Korea is essential to Japan's own security" and had indicated that Japan would concur in a U.S. request to use its military bases in Japan in defense of South Korea. The advent of the Tanaka government in 1972, in an atmosphere of detente, brought subtle changes in Japan's security posture toward the two Koreas. Foreign Minister Toshio Kimura stated that the government of the Republic of Korea was not the only legitimate government in Korea, denied that North Korea threatened South Korea, and linked

Japan's security not simply to the security of South Korea, but to the security of the entire Korean peninsula.

Japanese intellectuals, who had opposed the establishment of diplomatic relations with South Korea only, called for a policy of equidistance between the two Koreas. Kim Il Sung gave interviews to visiting editors of influential Japanese publications, expressing a desire for improved relations and increased trade with Japan. Japanese politicians from various parties, including the LDP, established a Dietmen's League for the Promotion of Japan–[North] Korean Friendship with over 240 members. A delegation from this group, headed by an LDP member, Chuji Kuno, visited Pyongyang in 1972 and signed a trade agreement with the DPRK Committee for the Promotion of International Trade stipulating a sizable increase in trade and an exchange of trade missions. The two parties urged the Japanese government to abandon its unfriendly attitude toward the DPRK and expressed optimism that efforts by the two peoples would lead to the establishment of diplomatic relations.

Japanese interest in increasing contacts with North Korea coincided with North Korea's decision to step up drastically its purchases of plants and machinery from Japan and Europe. Japanese businessmen responded with enthusiasm and set about organizing a delegation of business leaders to visit North Korea. Trade shot up rapidly, especially Japanese exports to North Korea, which increased ninefold from 1971 to 1974. North Korea sent a number of delegations to Japan, including one from the Committee for the Promotion of International Trade in 1972; several with interest in television and radio, steel, and cement in 1973; and an industrial and trade delegation in 1974. Japanese media representatives who visited North Korea portrayed an orderly, neat, rapidly developing society. Their praise of North Korea contrasted sharply with the steady stream of critical reporting on South Korea.

The establishment of diplomatic relations with China in 1972 created pressures for doing the same with North Korea. A number of LDP members joined members of opposition parties in organizing a National Council for the Normalization of Japan–North Korea relations in September 1973. Even the government departed from past policy by authorizing loans by the Export-Import Bank for the export of two plants to North Korea.

The enthusiasm for improving relations with North Korea was short-lived. The breakdown of North-South talks in 1973, the assassination attempt on Park Chung-hee, and the discovery of tunnels under the DMZ quickly soured the detente atmosphere. The Kim Dae Jung kidnapping strained relations between Seoul and Tokyo, as did the anger of South Koreans against Japan over the assassination incident and South Korean protests at Japanese actions improving relations with North

Korea. Business leaders, recognizing the risks to their interests in further aggravating relations with South Korea, cancelled the planned delegation to North Korea. The Japanese government decided not to authorize any more Export-Import bank loans for sales to North Korea.

The U.S. withdrawal from Vietnam in 1975 and Kim Il Sung's belligerent speech in Peking reinforced the Japanese government's policy of drawing back from improving relations with North Korea and concentrating instead on strengthening relations with South Korea. Prime Minister Takeo Miki, who had succeeded Tanaka, delicately reformulated the Japanese view of Korea so as to restore the stress on the importance of the security of the Republic of Korea to peace in Korea and to Japan.[48]

The policies of Miki and his successors were less restrictive of contacts between Japan and North Korea than Sato had been, but they were cautious and selective, with an eye to South Korean reactions. North Korea's default on its debts to Japanese creditors dampened the overblown optimism of 1972 and 1973 in the business community concerning trade prospects. The political opposition and left-wing intellectuals continued to criticize the Japanese government's one-sided relationship with South Korea and advocated the establishment of diplomatic relations with North Korea, but with no perceptible effect on government policy.

Trade

Trade between Japan and North Korea was qualitatively different from the negligible indirect trade between the Soviet Union and South Korea or the substantial but unacknowledged trade between China and South Korea. Japan traded openly with North Korea. The Japan External Trade Organization (JETRO) regularly published analyses of the trade and issued statistics on it. The Japanese media reported on it at length.

During the North Korea fever of the early 1970s, the big Japanese companies showed keen interest in doing business with North Korea, but their interest quickly cooled when Pyongyang defaulted on its debts. Most of the trade has been conducted by small firms owned by Koreans in Japan.

The primary problem besetting trade between Japan and North Korea has been the difficulty of establishing a firm schedule for the payment of interest and principal on North Korean debts of some $400 million incurred in the early 1970s. A rescheduling of payments agreed to in 1979 after prolonged negotiations had to be renegotiated in 1983 to extend the time for repayment of principal. Even interest payments were not always made on time. In late 1983 the North Koreans stopped making interest payments in retaliation for the Japanese sanctions imposed after the Rangoon bombing. North Korea's reputation as an unreliable debtor forced it to conduct most trade with Japan on a cash or barter basis. Not until 1979 did total trade exceed the level reached in 1974. Since then it has remained in the $400 to $500 million range, substantially less than the level of Chinese trade with South Korea in 1984 to 1985.[49]

Japan's trade with North Korea has had a political dimension not present in Chinese or Soviet trade with South Korea. The two countries have exchanged delegations for the purpose of promoting trade. Japanese politicians, following a pattern established in trade with China before the establishment of diplomatic relations, signed trade agreements with North Korean agencies and advocated the establishment of trade missions in Pyongyang and Tokyo. South Korea, while recognizing the impossibility of preventing trade between Japan and North Korea, has strenuously opposed these efforts by Japanese politicians to create a political framework for trade. The South Koreans also protested strongly the export of materials that would bolster North Korea's arms industry or would add to its military capability.

Exchange of Delegations

The exchange of persons between Japan and North Korea went far beyond the narrow limits of participation in international conferences and sports events constituting the bulk of the exchanges that China and the Soviet Union had with South Korea. Although no official negotiations occurred, such as that between Peking and Seoul over the hijacked plane, many politically significant trips took place. Japanese politicians visited Pyongyang rather freely, but trips to Japan by North Koreans were strictly limited by the Japanese government. The government, in principal, refused to admit political figures and required the North Koreans admitted to refrain from political activity in Japan. If one failed to observe this restriction, the South Koreans protested loudly to the Japanese government.

The leaders of the Japanese Socialist Party, North Korea's principal backer in Japan, made frequent trips to North Korea. The JSP's willingness to support publicly North Korea's position and to attack the position of the Japanese government toward Korea assured such visitors a warm welcome. A notable visit was the Fifth JSP Mission to North Korea led by Chairman Ichio Asukata in May 1978. The JSP and the KWP issued a joint communique asserting that the two parties had "reached an identity of views on all questions discussed." In the communique the JSP demanded the withdrawal of U.S. forces from South Korea and the abrogation of the Japan-ROK treaty. It denounced the "Park Chung-hee puppet clique" and expressed firm support for reunification of Korea on the terms put forward by North Korea.[50]

The Asukata mission encountered an unexpected change in North Korea's position concerning the establishment of diplomatic relations with Japan. In 1972 and 1973 North Korea urged the establishment of diplomatic relations between Pyongyang and Tokyo, asserting that Japanese diplomatic relations with both Koreas would not impede reunification. Kim Il Sung himself told the *Tokyo Shimbun* in February 1973 that "Japan–South Korea relations in no way preclude normalization of diplomatic relations between our country and Japan."[51] Previous joint communiqués had supported the establishment of diplomatic relations, and it had become a fundamental tenet in the JSP position on Japan-Korean relations. The communiqué issued during the Asukata visit, however, omitted reference to normalization. Asukata explained later at a press conference that the KWP now advocated deferring the establishment of diplomatic relations until after the reunification of Korea, on the ground that their establishment while Korea was divided would lead to cross-recognition.[52]

Headed by LDP member Chuji Kuno, delegations of the Dietmen's League, which had signed the trade agreement in 1972, also made repeated trips to Pyongyang. The League's joint communiques with the [North] Korean Society for Cultural Relations with Foreign Countries, like those of the JSP and KWP, generally supported the North Korean position, but in more restrained language. These delegations discussed with the North Koreans substantive matters such as trade, fisheries, and cultural exchanges. Patterned after similar delegations to China before 1972, they included LDP members as well as those from other parties and sought to develop unofficial relations with North Korea step by step.

Most delegations from Japan were politically sympathetic to North Korea. They included representatives of the Japan Committee for Supporting Korea's Independent and Peaceful Reunification, frequent delegations from Chosoren, and left-wing scholars and journalists. Numerous businessmen traveled back and forth. In September 1980 a seven-member LDP mission headed by former minister of labor Katsuji Fujii proposed a quasi-governmental trade agreement.

The proposed agreement did not materialize at that time, but Japanese big business was showing signs of renewed interest in trade with North Korea, probably encouraged by the agreement on debt rescheduling and the growth of North Korea's foreign trade. A number of leading businessmen, including Yoshiro Inayama, chairman of Nippon Steel Company and head of the Federation of Economic Organizations (Keidanren), established an East Asian Trade Research Council for the primary purpose of studying the prospects of expanding trade with North Korea. The organization avoided publicity so as to minimize adverse reactions in

South Korea, where many of the companies involved had valuable trade relations.[53]

In 1982 total visitors to Japan from North Korea numbered 246 persons, according to one estimate. Most travel was related to trade. Some thirty to forty groups visited Japan each year for this purpose.[54] These visits, like those of Japanese businessmen to North Korea attracted relatively little attention and created no political problems. The prime criterion applied by the Japanese government in deciding on the admission or exclusion of a North Korean delegation was whether it was likely to conduct "political activities" in Japan. Opinion differed on what constituted political activities, and the admission of certain delegations provoked strong adverse reactions in Seoul.

Delegations refused entry by the Japanese government included a delegation to a Chosoren convention in 1977 headed by a high North Korean government official and a delegation to the Second World Conference on the Unification of Korea in Tokyo in 1978. Han Dok Su, chairman of Chosoren, who had been elected a deputy to the Supreme People's Assembly in 1977, was denied permission to attend the Assembly meeting and return to Japan on the ground that the trip would be for political activity. In July 1983 a North Korean delegation declined to attend an antinuclear meeting in Japan to which it had been invited by the JSP, on the ground that the Japanese government's ban on political activities was too strict. Delegations and personages admitted to Japan included a delegation to an IPU conference in 1974; Kim Ki-nam, the editor-in-chief of the *Nodong Sinmun*, in 1978; a trade mission representing the Committee for the Promotion of International Trade in 1981; and a delegation from Pyongyang's Academy of Social Sciences to attend a conference of the Asian-African Legal Consultative Committee in 1983, at which South Korea was also represented. At this conference a ten-minute conversation at a reception between Japanese Foreign Minister Shintaro Abe and the head of the North Korean delegation attracted attention and caused uneasiness in Seoul.

The Dietmen's League, headed by Chuji Kuno, invited delegations in 1977 and again in 1981 representing the Society for Cultural Relations with Foreign Countries headed by Hyon Chun-kuk, a vice chairman of the society and a member of the Supreme People's Assembly. Hyon's visits alarmed South Korea because they appeared to be significant steps toward official relations between Tokyo and Pyongyang. The meetings involved members of the ruling parties of both countries, and they discussed such politically sensitive subjects as the establishment of unofficial trade missions in the two countries and the opening of air travel between them. The South Korean government protested strongly Hyon's press interviews in which he condemned political conditions in

South Korea.[55] The Japanese government agreed that Hyon had over-stepped the bounds and for several years thereafter declined to readmit him.

The Rangoon bombing in October 1983 temporarily halted the expansion of contacts between Japan and North Korea. The Japanese government banned the travel of Japanese officials to North Korea and of North Korean officials to Japan and prohibited contacts between its diplomats and those of North Korea. North Korea retaliated by adopting similar regulations—the mirror image of those adopted by Japan. Although the sanctions were mild and did not apply to unofficial contacts between Japanese and North Koreans, the chilling impact of the Rangoon atrocity, particularly on left-wing circles that had been friendly toward Pyongyang diminished for a time the desire to promote contacts. The number of Japanese visiting North Korea dropped to 798 in 1984, compared to 876 in 1983. North Korean visitors to Japan decreased sharply from 434 to 167.[56] Chuji Kuno, chairman of the Dietmen's League, who had led eight delegations to North Korea, and his deputy both lost their Diet seats in the December 1983 elections, thus further hampering the development of contacts with North Korea.

The Japanese government lifted its sanctions in January 1985, but even before that significant unofficial contacts had resumed. Four North Korean social scientists toured Japanese universities in May-June 1984. JSP Chairman Masashi Ishibashi spent six days in Pyongyang in September 1984. Exchanges gained momentum in 1985. In February a North Korean film crew arrived to make a movie in Japan. In April, Kim Ki-nam, editor-in-chief of the *Nodong Sinmun*, returned to Japan at the invitation of the JSP and expressed his political views freely to the Japanese press, which disturbed the South Koreans.[57] A JSP delegation, headed by the secretary-general, Makoto Tanabe, visited North Korea in May. In June a goodwill and friendship delegation arrived in Japan headed by Kim U-chong, chairman of the [North] Korean Japan Friendship Association and vice chairman of the Society for the Promotion of Cultural Relations with Foreign Countries. His host was Yoichi Tani, an LDP Diet member who had become acting chairman of the Dietmen's League. Kim reportedly met privately with senior LDP figures, including former prime minister Takeo Miki, causing speculation in Seoul that Japan might be moving closer to approving the establishment of trade offices in the two countries, which the Dietmen's League had long advocated.[58]

Trade-related activities also picked up. The Changwan Trade Company, established not long before to represent 250 North Korean factories in promoting trade with Western countries, and the only North Korean trading company to maintain an office in Tokyo, sent a delegation to

Japan in September to spend a month talking with Japanese companies.[59] About the same time Den Kawakatsu, chairman of the Nankai Electric Railway Company, visited Pyongyang and met with Kim Il Sung and Politburo member Ho Tam. Kawakatsu signed a private memorandum with Yi Song-nok, head of a committee for Asian trade and concurrently the vice minister of foreign trade, calling for increased efforts to enlarge the trade between Japan and North Korea through joint ventures and otherwise. Kawakatsu was the first topflight Japanese businessman to visit North Korea. When he returned, he reported on his trip to the East Asia Trade Research Council.[60]

Fisheries

The declaration of a 200-mile economic zone by the DPRK on August 1, 1977, together with a 50-mile "military zone" that foreign ships could enter only with Pyongyang's permission, barred Japanese fishermen from a large area of their traditional fishing waters. A fisheries agreement between the two countries was urgently needed to permit some continued fishing by Japanese in these waters. As a government-to-government agreement could not be concluded owing to the absence of diplomatic relations, the Dietmen's League sent a delegation to Pyongyang in September to conclude a private agreement. The negotiations stalled over insistence by the North Koreans that the Japanese government "guarantee" the agreement, and the two sides settled on an interim accord permitting Japanese fishing boats under 200 tons to fish without paying fees in the North Korean economic zone, but not in the military zone. The agreement was extended several times, but expired in June 1982 and was not renewed until October 1984.

North Korean patrol boats seized a number of Japanese fishing vessels and crews for entering the military zone or, after the fisheries agreement had expired, for fishing within the 200-mile economic zone. The North Koreans sometimes fined the fishermen, detained them for a few days, warned them against future infractions, and then released them after they had confessed to violating North Korean waters. In July 1984 the North Koreans fired on a Japanese fishing boat, killing its captain, and in October 1985 a North Korean patrol boat rammed and sank a Japanese fishing boat but rescued its crew. In November 1983 a Japanese ship captain and engineer were arrested at Nampo port for carrying to Japan on a previous trip a defector who had sneaked aboard and stowed away. The Japanese government rejected the North Korean demand that the defector be exchanged for them, as Japanese law prohibits the deportation of an illegal immigrant to a place where he might be persecuted. As of December 1986 the two Japanese seamen were still being held hostage in North Korea.

Japan and North Korea had no convenient channel through which to negotiate the settlement of incidents, such as the Chinese and South Koreans had developed in Hong Kong. The Japanese Red Cross Society would send a message to its counterpart in North Korea appealing for the return of the detained fishermen, but government officials declined to take any action, on the ground of the absence of diplomatic relations.

The JSP and South Korea

The JSP saw itself as an important link between Japan and North Korea in the absence of diplomatic relations between the two governments. It declined to acknowledge the legitimacy of the ROK and rejected contacts with that government or with the ruling party in South Korea. It had contacts only with the tiny United Socialist Party in South Korea, which had no significant political influence. After the DPRK declared its willingness to talk with the ROK, first in the form of tripartite talks and later in a North-South dialogue, some JSP members began to question the party's one-sided commitment to North Korea. The chairman of the financial and monetary committee, Sanji Muto, declared publicly in September 1984 that the JSP should recognize South Korea as a sovereign state. In November Koichi Yamamoto, a former secretary-general of the JSP, and three other former Diet members in the party defied the party leadership and visited South Korea in response to an invitation from the speaker of the ROK National Assembly.

In mid-1985, the debate between left-wing and right-wing factions in the JSP heated up. Party leaders, instead of almost totally rejecting contacts with South Koreans as in the past, began to give serious consideration to developing a relationship with the NKDP, the chief opposition party in South Korea, while still eschewing contacts with the government or the ruling party. In October 1985 Kim Young Sam met with Masashi Ishibashi, chairman of the JSP, and reached agreement in principle on an exchange of visits between the two parties.

The DJP took a dim view of the proposed exchange, particularly after the JSP's central executive committee reaffirmed the policy of cultivating friendly relations with the KWP and called for "coalition with South Korean forces that wish for peaceful reunification and restoration of democracy."[61] The JSP's leadership in effect rejected a written appeal from five senior party members for a radical change in the JSP's policy, including recognition of the ROK government and exchanges with all the political parties in South Korea. In order to firmly discourage exchanges between the JSP and the NKDP, DJP leaders not only urged the NKDP not to send a delegation to Japan, but strongly implied that a JSP delegation would be denied visas to make a return visit.[62] DJP leaders feared that exchanges between the JSP and the NKDP would stimulate LDP members in Japan to step up their contacts with North Korea.

The JCP and North Korea

The Japan Communist Party accepted the legitimacy of the DPRK and rejected that of the ROK, but it did not offer wholehearted support to the KWP, as the JSP did. On the contrary, the JCP published an article in 1979 in the party's theoretical journal by Tetsuzo Fuwa, secretary-general of the party's Central Committee, harshly condemning Kim Il Sung's cult of personality.[63] In April 1985 the JCP revised its party platform to acknowledge the existence of two governments in Korea. In a resolution presented at its party congress in November 1985, the JCP denounced the fatal shooting of a Japanese fisherman as a barbaric form of hegemonism practiced by the KWP, flouting the principles of scientific socialism and international law.[64]. Thus, the JCP, instead of providing a useful channel through which the DPRK could influence the Japanese, adopted a confrontational stance.

Trends in Japanese Contacts

Contacts between Japan and North Korea have risen and fallen over the years, but the trend has been unmistakably upward, both in numbers and in their political significance. The opposition JSP has taken the lead in furthering contacts, but, as happened in the process of normalizing relations with China, certain LDP members, in particular Chuji Kuno, became identified with this cause. Normalization of relations with North Korea was not, however, a hotly contested political issue in Japan as normalization with China had been. The pressure that advocates of normalization could bring to bear on the government was slight. The LDP leadership and government bureaucrats had their own reasons for allowing and even quietly encouraging contacts with Pyongyang. But the check on them was their concern with South Korea's reaction.

The Japanese government's policy toward contacts with North Korea rested on three basic principles. First, maintaining a good relationship with South Korea was essential for security, economic, and political reasons. Seoul would not be given a veto on Japanese contacts with North Korea, but these contacts would be held to a level that would not seriously harm the essential relationship with South Korea. Second, peace on the Korean peninsula was vital to Japan's security. Contacts between Japan and North Korea would penetrate the excessive isolation of that country and help to give the North Koreans a more realistic view of the world outside. Such contacts would also encourage contacts by the Soviets and Chinese with South Korea and by Americans with North Korea. Cross-contacts would improve prospects for North-South talks and would contribute to a decline in tension on the peninsula. Third, trade could be justified purely in terms of its economic value to Japan, but beyond that, drawing North Korea into the international economy through trade also would reduce the danger of war in Korea.

All Japanese governments subscribed to these principles. Some were more liberal than others in the range of contacts permitted, but their tactics had a number of features in common. They all favored expanding contacts through a step-by-step or "piling up" process. Politicians took this view in the hope that the piling up of cross-contacts would lead eventually to cross-recognition by the big powers and the evolution through North-South dialogue of a stable state of peaceful coexistence on the peninsula. Bureaucrats generally shared this outlook, but also often had parochial, practical reasons for favoring contacts. The Ministry of Trade and Industry (MITI) wanted to promote trade. The Ministry of Agriculture and Fisheries wanted more lasting and favorable fisheries agreements with North Korea. The Ministry of Transportation was interested in getting overflight rights for Japan Air Lines to shorten the route to Peking.

Spurred by these motivations, successive Japanese governments cautiously probed the limits of South Korean tolerance. Seoul was quick to protest proposals by Japanese delegations to establish permanent trade offices or news representatives in each other's capitals or to open air service between Japan and North Korea. The South Koreans feared that Japan would rush far ahead of China and the Soviet Union in the cross-contacts process. As of mid-1986, the Japanese government had not approved these proposals. It repeatedly assured the South Korean government that its policy of refusing recognition and diplomatic relations to North Korea had not changed. Still, the methodical testing of limits continued. When Japanese–South Korean relations were good and North-South dialogue was underway, the Japanese felt greater freedom to expand contacts with North Korea. When Japanese-South Korean relations were strained and North-South dialogue had broken off, they were more cautious.

Big Power Interaction

The big powers are impelled to engage in cross-contacts, first of all for practical reasons. Trade, fisheries, and participation in international activities all require some form of contact with the part of Korea with which they lack diplomatic relations. As the two Koreas augment their international activities in competition with each other, more occasions arise when such contacts cannot easily be avoided.

The extent to which the big powers pursue or permit cross-contacts cannot be explained entirely on the grounds of practical needs, however. They are valued also for the contribution they are presumed to make to the stability of the Korean peninsula. The Japanese subscribe more openly and explicitly to this conviction than do the other big powers. They join the United States in advocating cross-recognition as a means of diminishing the cold war atmosphere that has surrounded Korea, and they see the step-by-step expansion of cross-contacts as leading to that goal.

The Chinese are more reticent in public than the Japanese are in endorsing cross-contacts, but in private many scholars and officials see the expansion as both inevitable and desirable. Some go so far as to accept cross-recognition as the end result. From the Chinese viewpoint cross-recognition would remove the inhibitions on a much more fruitful interchange with South Korea than is possible today.

The Japanese and the Chinese both strongly favor North-South dialogue and see a direct connection between progress in the dialogue and greater freedom to expand cross-contacts. Each does what it can to encourage its Korean associate to move ahead in the dialogue. The pace of expansion of cross-contacts by one also affects the other. China's opening up to South Korea in 1984 and 1985 tended to reduce the constraints on Japan's cross-contacts with North Korea.

The Soviet Union has fallen behind China in the increase of cross-contacts with South Korea. Soviet officials have publicly opposed cross-recognition, while scholars and officials have privately expressed the view that it is probably inevitable. The Soviets have seemed less inclined than the Chinese and Japanese to encourage their Korean ally to make progress in the North-South dialogue. Furthermore, to the limited extent that they show an interest in the expansion of cross-contacts beyond a level that cannot be avoided, they tend to compare their level of activity with that of the United States, not that of Japan.

The South Koreans have sought the help of the Japanese in urging China to go further in expanding its contacts with South Korea. Similarly, the North Koreans have enlisted Chinese help in urging the United States to increase its contacts with North Korea. As in other aspects of their international rivalry, success may produce undesired as well as desired results. That is, an increase in China's contacts with South Korea tends to encourage Japan and the United States to increase their contacts with North Korea. An increase in U.S. contacts with North Korea would encourage increased Soviet and Chinese contacts with South Korea, as will be discussed in the next chapter. The precise pattern of increases in cross-contacts by the big powers cannot be foreseen, but increases by one stimulate increases by another. The probability is high that their aggregate growth will not only continue, but accelerate.

Notes

1. Research Center for Peace and Unification, *Korean Unification: Source Materials with an Introduction* (Seoul, 1976), p. 339.

2. *FBIS*, February 5, 1974, p. A6.

3. *FBIS*, July 27, 1974, pp. E1–E2; August 5, 1974, pp. D5–D6.

4. *FBIS*, November 11, 1974, pp. A3–A5.

5. *FBIS*, September 7, 1978, p. E6.

6. Interview, Washington, D.C., April 1979.

7. The World Ice Hockey Championship (Group C), which was originally to be held in Peking in March 1979, was shifted to another country (*Korea Herald*, February 18, 1979).

8. Interview, Seoul, October 1982.

9. *Far Eastern Economic Review*, November 12, 1982, pp. 43–44.

10. *Korea Herald*, September 28, 1979.

11. *Korea Herald*, December 16, 1983.

12. Interview, April 1979.

13. A Chinese specialist on Korean affairs, in a conversation with the author in December 1981, cited this tendency as an obstacle to contacts with South Korea, giving as an example the attendance at a conference in Seoul of a Chinese studying in the United States, which had been played up in the South Korean press.

14. *Korea Herald*, June 6, 1979.

15. Interview with a U.S. scholar, July 1981.

16. Interviews, Peking, December 1981.

17. Interview, Cambridge, Mass., January 1983.

18. Interview, Washington, D.C., September 25, 1984.

19. *Newsweek*, January 14, 1985, quoted in *Korea Herald*, January 9, 1985; *Washington Post*, April 28, 1985.

20. *Asian Wall Street Journal*, December 16, 1985.

21. Sam Jameson, *Los Angeles Times*, in *Korea Herald*, October 19, 1985; *China Business Review*, July–August 1985, p. 4.

22. *Asian Wall Street Journal*, December 16, 1985.

23. *Far Eastern Economic Review*, September 8, 1983, pp. 44–45.

24. Interview with South Korean official, November 1984.

25. Selig S. Harrison, *China, Oil and Asia: Conflict Ahead?* (New York: Columbia University Press, 1977), pp. 123–137.

26. *Korea Herald*, June 11, 1983.

27. *Korea Herald*, August 15, 1984.

28. *Washington Post*, August 26, 1985; *Korea Herald*, August 11, 1985, and September 17, 1985.

29. *New York Times*, March 24, 1985; *FBIS*, March 26, 1985, p. E1.

30. *Korea Herald,* March 30, 1985; *FBIS,* March 29, 1985, pp. E1–E2.
31. *Korea Herald,* April 3, 1985.
32. *Korea Herald,* April 20, 1985; *FBIS,* April 30, 1985, pp. E4–E5; *FBIS,* January 1, 1985, p. E1; *FBIS,* September 16, 1985, p. E1.
33. *Washington Post,* December 30, 1978.
34. *Korea Herald,* May 16, 1984.
35. Interview, Peking, December 1984.
36. *FBIS,* June 23, 1986, p. E5.
37. Chae-Jin Lee, *China's Korean Minority: The Politics of Ethnic Education* (Boulder, Colo.: Westview Press, 1986), pp. 4–5.
38. Ibid., p. 119.
39. *FBIS,* May 1, 1984, p. E2.
40. *Korea Herald,* March 27, 1984.
41. *Korea Herald,* October 20, 1984.
42. Chae-Jin Lee, *China's Korean Minority,* p. 128.
43. *Korea Herald,* July 12, 1985.
44. Chae-Jin Lee, *China's Korean Minority,* pp. 146–149. See also articles on visits to Yanbian by a Korean-American journalist, Peter Hyun, and a West German scholar (*Korea Herald,* October 2 and 23, 1984; January 28, 1986).
45. *Korea Herald,* March 4, 1984.
46. *Korea Herald,* November 8, 1985.
47. *Korea Newsreview,* January 22, 1983, p. 10; *Korea Herald,* February 11, 1983, and August 6, 1983.
48. For more details on the "North Korea euphoria" of 1972 and 1973 and its rapid decline see Yung H. Park, "Japan's Korean Policy and Her Perceptions and Expectations Regarding America's Role in Korea," in Jo, *U.S. Foreign Policy in Asia,* pp. 347–368; Hong N. Kim, "Japan's Policy Toward the Two Koreas and Korean Unification," in Kang and Yim, *Politics of Korean Unification,* pp. 172–190; Chong-Sik Lee, *Japan and Korea,* pp. 74–96; and Bae Ho Hahn, "Policy Toward Japan," in Koo and Han, *The Foreign Policy of the Republic of Korea,* pp. 184–195.
49. Chong-Sik Lee, *Japan and Korea,* p. 78.
50. *FBIS,* May 17, 1978, pp. D3–D6.
51. *Tokyo Shimbun,* February 3, 1973.
52. *Asahi,* May 18, 1978.
53. *Washington Post,* October 9, 1980.
54. *Asian Wall Street Journal,* June 29, 1981; *FBIS,* June 24, 1983, p. E1.
55. *Korea Herald,* June 21, 1981.
56. Japan, Ministry of Foreign Affairs, *Waga gaikyo no kinkyo 1984,* p. 81; *Waga gaikyo no kinkyo 1985,* p. 107.
57. *Korea Herald,* April 28, 1985.
58. *FBIS,* June 13, 1985, pp. E1–E3.
59. *FBIS,* September 26, 1985, p. C3.
60. *FBIS,* September 18, 1985, p. D8.
61. *Korea Herald,* November 26, 1985.
62. *Korea Herald,* January 11, 1986.
63. *Korea Herald,* September 1, 1979.
64. *Korea Herald,* November 14, 1985.

12

Toward Cross-recognition: U.S. Policy

The second half of the 1980s promises to be a critical period for the two Koreas. Both are experimenting with untried methods of accomplishing a smooth leadership succession. Both face difficult economic challenges. Both are committed to maintaining a high level of military readiness.

The international rivalry of the Koreas has entered a new phase. North-South talks, opened in response to domestic and external pressures, have encouraged the big powers to step up cross-contacts. The interplay between cross-contacts and North-South dialogue poses new tests to the Koreas and to the big powers as each nation pursues its sometimes contradictory objectives in an increasingly complicated arena. The extreme adversarial stance of each Korea backed solidly by its allies, characteristic of the cold war period, had begun to erode in the early 1970s and is undergoing more rapid erosion in the mid-1980s.

The United States, the only big power with military forces in Korea, has a key role to play. The revolution in transportation and communication has offset its geographical remoteness and resulted in a steadily deepening involvement in the affairs of its Korean ally. Disengagement from Korea, seriously considered in some quarters in the immediate aftermath of the U.S. withdrawal from Vietnam, no longer attracts forceful advocates. Remaining involved and working with the other big powers to help to bring about a more stable and peaceful situation on the Korean peninsula seems a more attractive alternative to most observers today.

Formulating a U.S. strategy toward Korea for the next ten years or so is made difficult by the complexity of that situation: the number of players involved, the various aspects of the Korean situation and the interaction among them, and the influence of global trends on the United States and East Asia. The principal elements of an appropriate U.S. strategy are the deterrence of conflict, the fostering of political stability and economic development in South Korea, the encouragement of North-South dialogue, and the furthering of the trend toward cross-recognition.

Deterrence of conflict requires no drastic policy change, only the refinement of past successful policies to take account of changing capabilities and changes in technology and military doctrine. Emerging obstacles to economic development can be overcome by the combined efforts of experienced South Korean bureaucrats and entrepreneurs. The U.S. government contribution should consist principally in opposing excessive resort to protectionism in the United States. The responsibility for the maintenance of political stability in South Korea rests primarily on the South Korean government and secondarily on the political opposition. Here both are breaking new ground and the future is murky. The scope for U.S. influence is narrow and the impact of specific actions difficult to predict. U.S. policies in all these areas will receive only cursory attention here.

The area which seems both the ripest for change and offering the broadest range of choices for the United States is in the encouragement of actions by the big powers to move the two Koreas toward a state of peaceful coexistence. Little attention has been given to formulating a long-term diplomatic strategy to this end, taking full advantage of the interest of all four powers in a more stable, less potentially dangerous Korean peninsula. Discussion of such a strategy will be the principal focus of this chapter.

Deterrence of Conflict

The deterrence of conflict in Korea must be the foremost objective of U.S. policy there. Other objectives, such as economic development, democratization, and healthy economic relations between South Korea and the United States are important in their own right and may also contribute to deterring conflict, but the deterrence of conflict must be the prime objective because without peace none of the other objectives can be achieved.

Prevention of war is also the prime objective for the South Koreans. Their military forces are equipped, trained, and deployed for defense, particularly for the defense of Seoul. They are willing to put up with the disadvantages of having U.S. troops on their soil because they see these forces as having been and likely to continue to be a most effective deterrent to a North Korean attack. The proximity of Seoul to the DMZ makes deterrence of an attack far preferable to being forced to defend against an attack, because any large-scale conflict would result in enormous damage to South Korea's industrial and population center, even if the South Koreans succeeded in pushing back the invaders and punishing them. The South Koreans would like to see Korea unified, but there is virtually no support in South Korea today for an attempt to unify Korea by force. There is no Syngman Rhee calling for a march north. Not only does North Korea have strong defenses, but South Korean officials, military and civilian, recognize that the United States and Japan would oppose an invasion of the North, and the Soviet Union and China would not permit the military defeat of North Korea by South Korea.

Assessing the intentions of North Korea is more difficult. Kim Il Sung has declared repeatedly, in public and in private, that North Korea has no intention of attacking South Korea. He has pointed out that North Korea did not take advantage of the Kwangju uprising to attack the South. Yet the extraordinary proportion of resources poured into the North Korean military buildup, the digging of tunnels, the attempted assassination of Park Chung-hee and Chun Doo Hwan, the encouragement of revolution in South Korea, and the stress on reunification on North Korean terms all strongly suggest that if they considered the circumstances favorable, the North Koreans would seek to unify Korea by force. The presence of U.S. forces clearly has been a powerful deterrent to any such attempt.

So long as U.S. forces remain committed to the defense of South Korea, the probability of a large-scale North Korean attack is low. Not only did Kim Il Sung and others of his generation experience the devastation wreaked by U.S. bombing during the Korean War, they have drummed that knowledge into the younger generation. Whether or not the leaders believe their propaganda that the United States would use nuclear weapons against them in a new war, they know that U.S. conventional weapons are many times more powerful and accurate than those used in the 1950s. That they would put at risk everything that they have built during the past three decades, of which they are justifiably proud, is difficult to believe. They regard the presence of U.S. forces in South Korea as the principal obstacle to reunification and single-mindedly concentrate their diplomatic and propaganda efforts on getting them out.

The behavior of the big powers toward Korea in recent years, as well as the logic of their geopolitical positions, argues persuasively that none of them favors the renewal of conflict in Korea. The costs and risks would be too great and the rewards too uncertain. Moscow's improvement of relations with Pyongyang since 1984 does not alter this judgment. The provision of MIG-23s and SA-3 missiles to North Korea has not significantly affected the balance of forces as the South Koreans are receiving F-16s and the U.S. forces remain committed.

The common interest of all the parties concerned, including North Korea, in avoiding large-scale war under the circumstances that prevail in Korea today makes such an eventuality unlikely during the coming ten years, unless the U.S. withdrew its forces, a radical change occurred in the international environment, or one of the Koreas suffered a severe breakdown of law and order.

Prevention of conflict thus requires the continuation in the main of U.S. policies followed in the recent past: maintenance of a sizable force in Korea, close cooperation with South Korean military forces through the combined command, and demonstrations of preparedness through joint military exercises. South Korea probably will gradually narrow the quantitative gap between its forces and those of North Korea by arms purchases and by the further expansion of the South Korean arms industry. A military balance between the indigenous forces of the two Koreas is a necessary but not sufficient condition for the ultimate withdrawal of U.S. forces. Only when a stable state of peaceful coexistence has evolved between them can U.S. forces be withdrawn with a reasonable assurance that war will not result.

The United States should resist the tendency to view U.S. forces in Korea as a contribution to regional defense, a counter to the Soviet military buildup in Northeast Asia.[1] Making South Korea a regional defense base for the United States comparable to bases in Japan or the Philippines would almost certainly result in the establishment of Soviet bases in North Korea. The acquisition of such bases by the superpowers not only would raise further the already high level of militarization of the Korean peninsula, but it would make far more difficult negotiations by the two Koreas to ease the military confrontation between them.

The United States should seriously consider the withdrawal of tactical nuclear weapons from South Korea. These weapons would be a useful supplement to U.S. and South Korean conventional forces in halting a North Korean assault, but they are not indispensable either in a conflict or as a deterrent. By supplying similar weapons to North Korea, the Soviet Union could quickly cancel out their military advantage to U.S.-South Korean forces. Moreover, the political cost of the first use of nuclear weapons against the conventional forces of a small Asian country would be extraordinarily high, particularly among the Japanese, who understandably are more sensitive to nuclear issues than other people. The use of nuclear weapons in Korea probably would cost the United States the freedom to use bases in Japan to support its forces defending South Korea. North Korean propaganda has focused increasingly on the presence of nuclear weapons in South Korea and has urged turning the

Korean peninsula into a nuclear-free zone. Given the questionable value of tactical nuclear weapons in South Korea, the U.S. and South Korean governments should consider whether at some point in the North-South negotiations their withdrawal could be traded for important concessions by North Korea.[2]

Political Stability

A mounting atmosphere of confrontation between the government and the opposition is likely in South Korea as 1988 approaches. The U.S. government has long maintained that it favors progress toward a more democratic system in South Korea and has criticized repressive acts by the government, sometimes publicly, more often privately. The opposition will probably try to get the United States more deeply involved in the hope of weakening the advantage of the party in power.

The extent of U.S. involvement in South Korea, particularly in the defense against the North Korean military threat, makes total detachment from South Korean politics impossible. Whatever the United States does or does not do, it will be perceived by Koreans as favoring one party or another. Fine-tuning intervention so as to encourage a more democratic process is extremely difficult. Probably the best that can be done is to maintain a general stance in support of democracy and human rights, while intervening occasionally in the more important cases, as was done to secure the commutation of Kim Dae Jung's death sentence in 1981.

Politics in South Korea since 1984 has been moving hesitantly, with advances and retreats, toward a more democratic system, a process on which the U.S. government can have only a marginal effect. William J. Butler, a New York lawyer and chairman of the International Commission of Jurists in Geneva, who accompanied Kim Dae Jung on his return to Korea in 1985, put it well.

> We have found out after years of heartache that there's very little in the final analysis that the United States can do to bring about institutional change in a foreign country. That change, if it is to come, has to come from within, from people who are committed and who build their own institutions in line with their own culture and value system. The imposition of U.S. will abroad has severe limitations, and although we get symbolic concessions by getting people out of jail or better prison conditions and saving lives sometimes, we have never been able to bring about institutional changes anywhere in the world. That has to come from people who live and die there. . . . We have to be patient, and we have to support local institutions that are fighting for that result [democracy]. That's true everywhere in the world.[3]

Economic Development

As one of the world leaders in the pace of its economic growth, South Korea is well placed to continue its advance, provided no severe deterioration of world economic conditions occurs. Even though it has accumulated the fourth largest foreign debt among developing countries, it has had no difficulty in making payments. Furthermore, it has slowed the increase in indebtedness, and its credit rating in the international banking community continues to be good. Prospects for achieving the average annual growth rate of around 7 percent needed to absorb the growing labor force are favorable.

The principal contribution that the United States can make to economic growth in South Korea is to keep its own market open to goods from that country. Actions taken against Korean producers of a number of commodities for unfair trade practices had not seriously affected the total volume of exports to the United States up to the end of 1985, but they had alarmed the South Korean government and business community. Efforts by the United States to speed up the opening of the Korean market to U.S. products and services encountered resistance but produced some results. Such problems cannot be avoided as economic relations between the United States and South Korea expand, but more should be done by both governments to keep the differences in perspective and to tone down emotional reactions while official negotiators seek to resolve the problems.

Encouraging North-South Dialogue

The only way to reduce tension on the Korean peninsula and ultimately to reach a condition of stable peaceful coexistence is through North-South dialogue, resulting in the creation of widening areas of interaction between the two Koreas. Diminishing reciprocal hostility and suspicion will be a long, slow process. The on-again, off-again negotiations that began in 1984 may seem to have produced little in the way of substantive results, yet they have advanced the dialogue to a point never reached before. Two unprecedented actions occurred, enveloped by each side in self-serving propaganda, but significant nevertheless: the delivery of relief goods from North to South and the actual reunion of small number of separated family members. More important than the actual accomplishments has been the change in attitude on the part of North Korea, from flat rejection of dialogue with the Chun government to willingness to conduct high-level negotiations with it, and from insistence on starting with broad political agreements to willingness to negotiate on small steps, such as family reunions.

The political pressures on both parties to continue the dialogue are considerable, as discussed in Chapter 6. Both would benefit from showing willingness to pursue detente—North Korea in its efforts to expand foreign trade and South Korea in its desire for successful hosting of the Olympic Games. The South Korean government would also benefit in terms of domestic political support and international image from taking initiatives to further dialogue. The big powers should take advantage of these favorable circumstances to use their influence to nudge the dialogue forward. They can do so in two ways. One is by publicly expressing support for the dialogue and privately encouraging the Korean government with which they have diplomatic relations to press forward with it. The other is by expanding cross-contacts with the other part of Korea.

North-South dialogue and cross-contacts interact in a complex manner. One motivation for pursuing dialogue—not the primary one, but an important by-product—is to improve prospects for cross-contacts. The South Koreans hope that their negotiations with North Korea will make it easier for China and the Soviet Union to expand contacts with them. The Chinese confirm privately that this is indeed the case. The Soviets tend to be reticent on the subject. The North Koreans hope that negotiations with South Korea will make it easier for the United States and Japan to have contacts with them. The Japanese demonstrated the validity of this proposition in the early 1970s and again in 1984 and 1985. The United States has been slower to respond. From the viewpoints of the two Koreas, dialogue cuts two ways, encouraging cross-contacts with both Seoul and Pyongyang. Thus, they contend with each other, exploiting dialogue to expand desired contacts, while trying to limit expansion of the undesired ones.

The effect of cross-contacts on dialogue is more difficult to demonstrate than the effect of dialogue on cross-contacts. In some circumstances, it can be argued plausibly that expansion of cross-contacts might deter one of the Koreas from engaging in dialogue. For example, when North Korea presses for official talks with the United States and refuses to talk with South Korea, a U.S. policy of expanding cross-contacts might encourage the North Koreans to believe that official talks with the United States would soon follow, thus causing them to hold firm against talking with South Korea. When North-South dialogue is underway and cross-contacts with both Koreas expanding, dialogue and cross-contacts seem to reinforce one another. Progress in either contributes to the climate of detente.

In its official conversations with the other big powers, the United States should seek to fashion a common public stance on the North-South dialogue as the indispensable means of lowering tension and the risk of war in Korea. The Chinese and Japanese have firmly supported the dialogue in their public statements and in their bilateral discussions of Korea. The Soviets have issued routine statements supporting in general the North Korean position on the dialogue, but have been less forthcoming than the Chinese. On the other hand, the Soviets have avoided explicit endorsement of the tripartite talks, which the North Koreans regard as more important than the bilateral dialogue, because such talks would address what North Koreans see as the fundamental problem: the presence of U.S. forces in Korea.

Thus, all the big powers have endorsed North-South talks in principle. What is needed is a more active show of interest in them, expressions of gratification when progress is made, and concern when obstacles crop up. The big powers should not become involved in the details of the talks, supporting positions taken by one side or the other on particular issues. Their stance should be that these are problems that can and should be resolved by the Koreans themselves. The big power role should be to encourage the two sides not to give up, but to keep working on the resolution of the problems, one by one.

In one way the United States is directly involved in North-South relations as the representative of the UN Command in the Military Armistice Commission. For many years the UN Command urged on the North Koreans a number of confidence-building measures, such as genuine demilitarization of the DMZ, advance notification of maneuvers, and invitations for North Korea to send observers to watch the Team Spirit exercises. North Korea turned them all down. The North Korean proposal of July 1985 for reducing the numbers and armaments of guards in the Joint Security Area and the MAC Headquarters Area was a new departure for North Korea. It may have been put forward in response to Chinese suggestions, because U.S. diplomats, when urged by the Chinese to respond to the tripartite talks proposal, sometimes countered that North Korean responsiveness to confidence-building measures would demonstrate seriousness of purpose.

The UN Command turned down the North Korean proposal on the ground that it would be to the military advantage of the North Koreans, but it made a counterproposal applying to other segments of the DMZ and stressing the need for periodic verification. As of mid-1986, negotiations on the matter continued. The United States should try through innovative proposals and persistent negotiations, in close consultation with South Korea, to reach agreement with the North Koreans on some confidence-building measures in the DMZ. A genuine willingness on the part of the North Koreans to negotiate on such measures would be a welcome change from the position taken by Kim Il Sung in his conversation with Congressman Stephen Solarz in 1980, when he brushed aside negotiations on such matters as not worth considering.

The North Koreans have tried to use the North-South dialogue as a form of pressure and a propaganda weapon against the Team Spirit exercise by suspending the dialogue in 1985 and again in 1986 while the exercise was going on. The United States and South Korea rightly declined to respond to this pressure by halting the exercise. Some linkage should exist, however, between military activities and the North-South dialogue, if the goal of reducing tension is to be attained. For years the practice was to enlarge the Team Spirit exercise year after year on the assumption that the larger the exercise the more realistic the training and the greater the deterrent effect. When North-South dialogue is underway, the promise of some restraint in military activities on both sides might improve the atmosphere and encourage progress in the talks.

Advantages of Cross-recognition

The United States, Japan, and South Korea have advocated cross-recognition of both Koreas as a means of creating a more stable environment for Korea. Cross-recognition would have a number of advantages. It would enhance understanding between the big powers and the two Koreas. Diplomatic missions of all four big powers in Seoul and Pyongyang would make possible direct, frequent conversations between big power diplomats and the two Korean foreign ministries, improving understanding of each other's attitudes and policies and reducing the scope for miscalculation. The establishment of diplomatic relations would also open the way to an increase in trade and other contacts, thus providing additional channels through which the countries concerned could learn about each other. Moreover, cross-recognition by the big powers would quickly lead to admission of both Koreas to the United Nations and their recognition by almost all states. The near-universal acceptance of the legitimacy of the two Koreas would weaken the inclination of each to question the legitimacy of the other, creating a sounder basis for dialogue and interaction. A lesser, but not insignificant advantage of cross-recognition would be the easing of tension between the Korean governments and their big power supporters that now arises from the compulsion to restrict their supporters' contacts with their rival. Finally, it would open up North Korea, giving that country's leadership and bureaucracy a more realistic understanding of the outside world.

Only North Korea obdurately opposes cross-recognition. The Soviet Union and China give rhetorical support to Pyongyang's position, but private comments, as well as their growing contacts with South Korea, are persuasive evidence that they would promptly establish diplomatic relations with Seoul if North Korea would drop its opposition. They see little possibility of the reunification of Korea in the foreseeable future, and a stable divided Korea would serve their interests as well as if not better than a united Korea.

The North Koreans insist that cross-recognition would freeze the division of Korea, preventing reunification. From the North Korean viewpoint, this argument has validity. Kim Il Sung clings to the hope that the present government in South Korea will be replaced by a government more amenable to the withdrawal of U.S. forces and the reunification of Korea on North Korean terms. Recognition of the present government by the Soviet Union and China, followed by the other Communist states and many Third World countries, would cut the ground from under North Korea's claim that South Korea is a puppet of the United States, unworthy of recognition as a legitimate state. That claim has already been weakened by Pyongyang's own willingness to conduct official negotiations with the Chun government, by growing contacts with South Korea by China and the Soviet Union, and by South Korea's rising prestige and influence in the world.

South Korea takes the view that diminishing the existing hostility between the two Koreas to a level where serious negotiations on some form of unification could begin, will take a very long time. Replacing mistrust with confidence in the other's intentions can be accomplished only through widening contacts and various forms of interaction between them, step by step. Thus, peaceful coexistence must be attained before unification becomes a realistic possibility. Cross-recognition would help to provide a stable international framework within which a state of peaceful coexistence could evolve. The South Koreans are confident that trends in the behavior and attitudes of states toward Korea increasingly validate their view of a realistic path toward unification, rather than that of the North Koreans.

Stimulating Cross-contacts

Cross-contacts prepare the way for eventual cross-recognition. It could be argued that instead of preparing the way, they serve as a substitute for cross-recognition. To the extent that states can carry on necessary business without diplomatic relations, diplomatic recognition can be deferred indefinitely. But the absence of diplomatic relations makes the conduct of interstate business awkward and difficult. As the business that a state or its citizens wish to conduct with one of the Koreas increases, so does the tendency to devise quasi-official or even official ways of conducting that business. Recent contacts between China and South Korea and between Japan and North Korea illustrate this trend.

Governments become less willing to yield to pressures from one Korean government to refrain from contacts with the other. They may hold off from taking the final step of diplomatic recognition for a long time, but they move steadily toward a greater use of official channels even in the absence of diplomatic relations. Gradually, North Korea's power to prevent cross-recognition will decline further. At some point, perhaps after Kim Il Sung leaves the scene, North Korea may realize that it has as much to gain from cross-recognition as South Korea has, perhaps more.

The big powers have wide discretion in regard to the pace at which they allow cross-contacts to expand. If they move in unison, the two Koreas cannot easily slow the process. Express agreements among the big powers on the expansion of cross-contacts are not feasible, but tacit understandings might well be realized on the desirability of moving ahead with them. Balance in the expansion of cross-contacts eases the process. Given the wide differences in the governmental systems of the big powers and in the nature of their interests in Korea, substantial imbalances in the types of cross-contacts and the pace at which they expand cannot be avoided. But the existence of a rough equivalence and a sense that all are moving ahead together, would permit cross-contacts to expand more rapidly.

South Korea, in principle, favors the expansion of cross-contacts as a way of enhancing the prospects for cross-recognition. Through its Nordpolitik, it pursues contacts with China and the Soviet Union. The South Korean government is uneasy, however, regarding the expansion of U.S. and Japanese contacts with North Korea. It fears that such contacts will increase more rapidly than the contacts of the Soviet Union and China with South Korea. It is particularly concerned at the unremitting effort by North Korea to draw the United States into an official dialogue.

North Korea, in principle, opposes both cross-contacts and cross-recognition, but its capacity to prevent cross-contacts has been declining. It is more sensitive than South Korea to the possibility that an increase in the cross-contacts it favors will stimulate an increase in undesirable cross-contacts. For example, Kim Il Sung told a Japanese politician in 1977 that he would like "in principle" to have U.S. correspondents visit North Korea, but he feared that such visits would lead to visits to South Korea by journalists of "a certain country" and increase the risk of cross-recognition.[4]

Cross-contacts Between the United States and North Korea

Before the 1970s the climate between the United States and North Korea was one of unmitigated hostility, highlighted by the capture of the *Pueblo* in 1968 and the shooting down of the EC-121 aircraft in 1969. U.S. passports bore a notation that they were not valid for travel to North Korea. No North Koreans came to the United States.

The changed climate in and around Korea in the early 1970s brought important changes. North Korea admitted two U.S. journalists in 1972.[5] The first North Korean officials arrived in the United States in 1973 to staff Pyongyang's Permanent Observer Mission at the United Nations. In 1974 the North Koreans proposed in a letter from the Supreme People's Assembly to the U.S. Congress to replace the Armistice Agreement with a peace treaty between Washington and Pyongyang.

In subsequent years, the North Koreans continued to press for an official dialogue with the United States, but they pursued unofficial contacts with the United States only halfheartedly, not zealously as the South Koreans did with the Soviet Union and China. A few Korean-American scholars were admitted to North Korea, but other U.S. scholars and news correspondents were denied admission. A number of Korean-Americans with relatives in North Korea made visits, looked after by the Korean Committee for Aiding Overseas Compatriots.

Incidents in the mid-1970s soured the atmosphere for the exchange of persons between North Korea and the United States: the ax-murders of two U.S. officers in the DMZ in 1976, the death of three of the four occupants of a U.S. helicopter shot down by the North Koreans after straying north of the DMZ in 1977, and charges by the North Koreans that the United States was violating its territory with high altitude SR-71 reconnaissance aircraft. A stream of denunciations of "U.S. imperialism" poured out of Pyongyang, tempered briefly after President Carter announced his intention to withdraw ground forces from South Korea, but turned up again when that program was suspended.

North Korea's hosting of the World Table Tennis Championships in April 1979 reopened the door to visits by U.S. citizens to North Korea. A table tennis team, accompanied by an interpreter, officials, and fifteen or so media representatives spent several days in Pyongyang. No reverse travel from North Korea to the United States occurred, however, because the North Koreans declined several invitations from U.S. sports organizations to participate in meets in the United States. Asked why the North Koreans refused to send teams to the United States, a North Korean sports official explained that South Korean teams were to compete in those events and the North Koreans "could not afford to give the impression that they would tolerate 'two Koreas.'" When it was pointed out to him that the North Koreans had competed with South Korean teams at the Asian Games in Bangkok, he responded that "Thailand is not the United States."[6]

In the fall of 1979 Pyongyang invited several members of Congress to visit North Korea. One member, Stephen Solarz (Democrat, New York), made the trip in July 1980.⁷ His invitation had been suggested by Prince Norodom Sihanouk, who offered Solarz and his group the hospitality of his palatial residence in Pyongyang. In response to a question by Solarz as to whether North Korea would approve cultural, scholarly, and other people-to-people exchanges, even in the absence of an official level dialogue, Kim Il Sung said that he would welcome such exchanges, which would contribute to mutual understanding and friendship.

The number of U.S. citizens visiting North Korea increased a little during subsequent years, but the North Koreans were selective, admitting some applicants and refusing others. Their reasons for the refusals were obscure. In one instance, they approved three of six persons who applied for a group visit and rejected the other three. Most of those admitted were scholars or Korean-Americans who had relatives in North Korea.⁸ The Committee for Aiding Overseas Compatriots stepped up its program of bringing Korean-Americans to meet with relatives, sometimes combining with the Committee for Peaceful Reunification of the Fatherland to arrange a seminar for the visitors, winding up with a "resolution" condemning the South Korean government and calling for the withdrawal of U.S. troops from South Korea.⁹ In 1984 the North Koreans invited several prominent U.S. citizens to visit North Korea, none of whom went.

Until 1985 no North Koreans came to the United States, other than those connected with the United Nations or the International Olympic Committee, plus an occasional Korean resident of Japan traveling on a North Korean passport. North Korean officials complained of the inequality of treatment.¹⁰ One reason for the difficulty was that North Koreans applying for entry to the United States were officials, not private scholars. The Canadian government declined to issue visas to a delegation invited to the Toronto conference of the Association for Asian Studies in 1981, when the leader of the delegation presented a diplomatic passport and the other members official passports. Another problem was the North Korean insistence that an institution sponsoring the visit of North Koreans had to exclude South Koreans from meetings arranged for the North Korean visitors. U.S. universities, the principal institutions interested in inviting North Koreans to this country, could not give such assurances. One of the North Koreans from Japan admitted to the United States as a scholar to attend a conference of the International Studies Association in Philadelphia in 1981 created a bad impression when he went on to attend a conference in Washington, D.C., at which Koreans hostile to the government of the ROK sought to pass a resolution backing the North Korean position on unification.

In November 1985 a breakthrough occurred. The director and a senior researcher from the Institute of History of the North Korean Academy of Social Sciences, accompanied by an interpreter, attended the Mid-Atlantic Regional Conference of the Association for Asian Studies at Washington, D.C. The two took part in a panel chaired by a Korean-American scholar, along with two historians from South Korea, presenting papers on historical topics. The taboo against participating with South Koreans in events on U.S. soil had been broken. The North Koreans might have decided earlier to modify that policy, for they had sent representatives to a meeting of the International Olympic Committee in Los Angeles in January 1984 preparing for the Olympic Games to be held that summer. Thus, it seems likely that they would have sent a team to the Los Angeles Olympics, had it not been for the Soviet boycott.

The slowness in the development of contacts between the United States and North Korea was due in part to Pyongyang's inability to fully control or predict the results. The North Koreans would have liked to admit only those who would report favorably on their country, but from their viewpoint the reporting by visiting U.S. journalists must have appeared more negative than positive. Even more worrisome was the fear that contacts with the United States would promote acceptance of the two-Koreas concept. They found themselves in a quandary. Pursuing contacts with the United States would encourage the Soviet Union and China to do the same with South Korea. Yet it must have been clear by the mid-1980s that refraining from contacts with the United States would not prevent the Chinese and the Soviets from having contacts with South Korea. They had little choice but to enter more vigorously into the competition.[11]

The South Korean government argued tenaciously against any contacts between the United States and North Korea. The South Koreans feared that if the North Koreans could establish a beachhead in the United States through unofficial contacts, they would be in a position to increase pressure on the U.S. government for an official dialogue. They also feared that the North Koreans could exploit opposition to the Chun government by some Koreans in the United States to build a political organization along the lines of the Chosoren in Japan. They accepted in principle the view that a balanced increase in cross-contacts by all the big powers with the two Koreas was desirable, but they were quick to point out any respect in which the United States seemed to be getting ahead of the Chinese and the Soviets. At the same time, they ignored those aspects, such as China's trade with South Korea, in which the United States lagged far behind.

The U.S. government, under this constant pressure from its South Korean ally, moved slowly and cautiously in permitting the expansion of contacts. It could not prevent travel by U.S. citizens to North Korea, but by refusing visas to North Koreans it could make Pyongyang less inclined to admit U.S. citizens. Cautious moves to allow the expansion of contacts were placed on hold for months by the Rangoon bombing and again by a dispute over a North Korean diplomat in New York accused of rape. The opening of North Korea had no influential constituency behind it in the United States as the opening of China had had. The North Korean market was inconsequential, at least until the North Koreans had resolved their debt problem. There was no significant pressure on the State department to adopt an activist policy. Moreover, one could not dismiss entirely the suspicion that North Koreans admitted ostensibly for nonpolitical purposes might engage in political activities, as some had in Japan.

A Long-term Strategy for the United States

The rigidity of the confrontation between the two Koreas and the complexity of big power involvement in it rule out any simple, short-term solution to the Korean problem. As Winston Churchill once said: "People think they can settle these obstinate world issues at one stroke. You can't do that. No one can do it. The essence of my policy is to get agreement about bits of a problem—to gain three or four years' easement."[12] The United States needs a long-term strategy to give direction and a degree of consistency to its tactical moves.

Diminishing the Saliency of Military Confrontation

A primary goal of U.S. policy should be to diminish the saliency of the military confrontation, which has heavily outweighed all other forms of interaction between the two Koreas. Diplomatic rivalry has increased in relative importance and the North-South dialogue has very recently opened the door a crack to the possibility of the exchange of persons and goods. But results from these attempts to increase the relative importance of such activities will be slow in coming, owing to the impact of the Rangoon bombing on the South Korean view of North Korea, the influence of the military on the governments on both sides, and the firmly established national practice of viewing each other primarily as military threats.

The United States can help to counter the tendency to overemphasize military confrontation by stressing the importance of restraint on the part of both the United States and the Soviet Union in supplying advanced weapons to the two Koreas and, as argued above, by refraining from basing in Korea forces designed for a regional mission, so long as the Soviet Union does the same. The United States should also press ahead with negotiating confidence-building measures in the DMZ and consult with the South Koreans on ways of limiting military exercises if substantial progress is made in North-South talks. The withdrawal of U.S. forces should be envisaged as occurring after South Korea has closed the quantitative gap in weaponry between its forces and those of North Korea, a peace treaty has replaced the armistice, and the two Koreas have established a stable state of coexistence.

Peaceful Coexistence First, Unification Second

A unified Korea should be the long-term goal of U.S. policy, in conformity with the homogeneous nature of the Korean people and the commitment to unification expressed by both Korean governments. But the United States should continue to support the view of the South Korean government that the lowering of tension between the two Koreas and the attainment of a stable state of peaceful coexistence is an essential prerequisite to serious negotiations on unification.

The international trend toward cross-recognition favors the South Korean viewpoint. The North Korean contention that the DPRK is the only legitimate government on the Korean peninsula, whereas the ROK is illegitimate and unworthy of international recognition, is constantly losing ground. The United States, together with Japan and South Korea, should continue vigorously advocating cross-recognition as offering a realistic framework to facilitate evolution of a state of peaceful coexistence between the two Koreas.

Some U.S. citizens have advocated that the United States, as the only big power with military forces in Korea, should accept the North Korean proposal for official talks. They argue that the United States would be in a better position to contribute to a settlement in Korea if it could talk officially with both parties. Advocates of Washington-Pyongyang talks fail to demonstrate convincingly, however, that the gains from this action would outweigh the probable damage to the primary channel through which lowered tension in Korea must be sought—the North-South dialogue. The opening of official talks between Washington and Pyongyang, without any comparable action by the Soviet Union and China toward South Korea, would reinforce North Korea's claim to be the legitimate government on the peninsula and weaken its incentive to talk seriously with the ROK. Hence, the United States should refrain from an official dialogue with North Korea until the Soviets and Chinese are prepared to do the same with South Korea.

For reasons discussed earlier, Japan, China, and the Soviet Union may feel more comfortable with a divided Korea than they would with a strong, unified Korea free to form an alliance with an adversary. Consequently, when serious negotiations between the two Koreas on unification become possible, these three powers might be more supportive of the negotiations if the end result were to be a unified neutral or neutralized state, free of nuclear weapons. Taking positions now on neutrality for a unified Korea would be premature, however. At the present stage, the task is to foster the North-South dialogue and to move toward cross-recognition by the balanced expansion of cross-contacts.

Expanding Cross-contacts

During 1984 to 1985 the Japanese and the Chinese took the lead in the expansion of cross-contacts. The United States and the Soviet Union, which lacked the economic and other incentives that drove the Japanese and Chinese, lagged behind. Political inhibitions limited U.S. and Soviet cross-contacts, but even if these were totally removed, their cross-contacts would not reach the Japanese and Chinese levels.

The political inhibitions on the expansion of contacts between the United States and North Korea have consisted primarily of North Korean uncertainties about their desirability and of South Korean opposition to them, which has made the United States cautious in approving visas. The North Koreans seem to have taken a more positive view of contacts recently. Consequently, a liberal U.S. policy of granting visas to bonafide nonpolitical visitors would be desirable, in the hope of gradually stimulating a larger two-way exchange.

The U.S. Department of State has been criticized for refusing to make exceptions to the rule limiting North Korean diplomats at the UN to a radius of 25 miles from New York City in order to permit them to attend meetings in other cities to which they have been invited. The South Koreans feel at a disadvantage because they have no diplomats stationed in Moscow or Peking, and they would protest strongly if North Korean diplomats in New York were permitted to travel about the United States to present their official views. It would be desirable, however, to allow the North Korean diplomats to attend international conferences in the United States to which they may be invited, just as South Korean officials have been allowed to attend international conferences in the Soviet Union and China.

Since the Korean War, the United States has maintained an embargo on trade and financial transactions with North Korea. The rapid expansion of China's trade with South Korea suggests that the time has come to reconsider that embargo. A possible approach might be to offer to lift it in exchange for an expression of willingness by the Soviet Union and China to trade openly with South Korea. A bargain of that sort should be explored quietly with those governments, even though a favorable response seems unlikely. Moscow and Peking probably prefer the current method of carrying on the trade while publicly denying its existence. As such a course of action is impractical for the United States, the U.S. embargo should be lifted as a means of widening the scope of cross-contacts, in exchange for appropriate concessions and assurances from the North Koreans.

The South Korean government probably will firmly oppose lifting the embargo. South Koreans tend to exaggerate the economic importance to North Korea of such a step and the contribution it could make to the North Korean arms industry. In fact, few if any products could be procured by North Korea from the United States that are not already available from Japan or Western Europe. The export of weapons and high technology would be banned by the same regulations that ban their export to the Soviet Union. North Korea's foreign exchange shortage would limit its purchases from the United States to a very low level. The effect would be primarily political—a signal to those North Koreans who favor expanding unofficial contacts with the United States.

South Korean opposition to the opening of trade between the United States and North Korea reflects the fear among many South Koreans that the resulting unofficial contacts would increase the probability of official contacts. It also relates to a basic difference among South Koreans as to policy toward North Korea. Some South Koreans argue that North Korea should be isolated as much as possible from contacts with the West—particularly the United States—until it is prepared to take a much more constructive attitude in the North-South dialogue. Others take the view that North Korea will take a more constructive attitude only after influences from outside give it a more realistic understanding of trends in the world. The "isolators" oppose the expansion of unofficial U.S. contacts with North Korea, while the "openers" favor them. Even the openers, however, want balance in the expansion of cross-contacts. They would oppose a rapid expansion of U.S. contacts with North Korea that would place them too far ahead of Soviet contacts with South Korea.

In this debate among South Koreans, the United States should side decisively with the openers. Creating more channels through which outside information and influence can flow into isolated North Korea not only would in time cause the North Koreans to take a more realistic view of trends in the world, but would also improve U.S. understanding of North Korea. Moreover, it would stimulate Soviet and Chinese contacts with South Korea, preparing the way for cross-recognition. South Korea's official endorsement of cross-recognition favors the openers, puts the isolators on the defensive, and strengthens U.S. influence on this issue.

In urging steps to open North Korea, one should not dismiss the North Korean government's capability to control and limit contacts to prevent the introduction of undesired ideas. In the long run, however, even the rigid views of that government are likely to change under the prolonged bombardment of influence from outside. Some change has been evident during the past several years, and the rate of change may well accelerate. China's opening to the outside, Chinese encouragement of the North Koreans to follow China's example, and the interest shown by some North Koreans in the Chinese model almost certainly will push Pyongyang toward opening the society further.

A prime requirement in a long-term strategy toward Korea is patience. The concrete results of the North-South dialogue will be slow in coming. Gaining North Korea's acceptance of cross-recognition probably will take a long time. The principal U.S. concern should be to keep the two processes moving toward the desired goal of a stable, peaceful coexistence between the two Koreas. Common big power interest in a stable Korea facilitates the task and affords scope for a more activist and imaginative policy than that followed in the recent past.

Notes

1. For arguments favoring a regional, strategic role for U.S. forces in Korea, see Norman D. Levin and Richard L. Sneider, "Korea in Postwar U.S. Security Policy," in Han, *After One Hundred Years*, pp. 269–270, and Yu-Nam Kim, "U.S.-Korean Security Interdependence with Special Reference to Northeast Asia," in Kwak and others, *U.S.-Korean Relations*, pp. 263–264.

2. See also Clough, *Deterrence and Defense in Korea*, pp. 55–57.

3. *Washington Post*, February 17, 1985, p. D8. For a balanced, but somewhat more activist view, see Stephen J. Solarz, "Promoting Democracy in The Third World: Lost Cause or Sound Policy?" *SAIS Review* 5, no. 2 (Summer-Fall 1985):139–153.

4. Interview with Hideo Den, Washington, D.C., February 1977.

5. Harrison Salisbury spent sixteen days in North Korea and published a series of articles in the *New York Times* in May–June 1972 and later described his experiences in a book *To Peking and Beyond* (New York: Quadrangle/The New York Times Book Co., 1973), pp. 189–221. Selig Harrison, Tokyo correspondent for the *Washington Post*, also visited North Korea the same year and published a series of articles in that newspaper.

6. Interview, Pyongyang, July 1980.

7. For a report on the trip see *The Korean Conundrum: A Conversation with Kim Il Sung.* Three correspondents and I accompanied Solarz on his trip.

8. Among the U.S. citizens admitted were the six Korean-American scholars who wrote of their impressions in Kim and Koh, *Journey to North Korea: Personal Perceptions;* also Lee Chong-Sik (University of Pennsylvania), Bruce Cumings (University of Washington), Karl Moscowitz and Terry MacDougall (Harvard), and Donald Zagoria (Hunter College). Others included: Maude and David Easter and Steve Thierman (American Friends Service Committee), and Thomas Reston (former spokesman, U.S. Department of State), John Burns (*New York Times*), and Walter Miller (Tokyo Bureau chief, Cox newspapers).

9. *FBIS,* July 19, 1983, p. D7; July 20, 1983, p. D7.

10. In 1981 the deputy chief of the North Korean mission to the UN asked for a meeting with the author in New York to complain that their admission of a number of U.S. scholars to North Korea had not been reciprocated by the United States.

11. North Korean anxiety at the progress being made by the United States and South Korea in promoting cross-contacts comes through clearly in a long article in the KWP's theoretical journal, *Kulloja,* in December 1983 entitled "Let Us Check and Frustrate the Maneuvers of the U.S. Imperialists to Fabricate Two Koreas" (*FBIS,* January 20, 1984, pp. D4–D12).

12. Lord Moran, *Churchill: Taken from the Diaries of Lord Moran* (Boston: Houghton Mifflin Co., 1966), p. 487.

Appendix 1

North Korea's Foreign Trade
(in millions of US$)

	Exports	Imports	Total
1977	511	712	1,223
1978	621	757	1,377
1979	1,316	1,254	2,571
1980[a]	1,099	1,122	2,220
1981	742	1,140	1,882
1982	1,023	1,178	2,201
1983	898	1,108	2,006

[a]China is excluded before 1980. Table includes twenty principal trading partners.
Source: Unpublished figures supplied by Japan External Trade Research Organization (JETRO), December 1984.

Appendix 2

United Nations Special Agency Meetings Held in Seoul

1. FAO

   - The Eighth FAO (Regional Conference) September 14, 1966
   - FAO/Asia and the Far East Commission on Agricultural Statistics (4th Session), October 6–12, 1972

2. WHO

   - WHO Regional Committee for the Western Pacific (16th Session), September 16–21, 1965
   - WHO Regional Committee for the Western Pacific (31st Session), September 22–28, 1981

3. UNESCO

   - UNESCO/Regional Workshop on Extraction, Separation, and Purification Techniques, August 22–September 2, 1977
   - UNESCO/Regional Training Course, Environmental Management, July 10–23, 1978
   - UNESCO/International Expert Meeting on Social Indicators of the Role of Children, May 12–15, 1980
   - UNESCO/Symposium on the Applicability of Indicators of Socio-Economic Change, September 1–4, 1981
   - UNESCO/International Symposium on the Relations Between Creative Workers, Artists, and Intellectuals, May 25–29, 1982
   - UNESCO/Meeting of Experts on Indicators of Culture and Communication, May 31–June 3, 1983
   - UNESCO/Regional Workshop on Forecasting of Scientific and Technological Manpower Requirement, September 5–10, 1983
   - UNESCO/5th Asian Symposium on Medical Plants and Spices, August 20–24, 1984

Appendix 3

North Korean Military Presence in Africa

State	Date	Military Training	Supply of Military Equipment
Tanzania	1972	20 personnel[s]	35 antiaircraft guns, 30 boxes of bullets
	1975	180 personnel, approx.[b]	
Somalia	1972	20 guerrilla trainers[s]	
	1972–1974	1,500 guerrillas[b]	
	1978	200 guerrilla trainers[s]	
	1979		Unknown number of small firearms, 500 boxes of bullets
Guinea Bissau	1975–1977	200 personnel, approx.,[s] 200 personnel[b]	
Zaire	1975	130 advisers, 7 woman-soldier trainers[s]	$20 million worth of equipment (such as small firearms, mortars, field pieces, tantamount to one division's equipment), 30 copies of Soviet T-62 tanks, 3 torpedo speedboats

389

State	Date	Military Training	Supply of Military Equipment
Madagascar	1978–1979	3 training personnel, 8 MIG-17 pilots, 1 technical assitance group (composed of 35 men).[s] According to International Institute for Strategic Studies, a 400-man combat troop is stationed in Madagascar.[s]	8 MIG-17 (loan), 18 14.5mm antiaircraft guns, 2 patrol boats
	1979	3 air force pilots[b]	
	1981	Unknown number of personnel[s]	
Uganda	1979	Advisory group (composed of 3 men)[s]	
	1980		4,000 AK rifles; North Korea is known to have supplied $40 million worth of weaponry to Uganda.
	1981	5 technicians, advisory group (composed of 20 men), 10 personnel, 6 personnel,[s] 30 army officers, 40 personnel, 40 personnel (for the purpose of intelligence training)[b]; unconfirmed sources report that a combat troop of around 300 men is participating in antiguerrilla operations.[s]	
Togo	1975		35 antiaircraft guns, 500 boxes of bullets, fatigues, etc.
	1976	5 training personnel[s]	
	1980	25 training personnel[s]	
Mozambique		Instructor group (unknown number)[s]	
Botswana	1978	Advisory group (composed of 40 men)[s]	
Zambia	1978	11–12 guerrilla trainers,[s] 40 instructors[s]	

Country	Date	Personnel	Armaments
Benin	1973–1978	30 personnel[b]	2 torpedo speedboats
	1977	Unknown number of training personnel[s]	
	1978	Unknown number of personnel[s]	
Seychelles	1980		Unknown number of AK rifles
Zimbabwe	1981	Advisory group (composed of 50 men),[s] 17 air force personnel[b]	Tank, armored car, heavy firearms
Equatorial Guinea	1975–1978		3 speedboats, small firearms, bullets
	1982	10 officers on probation,[b] 10 army doctors[b]	
Ethiopia	1979		40 million pounds worth of armaments
Central Africa			Unknown number of rifles
Organization of African Unity	1975–1978		2,000 rifles, 100 machine guns, 50 mortars, small firearms, 601 boxes of equipment for 1,000 soldiers
Polisario	1977–1980		1,000 AK rifles, 5,000 hand grenades, estimated 20 thousand tons of ammunition (such as armaments, bullets, parts)
Namibia	1978		20 boxes of rifles, 700 boxes of bullets, 20 boxes of hand grenades

Notes:
b = brought to North Korea for training
s = sent to conduct military training or otherwise assist African country
Source: South Korean official, 11 March 1983

Selected Bibliography

Allen, Richard C. *Korea's Syngman Rhee: An Unauthorized Portrait.* Rutland, Vt.: Charles E. Tuttle, 1960.

An, Tai Sung. *North Korea in Transition: From Dictatorship to Dynasty.* Westport, Conn.: Greenwood Press, 1983.

Asia Watch Committee. *Human Rights in Korea.* New York, 1985.

Berger, Carl. *The Korea Knot.* Philadelphia: University of Pennsylvania Press, 1957.

Boettcher, Robert. *Gifts of Deceit: Sun Myung Moon, Tongsun Park and the Korean Scandal.* New York: Holt, Rinehart, and Winston, 1980.

Bong, Baik. *Kim Il Sung: Biography* (3 vols.). Tokyo: Miraisha, 1969.

Bunge, Frederica M., ed. *South Korea: A Country Study.* American University for U.S. Department of the Army. Washington, D.C.: U.S. Government Printing Office, 1982.

_____. *North Korea: A Country Study.* American University for U.S. Department of the Army. Washington, D.C.: U.S. Government Printing Office, 1981.

Central Intelligence Agency. *Korea: The Economic Race Between the North and The South,* Report ER 78-10008. Washington, D.C.: CIA, National Foreign Assessment Center, January 1978.

Cho, Soon Sung. *Korea in World Politics 1940–1950: An Evaluation of American Responsibility.* Berkeley: University of California Press, 1967.

Chung, Chin O. *Pyongyang Between Peking and Moscow: North Korea's Involvement in the Sino-Soviet Dispute 1958–1975.* University: University of Alabama Press, 1978.

Chung, Joseph Sang-hoon. *The North Korean Economy: Structure and Development.* Stanford, Calif.: Hoover Institution Press, 1974.

Clough, Ralph N. *Deterrence and Defense in Korea: The Role of U.S. Forces.* Washington, D.C.: Brookings Institution, 1976.

Cole, David C., and Princeton N. Lyman. *Korean Development: The Interplay of Politics and Economics.* Cambridge: Harvard University Press, 1971.

Cumings, Bruce. *The Origins of the Korean War: Liberation and the Emergence of Separate Regimes, 1945–1949.* Princeton, N.J.: Princeton University Press, 1981.

Cumings, Bruce, ed. *Child of Conflict: The Korean-American Relationship, 1943–1953.* Seattle: University of Washington Press, 1983.

Gelman, Harry, and Norman D. Levin. *The Future of Soviet–North Korean Relations.* Santa Monica, Calif.: Rand Corporation, 1984.

Goodrich, Leland M. *Korea: A Study of U.S. Policy in the United Nations.* New York: Council on Foreign Relations, 1956.

Hahm, Pyong-Choon. *The Korean Political Tradition and Law.* Seoul: Hollym Corp., 1967.

Han, Sung-joo. *The Failure of Democracy in South Korea.* Berkeley: University of California Press, 1974.

Han, Sung-joo, ed. *After One Hundred Years: Continuity and Change in Korean-American Relations.* Seoul: Asiatic Research Center, Korea University, 1982.

Henderson, Gregory. *Korea: The Politics of the Vortex.* Cambridge: Harvard University Press, 1968.

Hinton, Harold C. *Korea Under New Leadership: The Fifth Republic.* New York: Praeger, 1983.

Jo, Yung-hwan, ed. *U.S. Foreign Policy in Asia.* Santa Barbara, Calif.: ABC-Clio, Inc., 1978.

Johnson, Stuart E., with Joseph A. Yager. *The Military Equation in Northeast Asia.* Washington, D.C.: Brookings Institution, 1979.

Kang, Young Hoon, and Yong Soon Yim, eds. *Politics of Korean Unification.* Seoul: Research Center for Peace and Unification, 1978.

Kihl, Young Whan. *Politics and Policies in Divided Korea: Regimes in Contest.* Boulder, Colo.: Westview Press, 1984.

Kim, C.I. Eugene, and B. C. Koh, eds. *Journey to North Korea: Personal Perceptions.* Berkeley: Institute of East Asian Studies, University of California, 1983.

Kim, Han-kyo, ed. *Studies on Korea: A Scholar's Guide.* Honolulu: University of Hawaii Press, 1980.

Kim, Ilpyong J. *Communist Politics in North Korea.* New York: Praeger, 1975.

Kim, Joungwon Alexander. *Divided Korea: The Politics of Development, 1945–1972.* Cambridge: Harvard University Press, 1975.

Kim, Kwan Bong. *The Korea-Japan Treaty Crisis and the Instability of the Korean Political System.* New York: Praeger, 1971.

Kim, Se-Jin. *The Politics of Military Revolution in Korea.* Chapel Hill: University of North Carolina Press, 1971.

Kim, Se-Jin, and Chi-won Kang, eds. *Korea: A Nation in Transition.* Seoul: Research Center for Peace and Unification, 1978.

Kiyosaki, Wayne S. *North Korea's Foreign Relations: The Politics of Accommodation, 1945–1975.* New York: Praeger, 1976.

Koh, Byung Chul. *The Foreign Policy Systems of North and South Korea.* Berkeley: University of California Press, 1984.

Koo, Youngnok, and Sung-joo Han, eds. *The Foreign Policy of the Republic of Korea.* New York: Columbia University Press, 1985.

Koo, Youngnok, and Dae-Sook Suh, eds. *Korea and the United States: A Century of Cooperation.* Honolulu: University of Hawaii Press, 1984.

Kuznets, Paul W. *Economic Growth and Structure in the Republic of Korea.* New Haven, Conn.: Yale University Press, 1977.

Kwak, Tae-Hwan, Wayne Patterson, and Edward A. Olsen, eds. *The Two Koreas in World Politics*. Seoul: Institute for Far Eastern Studies, Kyungman University, 1983.

Kwak, Tae-Hwan, John Chay, Soon Sung Cho, and Shannon McCune, eds. *U.S.-Korean Relations, 1882–1982*. Seoul: Kyungnam University Press, 1982.

Lee, Chae-Jin. *China's Korean Minority: The Politics of Ethnic Education*. Boulder, Colo.: Westview Press, 1986.

Lee, Chong-Sik. *Japan and Korea: The Political Dimension*. Stanford, Calif.: Hoover Institution Press, 1985.

_____. *The Korean Workers' Party: A Short History*. Stanford, Calif.: Hoover Institution Press, 1978.

_____. *The Politics of Korean Nationalism*. Berkeley: University of California Press, 1963.

Lee, Hahn-been. *Korea: Time, Change, and Administration*. Honolulu: East-West Center Press, 1968.

Lee, Mun Woong. *Rural North Korea Under Communism: A Study of Sociocultural Change*. Houston: Rice University Studies, vol. 62, no. 1, Winter, 1976.

Mason, Edward S., Mahn Je Kim, Dwight H. Perkins, Kwang Suk Kim, and David C. Cole. *The Economic and Social Modernization of the Republic of Korea*. Cambridge: Harvard University Press, 1980.

Matray, James I. *The Reluctant Crusade: American Foreign Policy in Korea, 1941–1950*. Honolulu: University of Hawaii Press, 1984.

Mitchell, Richard H. *The Korean Minority in Japan*. Berkeley: University of California Press, 1967.

Nam, Koon Woo. *The North Korean Communist Leadership, 1945–1965*. University: University of Alabama Press, 1974.

Oh, John Kie-chiang. *Korea: Democracy on Trial*. Ithaca, N.Y.: Cornell University Press, 1968.

Oliver, Robert T. *Syngman Rhee and American Involvement in Korea, 1942–1960*. Seoul: Panmun Book Co., Ltd., 1973.

_____. *Syngman Rhee: The Man Behind the Myth*. New York: Dodd, Mead & Co., 1954.

Paige, Glenn D. *The Korean Decision: June 24–30, 1950*. New York: Free Press, 1968.

Park, Jae Kyu, and Jun Gun Kim, eds. *The Politics of North Korea*. Seoul: Institute for Far Eastern Studies, Kyungnam University, 1979.

Rees, David. *Korea: The Limited War*. Baltimore: Penguin Books, Inc., 1964.

Republic of Korea, National Unification Board. *A White Paper on South-North Dialogue in Korea*. Seoul, December 1982.

Rhee, Yung Whee, Bruce Ross Larson, and Gary Pursell. *Korea's Competitive Edge: Managing the Entry into World Markets*. Baltimore, Md.: Johns Hopkins University Press (published for the World Bank), 1984.

Sandusky, Michael. *America's Parallel*. Alexandria, Va.: Old Dominion Press, 1985.

Scalapino, Robert A., and Jun-yop Kim, eds. *North Korea Today: Strategic and Domestic Issues*. Berkeley: Institute of East Asian Studies, University of California, 1983.

Scalapino, Robert A., and Chong-Sik Lee. *Communism in Korea* (2 vols.). Berkeley: University of California Press, 1972.

Solarz, Stephen J. *The Korean Conundrum: A Conversation with Kim Il Sung.* Report to the House Committee on Foreign Affairs, 97th Cong., 1st sess. Washington, D.C.: U.S. Government Printing Office, 1981.

Solomon, Richard H., ed. *Asian Security in the 1980s.* Santa Monica, Calif.: Rand Corporation, 1979.

Suh, Dae-Sook and Chae-Jin Lee, eds. *Political Leadership in Korea.* Seattle: University of Washington Press, 1976.

Talbott, Strobe, ed. *Khrushchev Remembers.* New York: Bantam Books, 1971.

U.S. Department of State. *North Korea: A Case Study in the Techniques of Takeover.* Department of State Publication No. 7118, Far Eastern Series No. 103, Washington, D.C.: U.S. Government Printing Office, 1961.

World Bank. *Korea: Development in a Global Context.* Washington, D.C., 1984.

Wright, Edward Reynolds, ed. *Korean Politics in Transition.* Seattle: University of Washington Press, 1975.

Yang, Sung Chul. *Korea and Two Regimes: Kim Il Sung and Park Chung Hee.* Cambridge, Mass.: Schenkman, 1981.

Zagoria, Donald A., ed. *Soviet Policy in East Asia.* New Haven, Conn.: Yale University Press, 1982.

Index

Advisory Council on Peaceful Unification Policy, 187
Afghanistan, 250, 260, 303(n56)
Agency for National Security Planning (ANSP), 180, 202. See also Korean Central Intelligence Agency
Agriculture
  and the division of Korea, 5, 6
  in North Korea, 49, 81–83, 154, 168–169
  in South Korea, 19, 69–72
  See also Land reform
Anticommunism, 45–46, 105, 329
Arms
  North Korean export of, 296–299, 304(n70)
  South Korean export of, 175, 299
  See also Nuclear weapons
Asian Games, 322–324, 351
Association of Southeast Asian Nations (ASEAN), 208, 213, 288

Banking industry, 75, 76–77, 152–153, 212
Brezhnev, Leonid I., 48
Bureaucracy, 42–44, 63(n12)
Burma, 182. See also Rangoon bombing

Carter, Jimmy
  on human rights, 216
  in Seoul, 118
  and U.S. presence in South Korea, 96, 191, 210, 211
Central People's Committee (CPC), 51
Cha Chi Chol, 36
Chaebol, 152
Chang Myon, 33, 39–40
Chiang Ching-kuo, 148
Chiang Kai-shek, 148
China. See People's Republic of China
Chinese–South Korean air incidents, 340–343
Chinese–South Korean sea incidents, 343–344
Choe Yong-gon, 266
Choi Kyu Ha, 124–125, 128
Chollima campaign, 60, 84, 86, 263–264
Cho Man-sik, 7, 11, 12
Chondogyo church, 30
Chong Chun-ki, 201
Chongjin, 264
Chosoren, 234–236, 240(n49), 357–358
Christian church, 30, 47, 221
Chu che, 55–56
  and economic stagnation, 51, 154–155, 161, 162, 165–166
  introduction of, 48, 49, 50
  and the nonaligned movement, 292, 316–317
  See also Kim Il Sung
Chun Doo Hwan, 69, 129, 138, 139
  assassination attempts on, 175, 181–183

foreign policy, 130–131, 233, 288–289, 334
  leadership ability, 130–131
  power consolidation by, 125–126, 127, 128, 129
  on reunification, 130, 187–189, 192, 201, 202
Chung Seung Hwa, 125, 126
Civil Defense Corps, 95
Civil unrest, 36–37, 39, 47, 126–127
  under Chun, 131–132, 134–138, 203, 218–219, 225
  in North Korea, 59–60
  North Korean instigation of, 17, 33, 50, 104–105, 137, 369
  under Park, 34, 35–36
  See also Political repression; Social change
Coal, 84, 157–158
Cold war, 1, 11, 14, 15, 23, 207, 256
Combined Forces Command, 97
Committee for the Peaceful Reunification of the Fatherland, 188, 198, 379
Committee for the Promotion of International Trade, 354
Communication, 113, 334, 351
Confederation of International Contracting Associations (CICA), 308
Confucianism, 29
  and North Korea, 30, 56, 144–145
  and South Korea, 42, 43, 47
Construction contracts, 79–80, 152
  in Libya, 287
  in the Middle East, 75, 79, 220, 306–307
Council for Mutual Economic Assistance (CMEA), 245
Council for the Promotion of Democracy, 132
Council for the Rapid Realization of Korean Independence, 9–10

Defections, 179–180, 193, 360
  Chinese, to South Korea, 342
Demilitarized Zone (DMZ)
  confidence-building measures in, 199–200, 374–375, 382
  military action near, 104, 105, 106, 175, 378
  See also 38th parallel
Democratic Confederal Republic of Koryo, 185–186, 278
Democratic Front for the Reunification of the Fatherland (DFRF), 118, 189
Democratic Justice Party (DJP), 132–134, 137, 139
  formation, 128–129
  and the JSP, 361–362
Democratic Korea Party (DKP), 129, 132–133
Democratic Party, 33, 39
Democratic People's Republic of Korea (DPRK). See North Korea
Democratic Republican Party (DRP), 34, 35, 36, 38, 125
Deng Xiaoping, 264, 267, 269